FIRE AND INK

Fire and Ink

An Anthology of Social Action Writing

∽ Edited by ∽

Frances Payne Adler,
Debra Busman, and
Diana García

The University of Arizona Press   Tucson

The University of Arizona Press
© 2009 The Arizona Board of Regents

www.uapress.arizona.edu

Library of Congress Cataloging-in-Publication Data
Fire and ink : an anthology of social action writing /
edited by Frances Payne Adler, Debra Busman, and Diana García.
        p.   cm.
    ISBN 978-0-8165-2793-9 (pbk. : alk. paper)
        1. Social problems—Literary collections.   2. Social action—Literary
collections.   3. Social justice—Literary collections.   4. American literature—
21st century.   I. Adler, Frances Payne, 1942–   II. Busman, Debra, 1953–
III. García, Diana, 1950–
    PS509.S5F57 2009
    810.8' 03556—dc22   2009017241

Manufactured in the United States of America on acid-free,
archival-quality paper.

14   13   12   11   10   09   6   5   4   3   2   1

Dedication

In memory of
Mahmoud Darwish (1941–2008),
Sekou Sundiata (1948–2007),
Gloria Anzaldúa (1942–2004),
June Jordan (1936–2002),
Toni Cade Bambara (1939–1995),
Audre Lorde (1934–1992), and
Langston Hughes (1902–1967).

May your words continue to inspire
others to act as you have inspired us.

Contents

3.   WRITING RACE, CLASS, GENDER, AND RESISTANCE

4. COMING INTO LANGUAGE

7. Releasing the Dragons: When the Prison Doors Are Opened

8. WAR AND OTHER FORMS OF VIOLENCE

9. WAGING PEACE/LOVE AS REVOLUTION

10. TALKING, TEACHING, AND IMAGINING: SOCIAL ACTION WRITING

Preface

What Is Social Action Writing?

Social action writing is a form of critical inquiry and an act of social responsibility. It speaks out against social injustice and refuses to acquiesce to the tyranny of silence. Deeply rooted in U.S. history, social action writers continue to bear witness to their lived experiences and those of their communities. They retrieve and reclaim stories that others have miswritten or are currently miswriting. As Gloria Anzaldúa reminds us in *This Bridge Called My Back*, "I write to record what others erase when I speak, to rewrite the stories others have miswritten about me, about you."

When a people loses control of its own narratives—both in the past and today—what continuously gets erased and "miswritten" are not only the stories of injustice—the daily and historically rooted realities of inequality and oppression—but also the equally important stories of resistance. These retrieved stories of injustice and resistance not only give heart, they remind us that we are not alone in the struggle, that others are outraged at injustice too, that others are working in brilliant and compassionate and creative ways to forge a more equitable future.

Unfortunately, we have yet to achieve this "equitable" future. As we write, the prison population soars over two million, making us the world's largest incarcerator of its citizens. Vigilante "minutemen" patrol the Mexican border. Pending xenophobic legislation misdirects the nation's attention to the brown, the "foreign," the working poor, as the foci of what is "illegal" in this country. Both in our own country and around the world, our civil rights have been compromised.

Following on the heels of the U.S. Patriot Act, the Military Commissions Act of 2006 had legitimized torture and provided the basis for the former president to round up both aliens and U.S. citizens, furthering a climate of fear and repression reminiscent of the 1950s McCarthy era, the Espionage Act of 1917, the Sedition Act of 1918, and the World War II internment camps. Though we are encouraged by the new president's tone of optimism and possibility and know that the previous administration's policies are being reviewed, it is crucial to speak out, to ensure that our leaders remain committed to change.

This commitment to change must begin with an end to the war in Iraq. As of April 11, 2009, according to antiwar.com, 4,271 U.S. troops have died, 31,169 have been wounded, and $3 billion dollars a week have been spent, totaling $612,571,268,433 and counting (costofwar. com). An October 2006 study in *Lancet* reported that more than 650,000 Iraqi men, women, and children had been killed since the invasion, and current estimates are well over a million. A faded bumper sticker reads, "I'm already against the Next War!"

Speaking of "equitable," what are the new silences? As we write, the economy falters and millions are out of work. Next year, and the years after that, where will we be? As you pick up this book and read it through the lens of your time, what will be happening in your community, in your country, in your world?

Centuries of walls of silence have been coming down, and social action writers have been witnessing and resisting injustice in poems and stories and personal essays. Prisoners have been writing about their abusive world behind bars. Women who have been raped and/or have become victims of incest have been taking back their truths, speaking out, writing about it. Peoples whose cultures have been stolen from them have been reclaiming them, taking back language and erased history. The gap between the rich and the poor in the United States has increased from 30-fold to 75-fold, and poems and stories about this class war are sweeping the country in readings, in poetry slams, and on Web sites. Poetry slams have become another form of critical inquiry. Even Counterpunch. org has a Poet's Basement.

In 2003, poetsagainstthewar.org drew thousands of poems within days. In 2008, with no end in sight to the war in Iraq, activist poets gathered at Split This Rock Poetry Festival in Washington, D.C. They came from across the country, a national network of writers for change, with readings by such poets as Sonia Sanchez, Patricia Smith, Martín Espada, Naomi Shihab Nye, and Carolyn Forché, among others—many of them contributors to this anthology.

As to the question of the taboo against social action writing or "political" writing: some writers inhabit a privileged realm that leaves them free to reflect on the perfect hurricane or a new hummingbird's nest.

Other writers' realities reflect on the aftermath of the hurricane. It is the need to privilege those alternate or non-mainstream realities now that compels us to name social action writing as a literary movement.

In response to this hunger for work that illuminates these alternate realities, creative writing programs around the nation brim with social action writings—ours at California State University Monterey Bay, June Jordan's Poetry for the People at Berkeley, Kelly Norman Ellis's program at Chicago State University (the home campus of Gwendolyn Brooks), and many others.

Why an anthology of social action writing? There is a body of knowledge among social action writers that has been accruing, and it is time to name it, gather samples of the work together, and include it with craft as a central part of the creative writing toolbox.

In our time of political turmoil, this cross-genre anthology of social action writing models some of the work for peace and justice by activist poets and writers. People are looking toward the poets and writers of our time for truth. Our lives are glutted with words, untrustworthy words—in advertising, in our legislators' speeches, in the media. Years ago, when Gonzalo Palacios, the then–Minister of Culture of Venezuela, visited the United States, he said, "When you want to know the truth about what's going on in a country, look to the artists and poets. The media may be in the pocket of the government. . . ."

Our students often don't see their lives reflected in the media, in public policy. They strive to break these silences with their poems and stories. Once taboo in creative writing programs at universities, political writing is percolating through our students. They are ready. Student enrollment in our Creative Writing and Social Action Program has tripled. Students have been choosing our major because they "want to DO something."

Finally, we admit, we created this anthology for ourselves, too. At least once each semester, one of us would exclaim, "We need a book!" No explanation was needed. We all knew which book. Our dream book would include writers of our time writing in response to the social injustices facing us. The pieces would be well crafted and speak out against oppression. They would speak in solidarity with those who are equally outraged at the injustices we witness.

For twelve years, we've been building a Creative Writing and Social Action Program at California State University Monterey Bay. We've housed the program in a new way—in an interdisciplinary humanities

and communication department rather than an English department—
to ground the students' writing in its cultural, political, and historical
contexts (see "Activism in Academia" in part 10, and our Web site: http://
hcom.csumb.edu/createwriting). For our purposes, we've had to rely on a
variety of poetry, short story, and creative nonfiction anthologies, looking
for that perfect balance of craft and social justice content. We never found
that one book. Instead, we supplemented. We placed copies of relevant
books and individual pieces on course reserve. We referred students to
additional writings and authors. We assigned research projects and were
delighted when our students unearthed pieces we had never discovered.
Whether focusing on welfare reform, prison reform, the environment,
physical or sexual abuse, or the dehumanization of migrant farm workers, our students examined their own experiences and the experiences of
those who are in no position to conduct such an examination.

How did we choose which writers to include? If there is a genesis for this
collection, the concepts of breaking silence, bearing witness, and celebrating resistance frame our selections. The anthology provides models of the
craft and courage it takes for social action writing. The poems, stories,
essays, and interviews are the ones that have influenced our students
over the years. In building the book, we have placed the student of social
action writing at the center of the design, grouping the collection according to cross-genre subject matter. In the introductions to the parts, and in
part 10—"Talking, Teaching, and Imagining: Social Action Writing"—we
have attempted to pass along some of our pedagogy and its applications.
We provide occasional historical background in the section introductions
but believe that it is the responsibility of the reader to do the background
reading and research. Why do we NOT know about this history?

Finally, in the long tradition of honoring the elders, we acknowledge
that each generation stands on the shoulders of those who have come
before, carrying on the legacy of resistance and the struggle for justice.
We honor many of our own elders and teachers, writers and theorists
such as Audre Lorde, Gloria Anzaldúa, Adrienne Rich, Dennis Brutus,
Ralph Salisbury, Henry Louis Gates, Jr., June Jordan, and Thich Nhat
Hanh, writers who have been so instrumental in forming the foundations
of this genre of contemporary social action writing, who have articulated
the power of "bearing witness," of refusing the erasure, of claiming the
power of naming one's self, narrating one's own story. We also welcome

the explosive energy coming from newer writers such as Arundhati Roy, Matthew Shenoda, Aya de Leon, Rigoberto Gonzalez, and Patricia Smith, among many others, who carry us forward with such wise and competent hands.

Gloria Anzaldúa writes, "Conocimiento es otro mode de conectar across colors and other differences to allies also trying to negotiate racial contradictions, survive the stresses and traumas of daily life, and develop a spiritual-imaginal-political vision together. Conocimiento shares a sense of affinity with all things and advocates mobilizing, organizing, sharing information, knowledge, insights, and resources with other groups."

We have edited this anthology to validate and value writers who are striving to learn about and expand on this body of social justice writing and who seek allies in this work. As we travel the country, doing readings and workshops on social action writing, we've been asked, "Are you going to publish a book?" This anthology is the answer to their question.

Frances Payne Adler, Debra Busman, Diana García
April 2009

Giving Thanks

An anthology of this size is possible only through the support and guidance of numerous family members, friends, our acupuncturist, colleagues, and writers. Your energy kept us sane and healthy.

We'd like to acknowledge and thank all of our contributors for their work and generosity. Their powerful words and ideas guided us in our creative vision for this book.

We'd like to thank our students for their commitment to their writing and for all they have taught us.

We could not have completed this anthology in a timely manner without the careful work of Karina Young, permissions editorial assistant, and Nicole St. Lawrence, biographical notes editorial assistant. Thank you for your crucial help.

Thank you to the Association of Writers and Writing Programs for supporting our presentations about social action writing over the years, and to those who joined us with questions and ideas and the fervor for social action writing, including AWP panelists Toi Derricotte, Kimberley Blaeser, Michele Kotter, and Brenda Cardenas.

The community at California State University Monterey Bay has been indispensable in our successful completion of this anthology. Thank you to the Division of Humanities and Communication faculty and to staff members Jacklyn Margo and Stacy Skibinski for their support and encouragement. CSUMB's Faculty Senate Research Committee awarded us a CSU grant to develop the proposal for the book. Troy Challenger and Erin Justice provided hours of generous technology support.

Finally, and most sincerely, our thanks to the wonderful people at the University of Arizona Press. Thank you, Patti Hartmann, senior editor; Kristen Buckles, acquiring editor; Nancy Arora, production editor; and Sarah O'Mahen, permissions specialist, for believing in the book from the start.

FIRE AND INK

∽ **I** ∽

BREAKING SILENCE/ THE POLITICS OF VOICE

Much of what is included in this book and in this first part focuses on writings that were not widely publishable prior to the late 1960s. The Civil Rights Movement, followed by the feminist and the gay and lesbian movements of the 1970s, precipitated a flowering of writing by the previously marginalized and disempowered throughout the country. The pieces in this opening part capture the whispered secrets, the muffled screams of outrage, and the stifled outbursts of those condemned to silence by the social norms of the United States leading up to the period following World War II.

The first piece in this section, Debra Busman's essay, "Some Serious Truths to Be Spoken," is a reminder to all writers that writing from the heart first requires us to learn how to listen, how to hear other truths. Some of the pieces that develop can be difficult and challenging, especially when the focus is on social action writing. For the teacher-writer, the ability to guide the interactions, discussions, and emotions that such writings evince highlights the complexity of how we respond, as a nation, to the social issues we face.

As writers, the call to witness such complex issues means that no subject is too fearful or shameful to address, either directly or obliquely. Committed writers realize they must confront governmental and political injustice. Janice Mirikitani, in her poem "Breaking Silence," meditates on the learned silence of the generation of Japanese-Americans who were interned during World War II, former internees who "were told/that silence was better/golden like our skin." In her poem "Frame," Adrienne

Rich presents a narrator who bears witness to what happens when a woman student remains silent in the face of an unjust arrest and mistreatment by two police officers.

Writing about or expressing one's reality can be a form of social action when one's identity does not conform to societal norms. Tracy Kelly, in her creative nonfiction piece "My Coming Out," presents a narrator who accepts her own identity and finally reveals she is gay. The narrator's mother responds, "I will pray for you." In her essay "Speaking in Tongues," Gloria Anzaldúa challenges the politics of voice when she writes that there is no wrong language for a would-be woman writer of color, only the struggle to write because "[w]e speak in tongues like the outcast and the insane."

Sometimes writers employ unexpected strategies to make their point. Linda McCarriston, in her poem "A Castle in Lynn," discloses a family tragedy through the voice of a father who recounts his abuse of his daughter. Chris Abani, in his poem "Ode to Joy," uses the voices of victims to document the torture and imprisonment he and other Nigerians faced at the hands of the military regime during the late 1980s.

Finally, in his essay "Introduction: On Bearing Witness," Henry Louis Gates, Jr., examines the body of work by African American writers who empower themselves and others when they name their own experience.

The point all these pieces make is that it may be painful but it remains critical to offer testimony about social and personal issues, because they are part of the larger political issues that require action.

You Gotta Be Ready for Some Serious Truth to Be Spoken

Debra Busman

To teach Creative Writing and Social Action means you gotta be ready for some serious truth to be spoken. When you ask students to break silence, to bear witness, to connect the meaning of their own personal lives within the larger societal frame, you gotta be ready for the truths that fly out, crawl out, peep out, and scream out from underneath the thick walls of practiced silence. You gotta be ready for stories of border crossings, coyotes and cops, night beatings, wife beatings, baby beatings, date rapes, gang rapes, daddy rapes, gunshots and chemo, pesticides, HIV, AZT, protease inhibitors, and the pink-cheeked 19-year-old who says, "Hey, next Tuesday I'll have *five years* clean and sober; can we have a cake in class?" You gotta be ready for stories that start out, "*Ese pinche* Columbus didn't have no stinkin' green card." You gotta be ready for the straight A student who has to leave school because her INS paperwork hasn't come through yet, and the social security number she gave at registration was the first nine numbers that came to her mind, and she cannot get financial aid because she is "illegal."

To teach Creative Writing and Social Action means you gotta be ready for all the stories, whether you want to hear them or not. When you ask students to speak the truths of their lives, you gotta be ready for the Stanford-bound future teacher of America who writes about being kicked out of the Navy for being too racist. You gotta be ready for the sweet-faced, curly-haired lover of Jesus who writes stories of his days as a violent skinhead, beating up Blacks, Jews, and queers. You gotta be ready for the stories the young man cannot yet share in class, scribbles slid under your office door, 4:30 a.m. e-mails, telling of his father's rage, the belt, the whiskey, the steel pipe slammed down hard on the thin nine-year-old boy body. The father's last words, before he left the child cowering in the corner, his back broken in two places: "Be a man, you pussy. I better not see you cry."

To teach Creative Writing and Social Action means you gotta be ready for war stories quite unlike those CNN sound bites of "precision bombs" and "surgical air strikes" spoon fed into the comfort of our living room TV sets during Desert Storm. You gotta be ready for the glassy-eyed reefer-smoking closeted ex-GI to suddenly bust out with long-held stories of 'friendly fire' and 'collateral damage,' stories told through choked sobs about retrieving the remains of his eight buddies, all under 20 years old, from their burned out carcass of a tank, bombed the night before by 'an American mistake.' You gotta be ready when he tells the class, "Man, you guys gotta know, war is not the fuckin' video game you think it is," when he tells stories of standing guard duty with no ammunition, stories of surrendering Iraqi soldiers shot en mass, thumbs and ears cut off for souvenirs, bodies bulldozed into shallow sand graves.

To teach Creative Writing and Social Action means you gotta be ready for these stories to share classroom space with the one by the retired prison guard, now a minister and college student, who writes of his experience as a young African American police officer on the scene with five white sheriffs in 1960's rural Mississippi when a 17-year-old gas station robbery suspect, a young Black man whose family he knew, was thrown into the back of a squad car, handcuffed, and locked inside with a 120-pound German Shepherd police dog that was ordered to attack. Then, when the writer describes the ensuing screams, the beer bellies, spit, and cigars, the white laughter, the blood, the horrific carnage told 40 years later with such immediacy and precision, you can only hold your heart and say, "Oh, good lord, why did I ever stress the importance of using sensory details, concrete language, and vivid imagery?"

To teach Creative Writing and Social Action means you gotta be ready to hear the stories held in private silence the past four years by a young woman working with the local Rape Crisis Center, stories about rape, domestic violence, child sexual abuse—things she says she didn't think you were "supposed to talk about in college," at least not until she took a women's studies class and Intro to Creative Writing. It means you gotta be ready for the young Japanese-American student who kind of drifts through class, quiet and respectful, suddenly shocked into con-sciousness by the poetry of Janice Mirikitani, suddenly alive and angry and writing poem after poem after poem about Executive Order 9066, model minorities, identity, resistance and rice, practically busting down your office door one day in his excitement to tell you he finally realized what he would write his senior capstone paper on. "The camps," he says. "I'm going to write about the camps. Both my grandmothers were sent to the internment camps. I'm going to interview them over break, get their stories, get the truth of my history." Then, you gotta be ready when he slumps into your office following spring break, crestfallen. "They wouldn't talk about it," he says. "They told me everything else, all about their lives before the war, how they decorated their houses, how they fell in love with their husbands; they told me all about my parents when they were babies, about their family businesses. But they wouldn't talk about the camps. They just shut up, looked at me funny, said, 'There is nothing to say.' It's weird; it scared me. Like whenever I brought it up, they just turned into some other people, like they weren't my grandmas any more. They are 80 years old. I don't want to hurt them, so I had to stop asking. What am I going to do? My project is ruined. I have no stories." And you have to tell him, "No, your project is not ruined. There are worlds within those silences. Your story is just beginning."

To teach Creative Writing and Social Action means you gotta be ready for the young blonde girl from a private high school in Sacramento's suburbs who rolls her Mabelline eyes the first day of class and says, "Is this going to be one of those courses where they try and ram that multicultural crap down your throat?" The same girl who, weeks later sits weeping in class, heart and mind open, listening to shared stories of INS thugs and deported grandfathers and pesticide-poisoned baby brothers, wheezing from asthma. Stories about cousins orphaned by police bombs dropped on fellow family MOVE members, seven- and nine-year-old brother and sister taken from their home, sitting in the Philadelphia police station, surrounded by cops watching the bombing live and in color on TV news, laughing, telling the children, "See those flames. See those tanks. That's your daddy inside there. That's your daddy we finally got right where he belongs." And the young, blonde, private-high-school student, who truly believed that California always belonged to the United States and that racism ended with the abolition of slavery, or at the very least after Martin Luther King Jr.'s "I have a dream" speech, turns her face to the class, Mabelline running down her cheeks, and says, "I'm so sorry. I didn't know. They never taught me about any of this. I'm so sorry. I just never knew." And her workshop buddy, Aisha, the self-described Pan Africanist revolutionary, takes the girl in her arms, rocks her softly. And Carlos, sitting in the back, can't help but shake his head, muttering: "Damn. And they got the nerve to tell me that *my people* are 'under-prepared' for college."

To teach Creative Writing and Social Action means you gotta be ready for the student who, having just listened to your best rap on the wonders of metaphoric imagery, says, "You know, Professor Busman, I mean I don't mean no disrespect or nothing, but, you know, all that stuff you been saying about metaphors and similes and shit, I mean, it's cool and everything, and I can see it working good in some poems, but my poem, you know, when I talk about that cop smashing the side of Bobby's skull with his stick, well, I don't want people to think that that noise sounds like anything *other* than the sound of a motherfuckin' pig's billy club crackin' up against the side of a brother's head. I mean *that's* the sound. It don't sound like nothing else. I don't want people *thinking* it sounds like something else. And, that line where I put my fist into that concrete wall out behind County General, I don't want people thinking that that feels like anything other than a fist into a concrete wall. Sometimes things ain't 'like' anything else; they just are what they are and the reader just gonna have to deal with it. You know what I'm saying?"

To teach Creative Writing and Social Action means that you gotta be ready to learn at least fifteen times more than whatever it is you think you have to teach. It means you gotta be ready to accept the fact that you can never really be ready for all the confusion, the grief, and the wonder that enters the classroom when students take you at your word and believe you really do want to hear the full and messy truths of all their "wild and precious" lives.

Breaking Silence

Janice Mirikitani

After forty years of silence
about the experience of Japanese
Americans in World War II concentration
camps, my mother testified before the
Commission on Wartime Relocation and
Internment of Japanese American
Civilians in 1981.

For my mother

There are miracles that happen
she said.
From the silences
in the glass caves of our ears,
from the crippled tongue,
from the mute, wet eyelash,
testimonies waiting like winter.
    We were told
that silence was better
golden like our skin,
    useful like
go quietly,
    easier like
don't make waves,
    expedient like
horse stalls and deserts.

"Mr. Commissioner . . .
. . . the U.S. Army Signal Corps confiscated
our property . . . it was subjected to
vandalism and ravage. All improvements
we had made before our incarceration
was stolen or destroyed . . .
I was coerced into signing documents
giving you authority to take . . ."
to take
to take.

My mother,
soft as tallow,
words peeling from her
like slivers of yellow flame.
Her testimony,
a vat of boiling water
surging through the coldest
bluest vein.
　　　She had come to her land
as shovel, hoe and sickle searing
reed and rock and dead brush,
labored to sinew the ground
to soften gardens pregnant with seed
awaiting each silent morning
birthing
fields of flowers,
mustard greens and tomatoes
throbbing like the sea.
　　　And then
All was hushed for announcements:
　　　"Take only what you can carry . . ."
We were made to believe our faces
betrayed us.
Our bodies were loud
with yellow screaming flesh
needing to be silenced
behind barbed wire.

"Mr. Commissioner . . .
. . . it seems we were singled out
from others who were under suspicion.
Our neighbors were of German and
Italian descent, some of whom were
not citizens . . . It seems we were
singled out . . ."

She had worn her work
like lemon leaves,
shining in her sweat,
driven by her dreams that honed
the blade of her plow.
The land she built
like hope
grew quietly
irises, roses, sweet peas
opening, opening.
       And then
all was hushed for announcements:
       ". . . to be incarcerated for your own good"
The sounds of her work
bolted in barracks . . .
silenced.

Mr. Commissioner . . .
So when you tell me I must limit
testimony,
when you tell me my time is up,
I tell you this:
Pride has kept my lips
pinned by nails
my rage coffined.
But I exhume my past
to claim this time.
My youth is buried in Rohwer,
Obachan's ghost visits Amache Gate.
My niece haunts Tule Lake.

Words are better than tears,
so I spill them.
I kill this,
the silence . . .

There are miracles that happen
she said,
and everything is made visible.
    We see cracks and fissures in our soil:
We speak of suicides and intimacies,
of longings lush like wet furrows,
of oceans bearing us toward imagined riches,
of burning humiliations and
crimes by the government.
Of self-hate and of love that breaks
through silences.
    We are lightning and justice.
    Our souls become transparent like glass
revealing tears for war-dead sons
red ashes of Hiroshima
jagged wounds from barbed wire.
    We must recognize ourselves at last.
    We are a rainforest of color
and noise.
    We hear everything.
    We are unafraid.

        Our language is beautiful.

(Quoted excerpts from my mother's testimony, modified with her
permission)

Frame

Adrienne Rich

Winter twilight. She comes out of the laboratory, last class of the day
a pile of notebooks slung in her knapsack, coat
zipped high against the already swirling
evening sleet. The wind is wicked and the
busses slower than usual. On her mind
is organic chemistry and the issue
of next month's rent and will it be possible to
bypass the professor with the coldest eyes
to get a reference for graduate school,
and whether any of them, even those who smile
can see, looking at her, a biochemist
or a marine biologist, which of the faces
can she trust to see her at all, either today
or in any future. The busses are worm-slow in the
quickly gathering dark. *I don't know her. I am*
standing though somewhere just outside the frame
of all this, trying to see. At her back
the newly finished building suddenly looks
like shelter, it has glass doors, lighted halls
presumably heat. The wind is wicked. She throws a
glance down the street, sees no bus coming and runs
up the newly constructed steps into the newly
constructed hallway. *I am standing all this time*
just beyond the frame, trying to see. She runs
her hand through the crystals of sleet about to melt
on her hair. She shifts the weight of the books
on her back. It isn't warm here exactly but it's

out of that wind. Through the glass
door panels she can watch for the bus through the thickening
weather. Watching so, she is not
watching for the white man who watches the building
who has been watching her. This is Boston 1979.
I am standing somewhere at the edge of the frame
watching the man, we are both white, who watches the building
telling her to move on, get out of the hallway.
I can hear nothing because I am not supposed to be
present but I can see her gesturing
out toward the street at the wind-raked curb
I see her drawing her small body up
against the implied charges. The man
goes away. Her body is different now.
It is holding together with more than a hint of fury
and more than a hint of fear. She is smaller, thinner
more fragile-looking than I am. *But I am not supposed to be*
there. I am just outside the frame
of this action when the anonymous white man
returns with a white police officer. Then she starts
to leave into the windraked night but already
the policeman is going to work, the handcuffs are on her
wrists he is throwing her down his knee has gone into
her breast he is dragging her down the stairs *I am unable*
to hear a sound of all this all that I know is what
I can see from this position there is no soundtrack
to go with this and I understand at once
it is meant to be in silence that this happens
in silence that he pushes her into the car
banging her head in silence that she cries out
in silence that she tries to explain she was only
waiting for a bus
in silence that he twists the flesh of her thigh
with his nails in silence that her tears begin to flow
that she pleads with the other policeman as if
he could be trusted to see her at all
in silence that in the precinct she refuses to give her name
in silence that they throw her into the cell

in silence that she stares him
straight in the face in silence that he sprays her
in her eyes with Mace in silence that she sinks her teeth
into his hand in silence that she is charged
with trespass assault and battery in
silence that at the sleet-swept corner her bus
passes without stopping and goes on
in silence. *What I am telling you*
is told by a white woman who they will say
was never there. I say I am there.

Ode to Joy

Chris Abani

John James, 14,
refused to serve his conscience up
to indict an innocent man.
Handcuffed to a chair, they tacked his penis
to the table
with a six inch nail
and left him there

to drip
to death
3 days later.

Risking death, an act insignificant
in the face of this child's courage,
we sang:

Oje wai wai,
Moje oje wai, wai.

Incensed,
they went
on a
killing rampage.

Guns
knives
truncheons

even canisters of tear gas,
fired close up or
directly into mouths, will
take the back
of
your head off
and many men
died singing
that night.

Notes caught
surprised,
suspended
as blows bloodied mouths,
clotting into silence.

A Castle in Lynn

Linda McCarriston

In the hometown tonight,
in the quiet before sleep,
a man strokes himself in the darkened
theater of memory. Best old

remembrance, he gets to play it
as slow as he needs, as his hand,
savvy tart of a million reruns,
plays the tune, plays the parts:

now hand is the hard bottom
of the girl. Now hand is full
of the full new breast. Now hand
—square hand, cruel as a spade—

splits the green girlwood of her body.
No one can take this from him now
ever, though she is for years a mother
and worn, and he is too old

to force any again. His cap hangs
on a peg by the door—plaid wool
of an elderly workingman's park-bench
decline. *I got there before*

the boys did, he knows, hearing
back to her pleading, back to her
sobbing, to his own voice-over
like his body over hers: laughter,

mocking, the elemental voice
of the cock, unhearted, in its own
quarter. *A man is king in his own
castle*, he can still say, having got

what he wanted: in a lifetime
of used ones, second-hand, one girl
he could spill like a shot of whiskey,
the whore only he could call *daughter*.

My Coming Out

Tracy Kelly

I begin coming out when I am seventeen. Standing in front of my neighbor's yard, he whispers in my ear, "Do you like girls?"

Hesitantly, I reply, "Yeah."

With a huge grin he says, "I knew it." I make him promise not to say a word to anyone.

I walk the block back home thinking how stupid of me. Now he thinks I'm gay. Halfway to my front door I begin to panic, knowing that somehow my mom will find out. This panic follows me throughout my life, knowing that one day the phone will ring and my mother's stern but loving voice will echo through from the other side.

That voice is my fear; it's the nervous sound in my head. In that split second I become fifteen again. I replay a midnight conversation I had with my mother as a sophomore in high school, her eyes staring deeply into mine and asking, "Tracy, are you gay?"

Remembering that moment, my stomach knots up as the words, "No, of course not," pour from my lips.

The memory of my mother's words, "Tracy, I could not handle having a gay child. It's the one thing I won't put up with," sparks my fear.

At that moment I enter the closet of oppression. I begin going out of my way to assert my heterosexuality. I engross myself in activities and surround myself with people who are openly homophobic. I spend my spare time at church meetings listening to a short balding man promising that God can cleanse and set me free from the perverted spirit that controls me. I devote the latter part of my high school days to praying and reading the Bible, believing that God will come in some bright light and make me whole.

I believe that somehow, someday, God will rid me of my perverted thoughts and fantasies. I wait, but God never comes. Resentment does. I begin to hate myself for being gay. I spend hours crying, begging to be normal, wishing my mother had never taught me to hate myself. I wish for a way off this emotional roller coaster, but it never comes to a stop. I graduate from high school angry, wanting to get away from everyone I know.

I take a part-time job with an environmental campaign in Venice, California, my first job. I love it. I work with a bunch of men and women who lived through the Sixties and Vietnam. One older man becomes very fond of me. We begin to spend lots of time together, mostly discussing my high school years and my family. From him I learn it is okay to like girls.

He has a friend, a tall black woman from Europe. He wants me to meet her. For the first time someone else embraces my sexual orientation. I become intimate with this woman, the first passionate affair of my life. As quickly as our affair begins, it ends. I am filled with the same self-hate. My hope was that by becoming sexual with another woman I would be okay with being lesbian. Boy was I wrong.

Instead I become more confused. I crawl deeper into my hole of self-hate. At the end of that summer I move to Alaska to attend college. I think moving away and attending a private Christian college will make God answer my prayer. I live in Alaska for two years. Not once does God drop by. After two years I am drained and confused. At the end of my rope, tired of praying and tired of waiting. I pack my bags and say good-bye. I jump on a plane and move back in with my parents.

I am determined to put my past behind me. I make new friends and spend my days rollerblading up and down the Venice Beach boardwalk. I bump into a sixteen-year-old boy from Gallup, New Mexico. He has used the last of his money to take a bus to Los Angeles. We connect, probably because we are both running from something.

After spending countless days on the beach together, I finally ask him why he left home. He tells me how he loves to dress in women's clothing but in Gallup, he was beaten up for it, so he came to Los Angeles. He has devised this plan of how he is going to work and save money to buy hormone shots. I am taken aback. I avoid him for a couple of days. We meet up again and I explain to him that he freaked me out a little because I am scared of being lesbian.

He, however, thinks it is great. During that summer he gets arrested for sleeping on the beach and is sent to county jail. While there, he is raped and beaten by some other inmates. I see him one last time before I leave to attend college at California State University Monterey Bay. After a couple of months, I go back to Venice Beach where some homeless kids I used to hang out with inform me that my friend was beaten up for dressing up as a girl by some guys on the beach. I cry that day and decide never to hide who I am.

In my heart I know we became friends for a reason. To honor that friendship, I begin to deal with my own self-hate. It starts with writing my mom a letter to explain how much I am hurting, but I do not feel comfortable telling her I am lesbian. So I tell her I will not be coming home for a while. I tell her I need to work out some personal issues. She agrees to give me space but assures me that she is here for me and so is God.

For the next several months, I spend countless hours writing about my childhood and reading books about coming out. But I still do not understand what it means to be a lesbian. Sure, I like having sex with girls, but I do not think guys are ugly or bad. Then the moment of reckoning comes, in the form of an email.

Late one afternoon while sitting in the Language Lab, I receive an email from a girl asking if I like girls. I stare at the screen for what seems like forever. The moment has come; can I trust myself to be honest? I type five different responses to that email. In the end, I take the easy way out. I tell her I am bisexual. It seems easier.

I am admitting I like girls. Eventually I date this girl. Late one night lying in bed staring at the ceiling, I say, "You want to know a secret about me? I'm gay." I think she always knew, but it's different to hear it from me. I lie there that night thinking I finally did it. I came out for something other than sex.

After this night I become more open with my sexual orientation. I begin to speak in classrooms on school campuses about coming out. I tell my coming out story to others. My life begins to fall into place. I have a wonderful girlfriend, school is going great, and I have begun spending time with my mom.

Then one day while speaking in a service learning class at California State University Monterey Bay, a student asks if I have told my parents. A little embarrassed, I reply no. I give all these excuses of why my parents do not need to know, but I feel in my heart like I am cheating myself. This innocent question sends me back into turmoil. I have to reexamine my life. In the process, I end my relationship with the first girl I loved.

The pain and self-reflection that comes along with that sends me back into the arms of my mother. Late one evening, sitting in her living room, she asks, "So what kind of relationship did you and that girl have?"

I stare blankly and then respond, "We don't really hang out anymore."

She replies, "I know, because you've been a little sad."

That day I explain to my mother my relationship. She sits attentively, saying nothing, just letting me talk. Finally, I think, it's okay. I can be gay.

After my rambling, my mother calmly stands up and looks down at me. In this dry, low voice she says, "Tracy, I love you, and the only one who can help you is God. I will pray for you." She bends over and hugs me. I don't know what to do or say. I say nothing. We go on with our day like nothing happened.

Thinking about this later, I am relieved that she didn't kick me out or perform an exorcism. She didn't get upset, she didn't scream, she didn't pull out the Bible and start quoting scriptures. Thank God she didn't break out the oil and go into revival mode. She was calm. It was not what I had expected.

I begin to think of our conversation as a step in the right direction. Just like coming out is a process for me, it is for her too. For me, though, the process is unavoidable. I cannot hide behind Bible scriptures or prayer cloths. Being gay is a part of who I am. Coming out is a lifelong journey. Coming out is something I encounter every time I meet new people, get a new job, visit family members, make a new friend, or visit the doctor. Coming out is a lifelong journey.

Speaking in Tongues

A Letter To 3rd World Women Writers

Gloria Anzaldúa

21 mayo 80

Dear mujeres de color, companions in writing—

I sit here naked in the sun, typewriter against my knee trying to visualize you. Black woman huddles over a desk in the fifth floor of some New York tenement. Sitting on a porch in south Texas, a Chicana fanning away mosquitoes and the hot air, trying to arouse the smoldering embers of writing. Indian woman walking to school or work lamenting the lack of time to weave writing into your life. Asian American, lesbian, single mother, tugged in all directions by children, lover or ex-husband, and the writing.

It is not easy writing this letter. It began as a poem, a long poem. I tried to turn it into an essay but the result was wooden, cold. I have not yet unlearned the esoteric bullshit and pseudo-intellectualizing that school brainwashed into my writing.

How to begin again. How to approximate the intimacy and immediacy I want. What form? A letter, of course.

My dear *hermanas*, the dangers we face as women writers of color are not the same as those of white women though we have many in common. We don't have as much to lose—we never had any privileges. I wanted to call the dangers "obstacles" but that would be a kind of lying. We can't *transcend* the dangers, can't rise above them. We must go through them and hope we won't have to repeat the performance.

Unlikely to be friends of people in high literary places, the beginning woman of color is invisible both in the white male mainstream world and in the white women's feminist world, though in the latter this is gradually changing. The *lesbian* of color is not only invisible, she doesn't even exist. Our speech, too, is inaudible. We speak in tongues like the outcast and the insane.

Because white eyes do not want to know us, they do not bother to learn our language, the language which reflects us, our culture, our spirit. The schools we attended or didn't attend did not give us the skills for writing nor the confidence that we were correct in using our class and ethnic languages. I, for one, became adept at, and majored in English to spite, to show up, the arrogant racist teachers who thought all Chicano children were dumb and dirty. And Spanish was not taught in grade school. And Spanish was not required in High School. And though now I write my poems in Spanish as well as English, I feel the rip-off of my native tongue.

> I *lack imagination* you say
>
> *No*. I lack language.
> The language to clarify
> my resistance to the literate.
> Words are a war to me.
> They threaten my family.
>
> To gain the word
> to describe the loss
> I risk losing everything.
> I may create a monster
> the word's length and body
> swelling up colorful and thrilling
> looming over my *mother*, characterized.
> Her voice in the distance
> *unintelligible illiterate*.
> These are the monster's words.[1]
>
> Cherríe Moraga

Who gave us permission to perform the act of writing? Why does writing seem so unnatural for me? I'll do anything to postpone it—empty the trash, answer the telephone. The voice recurs in me: *Who am I, a poor Chicanita from the sticks, to think I could write?* How dare I even considered becoming a writer as I stooped over the tomato fields bending, bending under the hot sun, hands broadened and calloused, not fit to hold the quill, numbed into an animal stupor by the heat.

How hard it is for us to *think* we can choose to become writers, much less *feel* and *believe* that we can. What have we to contribute, to give? Our own expectations condition us. Does not our class, our culture as well as the white man tell us writing is not for women such as us?

The white man speaks: *Perhaps if you scrape the dark off of your face. Maybe if you bleach your bones. Stop speaking in tongues, stop writing lefthanded. Don't cultivate your colored skins nor tongues of fire if you want to make it in a right-handed world.*

> "Man, like all the other animals, fears and is repelled by that which he does not understand, and mere difference is apt to connote something malign."[2]

I think, yes, perhaps if we go to the university. Perhaps if we become male-women or as middleclass as we can. Perhaps if we give up loving women, we will be worthy of having something to say worth saying. They convince us that we must cultivate art for art's sake. Bow down to the sacred bull, form. Put frames and metaframes around the writing. Achieve distance in order to win the coveted title "literary writer" or "professional writer." Above all do not be simple, direct, nor immediate.

Why do they fight us? Because they think we are dangerous beasts? Why *are* we dangerous beasts? Because we shake and often break the white's comfortable stereotypic images they have of us: the Black domestic, the lumbering nanny with twelve babies sucking her tits, the slant-eyed Chinese with her expert hand—"They know how to treat a man in bed"—the flat-faced Chicana or Indian, passively lying on her back, being fucked by the Man *a la* La Chingada.

The Third World woman revolts: *We revoke, we erase your white male imprint. When you come knocking on our doors with your rubber stamps to brand our faces with DUMB, HYSTERICAL, PASSIVE PUTA, PERVERT, when you come with your branding irons to burn MY PROPERTY on our buttocks, we will vomit the guilt, self-denial, and race-hatred you have force-fed into us right back into your mouth. We are done being cushions for your projected fears. We are tired of being your sacrificial lambs and scapegoats.*

I can write this and yet I realize that many of us women of color who have strung degrees, credentials, and published books around our necks like pearls that we hang onto for dear life are in danger of contributing to the invisibility of our sister-writers. "La Vendida," the sell-out.

The danger of selling out one's own ideologies. For the Third World woman, who has, at best, one foot in the feminist literary world, the temptation is great to adopt the current feeling-fads and theory fads, the latest half truths in political thought, the half-digested new age psychological axioms that are preached by the white feminist establishment. Its followers are notorious for "adopting" women of color as their "cause" while still expecting us to adapt to *their* expectations and *their* language.

How dare we get out of our colored faces. How dare we reveal the human flesh underneath and bleed red blood like the white folks. It takes tremendous energy and courage not to acquiesce, not to capitulate to a definition of feminism that still renders most of us invisible. Even as I write this I am disturbed that I am the only Third World woman writer in this handbook. Over and over I have found myself to be the only Third World woman at readings, workshops, and meetings.

We cannot allow ourselves to be tokenized. We must make our own writing and that of Third World women the first priority. We cannot educate white women and take them by the hand. Most of us are willing to help, but we can't do the white woman's homework for her. That's an energy drain. More times than she cares to remember, Nellie Wong, Asian American feminist writer, has been called by white women wanting a list of Asian American women who can give readings or workshops. We are in danger of being reduced to purveyors of resource lists.

Coming face to face with one's limitations. There are only so many things I can do in one day. Luisah Teish addressing a group of predominantly white feminist writers had this to say of Third World women's experience:

> "If you are not caught in the maze that (we) are in, it's very difficult to explain to you the hours in the day we do not have. And the hours that we do not have are hours that are translated into survival skills and money. And when one of those hours is taken away it means an hour not that we don't have to lie back and stare at the ceiling or an hour that we don't have to talk to a friend. For me it's a loaf of bread."

Understand.
My family is poor.
Poor. I can't afford
a new ribbon. The risk

of this one is enough
to keep me moving
through it, accountable.
The repetition like my mother's
stories retold, *each* time
reveals more particulars
gains more familiarity.

You can't get me in your car so fast.[3]

Cherríe Moraga

Complacency is a far more dangerous attitude than outrage.[4]

Naomi Littlebear

Why am I compelled to write? Because the writing saves me from this complacency I fear. Because I have no choice. Because I must keep the spirit of my revolt and myself alive. Because the world I create in the writing compensates for what the real world does not give me. By writing I put order in the world, give it a handle so I can grasp it. I write because life does not appease my appetites and hunger. I write to record what others erase when I speak, to rewrite the stories others have miswritten about me, about you. To become more intimate with myself and you. To discover myself, to preserve myself, to make myself, to achieve self-autonomy. To dispel the myths that I am a mad prophet or a poor suffering soul. To convince myself that I am worthy and that what I have to say is not a pile of shit. To show that I *can* and that I *will* write, never mind their admonitions to the contrary. And I will write about the unmentionables, never mind the outraged gasp of the censor and the audience. Finally, I write because I'm scared of writing, but I'm more scared of not writing.

Why should I try to justify why I write? Do I need to justify being Chicana, being woman? You might as well ask me to try to justify why I'm alive.

The act of writing is the act of making soul, alchemy. It is the quest for the self, for the center of the self, which we women of color have come to think as "other"—the dark, the feminine. Didn't we start writing to reconcile this other within us? We knew we were different, set apart, exiled from what is considered "normal," white-right. And as we internalized this exile, we came to see the alien within us and too often, as a result, we split apart from ourselves and each other. Forever after we have been in search of that self, that "other" and each other. And we return, in widening spirals and never to the same childhood place where it happened, first in our families, with our mothers, with our fathers. The writing is a tool for piercing that mystery but it also shields us, gives a margin of distance, helps us survive. And those that don't survive? The waste of ourselves: so much meat thrown at the feet of madness or fate or the state.

24 mayo 80

It is dark and damp and has been raining all day. I love days like this. As I lie in bed I am able to delve inward. Perhaps today I will write from that deep core. As I grope for words and a voice to speak of writing, I stare at my brown hand clenching the pen and think of you thousands of miles away clutching your pen. You are not alone.

> Pen, I feel right at home in your ink doing a pirouette, stirring the cobwebs, leaving my signature on the window panes. Pen, how could I ever have feared you. You're quite house-broken but it's your wildness I am in love with. I'll have to get rid of you when you start being predictable, when you stop chasing dust devils. The more you outwit me the more I love you. It's when I'm tired or have had too much caffeine or wine that you get past my defenses and you say more than what I had intended. You surprise me, shock me into knowing some part of me I'd kept secret even from myself. —Journal entry.

In the kitchen Maria and Cherríe's voices falling on these pages. I can see Cherríe going about in her terry cloth wrap, barefoot washing the dishes, shaking out the tablecloth, vacuuming. Deriving a certain pleasure watching her perform those simple tasks, I am thinking *they lied, there is no separation between life and writing.*

The danger in writing is not fusing our personal experience and world view with the social reality we live in, with our inner life, our history, our economics, and our vision. What validates us as human beings validates us as writers. What matters to us is the relationships that are important to us whether with our self or others. We must use what is important to us to get to the writing. *No topic is too trivial.* The danger is in being too universal and humanitarian and invoking the eternal to the sacrifice of the particular and the feminine and the specific historical moment.

The problem is to focus, to concentrate. The body distracts, sabotages with a hundred ruses, a cup of coffee, pencils to sharpen. The solution is to anchor the body to a cigarette or some other ritual. And who has time or energy to write after nurturing husband or lover, children, and often an outside job? The problems seem insurmountable and they are, but they cease being insurmountable once we make up our mind that whether married or childrened or working outside jobs we are going to make time for the writing.

Forget the room of one's own—write in the kitchen, lock yourself up in the bathroom. Write on the bus or the welfare line, on the job or during meals, between sleeping or waking. I write while sitting on the john. No long stretches at the typewriter unless you're wealthy or have a patron—you may not even own a typewriter. While you wash the floor or clothes listen to the words chanting in your body. When you're depressed, angry, hurt, when compassion and love possess you. When you cannot help but write.

Distractions all—that I spring on myself when I'm so deep into the writing when I'm almost at that place, that dark cellar where some "thing" is liable to jump up and pounce on me. The ways I subvert the writing are many. The way I don't tap the well nor learn how to make the windmill turn.

Eating is my main distraction. Getting up to eat an apple danish. That I've been off sugar for three years is not a deterrent nor that I have to put on a coat, find the keys and go out into the San Francisco fog to get it. Getting up to light incense, to put a record on, to go for a walk—anything just to put off the writing.

Returning after I've stuffed myself. Writing paragraphs on pieces of paper, adding to the puzzle on the floor, to the confusion on my desk making completion far away and perfection impossible.

26 mayo 80

Dear mujeres de color, I feel heavy and tired and there is a buzz in my head—too many beers last night. But I must finish this letter. My bribe: to take myself out to pizza.

So I cut and paste and line the floor with my bits of paper. My life strewn on the floor in bits and pieces and I try to make some order out of it working against time, psyching myself up with decaffeinated coffee, trying to fill in the gaps.

Leslie, my housemate, comes in, gets on hands and knees to read my fragments on the floor and says, "It's good, Gloria." And I think: *I don't have to go back to Texas, to my family of land, mesquites, cactus, rattlesnakes and roadrunners. My family, this community of writers. How could I have lived and survived so long without it. And I remember the isolation, re-live the pain again.*

"To assess the damage is a dangerous act,"[5] writes Cherríe Moraga. To stop there is even more dangerous.

It's too easy, blaming it all on the white man or white feminists or society or on our parents. What we say and what we do ultimately comes back to us, so let us own our responsibility, place it in our own hands and carry it with dignity and strength. No one's going to do my shitwork, I pick up after myself.

It makes perfect sense to me now how I resisted the act of writing, the commitment to writing. To write is to confront one's demons, look them in the face and live to write about them. Fear acts like a magnet; it draws the demons out of the closet and into the ink in our pens.

The tiger riding our backs (writing) never lets us alone. *Why aren't you riding, writing, writing?* It asks constantly till we begin to feel we're vampires sucking the blood out of too fresh an experience; that we are sucking life's blood to feed the pen. Writing is the most daring thing I have ever done and the most dangerous. Nellie Wong calls writing "the three-eyed demon shrieking the truth."[6]

Writing is dangerous because we are afraid of what the writing reveals: the fears, the angers, the strengths of a woman under a triple or quadruple oppression. Yet in that very act lies our survival because a woman who writes has power. And a woman with power is feared.

> What did it mean for a black woman to be an artist in our grand-mother's time? It is a question with an answer cruel enough to stop the blood. —Alice Walker[7]

I have never seen so much power in the ability to move and transform others as from that of the writing of women of color.

In the San Francisco area, where I now live, none can stir the audience with their craft and truthsaying as do Cherríe Moraga (Chicana), Genny Lim (Asian American), and Luisah Teish (Black). With women like these, the loneliness of writing and the sense of powerlessness can be dispelled. We can walk among each other talking of our writing, reading to each other. And more and more when I'm alone, though still in communion with each other, the writing possesses me and propels me to leap into a timeless, spaceless no-place where I forget myself and feel I am the universe. *This* is power.

It's not on paper that you create but in your innards, in the gut and out of living tissue—*organic writing* I call it. A poem works for me *not* when it says what I want it to say and *not* when it evokes what I want it to. It works when the subject I started out with metamorphoses alchemically into a different one, one that has been discovered, or uncovered, by the poem. It works when it surprises me, when it says something I have repressed or pretended not to know. The meaning and worth of my writing is measured by how much *I* put myself on the line and how much nakedness I achieve.

Audre said we need to speak up. Speak loud, speak unsettling things and be dangerous and just fuck, hell, let it out and let everybody hear whether they want to or not.[8]

Kathy Kendall

I say mujer mágica, empty yourself. Shock yourself into new ways of perceiving the world, shock your readers into the same. Stop the chatter inside their heads.

Your skin must be sensitive enough for the lightest kiss and thick enough to ward off the sneers. If you are going to spit in the eye of the world, make sure your back is to the wind. Write of what most links us with life, the sensation of the body, the images seen by the eye, the expansion of the psyche in tranquility: moments of high intensity, its movement, sounds, thoughts. *Even though we go hungry we are not impoverished of experiences.*

I think many of us have been fooled by the mass media, by society's conditioning that our lives must be lived in great explosions, by "falling in love," by being "swept off our feet," and by the sorcery of magic genies that will fulfill our every wish, our every childhood longing. Wishes, dreams, and fantasies are important parts of our creative lives. They are the steps a writer integrates into her craft. They are the spectrum of resources to reach the truth, the heart of things, the immediacy and the impact of human conflict.[9]

Nellie Wong

Many have a way with words. They label themselves seers but they will not see. Many have the gift of tongue but nothing to say. Do not listen to them. Many who have words and tongue have no ear, they cannot listen and they will not hear.

There is no need for words to fester in our minds. They germinate in the open mouth of the barefoot child in the midst of restive crowds. They wither in ivory towers and in college classrooms.

Throw away abstraction and the academic learning, the rules, the map and compass. Feel your way without blinders. To touch more people, the personal realities and the social must be evoked—not through rhetoric but through blood and pus and sweat.

Write with your eyes like painters, with your ears like musicians, with your feet like dancers. You are the truthsayer with quill and torch. Write with your tongues on fire. Don't let the pen banish you from yourself. Don't let the ink coagulate in your pens. Don't let the censor snuff out the spark, nor the gags muffle your voice. Put your shit on the paper.

We are not reconciled to the oppressors who whet their howl on our grief. We are not reconciled.

Find the muse within you. The voice that lies buried under you, dig it up. Do not fake it, try to sell it for a handclap or your name in print.

Love, Gloria

Notes

1. Cherríe Moraga, "It's the Poverty," in *Loving in the War Years*, an unpublished book of poems.

2. Alice Walker, "What White Publisher's Won't Print," in *I Love Myself When I Am Laughing—A Zora Neale Hurston Reader*, Alice Walker, editor (New York: The Feminist Press, 1979), p. 169.

3. Moraga, *Ibid*.

4. Naomi Littlebear, *The Dark of the Moon* (Portland: Olive Press, 1977), p. 36.

5. Cherríe Moraga's essay, see "La Güera."

6. Nellie Wong, "Flows from the Dark of Monsters and Demons: Notes on Writing," *Radical Woman Pamphlet* (San Francisco, 1979).

7. Alice Walker, "In Search of Our Mothers' Gardens: The Creativity of Black Women in the South," *MS*, May 1974, p. 60.

8. Letter from Kathy Kendall, March 10, 1980, concerning a writer's workshop given by Audre Lorde, Adrienne Rich, and Meridel LeSeur.

9. Nellie Wong, *Ibid*.

Introduction: On Bearing Witness

Henry Louis Gates, Jr.

> Histories cannot be more certain than when he who creates the
> things also narrates them.
> —Vico

Of the various genres that comprise the African-American literary tradition, none has played a role as central as has black autobiography. For
hundreds of black authors, the most important written statement that
they could make seems to have been the publication of their life stories.
Through autobiography, these writers could, at once, shape a public
"self" in language, and protest the degradation of their ethnic group by
the multiple forms of American racism. The ultimate form of protest,
certainly, was to register in print the existence of a "black self" that had
transcended the limitations and restrictions that racism had placed on
the personal development of the black individual.

The African-American tradition is distinctive in that an author typically publishes as a *first* book her or his autobiography, establishing her
or his presence and career as a writer through this autobiographical
act—rather than, as for most authors, at or near the end of a productive
career, or at least after an author's other works have, as it were, generated
sufficient interest in the life that has generated the author's oeuvre. A
familiar example of this phenomenon is Maya Angelou, who emerged
as a major American author with her marvelously compelling and lyrical
I Know Why the Caged Bird Sings (1968), but this is true as well for
many of the most prominent figures in the African-American tradition,
from Frederick Douglass to Itabari Njeri.

And curiously enough, the structural similarities among these autobiographies suggest that black writers turn to autobiographical texts
written by other black writers to pattern their own narratives. Claude

Brown, the author of *Manchild in the Promised Land* (1965), told a New York audience in 1990 that, when faced with the task of creating his autobiography, he carefully analyzed Frederick Douglass's slave narrative and Richard Wright's *Black Boy* to learn how other blacks had solved difficult matters of language and form, and then emulated the structure of their narratives. The evidence gained from reading hundreds of black autobiographies indicates that most of their authors underwent a similar process.

Deprived of access to literacy, the tools of citizenship, denied the rights of selfhood by law, philosophy, and pseudo-science, and denied as well the possibility, even, of possessing a collective history as a people, black Americans—commencing with the slave narratives in 1760—published their *individual* histories in astonishing numbers, in a larger attempt to narrate the collective history of "the race." If the individual black self could not exist before the law, it could, and would, be forged in language, as a testimony at once to the supposed integrity of the black self and against the social and political evils that delimited individual and group equality for all African-Americans. The will to power for black Americans was the will to write; and the predominant mode that this writing would assume was the shaping of a black self in words. And while fiction would seem to be the major genre practiced by black writers today, the impulse to testify, to chart the peculiar contours of the individual protagonist on the road to becoming, clearly undergirds even the fictional tradition of black letters, as the predominance of the first-person form attests. Constructed upon an ironic foundation of autobiographical narratives written by ex-slaves, the African-American tradition, more clearly and directly than most, traces its lineage—in the act of declaring the existence of a surviving, enduring ethnic self—to this impulse of autobiography.

But the potency of black autobiography is hardly restricted to the realm of high culture. I remember when Sammy Davis, Jr.'s, first autobiography, *Yes I Can!*, was published in 1965 and quickly became a bestseller, such a bestseller in fact that I was able to purchase it at our local newsstand in Piedmont, West Virginia, soon after the Watts riots. Davis's tale of woe and triumph was inspirational for me, and led me to search for other black autobiographies.

Searching for a key to unlock the madness of American racism, and strategies for my own survival of it, I avidly read, first, *The Autobiography of Malcolm X*, then Claude Brown's *Manchild in the Promised*

Land, as did everyone else in my family. It was through *Manchild* that I first encountered the careful record of a sensitive and articulate black adolescent's quest for selfhood and dignity in an urban world so very far away from my village in the hills of West Virginia. That the book nevertheless captured the terrors that every adolescent encounters on the crooked path to adulthood is perhaps most crudely evidenced by the fact that his book sold three million copies and was translated into fourteen languages in 1965.

The burden of the past plays itself out rather differently in the white and black literary traditions. For the scholar of Western literature, the weight of the authority of canonized texts and canonical critical interpretations can prove to be a confining barrier to creativity, innovation, and even improvisation, delimiting ways of seeing and restricting modes of analysis. The curse that the scholar of Western culture bears, then, is the presence of an enshrined collective cultural memory, one that can confine and delimit just as surely as it preserves continuity and enables the extension of tradition.

Paradoxically, however, the curse that the scholar of African and African-American Studies bears is the *absence* of a printed, catalogued, collective cultural memory. Despite the enormous interest in Black Studies since the late sixties, we still have relatively few of the sort of reference works—such as biographical dictionaries; annotated bibliographies; histories of disciplines; and especially encyclopedias, concordances, and dictionaries of black-language use—that allow the scholar to presume so very much about the subject at hand. These sorts of data, readily accessible to scholars in the traditional disciplines, can be enabling tools, allowing for the production of more sophisticated modes of analysis than are possible otherwise, when a scholar is forced virtually always to re-create from degree zero the historical and critical context in which she or he is working. The excitement generated by the production of scholarship in Black Studies stems from the certain knowledge that virtually all that one sees and writes can be novel and different, free of this burden of the canonized past, the prison-house of tradition. While historical and archival scholarship in Black Studies is revealing our traditions to be much fuller than we ever dreamed them to be, there nevertheless persists the suspicion that all we think, and see, and write is somehow new. Publishing criticism, for our generation of commentators, still feels like an inscription upon a small section of a large and black tabula rasa.

And yet *remembering* is one of the cardinal virtues emphasized by the culture itself—from subtle narrative devices such as repetition of line and rhythm (the sermon, black music, oral narration) to more public pageant modes of commemoration such as the observation of particular "black" holidays ("Juneteenth," Black History Month, Kwaanza) or their particular ways of observing, such as eating "Hoppin' John" on New Year's Day or reinterpreting the Fourth of July to make it analogous to Good Friday rather than to Easter. From Founder's Day ceremonies and family reunions, to the naming of black institutions after black historical figures—Wheatley, Carver, Dunbar, and Washington public schools have long been familiar, and now, of course, Martin Luther King schools and boulevards abound—or what we might think of as historical concepts or metaphors, such as the African Methodist Episcopal Church, African-Americans have been overtly concerned with what Toni Morrison has described in an apt phrase as "rememory," the systematic remembrance of things past.

Remembering has been encoded within the culture as a process precisely because blacks were denied access to their history systematically, both under slavery and after slavery. Under slavery, of course, they were denied access to the tools of formal memory—reading and writing. They were also denied access to their native languages and often even to the drum (deemed "subversive" by many masters, and correctly so, since it was the "home" of repetition and contained the code of a Pan-African language that all blacks could understand). Without a written language, as Hegel had it, there could be no ordered repetition or memory, and without memory, there could be no history. Without history, there could be no self. One abolitionist described in his memoirs an encounter with a slave that illustrates this point nicely: when the abolitionist asked after the slave's "self," he responded, "I ain't got no self." Without hesitation, the abolitionist responded to the black man, "Slave are you?" "That's what I is."

This connection among language, memory, and the self has been of signal importance to African-Americans, intent as they have had to be upon demonstrating both common humanity with whites and upon demonstrating that their "selves" were, somehow, as whole, integral, educable, and as noble as were those of any other American ethnic group. Scholars have long registered the relation in the African–American tradition between the declaration of selfhood and the public act of publication. Deprived of formal recognition of their subjectivity in Western arts and letters, in jurisprudence, and in all that signals full citizenship, African-Americans sought out the permanence of the book to write a rhetorical self into the nonexistence of language. "I write my self, therefore I am" could very well be taken as the motto of "the race" in this country. The perilous journey from object to subject is strewn with black autobiographies. "Unscathed by Slavery" could very well be the subtitle of the hundreds of slave narratives published by ex-slaves between 1760 and Booker T. Washington's *Up From Slavery* in 1901.

I was once led to speculate whether the very vitality of autobiography produced a concomitant nonvitality of the individualized black biography; whether the requisite energy necessary to proclaim that "I am" could not be dissipated in making that claim for another. In the African-American tradition, it appears, the channel of existence had to be transgressed by one's self, without the agency of a midwife. One's public initiation was a private act. One crossed that abyss by an act of individual will, positing humanity, selfhood, and citizenship with the stroke of a pen. Only in the biographical dictionary could these requisites of isolated initiation be transcended, biography as an iconographic act of hero-production was collective, a testament to the existence of "the negro," rather than isolated Negroes; parts, in the arbitrariness of alphabetical order, amounting to an African-American whole. Nurses and churchmen; club women and fraternal orders; free citizens of Cincinnati and freemasons—each had their collective biographical testimony, intended to create the collective features of "the race." But the black individual's concern was to create herself or himself, in words. As Barbara Mellix has put it so well, "I came to comprehend more fully the generative power of language. I discovered . . . that through writing one can continually bring new selves into being, each with new responsibilities and difficulties, but also with new possibilities. Remarkable power, indeed. I write and continually give birth to myself."

. . .

These testaments reveal that answers to questions of African-American identity in American society are not static, that they are dynamic constructions reflecting, and responding to, the dramatic changes in black-white and male-female American relations between antebellum America and the post–civil rights era. Despite shared concerns about the relation of the individual black talent to racist and sexist social structures evinced in all of this writing—and despite the formal relations that obtain among these texts—the pattern of response by black writers is full of infinite improvisation, like variations on two great themes. The silences that a contemporary reader may remark in the narrative of the ex-slave—silences on, for example, his or her own sexuality and misogyny—become, for a later generation, fundamental moments of revelation. We have come a long way from Samuel Delany's very personal account of his discovery of his own homosexuality or Itabari Njeri's frank account of her cousin's turn to the streets at age thirteen. . . . we can safely say that what it means to be a black person in America has proven richly various. As James Baldwin put it so well, "While the tale of how we suffer, and how we are delighted, and how we may triumph is never new, it always must be heard. There isn't any other to tell, it's the only light we've got in all this darkness . . . and this tale, according to that face, that body, those strong hands on those strings, has another aspect in every country, and a new depth in every generation." These stories endure as chronicles not merely of personal achievement, but of the impulse *to bear witness*.

WHERE I COME FROM

In answer to the question, where are you from, some of us may begin with a family name, a specific neighborhood, a town or city, a country, a place in time. Sometimes our answer requires a more complex response, one grounded in history or socioeconomics or culture. Some of us are privy to stories handed down through the generations that reflect on the heroic experiences of those who came before us. For others of us, stories about home or family hold sour or terrifying memories of their own.

Although not all lives are marred by violence, the burden of heightened sensitivity can yield richly etched narratives. For example, in Gary Soto's short story "The Jacket," he writes about a child who is given an ugly jacket "the color of day-old guacamole," all the family could afford. Powerless against poverty, the young boy's frustration and shame are palpable.

In his poem "Singing," Jacob Bloom memorializes a nineteenth-century Russian great-grandfather, beaten during a pogrom, who receives "something better than bread,/the name of a place, *America/where you would not have to live with your back/turned like a shield.*" Although Khadijah Queen, in her poem "The New Reb," places us squarely in the twenty-first century with a narrator who "turn[s] up Tupac another notch," her response to older images and symbols reminds us of our own nineteenth-century Civil War and our history of racial violence.

Viana Enedina Torres uses a variety of Spanish and Nahuatl phrases in her poem "There Ain't No Starbucks in the East Side" to exhort her people to reclaim their ancestry and reject the generations-old history of gang violence and poverty. Matthew Shenoda's poem "Where We Come From" also uses another language, in this case, Arabic, to depict a Middle East caught between violence and dreams, between machine guns, garbage, and "blue lotus songs." Forrest Hamer's "Goldsboro narrative #5: Elders the grandchildren of slaves" gives voice not only to the racial violence endured by residents of a southern town but also to the efforts of the elders to shield their children from that violence and intimidation.

Juan Felipe Herrera creates a surreal city and a mythological hero in his poem "The Return of Jake Condor" through alternating images of doom and ecstasy. Kimberly Blaeser's poem "Apprenticed to Justice" carries the "history of loss" and the "fertile ground/from which we will build/new nations." Ralph Salisbury's poem "A Fancy Dancer, Ascending Among Mountain Flowers" captures the heightened moment at which the figure embraces the world through dance and reclaims his place in his people's history.

Set in the Philippines during World War II, Amy Dixon's story "Chicken Blood" addresses the brutality of occupying armies and forms of resistance women and girls employ to survive. Other forms of resistance occur when a nation attempts to prevent immigrants seeking a better life from crossing the border. Ray Gonzalez's essay "Peace Grove" expresses the frustration of how home and personal identity are disrupted by borderland politics. His meditation on a grove of cottonwood trees planted by Pancho Villa as a symbol for peace on the Mexican side of the border in 1911 imagines the roots growing beyond the "vast poverty and squalor" of his neighborhood, perhaps overcoming the continuing diffidence of government officials.

Sometimes diffidence on the part of those who love us the most, our own family members, aggravates a childhood trauma, thus affecting a child's self-image and self-acceptance. Alice Walker's essay "Beauty: When the Other Dancer Is the Self" demonstrates how those early experiences shape and torment us. The struggle to overcome the trauma, and how family plays a role in that struggle, yields one answer for how we learn to love ourselves.

The Jacket

Gary Soto

My clothes have failed me. I remember the green coat that I wore in fifth and sixth grades when you either danced like a champ or pressed yourself against a greasy wall, bitter as a penny toward the happy couples.

When I needed a new jacket and my mother asked what kind I wanted, I described something like bikers wear: black leather and silver studs with enough belts to hold down a small town. We were in the kitchen, steam on the windows from her cooking. She listened so long while stirring dinner that I thought she understood for sure the kind I wanted. The next day when I got home from school, I discovered draped on my bedpost a jacket the color of day-old guacamole. I threw my books on the bed and approached the jacket slowly, as if it were a stranger whose hand I had to shake. I touched the vinyl sleeve, the collar, and peeked at the mustard-colored lining.

From the kitchen mother yelled that my jacket was in the closet. I closed the door to her voice and pulled at the rack of clothes in the closet, hoping the jacket on the bedpost wasn't for me but my mean brother. No luck. I gave up. From my bed, I stared at the jacket. I wanted to cry because it was so ugly and so big that I knew I'd have to wear it a long time. I was a small kid, thin as a young tree, and it would be years before I'd have a new one. I stared at the jacket, like an enemy, thinking bad things before I took off my old jacket whose sleeves climbed halfway to my elbow.

I put the big jacket on. I zipped it up and down several times, and rolled the cuffs up so they didn't cover my hands. I put my hands in the pockets and flapped the jacket like a bird's wings. I stood in front of the mirror, full face, then profile, and then looked over my shoulder as if someone had called me. I sat on the bed, stood against the bed, and combed my hair to see what I would look like doing something natural. I looked ugly. I threw it on my brother's bed and looked at it for a long time before I slipped it on and went out to the backyard, smiling a "thank you" to my mom as I passed her in the kitchen. With my hands in my pockets, I kicked a ball against the fence, and then climbed it to sit looking into the alley. I hurled orange peels at the mouth of an open garbage can and when the peels were gone I watched the white puffs of my breath thin to nothing.

I jumped down, hands in my pockets, and in the backyard on my knees I teased my dog, Brownie, by swooping my arms while making bird calls. He jumped at me and missed. He jumped again and again, until a tooth sunk deep, ripping an L-shaped tear on my left sleeve. I pushed Brownie away to study the tear as I would a cut on my arm. There was no blood, only a few loose pieces of fuzz. Damn dog, I thought, and pushed him away hard when he tried to bite again. I got up from my knees and went to my bedroom to sit with my jacket on my lap, with the lights out.

That was the first afternoon with my new jacket. The next day I wore it to sixth grade and got a D on a math quiz. During the morning recess Frankie T., the playground terrorist, pushed me to the ground and told me to stay there until recess was over. My best friend, Steve Negrete, ate an apple while looking at me, and the girls turned away to whisper on the monkey bars. The teachers were no help: they looked my way and talked about how foolish I looked in my new jacket. I saw their heads bob with laughter, their hands half-covering their mouths.

Even though it was cold, I took off the jacket during lunch and played kickball in a thin shirt, my arms feeling like Braille from goose bumps. But when I returned to class I slipped the jacket on and shivered until I was warm. I sat on my hands, heating them up, while my teeth chattered like a cup of crooked dice. Finally warm, I slid out of the jacket but a few minutes later put it back on when the fire bell rang. We paraded out into the yard where we, the sixth graders, walked past all the other grades to stand against the back fence. Everybody saw me. Although they didn't say out loud, "Man, that's ugly," I heard the buzz-buzz of gossip and even laughter that I knew was meant for me.

And so I went, in my guacamole jacket. So embarrassed, so hurt, I couldn't even do my homework. I received Cs on quizzes and forgot the state capitals and the rivers of South America, our friendly neighbor. Even the girls who had been friendly blew away like loose flowers to follow the boys in neat jackets.

I wore that thing for three years until the sleeves grew short and my forearms stuck out like the necks of turtles. All during that time no love came to me—no little dark girl in a Sunday dress she wore on Monday. At lunchtime I stayed with the ugly boys who leaned against the chain-link fence and looked around with propellers of grass spinning in our mouths. We saw girls walk by alone, saw couples, hand in hand, their heads like bookends pressing air together. We saw them and spun our propellers so fast our faces were blurs.

I blame that jacket for those bad years. I blame my mother for her bad taste and her cheap ways. It was a sad time for the heart. With a friend I spent my sixth-grade year in a tree in the alley waiting for something good to happen to me in that jacket, which had become the ugly brother who tagged along wherever I went. And it was about that time I began to grow. My chest puffed up with muscle and, strangely, a few more ribs. Even my hands, those fleshy hammers, showed bravely through the cuffs, the fingers already hardening for the coming fights. But that L-shaped rip on the left sleeve got bigger; bits of stuffing coughed out from its wound after a hard day of play. I finally Scotch-taped it closed, but in rain or cold weather the tape peeled off like a scab and more stuffing fell out until that sleeve shriveled into a palsied arm. That winter the elbows began to crack and whole chunks of green began to fall off. I showed the crack to my mother, who always seemed to be at the stove with steamed-up glasses, and she said there were children in Mexico who would love that jacket. I told her that this was America and yelled that Debbie, my sister, didn't have a jacket like mine. I ran outside, ready to cry, and climbed the tree by the alley to think bad thoughts and watch my breath puff white and disappear.

But whole pieces still casually flew off my jacket when I played hard, read quietly, or took vicious spelling tests at school. When it became so spotted that my brother began to call me "camouflage," I flung it over the fence into the alley. Later, however, I swiped the jacket off the ground and went inside to drape it across my lap and mope.

I was called to dinner: steam silvered my mother's glasses as she said grace; my brother and sister with their heads bowed made ugly faces at their glasses of powdered milk. I gagged too, but eagerly ate big rips of buttered tortilla that held scooped up beans. Finished, I went outside with my jacket across my arm. It was a cold sky. The faces of clouds were piled up, hurting. I climbed the fence, jumping down with a grunt. I started up the alley and soon slipped into my jacket, that green ugly brother who breathed over my shoulder that day and ever since.

Singing

Jacob Bloom

In 1791, after the partitions of the Polish-Lithuanian Common-
wealth, Catherine II established the Pale of Settlement, the territory
in western Russia in which Jews were forced to live. The Pale was
created to solve the "Jewish problem" in Russia. Large numbers of
Jews began to flee the Pale in the late nineteenth century to escape
pogroms and oppressive legislation. My great grandfather Hyman
Bloom was among them.

How dark it was in Minsk, in all the Pale,
where the tsar threw a heavy cloak of laws
over your head that stifled your song, your breath.
A giant shadow reigned as if death itself
hovered in the air and blocked the sun.
You wanted to run, but where?
The wall around you was there and not there,
as hard as stone but having none;
it could not be torn down like the one in the ghetto.
Fists made hard in the fields fell on you like hail,
and boots kicked in your empty stomach
as if it were an old door.
Strangers beat you if you opened your mouth
to let the Word out.
Smoke from fires set by hungry hands
rose up like mountains;
your house became a trail in the sky;
was it ash or snow that fell, was it day or night?
And still you lit the Sabbath candles,
still you prayed for light.

A friend gave you something better than bread,
the name of a place, *America*,
where you would not have to live with your back
turned like a shield, he said.
As to a blind man, one with ears to hear
and eyes to see the world through the word,
the vision of what could be came to you.
The darkness began to yield,
and your voice joined the others
who welcomed the dawn, who watched the sun rise,
who rejoiced at a land without smoke or shadow,
and you took flight.

The New Reb

Khadijah Queen

Drives a red four-by-four
Littered with stars and bars,
Rolls his eyes
As I turn up Tupac another notch.

It's a white man's world

And if I'm offended
By oversize tires,
Spit-chew and cowboy boots, flags
Resurrected as window-stickers,

Then I, too, ride with the dead.

There Ain't No Starbucks in the East Side

Viana Enedina Torres

This poem is dedicated to my querida Raza who, after 500 years of oppression and colonization, continues to remain stronger than ever throughout this constant struggle for respect and justicia!

There ain't no Starbucks in the East Side . . .
Where on Sundays the barrio's streets overflow
With low-riding, well-dressed, bien peinados raza
Cruising down Story and King.
Q-vo RAZA! Sal si puedes!
There ain't no Starbucks in the East Side . . .

Where brown dirty hills surround the barrio,
Browner than yesterday.
Where raza paleteros y vendedores de flores
Tiredly walk the streets, hoping to sell.
Adelante RAZA!
There ain't no Starbucks in the East Side . . .

Where barbed wire surrounds closed-in schools,
Where raza students learn from out-dated Eurocentric school books,
Denied college prep courses, and knowledge of their Chicano history.
Decolonizate RAZA!
There ain't no Starbucks in the East Side . . .

Where bad ass, hard core rucas y vatos kick it late at night
After the cruise looking bien chingones downing Budweisers,
And talking shit about the fucken chota who want to pass an anti
        cruising law.
Rise up RAZA! Brown is beautiful!
There ain't no Starbucks in the East Side . . .

Where 14 year old Chicanitas walk the streets late at night,
Talking about the fine ass guys they hooked up with outside
        McDonalds,
Where another silenced mujer puts up with her old man's abusive shit.
Que viva la fuerza de la mujer Chicana!
There ain't no Starbucks in the East Side . . .

Where the llanto of another Chicano echos through East San Carlos
        street,
While the billy club of a police officer crashes against the skull of
Fernando,
Who was pulled over for having a crack on his windshield.
507 hundred years of resistance RAZA!
There ain't no Starbucks in the East Side . . .

Where liquor stores, fast cash advancement centers,
And bars poison every street corner.
Where angry raza families mourn for yet another death caused by police
brutality.
Mexica Tiahui RAZA!
There ain't no Starbucks in the East Side . . .

Where the fucked up system controls our gente like puppets,
Contaminates our barrios, incarcerates us, sprays us with pesticides,
Injects us with chemical warfare, and feeds us with lies.
Where pinche políticos pump in drugs and guns to keep our
Strong voices silent and oppressed,
While they laugh as we continue to play their game and fall into their
death trap.
WAKE UP RAZA!
There ain't no Starbucks in the East Side.

Where We Come From

Matthew Shenoda

semi-automatic machine fire
barreling through
freedom for hire

our homelands becoming
first world garbage dumps

too much internal posturing
not enough external interrogation

rising from cane fields & potted mint leaves
naᶜnāᶜ breath & cellophane feet

eating *rummān* & *tamr hind*
escaping into juice-glitter

      in places where the list of murdered
      surpasses the dead by natural causes

hunger is not the birthright of the children

retinas glare with coals of sandstone

muddied waters are the fertile of servile

      in places where the list of murdered
      surpasses the dead by natural causes

children dream of parrot fish in coral sunshine

dusty streets are filled with bright fabric
'cause weaving is the art of prayer

trash heaps rise like sky-water

doves fly over waves crying

> in places where the list of murdered
> surpasses the dead by natural causes

mirrors reflect lies

ᶜafarīt lurk in crop soil

children learn from coal-burned corn

hieroglyphs speak truths

conquest sleeps in the neighbor's house

people hide colonial shoes under beds

someone walks on the dunes of ruin

we sing reality
through blue lotus songs

> in places where the list of murdered
> surpasses the dead by natural causes

politicians pay surgeons
to sew their eyes shut
& launch cannons in their ears

naᶜnāᶜ: Arabic; mint

rummān: pomegranate

tamr hind: Arabic; tamarind

ᶜ*afarīt*: Arabic; evil spirits or ghosts, similar to the West Indian "duppy"

Goldsboro narrative #5

Elders the grandchildren of slaves

Forrest Hamer

Long before the burning cross could flame
away into ashes, the elders arranged
to have the fire on the neighbor's lawn

doused, and by morning there was no
evidence for children that the
neighborhood had been visited. Sent

to my room to play, I overheard the worry
that had been snuffed a minute before,
and I looked out my window for even

a shadow on the Negro leader's yard.
When my grandfather told me that afternoon
how good I was, how much as good as anyone

else, I knew he was preparing my sister and me
for the day we would walk into a classroom
full of white children and find a seat.

It wasn't the news of the cross burning
that elders protected us from, not the news
of a bombed church somewhere else,

of Sunday-after-church lynchings, or
the real reason we would drink water
at home before going downtown, but

the bitterness and the worry and the fear,
quickenings that flare terrible,
recalling what their grandparents learned.

A child couldn't walk into that classroom
knowing what the elders knew. A child
wouldn't look for a seat in that room

if he knew what the elders knew. A child
wouldn't play outside even into dark
if the child really believed

visitors would come into his neighborhood
wearing white sheets so they could light up a night
elders might not be able to calm.

The Return of Jake Condor

Juan Felipe Herrera

For Alfredo Arreguín, Maga Robles, and Tom Lutz

It is a tiger that devours me, but, I am the tiger.
—Jorge Luis Borges

El Lobo banished by Meroliko, the lard-seller, roamed with the merchant's voice pinned to his reddish ears—stop killing, stop the bloodletting. Stop attacking the innocent. Go North. Learn the language of peace.

For years. Lobo wandered. And could not learn.

Still young, Lobo guffawed at the city center from afar. His tongue cleaned the fissures of his hind foot. He cracked scraps at night and by day took blows for stealing rotten vittles from the trash. At the margin where the rivers dumped disheveled animals, wiry torsos, doll heads, Lobo sipped the caked, sour porridge of the wealthy, the lice and the rice sculpted by the diligent and miniscule troops of ant colonies. Lobo ached under the eucalyptus, its velvety aromatic shade pleasurable and bitter.

The clouds were low and jagged as if torn from a neighboring village or slapped by the thunder of Tzontevitz Mountain, the throne of the Mayan witches. Lobo limped down to the foothills and for a moment gazed at his make-shift homeland—a rush of rust and sage-colored thorns and brambles, silvery rivers, the still-living medicine ferns that had lulled and healed him night upon countless night.

Outside the Mercado, under the umber shadows of the stone church, Meroliko, huckster jester, dressed in loose-legged muslin pantaloons and an oily over-sized shirt, pirouetted on top of an ancient empty wine cask. He bellowed into the yellow light air with his stout lungs and angelic mouth, in his modern tie, cowboy lizard boots, his hook nose and his deep woman face and turbulent, mysterious eyes, his tresses, his stench.

Hundreds of potato eaters faced him, beseeched him. With iodine stained crutches, bandages as long as the steeple above them, the tawdry, proud-shouldered lines leaned toward the tiny wedge table stacked with polished containers in front of Meroliko's shrunken podium. Tengo para todo—he bellowed. For all maladies.

For every pain, for every bone turned to chalkdust, for the eye, shattered, for the ear with one last string of wind, for the chest and its tender lacing, for the leg gone green and filled with black moss, for the scorpioned backbone, for the ragged wrists of the mother kneading sons into men, for the daughter's little wedding legs, for the ash man who once was a brilliant jewel at the betting parlours, for the face fixed with nail points and reddish rings, for you with envy and speckled dots of love's stuff now puffed into coppery cross-hatch patches on the cheek, for all lost souls down, down in the dungeons behind the locked snake-tailed purse of the soul. You there, yes, you! Meroliko let his high-pitched voice cut across the ragged multitudes. Take this ointment. Please, let bliss fill you. Come, you.

With his thick, child hands he unraveled a heavy can out of his net bag. Cebo, queridos, he called out.

Inside this tin container

se cura de todo. All is cured. Del codo, of the elbow, del estómago, of the stomach, del cerebro, of the brain, de la bola, of the ball inside, de la locura, of the mind gone, del ombligo desatado, of the unwound umbilicus, de la sangre impura, of foul blood, de la bilis, of bile, de las coyunturas, of all joints, del hambre, of hunger, de la sal en su vida, of the ills in your life, de las voces en la almohada de piedras, of the voices under the rubble pillow, de la sequía del anciano, of the elder's thirst, de la roña, of the welts, de las moscas que los persiguen, of the flies that follow you, de la gangrena, of gangrene, del diabetes, of diabetes, del corazón, of the heart, de la ronca voz hecha nudo en la garganta, of the hoarse voice knotted in the throat, de las siete flechas de los hechiceros, of the seven arrows of the witches, de la falta del dinero, of poverty, de la casa llena de sombras, of the house afflicted with shadows, de la lengua, of the tongue, de las rodillas, of the knees, del ovario cerrado, of the sealed ovary, de las bellezas que no florecen, of beauty that does not flourish, de toda la furia del mundo, of all the world's fury, de todas las guerras de cada uno hechas tiniebla para todos, para siempre, of each one's wars made thunderstorm for all, forever.

The dark tin disk lifted from the middle of his soft right hand. Cebo, he said as he gazed at the potato-eaters—Cebo de Lobo, Wolf Grease, my dears.

Lobo opened his flashing eyes. For a moment, he looked back. He was from Tzontevitz Mountain, an unapproachable, terrifying peak where his mother had left him to fend for himself. And where after a drought, Meroliko, the merchant, had found him weeping. As a child, his hair an auburn torch, he had been adopted by two wealthy men from a metropolis in the North Country. All the good things had come to him. A three-story house in the hills. A bed with two tables, games, cartoons that spoke of lives ascending into new dimensions. Filtered water in a ceramic bowl. Clean milk with large oatmeal cookies. Napkins embroidered, floral chairs and a mirror before him. He combed his hair, burped out loud, made incredible tawny faces—the face of the boy swollen with fear, the face of the rock star on the verge of a movie contract, the face of a rubbery squeak-voiced mermaid on the Saturday morning series called *Sirenita de Hoy*. He laughed louder than his two gentle, upscale keepers.

They had also given Lobo a name—Jake Condor. He wore it on occasion when he went shopping with his foster parents. In North Country, Lobo learned to walk on cement squares and to speak elegant dinner talk. At the choir he stepped to the front and let his raw voice float and flex in the air. In the schoolyard the girls noted the magnetic, shifting knives in his eyes.

One morning, noticing a loading truck door ajar, Lobo jumped in. He snickered and ate the sweets inside the cardboard boxes. The door slammed and he rumbled inside the eighteen-wheeler for a week.

As the seventh night fell, the truck was unloaded and, when the driver was gone, Lobo crawled out and slipped into an abandoned automobile. He woke to find himself on the outskirts of a small Indian town. Mango and papaya were sold by women dressed in faded, rainbow-colored shawls. A foreman fired a shot at him. Lobo ran up the mountain and hid under the thick incense of the tropical caved-in ovens of foliage. This earth was familiar. It was dark clay, fiery, powdered. It was wet from the sap of his broken face. He was back to his source.

Meroliko prepared his metal cans of miracle grease. It was four-thirty in the morning. The blue-white smoke in his occupied adobe shack drifted out of the holes on the earth wall to his right. He boiled beans over a small fire on the hard dirt floor. Three tortillas on the embers. One cup of black coffee. Four teaspoons of sugar. This would keep him for the rest of the day. His net bag hung over a stick on the wall. He rolled a tortilla doused with bean juice and dipped it into a tall jar of chile paste. Then, he opened his bag and counted his well-polished tin cans filled with Cebo. Cebito, Cebito, he whimpered tenderly to his array of refurbished tuna-cans. It was Sunday, market day, five days before the feast at the end of the year. He filled the cans from a bucket of pork lard pulled from scraps at the butcher's shop.

Vámonos, Cebito, make me rich and famous. Meroliko slapped his stomach and crossed himself as he stepped out of another hole at the end of the demolished street on the outskirts of the largest Indian city of the world. It was made of many names given by those that had used it, loved, swept, invaded, torn, caressed, dreamed, and hated it. Some names were poetic, such as City of the Lost Golden Songs. Some were enigmatic, such as Oxchú and Oltimo-Ta. Meroliko called his city Nuestra Señora del Todo. Our Lady of the All. But on the maps, the city didn't exist. The city had no name.

Under the rough-haired stars, Lobo fed a fire and drooled low notes of impossible joy. His left hind leg was shorter than his right. His jaw was scarred. After all these years, he had found his way. He was en route to Meroliko, Meroliko who was busy fooling the potato-eaters, the poorest of the poor with little dented painted cans of lies, promises, dreams, foggy lard, and curses. Lobo stood up on his hind legs in the yellow-red flame light. He faced Nuestra Señora del Todo. His comet-like eyes blurred with moon-pieces and mountain needles and cactus blades.

Apprenticed to Justice

Kimberly Blaeser

The weight of ashes
from burned out camps.
Lodges smoulder in fire,
animal hides wither
their mythic images shrinking
pulling in on themselves,
all incinerated
fragments
of breath bone and basket
rest heavy
sink deep
like wintering frogs.
And no dustbowl wind
can lift
this history
of loss.

Now fertilized by generations—
ashes upon ashes,
this old earth erupts.
Medicine voices rise like mists
white buffalo memories
teeth marks on birch bark
forgotten forms
tremble into wholeness.

And the grey weathered stumps,
trees and treaties
cut down
trampled for wealth.
Flat Potlatch plateaus
of ghost forests
raked by bears
soften rot inward
until tiny arrows of green
sprout
rise erect
rootfed
from each crumbling center.

Some will never laugh
as easily.
Will hide knives
silver as fish in their boot
hoard names
as if they could be stolen
as easily as land,
will paper their walls
with maps and broken promises,
scar their flesh
with this badge
heavy as ashes.

And this is a poem
for those
apprenticed
from birth.
In the womb
of your mother nation
heartbeats
sound like drums
drums like thunder
thunder like twelve thousand
walking

then ten thousand
then eight
walking away
from stolen homes
from burned-out camps
from relatives fallen
as they walked
then crawled
then fell.
This is the woodpecker sound
of an old retreat.
It becomes an echo.
an accounting
to be reconciled.
This is the sound
of trees falling in the woods
when they are heard,
of red nations falling
when they are remembered.
This is the sound
we hear
when fist meets flesh
when bullets pop against chests
when memories rattle hollow in stomachs.
And we turn this sound
over and over again
until it becomes
fertile ground
from which we will build
new nations
upon the ashes of our ancestors.
Until it becomes
the rattle of a new revolution
these fingers
drumming on keys.

A Fancy Dancer, Ascending Among Mountain Flowers

Ralph Salisbury

(For the Pygmy Mammoths of Wrangle Island, for all of the women
I have loved, from afar, or near, for Marianne Moore, who knew to
rhapsodize, and in memory of my father, whose Cherokee-Shawnee
stomp dancing would shake, and shape, my world.)

I am dancing to bees' zither rhythms, and, with
their gracious or drunkenly heedless permission,
am dancing with the scent
of centuries of millions of beautiful women with
each breath each step
through blossoms toward clouds
imperceptibly thins.

Without missing a molecule of more
and more ethereal air,
I'm dancing with timberline pines, which shrink, degree
by chilling degree, cone after generation of cone,
their sweet, sun after sun, season on season, growth,
as Pygmy Mammoths, my fellow mammals, gene
on gene, grew smaller, to survive,
as has, century after century, word
after compressed word, our poetry.

Particles of mineral syllables beneath
each foot's sole's eloquent cells,
I am dancing, with giddy expectation, on
stone only glaciers have carved, when,
out of some utterly beyond me lexicon,
dawn wind, a fancy dancer, from every tribe,
whirls petals faster than any man,
thought by exuberant thought jigging, toward summit and
exhaustion's rhapsodic anticipation of fulfillment, can.

Chicken Blood

Amy Samala Dixon

A small village in the costal mountains of the Philippines, during World War II

Malayah held the dead chicken tightly by its bound feet, over a large gray bowl. *Scrape, scrape, scrape.* Oldest Sister carefully sawed off the chicken's head with a long blade, its nasty, jagged teeth gleaming in the hot afternoon sun.

"Nini, don't waste any blood," she said, and walked away to clean the knife. Malayah stood, watching with morbid fascination as the deep-red liquid dripped into the bowl in an uneven stream. *Plop, plop, drip, dribble.* The heavy metallic scent of blood mingled with the odor of baked dirt and sweat in the heavy air. Her stomach clenched like an angry fist; she was almost mad with hunger. It took all of Malayah's concentration and energy to prevent herself from plunging her hand into the steamy stream of blood and licking it clean.

In her mind, she brought the neck to her chapped lips, drank the blood from the bird's body, sucked the marrow from its bones, ripped into its raw flesh with vicious teeth. Her fantasy sickened her, but she could not banish it. She clung tightly to visions of her family; they gave her the power to resist her selfish impulse, her stomach's urgent demand. She thought of Kuya and Oldest Sister, who had gone hungry for many days so she could eat. She thought of her six other older brothers and sisters, whose once strong arms were melting away like pats of Crisco on a hot skillet. She thought of Auntie the story teller, whose clear, intelligent eyes had become dull and glazed over. She tightened her grip, the rough bumps on the feet biting into her skin, pressed her bare toes hard against the hot dusty earth. After eternity had come and gone, Oldest Sister came out of the house again, took the chicken from Malayah's white-knuckled hands, and into the house. If they had rice, they could make ariscaldo, and one scrawny, starved chicken could feed their family of ten for several days. Malayah followed her sister into the house, and sat at the wooden table in their small kitchen. She ran her hands back and forth across the smooth, worn top, and thought of food. Rice. The staple that kept the people alive and fed year round. Even in Malayah's poor village, there had always been plenty of rice. But most of the country's rice could not be harvested that year, because of the war. The rice paddies had become battle fields, overrun with soldiers and death, and rice was rationed.

They left the blood outside for several hours, until it had turned fetid and sour. *I hope it's not me this time. Please, God, don't let it be me*, Malayah thought as she stared out the kitchen window at the bowl of blood on the ground outside her home.

Malayah listened with growing dread to the soft voices of her brothers and sisters, trying to decide who had to leave the relative safety of the mountains and travel into the Japanese occupied cities to pick up rice rations. The men couldn't go. If the Japanese even suspected a man of being part of the Philippine army, they would behead him, or worse. When Uncle Hilario was captured, they had buried him up to his neck, and poured a sticky, sugar glaze over his head to attract ants. Malayah shivered and brushed phantom insects off her arms. She remembered how he screamed as the ants swarmed over his eyes. Eaten alive.

Kuya glanced at Malayah, and his hard, black eyes softened a little, "You are too young to go," he told her. Relief washed over her, carrying away her dread and leaving a residue of fear in its wake. If she didn't go, that meant one of her sisters would have to. Oldest Sister held the family together; they couldn't spare her for even a day, Matring was too pretty, Auntie was too old.

In the end, Kuya and Oldest Sister decided that Yoli should go. She was barely twelve, and as thin and shapeless as a stick doll. She had no breasts to speak of, her hips were pointed angles, and her elbows and knees were huge knobs on her limbs. But girls younger than her had been taken, and the soldiers were getting less and less selective about the women and girls they kidnapped for the comfort camps. It was dangerous for any Filipina to go near the Japanese, but they would not survive much longer without rice. So Malayah, Oldest Sister, Matring, and Yoli went outside and knelt around the bowl.

Oldest Sister and Malayah dipped their hands into the warm, rancid blood and wiped their palms on Yoli's cheeks and forehead. Matring poured a cup of it into Yoli's smooth, straight hair, rubbing and scrunching her hair until it was knotted and matted with blood. Malayah smeared blood onto the simple homespun cloth of Yoli's homemade dress. They covered Yoli's arms and legs with the dark liquid, and let it harden into a sticky second skin on her stomach and back. Yoli dipped her feet in the bowl and covered them with dirt and dust. When they were through, Malayah almost didn't recognize her sister beneath the monster they had created.

The stench rose up around her in a cloud. Yoli's beautiful, shiny black hair was a dull, sick, rust-brown color. She looked and smelled like something rotting, but not one word of complaint escaped her lips. Malayah met Yoli's eyes. There was fear there, but also determination. Tears scalded both of their faces, smearing the blood on Yoli's cheeks even more.

"No . . ." Oldest Sister's voice was choked with emotion. "No one will want you now."

Yoli nodded. Malayah put her blood-covered hand in Oldest Sister's and held tight. She didn't move until Yoli's receding form faded into a blotch on the green and brown landscape.

Ariscaldo: A heavy, rice-based stew seasoned with ginger. It is usually made with chicken. First, chicken meat is cut into small pieces, and the chicken spine into sections, and everything is boiled (head, feet, spine, and meat) with ginger to make a broth. Then rice is boiled into the broth. It is very filling.

Comfort Camps: Filipino women and girls were kidnapped by the Japanese and sent to "comfort camps" where they were forced to sleep with Japanese soldiers, sometimes as many as 50 a day. When the comfort women were released from the camps at the end of the war, they were ostracized. Many of their families held them responsible, and thought they had brought shame upon the family.

Kuya: respected eldest brother

Nini: an affectionate name for the youngest girl in family

Peace Grove

Ray Gonzalez

The last house where I lived in El Paso was one mile from the Peace Grove, the cottonwoods Pancho Villa planted on the Mexican side of the Rio Grande near Juarez, where his rebel troops fought government soldiers in 1911. The battle lasted two days and was witnessed by hundreds of El Pasoans who camped along the river to watch. The Peace Grove was Villa's way of showing there could be peace, that the bloody Mexican Revolution could end. But the planting of the trees may have also been a signal to the U.S. and General John Pershing to leave the Mexicans alone to fight their own war. Even though they captured Juarez, Villa's army did not stay long. Two days later, they headed south into Chihuahua to continue the fight.

The idea of a revolutionary planting trees and the fact that the trees are standing today intrigued me when I lived in a tiny adobe house on the border of the two countries. From that house, one hundred yards from the Rio Grande, I saw thousands of illegal aliens, or as some of them preferred to be called, *mojados*, cross into the U.S. I stared every day at the crumbling huts of the Juarez *colonias* across the river.

The area behind my house was a favorite crossing point because the Rio Grande was very shallow west of downtown El Paso. The U.S. Border Patrol could not keep Mexicans out despite their constant patrolling of the area. The Peace Grove stood between the river and the low hills on the west end of Juarez, its neat rows of trees in sharp contrast to the decaying streets and houses, the broken walls painted turquoise, yellow, purple, or pink. The vast poverty and squalor spread for miles, blessed by the enduring limbs of the Peace Grove.

One evening after a sudden thunderstorm had rolled up from the south and swept through El Paso, I went for a walk on the levee road above the irrigation canal. It paralleled the river on the U.S. side. The black clouds moved slowly to the west and their bottom layers turned pink in the setting sun. Despite the heavy rain, the Rio Grande was nearly dry. It flowed in slow, muddy trails. As I walked south, I looked across the river at the cottonwoods and thought about my grandfather, Bonifacio Canales, who fought for Villa in the battle for Juarez. It was the only fighting he did during the revolution. He and my grandmother Julia had just been married. They were both fourteen years old and had fled Chihuahua for the border. When Villa's men entered Juarez, young *campesinos* chose sides, most of them deciding to help Villa take the town. After the victorious rebel army left, my grandparents fled to Arizona, where Bonifacio worked for the railroad in the Yaqui Indian labor camps until too much alcohol brought his early death in 1941.

I wondered what the young boys who fought for Villa thought about planting trees. Did anyone try to destroy the grove after Villa's departure? Did any of the rebels ever return to Juarez to see if the trees had grown? The rebels reminded me of several friends who had gone to Nicaragua in 1985, after the Sandinista Revolution, to show their support by joining local work brigades in planting trees in the war-torn country. They told me how U.S.-backed Contras later destroyed many of the crops in the countryside and burned the young trees the Americans had planted.

My thoughts were interrupted by the sound of tires screeching on gravel. I looked behind me at the Border Patrol car that pulled up in a frantic spin. The officer leaped out of the lime-green car and pointed a finger at me. "Hey, you wetback!" the Anglo officer sneered. "Got you, again!"

"Are you talking to me, Officer?" I smiled and spoke in my clearest Texas drawl. Yes, Chicanos can have good Texas accents when they want to.

"You speak English?" He approached with one hand on his holstered gun. He wore tiny sunglasses and sported a crewcut. He looked like he was in his early twenties.

"Yes. I probably speak it better than you."

He stood in front of me with his hands on his hips, uncertain what to do next. As we stared at each other, I could hear someone speaking Spanish across the river and the busy humming of traffic on Paisano Street to my right.

"You look like a wetback to me. Got any I.D.?"

I looked around to see if there were any potential witnesses nearby, but no one else was in sight. "Yes, I have a driver's license, but I don't think I have to show it to you, since I am an American citizen."

No muscle moved on the stony face behind the sunglasses. "Where do you live?"

I pointed to my house one hundred yards down the road. "Over there."

We both heard the squawking of his car radio and we stared at each other. "Yeah, I've seen you around here. Any wetbacks cross here?" He shook his head toward the river.

I shrugged and didn't answer. He shook his head again and walked briskly to his car. He gave me another look and climbed in. He pulled into reverse, made another loud turn on the narrow road, and screeched away in a thick trail of dust. I watched the car disappear around a bend, and then saw four Mexicans run across the road. They had been crouching behind the tall salt cedars that lined the street. They climbed the embankment and quickly vanished on Paisano toward downtown.

I laughed, but was angry. It was not the first time I had been stopped by the Border Patrol. They probably did have the right to ask for my I.D., but they usually backed down once they discovered that the brown-skinned person they were questioning was an English-speaking U.S. citizen who could report them to their superiors. I had called Border Patrol headquarters once when a patrol car pulled me and a friend over for no reason. The two officers stuck flashlights in our faces, didn't say a word to us, and drove off into the night. I reported them, but of course nothing happened.

I tried to forget this latest confrontation and kept walking to get a better view of the Peace Grove. I stopped another fifty yards down the road and looked across the river. The final light from the setting sun hit the trees and outlined them in orange. The combination of sunset and distant rain clouds cast a dark, burning glow over the western sky and washed over the Juarez colonias, making the houses look like they were on fire. I spotted a few people climbing the dirt streets to disappear over the tops of the hills. Several dogs barked and ran among the garbage that lay in the streets closest to the river.

I sat on the embankment of the levee road and watched the whole area turn darker. The river sparkled but barely moved. Its mud stretched in long layers of smooth sand for hundreds of yards. As I sat on the border of the two countries, watching the still group of full cottonwoods with their huge leaves, I realized that there was no border. Pancho Villa had planted those trees directly across from where I sat because that is where events dictated he should plant them. The two dozen trees, standing tall and healthy along the river, found their spot near the water because the line had been drawn there. It had been decided decades ago. No Mexican Revolution and no constant prowling of Border Patrol cars, nor the fact that thousands of people crossed this spot illegally, could affect the way the trees grew. They had no say in which direction the roots had spread since 1911.

I felt exhilarated and wanted to dig under the river with my bare hands to find the roots of the trees spreading across the river, covering this side. I wanted to know that the trees would absorb so much water that, sooner or later, they would dry the river, making the riverbed disappear. Then there would be no sign of a border! I wanted to see horses and Villa's troops digging to stick young trees into the mud across from me. I wanted to find El Pasoans sitting on the bank, having a good time, watching the planting instead of acting like war was a sporting event to watch, pass judgment on, then interfere with. I didn't know all the historical details behind the planting of the trees. My thoughts of roots coming toward me, underground, wiping out the levee road and the patrol cars, blended with the last light of the evening.

I heard a splash in the water, but could not see anything in the river. Smoke from wood stoves and an occasional electric light dotted the hills of the colonias. I rose and started to walk home, then heard angry voices across the river. I could barely make out two running figures as they moved through the Peace Grove. One of them shouted something I couldn't understand, and the angry voice of a woman replied, "¡*Vámonos!* ¡*Vámonos!*"

They stopped under a tree and argued in loud voices. The second figure was a man who tugged at the woman's dress. She shook him off, stepped a few feet back, and yelled something at him. He threw up his hands and joined her. They approached the river and began to wade across.

I turned away and headed home. When I reached the bend in the levee, I paused and looked for them. They crouched in the middle of the low river, two more waiting to enter, watching for *la migra*. I didn't see any patrol cars. The couple ran the rest of the way and blended into the darkness on this side. I kept walking, then heard a car engine start. The headlights of a patrol car blinded me and blocked my path. I stopped and waited for the officer, a different one this time, to get out and question me. I knew this meant I was going to take my time getting back to my house along the Rio Grande.

Beauty

When the Other Dancer Is the Self

Alice Walker

It is a bright summer day in 1947. My father, a fat, funny man with beautiful eyes and a subversive wit, is trying to decide which of his eight children he will take with him to the county fair. My mother, of course, will not go. She is knocked out from getting most of us ready: I hold my neck stiff against the pressure of her knuckles as she hastily completes the braiding and then beribboning of my hair.

My father is the driver for the rich old white lady up the road. Her name is Miss Mey. She owns all the land for miles around, as well as the house in which we live. All I remember about her is that she once offered to pay my mother thirty-five cents for cleaning her house, raking up piles of her magnolia leaves, and washing her family's clothes, and that my mother—she of no money, eight children, and a chronic earache—refused it. But I do not think of this in 1947. I am two and a half years old. I want to go everywhere my daddy goes. I am excited at the prospect of riding in a car. Someone has told me fairs are fun. That there is room in the car for only three of us doesn't faze me at all. Whirling happily in my starchy frock, showing off my biscuit-polished patent-leather shoes and lavender socks, tossing my head in a way that makes my ribbons bounce, I stand, hands on hips, before my father. "Take me, Daddy," I say with assurance; "I'm the prettiest!"

Later, it does not surprise me to find myself in Miss Mey's shiny black car, sharing the back seat with the other lucky ones. Does not surprise me that I thoroughly enjoy the fair. At home that night I tell the unlucky ones all I can remember about the merry-go-round, the man who eats live chickens, and the teddy bears, until they say: that's enough, baby Alice. Shut up now, and go to sleep.

It is Easter Sunday, 1950. I am dressed in a green, flocked, scalloped-hem dress (handmade by my adoring sister, Ruth) that has its own smooth satin petticoat and tiny hot-pink roses tucked into each scallop. My shoes, new T-strap patent leather, again highly biscuit-polished. I am six years old and have learned one of the longest Easter speeches to be heard that day, totally unlike the speech I said when I was two: "Easter lilies / pure and white / blossom in / the morning light." When I rise to give my speech I do so on a great wave of love and pride and expectation. People in the church stop rustling their new crinolines. They seem to hold their breath. I can tell they admire my dress, but it is my spirit, bordering on sassiness (womanishness), they secretly applaud.

"That girl's a little *mess*," they whisper to each other, pleased.

Naturally I say my speech without stammer or pause, unlike those who stutter, stammer, or, worst of all, forget. This is before the word "beautiful" exists in people's vocabulary, but "Oh, isn't she the *cutest* thing!" frequently floats my way. "And got so much sense!" they gratefully add . . . for which thoughtful addition I thank them to this day.

It was great fun being cute. But then, one day, it ended.

I am eight years old and a tomboy. I have a cowboy hat, cowboy boots, checkered shirt and pants, all red. My playmates are my brothers, two and four years older than I. Their colors are black and green, the only difference in the way we are dressed. On Saturday nights we all go to the picture show, even my mother; Westerns are her favorite kind of movie. Back home, "on the ranch," we pretend we are Tom Mix, Hopalong Cassidy, Lash LaRue (we've even named one of our dogs Lash LaRue); we chase each other for hours rustling cattle, being outlaws, delivering damsels from distress. Then my parents decide to buy my brothers guns. These are not "real" guns. They shoot "BBs," copper pellets my brothers say will kill birds. Because I am a girl, I do not get a gun. Instantly I am relegated to the position of Indian. Now there appears a great distance between us. They shoot and shoot at everything with their new guns. I try to keep up with my bow and arrows.

One day while I am standing on top of our makeshift "garage"— pieces of tin nailed across some poles—holding my bow and arrow and looking out toward the fields, I feel an incredible blow in my right eye. I look down just in time to see my brother lower his gun.

Both brothers rush to my side. My eye stings, and I cover it with my hand. "If you tell," they say, "we will get a whipping. You don't want that to happen, do you?" I do not. "Here is a piece of wire," says the older brother, picking it up from the roof; "say you stepped on one end of it and the other flew up and hit you." The pain is beginning to start. "Yes," I say. "Yes, I will say that is what happened." If I do not say this is what happened, I know my brothers will find ways to make me wish I had. But now I will say anything that gets me to my mother.

Confronted by our parents we stick to the lie agreed upon. They place me on a bench on the porch and I close my left eye while they examine the right. There is a tree growing from underneath the porch that climbs past the railing to the roof. It is the last thing my right eye sees. I watch as its trunk, its branches, and then its leaves are blotted out by the rising blood.

I am in shock. First there is intense fever, which my father tries to break using lily leaves bound around my head. Then there are chills: my mother tries to get me to eat soup. Eventually, I do not know how, my parents learn what has happened. A week after the "accident" they take me to see a doctor. "Why did you wait so long to come?" he asks, looking into my eye and shaking his head. "Eyes are sympathetic," he says. "If one is blind, the other will likely become blind too."

This comment of the doctor's terrifies me. But it is really how I look that bothers me most. Where the BB pellet struck there is a glob of whitish scar tissue, a hideous cataract, on my eye. Now when I stare at people—a favorite pastime, up to now—they will stare back. Not at the "cute" little girl, but at her scar. For six years I do not stare at anyone, because I do not raise my head.

Years later, in the throes of a mid-life crisis, I ask my mother and sister whether I changed after the "accident." "No," they say, puzzled. "What do you mean?"

What do I mean?

I am eight, and, for the first time, doing poorly in school, where I have been something of a whiz since I was four. We have just moved to the place where the "accident" occurred. We do not know any of the people around us because this is a different county. The only time I see the friends I knew is when we go back to our old church. The new school is the former state penitentiary. It is a large stone building, cold and drafty, crammed to overflowing with boisterous, ill-disciplined children. On the third floor there is a huge circular imprint of some partition that has been torn out.

"What used to be here?" I ask a sullen girl next to me on our way past to lunch.

"The electric chair," says she.

At night I have nightmares about the electric chair, and about all the people reputedly "fried" in it. I am afraid of the school, where all the students seem to be budding criminals.

"What's the matter with your eye?" they ask, critically.

When I don't answer (I cannot decide whether it was an "accident" or not), they shove me, insist on a fight.

My brother, the one who created the story about the wire, comes to my rescue. But then brags so much about "protecting" me, I become sick.

After months of torture at the school, my parents decide to send me back to our old community, to my old school. I live with my grandparents and the teacher they board. But there is no room for Phoebe, my cat. By the time my grandparents decide there *is* room, and I ask for my cat, she cannot be found. Miss Yarborough, the boarding teacher, takes me under her wing, and begins to teach me to play the piano. But soon she marries an African—a "prince," she says—and is whisked away to his continent.

At my old school there is at least one teacher who loves me. She is the teacher who knew me "before I was born" and bought my first baby clothes. It is she who makes life bearable. It is her presence that finally helps me turn on the one child at the school who continually calls me "one-eyed bitch." One day at school I simply grab him by his coat and beat him until I am satisfied. It is my teacher who tells me my mother is ill.

My mother is lying in bed in the middle of the day, something I have never seen. She is in too much pain to speak. She has an abscess in her ear. I stand looking down on her, knowing that if she dies, I cannot live. She is being treated with warm oils and hot bricks held against her cheek. Finally a doctor comes. But I must go back to my grandparents' house. The weeks pass but I am hardly aware of it. All I know is that my mother might die, my father is not so jolly, my brothers still have their guns, and I am the one sent away from home.

"You did not change," they say.
Did I imagine the anguish of never looking up?

I am twelve. When relatives come to visit I hide in my room. My cousin Brenda, just my age, whose father works in the post office and whose mother is a nurse, comes to find me. "Hello," she says. And then she asks, looking at my recent school picture, which I did not want taken, and on which the "glob," as I think of it, is clearly visible, "You still can't see out of that eye?"

"No," I say, and flop back on the bed over my book.

That night, as I do almost every night, I abuse my eye. I rant and rave at it, in front of the mirror. I plead with it to clear up before morning. I tell it I hate and despise it. I do not pray for sight. I pray for beauty.

"You did not change," they say.

I am fourteen and baby-sitting for my brother Bill, who lives in Boston. He is my favorite brother and there is a strong bond between us. Understanding my feelings of shame and ugliness he and his wife take me to a local hospital, where the "glob" is removed by a doctor named O. Henry. There is still a small bluish crater where the scar tissue was, but the ugly white stuff is gone. Almost immediately I become a different person from the girl who does not raise her head. Or so I think. Now that I've raised my head I win the boyfriend of my dreams. Now that I've raised my head I have plenty of friends. Now that I've raised my head classwork comes from my lips as faultlessly as Easter speeches did, and I leave high school as valedictorian, most popular student, and *queen*, hardly believing my luck. Ironically, the girl who was voted most beautiful in our class (and was) was later shot twice through the chest by a male companion, using a "real" gun, while she was pregnant. But that's another story in itself. Or is it?

"You did not change," they say.

It is now thirty years since the "accident." A beautiful journalist comes to visit and to interview me. She is going to write a cover story for her magazine that focuses on my latest book. "Decide how you want to look on the cover," she says. "Glamorous, or whatever."

Never mind "glamorous," it is the "whatever" that I hear. Suddenly all I can think of is whether I will get enough sleep the night before the photography session: if I don't, my eye will be tired and wander, as blind eyes will.

At night in bed with my lover I think up reasons why I should not appear on the cover of a magazine. "My meanest critics will say I've sold out," I say. "My family will now realize I write scandalous books."

"But what's the real reason you don't want to do this?" he asks.

"Because in all probability," I say in a rush, "my eye won't be straight."

"It will be straight enough," he says. Then, "Besides, I thought you'd made your peace with that."

And I suddenly remember that I have.

I remember:

I am talking to my brother Jimmy, asking if he remembers anything unusual about the day I was shot. He does not know I consider that day the last time my father, with his sweet home remedy of cool lily leaves, chose me, and that I suffered and raged inside because of this. "Well," he says, "all I remember is standing by the side of the highway with Daddy, trying to flag down a car. A white man stopped, but when Daddy said he needed somebody to take his little girl to the doctor, he drove off."

I remember:

I am in the desert for the first time. I fall totally in love with it. I am so overwhelmed by its beauty, I confront for the first time, consciously, the meaning of the doctor's words years ago: "Eyes are sympathetic. If one is blind, the other will likely become blind too." I realize I have dashed about the world madly, looking at this, looking at that, storing up images against the fading of the light. *But I might have missed seeing the desert!* The shock of that possibility—and gratitude for over twenty-five years of sight—sends me literally to my knees. Poem after poem comes—which is perhaps how poets pray.

On Sight

I am so thankful I have seen
The Desert
And the creatures in the desert
And the desert Itself.

The desert has its own moon
Which I have seen
With my own eye.
There is no flag on it.

Trees of the desert have arms
All of which are always up
That is because the moon is up
The sun is up
Also the sky
The stars
Clouds
None with flags.

If there *were* flags, I doubt
the trees would point.
Would you?

But mostly, I remember this:

I am twenty-seven, and my baby daughter is almost three. Since her birth I have worried about her discovery that her mother's eyes are different from other people's. Will she be embarrassed? I think. What will she say? Every day she watches a television program called "Big Blue Marble." It begins with a picture of the earth as it appears from the moon. It is bluish, a little battered-looking, but full of light, with whitish clouds swirling around it. Every time I see it I weep with love, as if it is a picture of Grandma's house. One day when I am putting Rebecca down for her nap, she suddenly focuses on my eye. Something inside me cringes, gets ready to try to protect myself. All children are cruel about physical differences, I know from experience, and that they don't always mean to be is another matter. I assume Rebecca will be the same.

But no-o-o-o. She studies my face intently as we stand, her inside and me outside her crib. She even holds my face maternally between her dimpled little hands. Then, looking every bit as serious and lawyerlike as her father, she says, as if it may just possibly have slipped my attention: "Mommy, there's a *world* in your eye." (As in, "Don't be alarmed, or do anything crazy.") And then, gently, but with great interest: "Mommy, where did you *get* that world in your eye?"

For the most part, the pain left then. (So what, if my brothers grew up to buy even more powerful pellet guns for their sons and to carry real guns themselves. So what, if a young "Morehouse man" once nearly fell off the steps of Trevor Arnett Library because he thought my eyes were blue.) Crying and laughing I ran to the bathroom, while Rebecca mumbled and sang herself off to sleep. Yes indeed, I realized, looking into the mirror. There *was* a world in my eye. And I saw that it was possible to love it: that in fact, for all it had taught me of shame and anger and inner vision, I *did* love it. Even to see it drifting out of orbit in boredom, or rolling up out of fatigue, not to mention floating back at attention in excitement (bearing witness, a friend has called it), deeply suitable to my personality, and even characteristic of me.

That night I dream I am dancing to Stevie Wonder's song "Always" (the name of the song is really "As," but I hear it as "Always"). As I dance, whirling and joyous, happier than I've ever been in my life, another bright-faced dancer joins me. We dance and kiss each other and hold each other through the night. The other dancer has obviously come through all right, as I have done. She is beautiful, whole and free. And she is also me.

Writing Race, Class, Gender, and Resistance

"... [H]ow come we ain't in on it?" Sylvia, the narrator in Toni Cade Bambara's story "The Lesson" asks herself when confronted with shattering evidence that she is one of the have-nots. Her question mirrors that of the writers in this section as they address the inequities and power disparities prevalent in our country. These readings remind us that we don't have to travel to distant countries to educate ourselves about the continuing imperative to question and challenge institutionalized privilege.

In her story "like a woman," Debra Busman distills the reality of surviving as a homeless teenager, whether as a drug dealer, a prostitute, or a Winchell's counterperson. The narrator's raw description of why she turns to the sex trade, that "I was getting fucked anyway so I figured I might as well get paid for it, right," captures the character's heartbreaking combination of youthful bravado and hopelessness. We cheer for her when she says, "Those girls never did stop trying to get me into a dress, but, like my smile at the donut store, it just wasn't gonna happen." We cheer louder when she spits into the coffee of the pigs who brag about the "hippies, whores, and dykes they've raped and messed up good," ignoring her presence, an unsubtle reminder that in their world, the invisible narrator and her invisible friends exist only to serve or abuse. They have no other identity.

Despite the enactment of the Civil Rights Act in 1964, racism remains a constant issue for persons of color in the United States. Unfortunately, society's thin veil of civility fails to protect those who are constantly forced to recognize their own powerlessness. As Sekou Sundiata reiterates in the refrain to his poem "Blink Your Eyes," "All depends, all depends on the skin,/all depends on the skin you're living in." For those who bear the weight of centuries of genocide, the perception versus the reality of privilege presents its own dilemma. Determined resistance in the face of centuries of colonial oppression infuses Marilyn Chin's poem "Blues on Yellow."

Individual writers may negotiate and come to terms with society's racialized perception of beauty, as in Diana García's poem "Las Rubias," but the challenge of protecting succeeding generations from racist attacks remains a constant challenge.

Lucille Clifton's narrator in "poem to my uterus" questions what becomes of her identity as a woman when she loses her uterus. The narrator rages, "they want to cut you out," and despairs, "where am i going/old girl/without you." Clifton layers a series of increasingly graphic metaphors, from the comfortable and well-worn "sock" and "stocking i will not need" to "my estrogen kitchen" and "my black bag of desire," to convey the narrator's complex and conflicted emotions as she mourns the loss of an intact sense of self, understandable to any woman who faces a hysterectomy.

The blues as poetic expression offers us a narrator recreating a mother's escape from a womanizing, high-control man in Kelly Norman Ellis's poem "Daddy Blues." Ellis uses repetition and rhyme to tell the story of a young mother who knows "A woman gotta taste air/For to satisfy her soul." We cheer for this mother brave enough to leave a man who "lied about his women/And cut off both mama's wings," but in the last line we find ourselves unnerved by the image of being "[m]et at the station by her daddy's wide mouth frown."

In a parallel vein, Minnie Bruce Pratt, in her poem "Standing in the Elevator," paints the precise moment when the narrator recognizes the privileges afforded to "the guys at the top" who "make the money" versus the lack of privilege of those who "know how/to make things with each other," because that's what they want to do.

Chitra Banerjee Divakaruni's poem "The Brides Come to Yuba City" connects us to the lives of women seeking a new and better life. Like the mother in "Daddy Blues," the journey can sometimes lead to a questionable end, as in the case of the newly arrived 16-year-old Harvinder, married to a 52-year-old man she has never met, who will that night "open her legs to him." The anonymous narrator, one of the brides, ends the poem with the line, "We cannot recognize a single face," referring to the men, their husbands, who "walk and walk/without advancing."

Even as the narrators in several of the preceding poems explore what it means to be a woman—such as in Jamaica Kincaid's "Girl," with a litany of "this is how . . ." instructions being passed down from mother to daughter—the narrator in Gary Gildner's poem "First Practice" begins the journey of understanding what it is to become a man. Gildner creates a brutal character in the form of the coach "with the short cigar" who instructs the boys, "if/there were any girls present/for them to leave now." With a few short lines, Gildner sketches the coach's lesson, one of winning at all costs. The coach instructs the boys to line up facing each other and tells them, "across the way . . ./is the man you hate most/in the world." We may not understand what kind of scrimmage this is, but we do understand the meaning behind the coach's original statement when he adds, "I don't want to see/any marks when you're dressed."

If only developing a sense of identity around the issue of gender was as easy as the coach in Gildner's poem suggests. From the time we are born, we spend our lives looking to those we admire and those we detest, seeking hints of the kind of person we might become and the kind of person we hope never to become. We want this person's kindness, that one's ability to carry on a conversation with anyone in a room, another's ease and grace in their body. The formation of identity comes to us through a myriad of clues. We are social sponges, practicing our identities at the playground among our peers. We begin to develop a sense of who we are even as we line up for our first school photos.

With an economy of dialogue, Tommi Avicolli Mecca provides a crystalline example of how to capture the relationship between family members in his story "He Defies You Still: The Memoirs of a Sissy." In the story, the father orders his son, "Don't say another word. Just get over there and walk right—walk like a man." In those few words, we recognize the father's fear and distaste. We want to believe the father is concerned more for his son than for himself, but the command to "walk right" makes us dread reading further into the story.

Writers may be able to recognize and reflect on their own privileges, but one's own privileges, to the extent that they exist, are not transferable. Zachary Knapp reflects on this lesson when he recounts how he is unable to protect his mentor, a Mexican immigrant tenant-farmer, from the sting of racism in his essay "Terreno."

Frances Payne Adler's account, "The Fear That Doesn't," underscores the perils faced by those who may look privileged but whose ancestry renders them members of historically oppressed groups. Even at a distance of decades and generations, the need to resist governmentally sanctioned oppression requires constant vigilance.

For his part, in his essay "White Skin Privilege," Harlon Dalton suggests that because of "White skin privilege," "White ethnics" fail to understand or see themselves in racial terms. He prods us to recognize the "troublesome consequence of race obliviousness" and suggests that the implications of not doing so foreclose the possibility of social justice.

The Lesson

Toni Cade Bambara

Back in the days when everyone was old and stupid or young and foolish and me and Sugar were the only ones just right, this lady moved on our block with nappy hair and proper speech and no makeup. And quite naturally we laughed at her, laughed the way we did at the junk man who went about his business like he was some big-time president and his sorry-ass horse his secretary. And we kinda hated her too, hated the way we did the winos who cluttered up our parks and pissed on our handball walls and stank up our hallways and stairs so you couldn't halfway play hide-and-seek without a goddamn gas mask. Miss Moore was her name. The only woman on the block with no first name. And she was black as hell, 'cept for her feet, which were fish-white and spooky. And she was always planning these boring-ass things for us to do, us being my cousin, mostly, who lived on the block cause we all moved North the same time and to the same apartment then spread out gradual to breathe. And our parents would yank our heads into some kinda shape and crisp up our clothes so we'd be presentable for travel with Miss Moore, who always looked like she was going to church, though she never did. Which is just one of the things the grownups talked about when they talked behind her back like a dog. But when she came calling with some sachet she'd sewed up or some gingerbread she'd made or some book, why then they'd all be too embarrassed to turn her down and we'd get handed over all spruced up. She'd been to college and said it only right that she should take responsibility for the young ones' education, and she not even related by marriage or blood. So they'd go for it. Specially Aunt Gretchen. She was the main gofer in the family. You got some ole dumb shit foolishness you want somebody to go for, you send for Aunt Gretchen. She been screwed into the go-along for so long, it's a blood-deep natural thing with her. Which is how she got saddled with me and Sugar and Junior in the first place while our mothers were in a la-de-da apartment up the block having a good ole time.

So this one day Miss Moore rounds us all up at the mailbox and it's pure-dee hot and she's knockin herself out about arithmetic. And school suppose to let up in summer I heard, but she don't never let up. And the starch in my pinafore scratching the shit outta me and I'm really hating this nappy-head bitch and her goddamn college degree. I'd much rather go to the pool or to the show where it's cool. So me and Sugar leaning on the mailbox being surly, which is a Miss Moore word. And Flyboy checking out what everybody brought for lunch. And Fat Butt already wasting his peanut-butter-and-jelly sandwich like the pig he is. And Junebug punchin on Q.T.'s arm for potato chips. And Rosie Giraffe shifting from one hip to the other waiting for somebody to step on her foot or ask her if she from Georgia so she can kick ass, preferably Mercedes'. And Miss Moore asking us do we know what money is, like we a bunch of retards. I mean real money, she say, like it's only poker chips or monopoly papers we lay on the grocer. So right away I'm tired of this and say so. And would much rather snatch Sugar and go to the Sunset and terrorize the West Indian kids and take their hair ribbons and their money too. And Miss Moore files that remark away for next week's lesson on brotherhood, I can tell. And finally I say we oughta get to the subway cause it's cooler and besides we might meet some cute boys. Sugar done swiped her mama's lipstick, so we ready.

So we heading down the street and she's boring us silly about what things cost and what our parents make and how much goes for rent and how money ain't divided up right in this country. And then she gets to the part about we all poor and live in the slums, which I don't feature. And I'm ready to speak on that, but she steps out in the street and hails two cabs just like that. Then she hustles half the crew in with her and hands me a five-dollar bill and tells me to calculate 10 percent tip for the driver. And we're off. Me and Sugar and Junebug and Flyboy hangin out the window and hollering to everybody, putting lipstick on each other cause Flyboy a faggot anyway, and making farts with our sweaty armpits. But I'm mostly trying to figure how to spend this money. But they all fascinated with the meter ticking and Junebug starts laying bets as to how much it'll read when Flyboy can't hold his breath no more. Then Sugar lays bets as to how much it'll be when we get there. So I'm stuck. Don't nobody want to go for my plan, which is to jump out at the next light and run off to the first bar-b-que we can find. Then the driver tells us to get the hell out cause we are there already. And the meter reads eighty-five cents. And I'm stalling to figure out the tip and Sugar say give him a dime. And I decide he don't need it bad as I do, so later for him. But then he tries to take off with Junebug foot still in the door so we talk about his mama something ferocious. Then we check out that we on Fifth Avenue and everybody dressed up in stockings. One lady in a fur coat, hot as it is. White folks crazy.

"This is the place," Miss Moore say, presenting it to us in the voice she uses at the museum. "Let's look in the windows before we go in."

"Can we steal?" Sugar asks very serious like she's getting the ground rules squared away before she plays. "I beg your pardon," say Miss Moore, and we fall out. So she leads us around the windows of the toy store and me and Sugar screamin, "This is mine, that's mine, I gotta have that, that was made for me, I was born for that," till Big Butt drowns us out.

"Hey, I'm goin to buy that there."

"That there? You don't even know what it is, stupid."

"I do so," he say punchin on Rosie Giraffe. "It's a microscope."

"Whatcha gonna do with a microscope, fool?"

"Look at things."

"Like what, Ronald?" ask Miss Moore. And Big Butt ain't got the first notion. So here go Miss Moore gabbing about the thousands of bacteria in a drop of water and the somethinorother in a speck of blood and the million and one living things in the air around us is invisible to the naked eye. And what she say that for? Junebug go to town on that "naked" and we rolling. Then Miss Moore ask what it cost. So we all jam into the window smudgin it up and the price tag say $300. So then she ask how long'd take for Big Butt and Junebug to save up their allowances. "Too long," I say. "Yeh," adds Sugar, "outgrown it by that time." And Miss Moore say no, you never outgrow learning instruments. "Why, even medical students and interns and," blah, blah, blah. And we ready to choke Big Butt for bringing it up in the first damn place.

"This here costs four hundred eighty dollars," say Rosie Giraffe. So we pile up all over her to see what she pointin out. My eyes tell me it's a chunk of glass cracked with something heavy, and different-color inks dripped into the splits, then the whole thing put into a oven or something. But for $480 it don't make sense.

"That's a paperweight made of semi-precious stones fused together under tremendous pressure," she explains slowly, with her hands doing the mining and all the factory work.

"So what's a paperweight?" asks Rosie Giraffe.

"To weight paper with, dumbbell," say Flyboy, the wise man from the East.

"Not exactly," say Miss Moore, which is what she say when you warm or way off too. "It's to weigh paper down so it won't scatter and make your desk untidy." So right away me and Sugar curtsy to each other and then to Mercedes who is more the tidy type.

"We don't keep paper on top of the desk in my class," say Junebug, figuring Miss Moore crazy or lyin one.

"At home, then," she say. "Don't you have a calendar and a pencil case and a blotter and a letter-opener on your desk at home where you do your homework?" And she know damn well what our homes look like cause she noseys around in them every chance she gets.

"I don't even have a desk," say Junebug. "Do we?"

"No. And I don't get no homework neither," say Big Butt.

"And I don't even have a home," say Flyboy like he do at school to keep the white folks off his back and sorry for him. Send this poor kid to camp posters, is his speciality.

"I do," say Mercedes. "I have a box of stationery on my desk and a picture of my cat. My godmother bought the stationery and the desk. There's a big rose on each sheet and the envelopes smell like roses."

"Who want to know about your smelly-ass stationery," say Rosie Giraffe fore I can get my two cents in.

"It's important to have a work area all your own so that . . ."

"Will you look at this sailboat, please," say Flyboy, cuttin her off and pointin to the thing like it was his. So once again we tumble all over each other to gaze at this magnificent thing in the toy store which is just big enough to maybe sail two kittens across the pond if you strap them to the posts tight. We all start reciting the price tag like we in assembly. "Handcrafted sailboat of fiberglass at one thousand one hundred ninety-five dollars."

"Unbelievable," I hear myself say and am really stunned. I read it again for myself just in case the group recitation put me in a trance. Same thing. For some reason this pisses me off. We look at Miss Moore and she lookin at us, waiting for I dunno what.

"Who'd pay all that when you can buy a sailboat set for a quarter at Pop's, a tube of glue for a dime, and a ball of string for eight cents? It must have a motor and a whole lot else besides," I say. "My sailboat cost me about fifty cents."

"But will it take water?" say Mercedes with her smart ass.

"Took mine to Alley Pond Park once," say Flyboy. "String broke. Lost it. Pity."

"Sailed mine in Central Park and it keeled over and sank. Had to ask my father for another dollar."

"And you got the strap," laugh Big Butt. "The jerk didn't even have a string on it. My old man wailed on his behind."

Little Q.T. was staring hard at the sailboat and you could see he wanted it bad. But he too little and somebody'd just take it from him. So what the hell. "This boat for kids, Miss Moore?"

"Parents silly to buy something like that just to get all broke up," say Rosie Giraffe.

"That much money it should last forever," I figure.

"My father'd buy it for me if I wanted it."

"Your father, my ass," say Rosie Giraffe getting a chance to finally push Mercedes.

"Must be rich people shop here," say Q.T.

"You are a very bright boy," say Flyboy. "What was your first clue?" And he rap him on the head with the back of his knuckles, since Q.T. the only one he could get away with. Though Q.T. liable to come up behind you years later and get his licks in when you half expect it.

"What I want to know is," I says to Miss Moore though I never talk to her, I wouldn't give the bitch that satisfaction, "is how much a real boat costs? I figure a thousand'd get you a yacht any day."

"Why don't you check that out," she says, "and report back to the group?" Which really pains my ass. If you gonna mess up a perfectly good swim day least you could do is have some answers. "Let's go in," she say like she got something up her sleeve. Only she don't lead the way. So me and Sugar turn the corner to where the entrance is, but when we get there I kinda hang back. Not that I'm scared, what's there to be afraid of, just a toy store. But I feel funny, shame. But what I got to be shamed about? Got as much right to go in as anybody. But somehow I can't seem to get hold of the door, so I step away for Sugar to lead. But she hangs back too. And I look at her and she looks at me and this is ridiculous. I mean, damn, I have never ever been shy about doing nothing or going nowhere. But then Mercedes steps up and then Rosie Giraffe and Big Butt crowd in behind and shove, and next thing we all stuffed into the doorway with only Mercedes squeezing past us, smoothing out her jumper and walking right down the aisle. Then the rest of us tumble in like a glued-together jigsaw done all wrong. And people lookin at us. And it's like the time me and Sugar crashed into the Catholic church on a dare. But once we got in there and everything so hushed and holy and the candles and the bowin and the handkerchiefs on all the drooping heads, I just couldn't go through with the plan. Which was for me to run up to the altar and do a tap dance while Sugar played the nose flute and messed around in the holy water. And Sugar kept givin me the elbow. Then later teased me so bad I tied her up in the shower and turned it on and locked her in. And she'd be there till this day if Aunt Gretchen hadn't finally figured I was lying about the boarder takin a shower.

Same thing in the store. We all walkin on tiptoe and hardly touchin the games and puzzles and things. And I watched Miss Moore who is steady watchin us like she waitin for a sign. Like Mama Drewery watches the sky and sniffs the air and takes note of just how much slant is in the bird formation. Then me and Sugar bump smack into each other, so busy gazing at the toys, specially the sailboat. But we don't laugh and go into our fat-lady bump-stomach routine. We just stare at that price tag. Then Sugar run a finger over the whole boat. And I'm jealous and want to hit her. Maybe not her, but I sure want to punch somebody in the mouth.

"Watcha bring us here for, Miss Moore?"

"You sound angry, Sylvia. Are you mad about something?" Give me one of them grins like she tellin a grown-up joke that never turns out to be funny. And she's lookin very closely at me like maybe she plannin to do my portrait from memory. I'm mad, but I won't give her that satisfaction. So I slouch around the store bein very bored and say, "Let's go."

Me and Sugar at the back of the train watchin' the tracks whizzin by large then small then gettin gobbled up in the dark. I'm thinkin about this tricky toy I saw in the store. A clown that somersaults on a bar then does chin-ups just cause you yank lightly at his leg. Cost $35. I could see me askin my mother for a $35 birthday clown. "You wanna who that costs what?" she'd say, cockin her head to the side to get a better view of the hole in my head. Thirty-five dollars could buy new bunk beds for Junior and Gretchen's boy. Thirty-five dollars and the whole household could go visit Granddaddy Nelson in the country. Thirty-five dollars would pay for the rent and the piano bill too. Who are these people that spend that much for performing clowns and $1,000 for toy sailboats? What kinda work they do and how they live and how come we ain't in on it? Where we are is who we are, Miss Moore always pointin out. But it don't necessarily have to be that way, she always adds then waits for somebody to say that poor people have to wake up and demand their share of the pie and don't none of us know what kind of pie she talkin about in the first damn place. But she ain't so smart cause I still got her four dollars from the taxi and she sure ain't gettin it. Messin up my day with this shit. Sugar nudges me in my pocket and winks.

Miss Moore lines us up in front of the mailbox where we started from, seem like years ago, and I got a headache for thinkin so hard. And we lean all over each other so we can hold up under the draggy-ass lecture she always finishes us off with at the end before we thank her for borin us to tears. But she just looks at us like she readin tea leaves. Finally she say, "Well, what did you think of F. A. O. Schwarz?"

Rosie Giraffe mumbles, "White folks crazy."

"I'd like to go in there again when I get my birthday money," says Mercedes, and we shove her out the pack so she has to lean on the mailbox by herself.

"I'd like a shower. Tiring day," say Flyboy.

Then Sugar surprises me by saying. "You know, Miss Moore, I don't think all of us here put together eat in a year what that sailboat costs." And Miss Moore lights up like somebody goosed her. "And?" she say, urging Sugar on. Only I'm standin on her foot so she don't continue.

"Imagine for a minute what kind of society it is in which some people can spend on a toy what it would cost to feed a family of six or seven. What do you think?"

"I think," say Sugar pushing me off her feet like she never done before, cause I whip her ass in a minute, "that this is not much of a democracy if you ask me. Equal chance to pursue happiness means an equal crack at the dough, don't it?" Miss Moore is besides herself and I am disgusted with Sugar's treachery. So I stand on her foot one more time to see if she'll shove me. She shuts up, and Miss Moore looks at me, sorrowfully I'm thinkin. And somethin weird is going on, I can feel it in my chest.

"Anybody else learn anything today?" lookin dead at me. I walk away and Sugar has to run to catch up and don't even seem to notice when I shrug her arm off my shoulder.

"Well, we got four dollars anyway," she says.

"Uh hunh."

"We could go to Hascombs and get half a chocolate layer and then go to the Sunset and still have plenty money for potato chips and ice-cream sodas."

"Uh hunh."

"Race you to Hascombs," she say.

We start down the block and she gets ahead which is O.K. by me cause I'm going to the West End and then over to the Drive to think this day through. She can run if she want to and even run faster. But ain't nobody gonna beat me at nuthin.

like a woman

Debra Busman

The other girls tell me I am going to have to dress "like a woman" if I'm going to make it on the street. "Screw you," I laugh. "I've been fucked all my life and I've never had to wear a dress yet."

"Just tryin' to help you out, girl," they call out as they walk on down Santa Monica Boulevard, ankles bowed out over wobbly spike heels, popping their gum and adjusting their spaghetti strap bras as if they had something special going on down there. Don't none of us, 'cept Lisa have any tits yet and even if I had 'em I wasn't about to go dressin' in no drag shit. For one thing, it costs too much and I've got better things to do with my money. And for another thing I can't hardly walk in that shit, much less run. Or fight. Some girls can, tho. I seen one girl whip off those fuck me pumps and bust some motherfucker trying to get something for nothing across the side of his head quicker than I could have cracked his nuts. Said she fucked up his eardrum cuz she got the pointy part right inside his ear hole and see, check out that blood, girl. I think she was just feeling good cuz she got his wallet, messed him up, and didn't even break a heel.

It was good for me, cuz she made a buy with the joker's money. That was before I was living on the streets. I just came down to deal, mostly pot but sometimes opium and acid. You had to carry if you wanted to run the serious shit and it wasn't my style. They all laughed and called me Mahatma cuz I was always reading Gandhi and Thoreau and shit about nonviolence and revolution and civil disobedience, but we was all tight anyway. We watched each other's backs and they knew I could fight like a motherfuckin' crazy person if I got pushed too far or somebody I hung out with was being messed up. There was no doubt but that I'd kill somebody if I had a gun, so it was better to just stick to dealing pot and reading my books. I had a lot of reading to do.

So, yeah, now I'm working the trade. I didn't particularly want to but there aren't exactly a lot of career opportunities for 15-year-old girls living on the streets of LA. The truth is I was getting fucked anyway so I figured I might as well get paid for it, right. You couldn't sleep anywhere without waking up to find some guy's dick poking around looking for some hole, didn't matter which one. Seems like ever since I can remember I been waking up to find some big hairy thing climbing on or off of me. I got tired of the shit and thought, hell, I can't get any sleep anyway, I'm going to make somebody pay for this shit. At least now I'm calling the shots and making some money. And I was right. Don't need no fancy drag dress. There is plenty of trade. I do all right. Lots of hairy guys just dying to pay for bait. Tell me I remind them of their daughter and then tell me how they want me to fuck them. They got some messed up shit, man, but the money's good. Better than working at McDonalds, right?

∽ ∽

Pigs and Donuts

"Hey, Baby, bring us some more coffee, will ya?" I spit in their coffee. And carry it to their table, talking to my body like it was somebody else, "Now, don't you mess me up here, we can't show no fear, ok. We just go in and out real smooth, no shaking, no tripping, no spilling. We just gonna set this shit down on the table real calm and professional like we're some college girl and then we gonna get back behind the counter." When I get my feet all talked into not stumbling and my hands convinced they gonna set the coffee down *on the table* and not in the faces or crotches of these motherfucking pigs I got to wait on, then I move. But it's all gotta happen real fast, these jokers don't like to wait. I tried for awhile to talk my mouth into smiling like a straight girl but it wasn't gonna happen so I let it slide. It wasn't ever my mouth they looked at anyway.

So, here I am working graveyard shift at Winchell's Donut House on Ventura Boulevard. I didn't last too long on the streets. It was ok, I mean, the money was easy and it felt good to be setting the price and terms for something that was gonna get taken from me anyway. And me and the other girls, we was tight and boy we had us some good times. For about a week or two. Got us formed all together like a pack of wild dogs (they called 'em "worker collectives" in the books I read, but I knew what they meant) and for awhile nobody messed with us. Some john dick or hairy try and pull something too kinky or not pay you or some shit and the other girls would be on his ass like white on rice. For some of 'em that was their favorite part of the trade. Yeah, we had some good times. Those girls never did stop trying to get me into a dress, but, like my smile at the donut store, it just wasn't gonna happen. And they still called me Mahatma and made fun of my books and I still called them queens and told 'em they'd never look as pretty as the boys round the corner in West Hollywood. We was tight. But it all got fucked up. For one thing, the shiny boys who dealt and carried wanted a piece of the action. They didn't think no females should be making that kind of money without givin' it to poppa, so we had some problems. Also, we couldn't do nothing about the police. Seemed like no matter how many we sucked and fucked, they just kept coming back round. They fucking multiplied like bunnies. They must have had the whole damn police force working vice and narcotics so they could get laid and stoned and then make some money from the payoffs and the stash they stole on busts.

But, hey, check it out. Here I am again surrounded by the mother-fuckers. Come to find out my boss has a deal with the police that if they come around his store a lot for "protection," he (which means I) will give them free coffee and donuts. The truth is I would much rather be robbed than protected, in fact I was working the last two times this store went down and it was cool. These brothers came in with weapons and all and I didn't even have to tell my body nothin. My feet stayed calm, my hands were steady and, damn if my mouth wasn't grinning wide and pretty as I asked them if they'd like some jelly donuts to go with the cash drawer I was emptying for them.

But that was just twice. The rest of the time, night after night I have to serve these pigs coffee and listen to them go off braggin' about the niggers beaners spics and faggots whose heads they've cracked and the hippies whores and dykes they've raped and messed up good. Like now they're talkin' right in front of me like I don't even exist except to bring them more donuts, which I guess is good since I belong to a few of the categories they like to fuck with and my friends belong to the rest. But it freaks me out to be so invisible, even tho it saves my ass. It's like I'm in some sort of nazi spy movie and it's only the whiteness of my skin and this thin white polyester donut uniform that keeps them from recognizing me as the enemy and killing me, too. And I keep thinking I ought to be doing something more than spitting in their coffee. My hands say, just give us a gun and we promise you we will not shake or tremble and in my mind I see their bodies sprawled out all over the floors I have to scrub each night.

But the truth is I just stay invisible and try and keep from showing my fear. It's all I can do to not throw up or piss on myself and I cannot stop the sweat from running down my back and sides. And so I sweep the floors, wipe the counters, load the glazes, and lay out the chocolate sprinkles in seven crooked rows.

Blink Your Eyes

Sekou Sundiata

Remembering Sterling A. Brown

I was on my way to see my woman
but the Law said I was on my way
thru a red light red light red light
and if you saw my woman
you could understand,
I was just being a man.
It wasn't about no light
it was about my ride
and if you saw my ride
you could dig that too, you dig?
Sunroof stereo radio black leather
bucket seats sit low you know,
the body's cool, but the tires are worn.
Ride when the hard time come, ride
when they're gone, in other words
the light was green.

I could wake up in the morning
without a warning
and my world could change:
blink you eyes.
All depends, all depends on the skin,
all depends on the skin you're living in

Up to the window comes the Law
with his hand on his gun
what's up? what's happening?
I said I guess
that's when I really broke the law.
He said *a routine, step out the car*
a routine, *assume the position.*
Put your hands up in the air
you know the routine, like you just don't care.
License and registration.
Deep was the night and the light
from the North Star on the car door, deja vu
we've been through this before,
why did you stop me?
Somebody had to stop you.
I watch the news, you always lose.
You're unreliable, that's undeniable.
This is serious, you could be dangerous.

I could wake up in the morning
without a warning
and my world could change:
blink you eyes.
All depends, all depends on the skin,
all depends on the skin you're living in

New York City, they got laws
can't no bruthas drive outdoors,
in certain neighborhoods, on particular streets
near and around certain types of people.
They got laws.
All depends, all depends on the skin
all depends on the skin you're living in.

Blues on Yellow

Marilyn Chin

The canary died in the gold mine, her dreams got lost in the sieve.
The canary died in the gold mine, her dreams got lost in the sieve.
Her husband the crow killed under the railroad.
                                    the spokes dost shorn his wings.

Something's cooking' in Chin's kitchen, ten thousand yellow
    bellied sap suckers baked in a pie.
Something's cooking' in Chin's kitchen, ten thousand yellow
    bellied sap suckers baked in a pie.
Something's cookin' in Chin's kitchen, die die yellow bird, die die.

O crack an egg on the griddle, yellow will ooze into white.
O crack an egg on the griddle, yellow will ooze into white.
Run, run, sweet little Puritan, yellow will ooze into white.

If you cut my yellow wrists, I'll teach my yellow toes to write.
If you cut my yellow wrists, I'll teach my yellow toes to write.
If you cut my yellow fists, I'll teach my yellow feet to fight.

Do not be afraid to perish, my mother, Buddha's compassion is nigh.
Do not be afraid to perish, my mother, our boat will sail tonight.
Your babies will reach the promiseland, the stars will be their guide.

I am so mellow yellow, mellow yellow. Buddha sings in my veins.
I am so mellow yellow, mellow yellow. Buddha sings in my veins.
O take me to the land of the unreborn, there's no life on earth
    without pain.

(The verses could be sung in any order and could be
repeated an infinite number of times.)

Las Rubias

Diana García

1.

dear modern women's magazine the ads say you can be a
breck model too but I know that's not true at least not unless
they bleach my skin to white and lighten
up my curls a bit and that's the rub isn't it because they are
curls not folding underneath my chin straight hair but kinky
curls that like to sneak into my ears and another thing those
motherdaughter shampoo ads daughter smiling with
straight ahead blue eyes naturally and mother smiling down
at daughter except my mom and I would have to rouge our
cheeks like heck to pink them that cashmere shade you use
in your ads yours very truly

2.

I dreamt they queened me
for the county fair.
There I stood,
tiara hooked to my head
waving fake nails
to the crowd,
bra straps pinned
to my sweetheart neckline,
bra straps digging
into my shoulders,
my gym coach squeezing
my shoulders, shaking
me awake.
I could run for Indian

princess, not the queen,
she said, too short,
but I knew the score
as she snatched away
the queen instructions:
doeskin looks better
on Mexican skin.

3.

Admittedly I broke with him first: my first boyfriend, the first boy
I ever kissed, serving kisses beneath the pines against the smell
of aftershave and grilled chicken during the annual church dinner.
But to replace me with Laurie's ash blond hair, install her in the
student council office, play kissypoo games with her before my eyes,
her sharp nose more needle-like each day? How could his mother
let him? I bet her mother didn't know how dark his nipples were.

4.

I like that white meat, my brother writes
from his ship in the Mediterranean.
And blond hair, hair down to their ass
and below if you know what I mean.
I know what he means, this
sinvergüenza, this desgraciado,
this no-respecter of me or my mother,
this brother I never answer.

5.

At the mariachi concert, Spanish rising from
all sides, our matched curls black against the
honey-strawberry-platinum sea around us, my best
friend mutters, *I've never seen so many rubias
since the last time we went to the beach.*

6.

About those cellophaned streaks in my hair:
I didn't want to do it. I strayed slightly or completely.
I bench pressed 65 pounds. I found my body again.
My washboarded abs and ripped buttocks called for accents.

So I stripped from selected lengths what made my hair black.
I strutted young again. I reeked bold. I turned white
overnight from some dubious shock.

7.
Around and through her hair, the setting sun backlights her face,
flushes her cheekbones lit from within by bottles of good red wine.
Her blond hair conducts sun and breeze and friends and I crescendo.

I see what others must see, not what she sees when she inspects her
image, the spreading gray that draws a line between youth and age.
I lean into her hair as we nestle together beside the Pacific.

And I recall Linda, the curly blond farmer's daughter, how we played
on the monkey bars the first day of school, how we crouched below
the sky, arms hooked at the elbows and swore we'd always be friends.

8.
Dear my son,
I hoped you would never
feel the sting of being
dark-skinned, your
black waving hair that curls
at the neck, your lips
traced by darker skin
so like mine. But
take heart: we are
the birds of paradise
against a gold-lit world.

poem to my uterus

Lucille Clifton

you   uterus
you have been patient
as a sock
while i have slippered into you
my dead and living children
now
they want to cut you out
stocking i will not need
where i am going
where am i going
old girl
without you
uterus
my bloody print
my estrogen kitchen
my black bag of desire
where can i go
barefoot
without you
where can you go
without me

Daddy Blues

Kelly Norman Ellis

Mama left Daddy on a train headed Mississippi south
Mama left Daddy on a train headed down south
On the City of New Orleans,
She cried and covered her mouth

I was a lee lil' baby
Cryin' on my Mama's knee
Lee lil' baby
Crying on my mama's knee
Daddy watched us ride
And hollored, "Baby, please don't leave me"

Sweet baby girl don't shake yo head and cry
Sweet baby girl don't rub yo eyes and cry
You'll see yo daddy sho'nuff by and by

Mama said he was a redbone
A pretty high yella thang
Mama said he was redbone
A pretty high yella thang
But he lied bout his women
And cut off both mama's wings

Couldn't breathe in Chicago, so Mama say she had to roll
Couldn't breathe in Chicago, Mama say she had to roll
A woman gotta taste air
For to satisfy her soul

Sweet baby girl don't hang yo head and cry
Sweet baby girl don't hang yo head and cry
You'll hear yo daddy's song by and by

Just a tender woman chile
With a baby riding on her hip
Just a tender woman chile
With a baby riding her hip
Still feel my daddy's warm sugar on her lips

Mama rocked me from Chicago
To a salty Pearl River town
Rocked me from Chicago
To that salty Pearl River town
Met at the station by her daddy's wide mouth frown

Standing in the Elevator

Minnie Bruce Pratt

There's the awkward moment when the elevator doors close,
and we try not to breathe as loud as the big animals we are.
No words, because there's too much to say and nothing
for our hands to do except punch the down button again.
We don't need some fancy research to tell us how we want
to be together, standing over a table strewn with puzzle
pieces, lifting one jagged edge to fit against another,
to match the piece of blue sky you just made. Sure, we're
in here because we need the money but it means nothing
by itself. Like the day the power failed, some of us stuck
in the elevator, and the building burning from the top down.
The cleaning guy had just his bucket and a squeegee blade.
He jimmied the doors open, he forced the steel doors apart,
in the vague light from the windows five people could see
enough to find their way out. When I was out of work,
and some guy at a stoplight asked to clean my windshield
for a dollar, I thought of that. I thought I'd never hear
our niagara of sound going up the stairs again, or step,
immersed, into tens of thousands rushing to work. One molecule
in the many, carried along toward the purpose of our day.
It's never really about the money, except for the guys at the top.
They know how to make the money. We know how
To make things with each other. That's what we want to do.

The Brides Come to Yuba City

Chitra Banerjee Divakaruni

The sky is hot and yellow, filled
with blue screaming birds. The train
heaved us from its belly
and vanished in shrill smoke.
Now only the tracks
gleam dull in the heavy air,
a ladder to eternity, each receding rung
cleaved from our husbands' ribs.
Mica-flecked, the platform
dazzles, burns up through thin
chappal soles, lurches
like the ship's dark hold,
blurred month of nights, smell of vomit,
a porthole like the bleached iris
of a giant unseeing eye.

Red-veiled, we lean into each other,
press damp palms, try
broken smiles. The man
who met us at the ship whistles
a restless *Angrezi* tune
and scans the fields. Behind us,
the black wedding trunks, sharp-edged,
shiny, stenciled with strange men-names
our bodies do not fit into:
Mrs. Baldev Fohl, Mrs. Kanwal Bains.
Inside, folded like wings,
bright *salwar kameezes* scented
with sandalwood. For the men,

kurtas and thin white gauze
to wrap their uncut hair.
Laddus from Jullundhar, sugar-crusted,
six kinds of lentils, a small bag
of *bajra* flour. Labeled in our mothers'
hesitant hands, pickled mango and lime,
packets of seeds—*methi, karela, saag*—
to burst from this new soil
like green stars.

He gives a shout, waves
at the men, their slow
uneven approach. We crease our eyes
through the veils' red film,
cannot breathe. Thirty years
since we saw them. Or never,
like Harvinder, married last year
at Hoshiarpur to her husband's photo,
which she clutches tight to her
to stop the shaking. He is fifty-two,
she sixteen. Tonight—like us all—
she will open her legs to him.

The platform is endless-wide.
The men walk and walk
without advancing. Their lined,
wavering mouths, their
eyes like drowning lights.
We cannot recognize a single face.

Note: Yuba City in northern California was settled largely by Indian railroad workers around the 1900s. Due to immigration restrictions, many of them were unable to bring their families over—or, in the case of single men, go back to get married—until the 1940s.

Girl

Jamaica Kincaid

Wash the white clothes on Monday and put them on the stone heap; wash the color clothes on Tuesday and put them on the clothesline to dry; don't walk barehead in the hot sun; cook pumpkin fritters in very hot sweet oil; soak your little cloths right after you take them off; when buying cotton to make yourself a nice blouse, be sure that it doesn't have gum on it, because that way it won't hold up well after a wash; soak salt fish overnight before you cook it; is it true that you sing benna in Sunday school?; always eat your food in such a way that it won't turn someone else's stomach; on Sundays try to walk like a lady and not like the slut you are so bent on becoming; don't sing benna in Sunday school; you mustn't speak to wharf-rat boys, not even to give directions; don't eat fruits on the street—flies will follow you; *but I don't sing benna on Sundays at all and never in Sunday school;* this is how to sew on a button; this is how to make a buttonhole for the button you have just sewed on; this is how to hem a dress when you see the hem coming down and so to prevent yourself from looking like the slut I know you are so bent on becoming; this is how you iron your father's khaki shirt so that it doesn't have a crease; this is how you iron your father's khaki pants so that they don't have a crease; this is how you grow okra—far from the house, because okra tree harbors red ants; when you are growing dasheen, make sure it gets plenty of water or else it makes your throat itch when you are eating it; this is how you sweep a corner; this is how you sweep a whole house; this is how you sweep a yard; this is how you smile to someone you don't like too much; this is how you smile at someone you don't like at all; this is how you smile to someone you like completely; this is how you set a table for tea; this is how you set a table for dinner; this is how you set a table for dinner with an important guest; this is how you set a table for lunch; this is how you set a table for breakfast; this is how to behave in the presence of men who don't know you very well, and this way they won't recognize immediately the slut I have warned you against becoming; be sure to wash every day, even if it is with your own spit; don't squat down to play marbles—you are not a boy, you know; don't pick other people's flowers—you might catch something; don't throw stones at blackbirds, because it might not be a blackbird at all; this is how to make a bread pudding; this is how to make doukona; this is how to make pepper pot; this is how to make a good medicine for a cold; this is how to make a good medicine to throw away a child before it even becomes a child; this is how to catch a fish; this is how to throw back a fish you don't like, and that way something bad won't fall on you; this is how to bully a man; this is how a man bullies you; this is how to love a man, and if this doesn't work there are other ways, and if they don't work don't feel too bad about giving up; this is how to spit up in the air if you feel like it, and this is how to move quick so that it doesn't fall on you; and this is how to make ends meet; always squeeze bread to make sure it's fresh; *but what if the baker won't let me feel the bread?*; you mean to say that after all you are really going to be the kind of woman who the baker won't let near the bread?

benna: Calypso music
doukona: a spicy plantain pudding

First Practice

Gary Gildner

After the doctor checked to see
we weren't ruptured,
the man with the short cigar took us
under the grade school,
where we went in case of attack
or storm, and said
he was Clifford Hill, he was
a man who believed dogs
ate dogs, he had once killed
for his country, and if
there were any girls present
for them to leave now.
                  No one
left. OK, he said, he said I take
that to mean you are hungry
men who hate to lose as much
as I do. OK. Then
he made two lines of us
facing each other,
and across the way, he said,
is the man you hate most
in the world,
and if we are to win
that title I want to see how.
But I don't want to see
any marks when you're dressed,
he said. He said, *Now.*

He Defies You Still

The Memoirs of a Sissy

Tommi Avicolli Mecca

Scene One:

A homeroom in a Catholic high school in South Philadelphia. The boy sits quietly in the first aisle, third desk, reading a book. He does not look up, not even for a moment. He is hoping no one will remember he is sitting there. He wishes he were invisible. The teacher is not yet in the classroom so the other boys are talking and laughing loudly.

Suddenly, a voice from beside him: "Hey, you're a faggot, ain't you?"

The boy does not answer. He goes on reading his book, or rather pretending he is reading his book. It is impossible to actually read now.

"Hey, I'm talking to you!"

The boy still does not look up. He is so scared his heart is thumping madly. But he can't look up.

"Faggot, I'm talking to you!"

To look up is to meet the eyes of the tormentor.

Suddenly a sharp pencil point is thrust into the boy's arm. He jolts, shaking off the pencil, aware that there is blood seeping from the wound.

"What did you do that for?" he asks timidly.

"Cause I hate faggots," the other boy says, laughing. Some other boys begin to laugh, too. A symphony of laughter. The boy feels as if he's going to cry. But he must not cry. Must not cry. So he holds back the tears and tries to read the book again. He must read the book. Read the book.

When the teacher arrives a few minutes later, the class quiets down. The boy does not tell the teacher what has happened. He spits on the wound to clean it, dabbing it with a tissue until the bleeding stops. For weeks he fears some dreadful infection from the lead in the pencil point.

Scene Two:

The boy is walking home from school. A group of boys (two, maybe three, he is not certain) grab him from behind, drag him into an alley, and beat him up. When he gets home, he races up to his room, refusing dinner ("I don't feel well," he tells his mother through the locked door) and spends the night alone in the dark wishing he would die. . . .

These are not fictitious accounts—I *was* that boy. Having been branded a sissy by neighborhood children because I preferred jump rope to baseball and dolls to playing soldiers, I was often taunted with "hey sissy" or "hey faggot" or "yoo hoo, honey" when I left the house.

To avoid harassment, I spent many summers alone in my room. I went out on rainy days when the street was empty.

I came to like being alone. I didn't need anyone, I told myself over and over. I was an island. Contact with others meant pain. Alone, I was protected. I began writing poems, then short stories. There was no reason to go outside anymore. I had a world of my own.

> In the schoolyard today
> they'll single you out
> Their laughter will leave your ears ringing
> like the church bells
> that once awed you . . .

School was one of the more painful experiences of my youth. The neighborhood bullies could be avoided. The taunts of the children living in those endless row houses could be evaded by staying in my room. But school was something I had to face day after day for some two hundred mornings a year.

I had few friends in school. Some kids would talk to me, but few wanted to be known as my close friend. Afraid of labels. If I was a sissy, then they would be sissies, too. I was condemned to loneliness.

Fortunately, a new boy moved into our neighborhood and befriended me; he wasn't afraid of the labels. He protected me when the other guys threatened to beat me up. He walked me home from school; he broke through the terrible loneliness. We were in third or fourth grade at the time.

We spent a summer or two together. Then his parents sent him to camp and I was once again confined to my room.

Scene Three:

High school lunchroom. The boy sits at a table near the back of the room. Without warning, his lunch bag is grabbed and tossed to another table. Someone opens it and confiscates a package of Tastykakes; another boy takes the sandwich. The empty bag is tossed back to the boy, who stares at it, dumbfounded. He should be used to this; it has happened before.

Someone says, "Faggot," laughing. There is always laughter. It does not annoy him anymore.

There is no teacher nearby. There is never a teacher around. And what would he say if there were? Could he report the crime? He would be jumped after school if he did. Besides, it would be his word against theirs. Teachers never noticed anything. They never heard the taunts. Never heard the word, "faggot." They were the great deaf mutes, pillars of indifference; a sissy's pain was not relevant to history and geography and god made me to love honor and obey him, amen.

The boy reaches into his pocket for some money, but there's only a few coins. Always just a few coins. He cleans windshields at his father's gas station on Saturdays and Sundays to earn money. But it's never much. Only enough now to buy a carton of milk and some cookies. Only enough to watch the other boys eat and laugh, hoping they'll choke on their food. . . .

Scene Four:

High school religion class. Someone has a copy of *Playboy*. Father N. is not in the room yet; he's late, as usual. Someone taps the boy roughly on the shoulder. He turns. A finger points to the centerfold model, pink fleshy body, thin and sleek. Almost painted. Not real. The other asks in a mocking voice, "Hey, does she turn you on? Look at those tits!"

The boy smiles, nodding meekly; turns away.

The other jabs him harder on the shoulder, "Hey, what'samatter, don't you like girls?"

Laughter. Thousands of mouths; unbearable din of laughter. In the arena thumbs down. Don't spare the queer.

"Wanna suck my dick, huh? That turn you on, faggot!"

What did being a sissy really mean? It was a way of walking (from the hips rather than the shoulders); it was a way of talking (often with a lisp or in a high-pitched voice); it was a way of relating to others (gently, not wanting to fight, or hurt anybody's feelings). It was being intelligent ("an egghead" they called it sometimes); getting good grades. It meant not being interested in sports, not playing football in the street after school, not discussing teams and scores and playoffs. And it involved not showing a fervent interest in girls, not talking about scoring or tits or *Playboy* centerfolds. Not concealing pictures of naked women in your history book; or porno books in your locker.

On the other hand, anyone could be a "faggot." It was a catchall. If you did something that didn't conform to the acceptable behavior of the group, then you risked being called a faggot. It was the most commonly used putdown. It kept guys in line. They became angry when somebody called them a faggot. More fights started over calling someone a faggot than anything else. The word had power. It toppled the male ego, shattered his delicate facade, violated the image he projected. He was tough. Without feeling. Faggot cut through all this. It made him vulnerable. Feminine. And feminine was the worst thing he could possibly be. Girls were fine for fucking, but no boy in his right mind wanted to be like them. A boy was the opposite of a girl. He was not feminine. He was not feeling. He was not weak.

Just look at the gym teacher who growled like a dog; or the priest with the black belt who threw kids against the wall in rage when they didn't know their Latin. They were men, they got respect.

But not the physics teacher who preached pacifism during lectures on the nature of atoms. Everybody knew what he was—and why he believed in the antiwar movement.

Scene Five:

Father: I wanna see you walk, Mark.

Mark: What do you mean?

Father: Just walk, Mark.

Mark: (Starts to walk) I don't understand.

Father: That's it, just walk.

Mark: (Walks back and forth)

Father: Now come here.

(Mark approaches; father slaps him across the face, hard)

Mark: What was that for?

Father: I want you to walk right now.

Mark: What do you mean?

Father: Stop fooling around, Mark, I want you to walk like a man.

Mark: Dad, I . . .

Father: (Interrupting) Don't say another word. Just get over there and walk right—walk like a man.

My parents only knew that the neighborhood kids called me names. They begged me to act more like the other boys. My brothers were ashamed of me. They never said it, but I knew. Just as I knew that my parents were embarrassed by my behavior.

At times, they tried to get me to act differently. Once my father lectured me on how to walk right. I'm still not clear on what that means. Not from the hips, I guess; don't "swish" like faggots do.

A nun in elementary school told my mother at open house that there was "something wrong with me." I had draped my sweater over my shoulders like a girl, she said. I was a smart kid, no complaints about my grades, but I should know better than to wear my sweater like a girl.

My mother stood there, mute. I wanted her to say something, to chastise the nun, to defend me. But how could she? This was a nun talking—representative of Jesus, protector of all that was good and decent.

An uncle once told me I should start "acting like a boy" instead of a girl. Everybody seemed ashamed of me. And I guess I was ashamed of myself, too. It was hard not to be.

Scene Six:

Priest: Do you like girls, Mark?

Mark: Uh-huh.

Priest: I mean REALLY like them?

Mark: Yeah—they're okay.

Priest: There's a role they play in your salvation. Do you understand it, Mark?

Mark: Yeah.

Priest: You've got to like girls. Even if you should decide to enter the seminary, it's important to keep in mind God's plan for a man and a woman. . . .

Catholicism of course condemned homosexuality. Effeminancy was tolerated as long as the effeminate person did not admit to being gay. Thus, priests could be effeminate because they weren't gay.

As a sissy, I couldn't count on support from the church. A male's sole purpose in life was to father children—souls for the church to save. The only hope a homosexual had of attaining salvation was to remain totally celibate. Don't even think of touching another boy. To think of a sin was a sin. And to sin was to put a mark on the soul. Sin—led to hell. There was no way around it. If you sinned, you were doomed.

Realizing I was gay wasn't an easy task. Although I knew I was attracted to boys by the time I was about eleven, I didn't connect this attraction to homosexuality. I was not queer. Not I. I was merely appreciating a boy's good looks, his fine features, his proportions. It didn't seem to matter that I didn't appreciate a girl's looks in the same way. There was no twitching in my thighs when I gazed upon a beautiful girl. But I wasn't queer.

We sat through endless English classes, and history courses about the wars between men who were not allowed to love each other. No gay history was ever taught. You're just a faggot. Homosexuals had never contributed to the human race. God destroyed the queers in Sodom and Gommorrah.

I resisted that label—queer—for the longest time. Even when everything pointed to it, I refused to see it. I was certainly not queer. Not I.

Near the end of my junior year in high school, most of the teasing and taunting had let up. Now I was just ignored. Besides, I was getting a reputation for being a hippie, since I spoke up in social studies classes against the war, and wore my hair as long as I could without incurring the wrath of the administration. When your hair reached a certain length, you were told to get a haircut. If you didn't, you were sent down to the vice principal's office, where you were given a haircut.

I had a friend toward the end of junior year; his name was Joe. He introduced me to Jay at the bowling alley in South Philadelphia. I knew immediately I was in love with Jay.

A relationship developed. It was all very daring; neither of us understood what was happening. I still rejected the label. I wasn't queer. He wasn't queer. But I knew I was in love with him. I told myself that all the time. Yet I wasn't a homosexual.

Franny was a queer. He lived a few blocks away. He used to dress in women's clothes and wait for the bus on the corner. Everybody laughed at Franny. Everybody knew he was queer.

Then one night, Halloween, a chilly October night, Jay called:

Scene Seven:

. . . "What?"

"It's wrong."

"What's wrong."

Tossing in my sleep—sweating. It was the winter of '69. The heavy woolen cover became a thick shroud on top of me. The heat pricked me like so many needles.

"Why can't I see you tonight?"

"We can't see each other anymore. . . ."

My heart was an acrobat. It leaped like a frog. Landed in a deep puddle. Help, it shouted. It was going down for the third time.

"Why?" I felt nauseous. I was going to vomit.

"We can't. I've got to go."

"Wait—!"

"What?"

There were tears running down my cheeks in streams that left a salty residue at the corners of my lips. The record player in the background shut off, closing me in. The walls of the room collapsed. I was entombed.

"Please, talk to me. I can't let you go like this. I want to know what's wrong. Please . . ."

"I can't see you anymore. It's over. It was a mistake."

"It wasn't a mistake, Jay. I—I love you."

"Don't say that!" Voice quivering; don't force me to see things I don't want to see right now.

"But I do. And you love me. Admit it. Don't break it off now. Admit it. Admit that you love me."

"I've got to go."

"You can't go. Admit it!"

"Goodbye."

"Jay?"

Silence.

We learned about Michelangelo, Oscar Wilde, Gertrude Stein—but never that they were queer. They were not queer. Walt Whitman, the "father of American poetry," was not queer. No one was queer. I was alone, totally unique. One of a kind. Except for Franny, who wore dresses and makeup. Where did Franny go every night? Were there others like me somewhere? Another planet, perhaps?

In school, they never talked of queers. They did not exist. The only hint we got of this other species was in religion class. And even then it was clouded in mystery—never spelled out. It was a sin. Like masturbation. Like looking at *Playboy* and getting a hard-on. A sin.

Once a progressive priest in senior-year religion class actually mentioned homosexuals—he said the word, broke the silence—but he was talking about homosexuals as pathetic and sick. Fixated at some early stage; penis, anal, whatever. Only heterosexuals passed on to the nirvana of sexual development.

No other images from the halls of the Catholic high school except those the other boys knew: swishy faggot sucking cock in an alley somewhere, grabbing asses in the bathroom. Never mentioning how straight boys craved blow jobs, too.

It was all a secret. You were not supposed to talk about queers. Whisper maybe. Laugh about them, yes. But don't be open, honest; don't try to understand. Don't cite their accomplishments. No history faces you this morning. You're a faggot. No history—a faggot.

Epilogue:

The boy marching down Spruce Street. Hundreds of queers. Signs proclaiming gay pride. Speakers. Tables with literature from gay groups. A miracle, he is thinking. Tears are coming loose now. Someone hugs him.

> You could not control
> the sissy in me
> nor could you exorcise him
> nor electrocute him
> You declared him illegal illegitimate
> insane and immature
> but he defies you still.

Terreno

Zachary Knapp

For a few thick moments apricots orbit in sunny colonies, and then, with a *whoosh*, the tree and fruit whip past. On this country road, row after orchard row disappears behind us and our eyes re-focus, only for a moment, on the fleeting trees, glimmering leaves, and crimson fruits ahead. Alejandro slows down as one by one, signs replace trees. "Private Property, No Trespassing" on the left, "Beware of Dog" and "McMurtry Brothers Fencing" on the right. Gravel grates and crunches under the Chevy's tires, stating our presence like signal guns. The flatbed's hooks and boards bounce, clang, and rattle. I imagine an old shopping cart rolling through a cobble-floored monastery. Alejandro eases his truck up the gravel road to the brown, one-story wood and stucco ranch house. We've driven up and down old, crumbly edged roads for the last hour, but now he's sure this is the place. In line next to the house is an immediate family of carport, garage, and three sheds all the same color. He parks near the sheds and I follow his lead as he opens his door.

"*¿Ellos saben que estamos viniendo?*" I ask one more time, hoping we are expected. He answers as he did before, a quick "*Sí*" and then an even quicker explanation. Torrents of Spanish rush through my ears and I try to catch familiar words and piece sentences together. I don't understand everything when he speaks so fast.

A plastic tricycle, two miniature bikes, and other toys spill out of the carport on the path to the front door. My friend and I walk side by side as if we were partners in this venture. I like this feeling as we talk about land, the number of wells and irrigation potential, the future crops we want to try. My imagination whirls in dreams about farming, marketing schemes, and growing melons in a warm valley away from the coastal fog. I wish I were in the land hunt with Alejandro. Instead of school, I'd spend the next year learning from, and farming with, my friend and mentor. I realize though that I haven't earned it yet like Alejandro. It's his time, and mine will come if I can match his perseverance.

Alejandro slows down as we approach the door. It opens before we get there. I'm suddenly in front as he steps back behind me. The immediacy of my task swoons over me like the smell of freshly harvested cilantro, and I don't feel qualified for the position he just gave me.

A stocky and weathered man stands in the doorway. His tanned skin, strong build, and well-used Wranglers draw my mind back to the "McMurtry Brothers" sign and the cattle fences we passed on the way here. A gruff "Hi" breaks through his bushy light brown and gray mustache. He doesn't smile, and it's obvious he wants an explanation for the kid with a blonde pony tail and the middle-aged Mexican man behind him. Thinking back to the "No Trespassing" signs on the road, I get the feeling he doesn't answer his door much.

The explanation is mine to give; Alejandro doesn't speak English. He brought me here to help translate in his search for farming land to lease next season. I feel the vertigo of a newborn calf's first shaky step as I stand between the rancher with land and my Mexican friend who needs land.

"Hi," I say. The adrenaline that gets me through last-minute class presentations kicks in.

"I'm Zachary and this is Alejandro." He steps out of the doorway and takes my extended hand. I consciously look him in the eye and match his firm grasp, our hands like coupling railroad cars. This is how I learned to make a good impression, and I know he was taught the same.

"I'm Bill," he says and shakes Alejandro's hand. I get a sense the railroad cars didn't couple, one just bumped the other. Without stepping forward, Alejandro muffles a quick "Hi," and looks at me instead of the rancher.

"Alejandro is looking for land to rent next season. Is this the right place? You do have land for rent, don't you?" Before he can answer I add, "He doesn't speak English, and so I'm here just to translate."

"We might have land. Green Organics hasn't decided yet if they want the extra fifty acres we're rentin' out this year." He makes it clear they have first priority. Feeling we're already behind, I try to give him some background.

"Alejandro is farming right now on land owned by a small farm education program that's targeted to Spanish-speaking folks and their families. He graduated from this program two years ago, and now his time is up to stay on this land, and he needs new land to rent." The words stream out in a single breath, my hands beckoning forward as if they could speed his understanding. I can tell he doesn't get it.

Alejandro stands still behind me. I turn so I can speak to them both. For the first time, my friend is without his almost cocky confidence. It's clear he doesn't understand what the man said about the land his future might depend on. His stature hangs heavy like a dripping wet towel.

"*El dijo que un otra compañía posible va rentar el terreno, y este compañía tiene el prioridad,*" I translate to Alejandro in my simple Spanish, the language he and the other farmers in the program help me with every day.

"I have to talk to my dad and my brother about it," Bill adds.

"*El tiene que hablar con su padre y hermano acerca esto.*"

"We'll probably know in a few days."

"*Ellos problamente van decidir en pocos dias.*"

Alejandro nods and looks only at me. The roles have changed. I wish it were the usual way, with me looking to him. My stomach doubles over like kneaded dough as I try to think of what to ask next. I am responsible for representing my friend, making an impression for him. How can it be that suddenly he can't represent himself? I want Bill to see Alejandro as I know him. The man with the big blue Ford tractor, the newest tractor on the farm. The farmer who started with nothing six years ago and now has the tractor and its implements, three flatbed trucks, and people working for him every day. He harvests almost every morning, starting work when most people's alarms are an hour away from ringing. Often I see him doing tractor work until nine or ten at night. He told me about the mildew in my beets before I even thought to check for it, and he is the one the others and I go to with our questions.

These things aren't something you put on a resume; you don't hand the man you want to rent from your tractor shop receipt, or a log of last week's hours. You don't have someone else tell him that you're respected and looked up to. These accomplishments come out in character, they come out when you meet someone and leave them with a positive feeling. In my culture, the hand and the eye are so important, confidence is important. How do I do this for someone else? How can Bill really meet Alejandro when Alejandro is too intimidated and self-conscious to face him at my side? I wonder if Bill realizes the power disparity in the situation. Will he rent land to a man he can't talk to? A man he only knows by translation through some long-haired kid?

I'm not sure what to say next.

"So it's fifty acres?" It sounds like an intelligent question.

"Yeah, it's that parcel past this first pasture on the other side of the road." Bill points to the stubby bronze field with a back wall of sun-bleached mountains. It is the field we veered away from to drive up to his house.

"Is the land certified organic?" I ask, trying to do the business my friend brought me here to do. Alejandro has told me it is, but shouldn't I double check.

"It's all ready to be, nothing but cows have been on it for at least . . . I don't know, forty years."

I translate to Alejandro. He looks at me and says, "*Sí.*" At this point the three of us don't know what to do. Bill reaches in his back pocket and pulls out his wallet.

"Here's my card to get a hold of me." He hands me a card with the *McMurtry Brothers Fencing* logo. "Does he have a number where I can get a hold of him?" he asks, nodding toward Alejandro. I turn to my friend, his expression more confused than before.

"*¿Tienes una numero donde El puede llamarte?*"

"*Sí, tengo,*" he says and pulls a stack of assorted business cards from his wallet. Soft with rounded corners, the cards advertise tractor repair, irrigation supplies, seed companies, and brokers promising good returns. Shuffling through them, he finds one he doesn't need and looks up. I can tell he wants a pen and I hand him the one in my pocket. We huddle together as he crosses out the business logo and carefully prints his name and cell phone number.

"*Este es mi cellular,*" he says. And hands the card to me. I pass it to Bill. He glances at it and says he'll let us know next week.

"Great, thank you," I force out enthusiasm.

"But I don't know," he adds. "You got to think what a big operation like Green Organics will say. Are they going to want to deal with having a little guy next door?"

Bill turns to go back into his door and stops.

"How much is he expecting to pay?" he asks, again looking at me with a nod toward Alejandro. On the way here, Alejandro told me what they were asking.

"Uh, about two fifty an acre, more or less."

"That's in the ballpark," he replies and shuts the door. Without speaking, Alejandro and I walk back to his truck. We drive out the way we came, the land for rent directly in front of us.

"*Está bien, este terreno,*" Alejandro says one more time.

⌢ ⌢

It's Friday evening, a week after our trip to look at the land and Alejandro hasn't heard back from Bill. Alejandro and I stand in front of his truck, and he asks me to call for him. This time of day an orange glow creeps over the fields. First basting the tips of flowering corn, it drizzles down stalks, creeps through branches, trickles over leaves, and finally ignites the low-lying lettuce and new seedlings. A moist northwest wind presses against our jackets; it warns of a fog battalion, mounted and advancing towards us. He dials and hands me the phone.

"Hello."

"Hi, may I speak to Bill please?"

"Speaking."

"Hi Bill, this is Zachary Knapp. I came out last week with Alejandro and talked to you about the land for rent."

Before I can ask if it's available, he jumps in.

"Nope, sorry, we don't have any land for you."

"Oh, OK," I say, not expecting such quick denial.

"OK, bye." He hangs up.

I look up at Alejandro. He knows the call was too short. Once again, for a split second, he looks different, heavy shoulders, powerless like an engine stalled on a hill's crest. He straightens, regains his poise, and looks past me to the fields.

"*Está bien. Yo se de otro rancho con mejor terreno.*" I know it's a bluff. He'll never be a victim in front of me, or to himself.

The Fear That Doesn't

Frances Payne Adler

for Bessie Weisman Plonsky

Let me tell you a story. I moved from California a few years ago to La Crosse, Wisconsin, into a big old house on 15th Street. It was built around the turn of the century, large oak-framed windows, two sun porches. The day I carried my bags through the door, my landlord was painting the kitchen, white paint on his fingers, his hair. I loved the place immediately. But for the carpets. I picked up the corner of the living-room carpet and found beautiful hardwood floors underneath.

I asked him if he would take up the carpets. He was reluctant, but agreed, and we set about lifting the carpets the next day, pulling out carpet tacks, and scraping off dried glue. I was thrilled: the floors—the original hundred-year-old floors—were in wonderful shape. My landlord began to talk about bringing in a sander and then spreading a Verathane finish. No, no, I insisted, none of that. These are just fine. I like the scratches, the spots just as they are. I want the history of the families who have lived here to keep walking through this home.

On his way out, we stood talking on the front porch. At some point, I looked above my head. On the doorframe was a *mezzuzeh*. My eyes filled with tears. I was pleased, surprised. Jews had lived here before me.

What's that? he asked. It contains Jewish blessings, I said, they're rolled up inside. Anyone who enters here is blessed.

I've owned this place fifteen years, he said. Never noticed it.

After he left, I removed the layers of paint from the old mezzuzeh and tacked up mine, just a little below, and parallel to it.

Let me tell you another story. My landlord's heritage is German. I am Jewish. He is a kind, thoughtful, hard-working man. I am a kind, thoughtful, hard-working woman. We are friends. He came over last week to fix my oven. (This is not a metaphor. This really happened.) One of the heating elements had exploded one day, and needed replacing. I'd been working at the kitchen table, before he arrived, writing, thinking, reading about the Holocaust. We talked, as he leaned in and out of his toolbox and the oven.

When I was in the Army, he said, I visited Auschwitz. It scared me.

In what way, I asked.

Well, you know that I'm of German descent, he said. And I'm the kind of guy who likes to do things right. It scared me to think of what I might have done, had I lived there then, and been indoctrinated into those values. It scared me.

He fitted the new heating element into the bottom of the oven and, latching up his toolbox, he said, I have a friend here in La Crosse who doesn't believe it happened.

What didn't, I asked.

The Holocaust. At least not to the extent they claim.

Are you kidding? (I had heard and read that there were people who thought this way.) What about all the documentation, the photographs?

Well, *he* would say, you can always take a picture of the same 400 bodies over and over.

This is the shape of the Fear That Doesn't Go Away: I thought about moving out. Packing my books, *You're only allowed one bag*, leaving in the night, that night.

Let me tell you another story. My grandmother left in the night. She was thirteen. It was just before the turn of the century, in Russia. Carpenters were building the floor of the house I was living in in Wisconsin, when my grandmother Bessie Weisman left Seredna, a little town on the Russian-Polish border. She had lived there with her parents, her sisters, brothers, they were Orthodox Jews, they owned a small general store, they sold thread, barley, coffee. It was a time of pogroms. One day, she was helping her father in the store, and some Russian soldiers came in, ordered some coffee. She carried it to them from the samovar, and one of them grabbed her breast. She spilled (threw?) the hot coffee at him, burned his face, he threw her to the floor and beat her. It was after that that she asked her family why they stayed there. She wanted to leave, this was not new, she had had enough of pogroms. They said no, this was their home, they had been there for generations, they would stay. She wrote her uncle in New York, asked him for boat fare, she would come to New York and work until she paid back his money. She walked thirty miles to the nearest port, got on a boat, by herself, and came to Ellis Island. She was thirteen years old.

A month later, her sisters left too. They went to Poland. To a town called Lodz. Four hundred thousand Jews were murdered by the Nazis at Chelmo, a town fifty miles northwest of Lodz. Two Jews survived. They were not my aunts.

The rest of the family who stayed in Seredna were taken to Auschwitz. *You're only allowed one bag*, leaving in the night, that night.

from White Skin Privilege

Harlon Dalton

Most White people, in my experience, tend not to think of themselves in racial terms. They know that they are White, of course, but mostly that translates into being not Black, not Asian-American, and not Native American. Whiteness, in and of itself, has little meaning.

For a significant chunk, the inability to "get" race, and to understand why it figures so prominently in the lives of most people of color, stems from a deep affliction—the curse of rugged individualism. All of us, to some degree, suffer from this peculiarly American delusion that we are individuals first and foremost, captains of our own ships, solely responsible for our own fates. When taken to extremes, this ideal is antagonistic to the very idea of community. Even families cease to be vibrant social organisms; instead they are viewed as mere incubators and support systems for the individuals who happen to be born into them.

For those who embrace the rugged individualist ideal with a vengeance and who have no countervailing experience of community, the idea that a person's sense of self could be tied to that of a group is well-nigh incomprehensible. Collective concerns can only be interpreted as "groupthink"; collective responsibility as some strange foreign ideology. I frankly despair of being able to reach such people. Fortunately, most Americans, whatever their professed ideals, know from personal experience what community feels like. They are meaningfully connected to something smaller than the nation and larger than themselves.

For some, the tie is to a particular region of the country. I have a former colleague, for example, whose West Texas accent seemed to get stronger the longer he remained away from home. For others, the connection is to a religious community, or to a profession, or to a community defined by shared ideals or aspirations, such as Alcoholics Anonymous and the Benevolent and Protective Order of Elks. Perhaps most significantly, many Americans eagerly lay claim to their ethnic heritage. It is, for them, a rich source of comfort, pride, and self-understanding. It provides shape and texture to their lives.

So-called White ethnics are not alone in this respect. Hyphenated Americans of all colors draw great strength from their ethnic roots, and take pride in those characteristics that make their ethnic group distinctive. Ethnicity is as significant a social force for Vietnamese-Americans living in Virginia and Chinese-Americans living in the borough of Queens as it is for Irish-Americans in South Boston and Polish-Americans in Chicago. Chicanos, Salvadorans, Puerto Ricans, and Cuban-Americans readily distinguish among one another even though their Anglo neighbors can't (or don't bother trying to) tell them apart. West Indians and U.S.–born African-Americans are as distinct from one another as steel drums are from saxophones. Lakota Sioux are not Navajo are not Pequot are not Crow.

On the other hand, from what I have observed, people who trace their ethnic roots to Europe tend to think quite differently about race than do people who hail from the rest of the world. Most non-White ethnics recognize that, at least in the American context, they have a race as well as an ethnicity. They understand full well that the quality of their lives is affected by these two social categories in distinct ways. White ethnics, on the other hand, are much less likely to think of themselves in racial terms. Like Whites who don't identify strongly with any ethnic group, they tend to take race for granted or to view it as somehow irrelevant.

At the same time, many White ethnics rely on their experience of ethnicity to draw conclusions about the operation of race in America. Drawing parallels makes sense to them because they regard White ethnicity and non-White race as being more or less equivalent. However, as the average Korean-American or Haitian immigrant can attest, despite their surface similarities, race and ethnicity are very different creatures.

Ethnicity is the bearer of culture. It describes that aspect of our heritage that provides us with a mother tongue and that shapes our values, our worldview, our family structure, our rituals, the foods we eat, our mating behavior, our music—in short, much of our daily lives. We embody our ethnicity without regard for the presence or absence of other ethnic groups. Of course, ethnic groups influence one another in myriad ways, and more than occasionally come into conflict. But they do not need each other to exist.

In contrast, races exist only in relation to one another. Whiteness is meaningless in the absence of Blackness; the same holds in reverse.

Moreover, race itself would be meaningless if it were not a fault line along which power, prestige, and respect are distributed. Thus, during the war in Vietnam the North Vietnamese did not distinguish between Black Americans and White ones, since both seemed equally powerful with an M-16 in their hands. While ethnicity determines culture, race determines social position. Although the members of a given ethnic group may, for a time, find themselves on the bottom by virtue of their recent arrival, their lack of language or job skills, or even because of rank discrimination, that position usually is not long-term. *Race* and hierarchy, however, are indelibly wed.

Despite this distinction, much confusion is generated by the fact that for most American Blacks (excluding, for example, recent immigrants from the Caribbean), race and ethnicity are inextricably intertwined. The particulars of our African cultural heritage were largely, though not completely, destroyed by slavery. Part of what made the television miniseries *Roots* such a powerful experience for so many of us was that the protagonist was able to trace his heritage not only to a generic African continent but to a particular country, particular village, and particular tribe. We long for that kind of deep rootedness, but mostly we have to make do. From the remnants of our various African cultures, the rhythms of our daily existence, and the customs of our new home, especially the rural South and the urban inner city, we developed a uniquely African-American culture, with its own music, speech patterns, religious practices, and all the rest.

The emergence in the 1980s of the term "African-American" was meant to supply a label for our ethnicity that is distinct from the one used for race. Most people, however, continue to use the term "Black" to refer to both. "White," on the other hand, refers only to race. It has no particular cultural content. In ethnic terms, a random White person wandering through New York's Metropolitan Museum of Art could as easily be Irish-American, an immigrant from Greece, a Lithuanian transplant, or a Texan on vacation.

Why do most White people not see themselves as having a race? In part, race obliviousness is the natural consequence of being in the driver's seat. We are all much more likely to disregard attributes that seldom produce a ripple than we are those that subject us to discomfort. For example, a Reform Jewish family living in, say, Nacogdoches, Texas, will be more acutely aware of its religious/ethnic heritage than will the Baptist family next door. On the other hand, if that same family moved to the

Upper West Side of Manhattan, its Jewishness would probably be worn more comfortably. For most Whites, race—or more precisely, their own race—is simply part of the unseen, unproblematic background.

Whatever the reason, the inability or unwillingness of many White people to think of themselves in racial terms has decidedly negative consequences. For one thing, it produces huge blind spots. It leaves them baffled by the amount of energy many Blacks pour into questions of racial identity. It makes it difficult for them to understand why many (but by no means all) Blacks have a sense of group consciousness that influences the choices they make as individuals. It blinds Whites to the fact that their lives are shaped by race just as much as are the lives of people of color. How they view life's possibilities; whom they regard as heroes; the extent to which they feel the country is theirs; the extent to which that belief is echoed back to them; all this and more is in part a function of their race.

This obliviousness also makes it difficult for many Whites to comprehend why Blacks interact with them on the basis of past dealings with other Whites, and why Blacks sometimes expect them to make up for the sins of their fathers, and of their neighbors as well. Curiously enough, many of the same folk wouldn't think twice about responding to young Black males as a type rather than as individuals.

Far and away the most troublesome consequence of race obliviousness is the failure of many to recognize the privileges our society confers on them because they have white skin. White skin privilege is a birthright, a set of advantages one receives simply by being born with features that society values especially highly.

COMING INTO LANGUAGE

Children of those who work in heat and soil, offspring of those who lack formal education, those who live in—or come to—our country with a first language other than "standard" English, have a ragged connection to a language that speaks to them from radio and television, from the mouths of those who stand in front of a classroom or behind the counter at a bank. Heads bowed, eyes lowered, their bodies speak of respect for those in authority. Authority does not recognize their primal language of survival. The pieces in this section offer alternative insights into the complexities of language usage, whether as acts of survival or as acts of resistance.

In the first piece, Hisaye Yamamoto DeSoto offers us the complacent character of Esther Kuroiwa in the short story "Wilshire Bus." When a racist passenger verbally attacks a Chinese couple on the bus, Esther Kuroiwa does not defend the couple and then is startled to realize that she is "gloating" because she is Japanese, not Chinese. When the verbally abusive passenger ends with, "So clear out, all of you, and remember to take every last one of your slant-eyed pickaninnies with you!" as he leaves the bus, she realizes she has been included in this verbal attack. Yamamoto DeSoto's unsparing depiction of Kuroiwa results in an unforgettable character.

In her series of letters "Not Editable," Chrystos describes the process of writing, of using language, as that of the "blanket to pull me through." She arrives at the realization that writing is the place where she "marr[ies] the work" to "[n]aming my version of truth" and a growing sense of self.

June Jordan, in her essay "Nobody Mean More to Me Than You/ And the Future Life of Willie Jordan," questions the United States's "strange" and "tenuous" adherence to a "Standard English." She uses the story of a former student to illustrate how navigating our educational system often requires that "we completely surrender our own voice, hoping to please those who will never respect anyone different from themselves." Jordan's essay depicts her students' excitement at defining and using black English, and then her students' subsequent dismay when they realize their new-found skills won't help their friend Willie Jordan find justice for his brother's murder.

In the wake of dealing with a tumor that turns out to be benign, Audre Lorde reconsiders her life in her essay "The Transformation of Silence into Language and Action" and arrives at the insight that "what I most regretted were my silences." She describes how she spent her life waiting for someone else to speak out against injustices. She admits she feared others' "contempt, of censure, . . . of challenge" if she did so, a position with which many of us can identify. A fear of death places these other fears into perspective when she ultimately realizes, "My silences had not protected me. Your silence will not protect you," a powerful piece of advice for any of us.

In Li-Young Lee's poem "Persimmons," the narrator explores the challenge of learning how to use the precise word, a challenge many in this country face. Even as the narrator recounts how, as a young student, words such as "*fight* and *fright, wren* and *yarn*" got him into trouble, we applaud the narrator's understanding of deeper concepts such as resistance, love, and regret.

Finally, in his essay "Coming into Language," Jimmy Santiago Baca returns to a time when he discovered his voice and learns, as does Chrystos in her letter "Not Editable," that to write is to survive. For Baca, the process of placing the "first words on the page" is comparable to feeling "an island rising beneath my feet like the back of a whale."

Wilshire Bus

Hisaye Yamamoto DeSoto

Wilshire Boulevard begins somewhere near the heart of downtown Los Angeles and, except for a few digressions scarcely worth mentioning, goes straight out to the edge of the Pacific Ocean. It is a wide boulevard and traffic on it is fairly fast. For the most part, it is bordered on either side with examples of the recent stark architecture that favors a great deal of glass. As the boulevard approaches the sea, however, the landscape becomes a bit more pastoral, so that the university and the soldiers' home there give the appearance of being huge country estates.

Esther Kuroiwa got to know this stretch of territory quite well while her husband, Buro, was in one of the hospitals at the soldiers' home. They had been married less than a year when his back, injured in the war, began troubling him again, and he was forced to take three months of treatments at Sawtelle before he was able to go back to work. During this time, Esther was permitted to visit him twice a week, and she usually took the yellow bus out on Wednesdays because she did not know the first thing about driving and because her friends were not able to take her—except on Sundays. She always enjoyed the long bus ride very much because her seat companions usually turned out to be amiable, and if they did not, she took vicarious pleasure in gazing out at the almost unmitigated elegance along the fabulous street.

It was on one of these Wednesday trips that Esther committed a grave sin of omission that caused her later to burst into tears and that caused her acute discomfort for a long time afterward whenever something reminded her of it.

The man came on the bus quite early, and Esther noticed him briefly as he entered because he said gaily to the driver, "You robber. All you guys do is take money from me every day, just for giving me a short lift!"

Handsome in a red-faced way, greying, medium of height, and dressed in a dark gray sport suit with a yellow-and-black flowered shirt, he said this in a nice, resonant, carrying voice that got the response of a scattering of titters from the bus. Esther, somewhat amused and classifying him as a somatotonic, promptly forgot about him. And since she was sitting alone in the first regular seat, facing the back of the driver and the two front benches facing each other, she returned to looking out the window.

At the next stop, a considerable mass of people piled on and the last two climbing up were an elderly Oriental man and his wife. Both were neatly and somberly clothed, and the woman, who wore her hair in a bun and carried a bunch of yellow and dark red chrysanthemums, came to sit with Esther. Esther turned her head to smile a greeting (well, here we are, Orientals together on a bus), but the woman was watching, with some concern, her husband who was asking directions of the driver.

His faint English was inflected in such a way as to make Esther decide he was probably Chinese, and she noted that he had to repeat his question several times before the driver could answer it. Then he came to sit in the seat across the aisle from his wife. It was about then that a man's voice, which Esther soon recognized as belonging to the somatotonic, began a loud monologue in the seat just behind her. It was not really a monologue, since he seemed to be addressing his seat companion, but this person was not heard to give a single answer. The man's subject was a figure in the local sporting world who had a nice fortune invested in several of the shining buildings the bus was just passing.

"He's as tight-fisted as they make them, as tight-fisted as they come," the man said. "Why, he wouldn't give you the sweat of his . . ." He paused here to rephrase his metaphor, ". . . wouldn't give you the sweat off his palm!"

And he continued in this vein, discussing the private life of the famous man so frankly that Esther knew he must be quite drunk. But she listened with interest, wondering how much of this diatribe was true, because the public legend about the famous man was emphatic about his charity. Suddenly, the woman with the chrysanthemums jerked around to get a look at the speaker, and Esther felt her giving him a quick but thorough examination before she turned back around.

"So you don't like it?" the man inquired, and it was a moment before Esther realized that he was now directing his attention to her seat neighbor.

"Well, if you don't like it," he continued, "why don't you get off this bus, why don't you go back where you came from? Why don't you go back to China?"

Then, his voice growing jovial, as though he were certain of the support of the bus in this at least, he embroidered on this theme with a new eloquence, "Why don't you go back to China, where you can be coolies working in your bare feet out in the rice fields? You can let your pigtails grow and grow in China. Alla samee, mama, no tickee no shirtee. Ha, pretty good, no tickee no shirtee!"

He chortled with delight and seemed to be looking around the bus for approval. Then some memory caused him to launch on a new idea. "Or why don't you go back to Trinidad? They got Chinks running the whole she-bang in Trinidad. Every place you go in Trinidad . . ."

As he talked on, Esther, pretending to look out the window, felt the tenseness in the body of the woman beside her. The only movement from her was the trembling of the chrysanthemums with the motion of the bus. Without turning her head, Esther was also aware that a man, a mild-looking man with thinning hair and glasses, on one of the front benches was smiling at the woman and shaking his head mournfully in sympathy, but she doubted whether the woman saw.

Esther herself, while believing herself properly annoyed with the speaker and sorry for the old couple, felt quite detached. She found herself wondering whether the man meant her in his exclusion order or whether she was identifiably Japanese. Of course, he was not sober enough to be interested in such fine distinctions, but it did matter, she decided, because she was Japanese, not Chinese, and therefore in the present case immune. Then she was startled to realize that what she was actually doing was gloating over the fact that the drunken man had specified the Chinese as the unwanted.

Briefly, there bobbled on her memory the face of an elderly Oriental man whom she had once seen from a streetcar on her way home from work. (This was not long after she had returned to Los Angeles from the concentration camp in Arkansas and been lucky enough to get a clerical job with the Community Chest.) The old man was on a concrete island at Seventh and Broadway, waiting for his streetcar. She had looked down on him benignly as a fellow Oriental from her seat by the window, then been suddenly thrown for a loop by the legend on a large lapel button on his jacket. I AM KOREAN, said the button.

Heat suddenly rising to her throat, she had felt angry, then desolate and betrayed. True, reason had returned to ask whether she might not, under the circumstances, have worn such a button herself. She had heard rumors of I AM CHINESE buttons. So it was true then; why not I AM

KOREAN buttons, too? Wryly, she wished for an I AM JAPANESE button, just to be able to call the man's attention to it. "Look at me!" But perhaps the man didn't even read English, perhaps he had been actually threatened, perhaps it was not his doing—his solicitous children perhaps had urged him to wear the badge.

Trying now to make up for her moral shabbiness, she turned toward the little woman and smiled at her across the chrysanthemums, shaking her head a little to get across her message (don't pay any attention to that stupid old drunk, he doesn't know what he's saying, let's take things like this in our stride). But the woman, in turn looking at her, presented a face so impassive yet cold, and eyes so expressionless yet hostile, that Esther's overture fell quite flat.

Okay, okay, if that's the way you feel about it, she thought to herself. Then the bus made another stop, and she heard the man proclaim ringingly, "So clear out, all of you, and remember to take every last one of your slant-eyed pickaninnies with you!" This was his final advice as he stepped down from the middle door. The bus remained at the stop long enough for Esther to watch the man cross the street with a slightly exploring step. Then, as it started up again, the bespectacled man in front stood up to go and made a clumsy speech to the Chinese couple and possibly to Esther. "I want you to know," he said, "that we aren't all like that man. We don't all feel the way he does. We believe in an America that is a melting pot of all sorts of people. I'm originally Scotch and French myself." With that, he came over and shook the hand of the Chinese man.

"And you, young lady," he said to the girl behind Esther, "you deserve a Purple Heart or something for having to put up with that sitting beside you."

Then he, too, got off.

The rest of the ride was uneventful, and Esther stared out the window with eyes that did not see. Getting off at last at the soldiers' home, she was aware of the Chinese couple getting off after her, but she avoided looking at them. Then, while she was walking towards Buro's hospital very quickly, there arose in her mind some words she once read and let stick in her craw: "People say, do not regard what he says, now he is in liquor. Perhaps it is the only time he ought to be regarded."

These words repeated themselves until her saving detachment was gone every bit and she was filled once again in her life with the infuriatingly helpless, insidiously sickening sensation of there being in the world nothing solid she could put her finger on, nothing solid she could come to grips with, nothing solid she could sink her teeth into, nothing solid.

When she reached Buro's room and caught sight of his welcoming face, she ran to his bed and broke into sobs that she could not control. Buro was amazed because it was hardly her first visit and she had never shown such weakness before, but solving the mystery handily, he patted her head, looked around smugly at his roommates, and asked tenderly, "What's the matter? You've been missing me a whole lot, huh?" And she, finally drying her eyes, sniffed and nodded and bravely smiled and answered him with the question, yes, aren't women silly?

Not Editable

Chrystos

September 3, 1983

Gloria, dear sister,

I begin to write a little   typed snatches   I ask myself if they
are "Art"   I have lost shreds of myself my confidence and my judgment   No coherence   my past work came from someone I can't
be anymore   I'm changing don't know where I'm going   no
anchors   no bag to stay inside of   form makes me restless   I
am not editable

This one [woman] thinks I'm a Real Artist   (WHAT is a real
artist? I don't do enough work to be one myself)   I have soul she
says   yeah I think   you wanna buy some?

I am so afraid always under my tough exterior   I don't really believe
I have anything unique to say   I've always written from some compul-
sion, the necessity to make some damn sense somewhere   a tool of
survival   never been art to me   Colors are different   I am going
to start to cry and I don't know why   even the dahlias hurt that gave
me such joy a few hours ago   I've never been here before   always
circumvented it with drug overdoses or hospital   stays from suicide attempts   anything to distract me from   this unconnected
anguish   these letters are masks you know   it is my journal that is
my best self   if there is a best self   I am still trying to find it   find
my way to bone honesty

September 5, 1983

I want a world to be like the dahlias this morning that shock me as I pass
by them with handfuls of dirty clothes   they pulse with life   they
sing it   they are coming right out of their skins with it   I retreat

inside myself and wonder what I am supposed to do here   I keep returning to the same answer   make some dahlia beauty   force it down their throats   wake them up   the sun comes over the edge of the building and shines down on my wet face   the rainbows in my eyelashes   the music   hammered dulcimer and celtic harp

the wild roses are so still and the boat hulls gleam with dew   I am lonely because I am pierced with life and so much is dead   there must be some place for me   I've been taught so well that functioning is the appearance of knowing what one is doing   at the dahlia farm I belonged   I was at home in those tall fat flowers blazing profuse and generous and full   I want to plant myself in her field and die back in the fall

I am sure that if I knew others who wrote or painted or SOMETHING   I would feel much differently   but those I know are ordinary folks   I used to seek them out   afraid I would get a big head if I didn't   thought it was so snobbish to only want other creative geniuses for friends   now I feel that anyone else will literally drive me mad   I have decided to open more deeply in letters because I don't have to hold back anything or be correct or any of that shit   and your power is equal to mine, different, very different but you are not afraid of me   that is such a relief

I do want very much to be a good writer   but I am tired of the conventions of poems   I don't know what to do about form   the only "form" that doesn't feel restrictive is letters   I'm afraid I don't make "sense" when I try to move that immediacy to other forms   I'll always write poems of course, but I want to make something else,   something new   a joint dialogue or a chorus or something that is very definitely not a "novel"   because they aren't novel anymore

August 21, 1983

I've been calling myself "Captain C" to bring home the fact that *I'm* in charge of my life and if I don't make manifest the beauty I carry in my heart, *use* my gifts—the regret and anger will poison me.

I am beginning to understand the idea of marrying the work. I am wondering why I obsessively save scraps of paper and everyone's letters. I know why. They prove my existence, that I'm cared for a little. That has always seemed necessary to verify through accumulation. Knowing why doesn't stop me.

I ache to belong somewhere, to some place, to some compassionate fellow travelers, to an idea larger than myself. But I make a lousy true believer. Authority is the worst tyranny. Why are we so dependent and rebellious with it?

I vaguely think of churning out art to support myself instead of cleaning toilets but I'll never be interested in success. I want something vastly more difficult—spiritual release, inner and world peace, a body of work I can heal myself through. My materialism is spiritual.

I am a hole rather than a whole. Change screams through me yet I cannot close that gaping wound. It is only when I work that I seem to have a core. I want to be an artist. I fight so many ghost demons just to *say* that. As the wind blows these papers, I wonder if my life has any meaning. I feel so random.

Writing has always been my blanket to pull me through.

Always written to *survive*. A desperation to it. Naming my version of truth to preserve my "sanity" because they are so very busy trying to snatch it away. I'm more sure of my drawings. I go into another state when I draw. Maybe I don't love words as much as I do colors. It's words I'm unsure of. Words are mushy. A line feels so *there*.

I want to spend the next *three* weeks sitting in this chair continuing this letter for you with breaks to eat and piss. *Then* I might begin to find the root . . . writing is mostly discarding fear *isn't it*? Trusting that one's private voice can give voice for others. Is it necessary to publish though? That's *my* current dilemma.

Yours,
Boca Caliente

Nobody Mean More to Me Than You[1] And the Future Life of Willie Jordan

July, 1985

June Jordan

Black English is not exactly a linguistic buffalo; as children, most of the thirty-five million Afro-Americans living here depend on this language for our discovery of the world. But then we approach our maturity inside a larger social body that will not support our efforts to become anything other than the clones of those who are neither our mothers nor our fathers. We begin to grow up in a house where every true mirror shows us the face of somebody who does not belong there, whose walk and whose talk will never look or sound "right," because that house was meant to shelter a family that is alien and hostile to us. As we learn our way around this environment, either we hide our original word habits, or we completely surrender our own voice, hoping to please those who will never respect anyone different from themselves: Black English is not exactly a linguistic buffalo, but we should understand its status as an endangered species, as a perishing, irreplaceable system of community intelligence, or we should expect its extinction, and, along with that, the extinguishing of much that constitutes our own proud and singular identity.

What we casually call "English," less and less defers to England and its "gentlemen." "English" is no longer a specific matter of geography or an element of class privilege; more than thirty-three countries use this tool as a means of "intranational communication."[2] Countries as disparate as Zimbabwe and Malaysia, or Israel and Uganda, use it as their non-native currency of convenience. Obviously, this tool, this "English," cannot function inside thirty-three discrete societies on the basis of rules and values absolutely determined somewhere else, in a thirty-fourth other country, for example.

In addition to that staggering congeries of non-native users of English, there are five countries, or 333,746,000 people, for whom this thing called "English" serves as a native tongue.[3] Approximately 10 percent of these native speakers of "English" are Afro-American citizens of the U.S.A. I cite these numbers and varieties of human beings dependant on "English" in order, quickly, to suggest how strange and how tenuous is any concept of "Standard English." Obviously, numerous forms of English now operate inside a natural, an uncontrollable, continuum of development. I would suppose "the standard" for English in Malaysia is not the same as "the standard" in Zimbabwe. I know that standard forms of English for Black people in this country do not copy that of whites. And, in fact, that structural differences between these two kinds of English have intensified, becoming more Black, or less white, despite the expected homogenizing effects of television[4] and other mass media.

Nonetheless, white standards of English persist, supreme and unquestioned, in these United States. Despite our multi-lingual population, and despite the deepening Black and white cleavage within that conglomerate, white standards control our official and popular judgments of verbal proficiency and correct, or incorrect, language skills, including speech. In contrast to India, where at least fourteen languages co-exist as legitimate Indian languages, in contrast to Nicaragua, where all citizens are legally entitled to formal school instruction in their regional or tribal languages, compulsory education in America compels accommodation to exclusively white forms of "English." White English, in America, is "Standard English."

This story begins two years ago. I was teaching a new course, "In Search of the Invisible Black Woman," and my rather large class seemed evenly divided between young Black women and men. Five or six white students also sat in attendance. With unexpected speed and enthusiasm we had moved through historical narratives of the nineteenth century to literature by and about Black women, in the twentieth. I had assigned the first forty pages of Alice Walker's *The Color Purple*, and I came, eagerly, to class that morning:

"So!" I exclaimed, aloud. "What did you think? How did you like it?"

The students studied their hands, or the floor. There was no response. The tense, resistant feeling in the room fairly astounded me.

At last, one student, a young woman still not meeting my eyes, muttered something in my direction:

"What did you say?" I prompted her.

"Why she have them talk so funny. It don't sound right."

"You mean the language?"

Another student lifted his head: "It don't look right, neither. I couldn't hardly read it."

At this, several students dumped on the book. Just about unanimously, their criticisms targeted the language. I listened to what they wanted to say and silently marveled at the similarities between their casual speech patterns and Alice Walker's written version of Black English.

But, I decided against pointing to these identical traits of syntax; I wanted not to make them self-conscious about their own spoken language—not while they clearly felt it was "wrong." Instead I decided to swallow my astonishment. Here was a negative Black reaction to a prize-winning accomplishment of Black literature that white readers across the country had selected as a best seller. Black rejection was aimed at the one irreducibly Black element of Walker's work: the language—Celie's Black English. I wrote the opening lines of *The Color Purple* on the blackboard and asked the students to help me translate these sentences into Standard English:

> *You better not never tell nobody but God. It'd kill your mammy.*
> Dear God,
> I am fourteen years old. I have always been a good girl. Maybe you can give me a sign letting me know what is happening to me.
> Last spring after Little Lucious come I heard them fussing. He was pulling on her arm. She say it too soon, Fonso. I aint well. Finally he leave her alone. A week go by, he pulling on her arm again. She say, Naw, I ain't gonna. Can't you see I'm already half dead, an all of the children.[5]

Our process of translation exploded with hilarity and even hysterical, shocked laughter: The Black writer, Alice Walker, knew what she was doing! If rudimentary criteria for good fiction includes the manipulation of language so that the syntax and diction of sentences will tell you the identity of speakers, the probable age and sex and class of speakers, and even the locale—urban/rural/southern/western—then Walker had written, perfectly. This is the translation into Standard English that our class produced:

*Absolutely, one should never confide in anybody besides God. Your
secrets could prove devastating to your mother.*
Dear God,

I am fourteen years old. I have always been good. But now, could
you help me to understand what is happening to me?

Last spring, after my little brother, Lucious, was born, I heard
my parents fighting. My father kept pulling at my mother's arm. But
she told him, "It's too soon for sex, Alfonso. I am still not feeling
well." Finally, my father left her alone. A week went by, and then he
began bothering my mother, again: Pulling her arm. She told him,
"No, I won't! Can't you see I'm already exhausted from all of these
children?"

(Our favorite line was "It's too soon for sex, Alfonso.")

Once we could stop laughing, once we could stop our exponentially
wild improvisations on the theme of Translated Black English, the students pushed me to explain their own negative first reactions to their
spoken language on the printed page. I thought it was probably akin to
the shock of seeing yourself in a photograph for the first time. Most of
the students had never before seen a written facsimile of the way they
talk. None of the students had ever learned how to read and write their
own verbal system of communication: Black English. Alternatively, this
fact began to baffle or else bemuse and then infuriate my students. Why
not? Was it too late? Could they learn how to do it, now? And, ultimately,
the final test question, the one testing my sincerity: Could I teach them?
Because I had never taught anyone Black English and, as far as I knew,
no one, anywhere in the United States, had ever offered such a course,
the best I could say was "I'll try."

He looked like a wrestler.

He sat dead center in the packed room and, every time our eyes
met, he quickly nodded his head as though anxious to reassure, and
encourage, me.

Short, with strikingly broad shoulders and long arms, he spoke with
a surprisingly high, soft voice that matched the soft bright movement
of his eyes. His name was Willie Jordan. He would have seemed even
more unlikely in the context of Contemporary Women's Poetry, except
that ten or twelve other Black men were taking the course, as well. Still,

Willie was conspicuous. His extreme fitness, the muscular density of his presence underscored the riveted, gentle attention that he gave to anything anyone said. Generally, he did not join the loud and rowdy dialogue flying back and forth, but there could be no doubt about his interest in our discussions. And, when he stood to present an argument he'd prepared, overnight, that nervous smile of his vanished and an irregular stammering replaced it, as he spoke with visceral sincerity, word by word.

That was how I met Willie Jordan. It was in between "In Search of the Invisible Black Women" and "The Art of Black English." I was waiting for Departmental approval and I supposed that Willie might be, so to speak, killing time until he, too, could study Black English. But Willie really did want to explore Contemporary Women's Poetry and, to that end, volunteered for extra research and never missed a class.

Toward the end of that semester, Willie approached me for an independent study project on South Africa. It would commence the next semester. I thought Willie's writing needed the kind of improvement only intense practice will yield. I knew his intelligence was outstanding. But he'd wholeheartedly opted for "Standard English" at a rather late age, and the results were stilted and frequently polysyllabic, simply for the sake of having more syllables. Willie's unnatural formality of language seemed to me consistent with the formality of his research into South African apartheid. As he projected his studies, he would have little time, indeed, for newspapers. Instead, more than 90 percent of his research would mean saturation in strictly historical, if not archival, material. I was certainly interested. It would be tricky to guide him into a more confident and spontaneous relationship both with language and apartheid. It was going to be wonderful to see what happened when he could catch up with himself, entirely, and talk back to the world.

September, 1984: Breezy fall weather and much excitement! My class, "The Art of Black English," was full to the limit of the fire laws. And, in Independent Study, Willie Jordan showed up, weekly, fifteen minutes early for each of our sessions. I was pretty happy to be teaching, altogether!

I remember an early class when a young brother, replete with his ever present pork-pie hat, raised his hand and then told us that most of what he'd heard was "all right" except it was "too clean." "The brothers on the street," he continued, "they mix it up more. Like 'fuck' and 'motherfuck.'

Or like 'shit.'" He waited. I waited. Then all of us laughed a good while, and we got into a brawl about "correct" and "realistic" Black English that led to Rule 1.

Rule 1: *Black English is about a whole lot more than mothafuckin.*
As a criterion, we decided, "realistic" could take you anywhere you want to go. Artful places. Angry places. Eloquent and sweetalkin' places. Polemical places. Church. And the local Bar & Grill. We were checking out a language, not a mood or a scene or one guy's forgettable mouthing off.

It was hard. For most of the students, learning Black English required a fallback to patterns and rhythms of speech that many of their parents had beaten out of them. I mean, *beaten.* And, in a majority of cases, correct Black English could be achieved only by striving for *incorrect* Standard English, something they were still pushing at, quite uncertainly. This state of affairs led to Rule 2.

Rule 2: *If it's wrong in Standard English it's probably right in Black English, or, at least, you're hot.*
It was hard. Roommates and family members ridiculed their studies, or remained incredulous, "You *studying* that shit? At school?" But we were beginning to feel the companionship of pioneers. And we decided that we needed another rule that would establish each one of us as equally important to our success. This was Rule 3.

Rule 3: *If it don't sound like something that come out somebody mouth then it don't sound right. If it don't sound right then it ain't hardly right. Period.*
This rule produced two weeks of compositions in which the students agonizingly tried to spell the sound of the Black English sentence they wanted to convey. But Black English is, preeminently, an oral/spoken means of communication. *And spelling don't talk.* So we needed Rule 4.

Rule 4: *Forget about the spelling. Let the syntax carry you.*
Once we arrived at Rule 4 we started to fly because syntax, the structure of an idea, leads you to the world view of the speaker and reveals her values. The syntax of a sentence equals the structure of your consciousness. If we insisted that the language of Black English adheres to a distinctive Black syntax, then we were postulating a profound difference between white and Black people, *per se.* Was it a difference to prize or to obliterate?

There are three qualities of Black English—the presence of life, voice, and clarity—that testify to a distinctive Black value system that we became excited about and self-consciously tried to maintain.

1. Black English has been produced by a pre-technocratic, if not anti-technological, culture. More, our culture has been constantly threatened by annihilation or, at least, the swallowed blurring of assimilation. There-fore, our language is a system constructed by people constantly needing to insist that we exist, that we are present. Our language devolves from a culture that abhors all abstraction, or anything tending to obscure or delete the fact of the human being who is here and now/the truth of the person who is speaking or listening. Consequently, *there is no passive voice construction possible in Black English*. For example, you cannot say, "Black English is being eliminated." You must say, instead, "White people eliminating Black English." The assumption of the presence of life governs all of Black English. Therefore, overwhelmingly, *all action takes place in the language of the present indicative*. And every sentence assumes the living and active participation of at least two human beings, the speaker and the listener.

2. A primary consequence of the person-centered values of Black English is the delivery of voice. If you speak or write Black English, your ideas will necessarily possess that otherwise elusive attribute, *voice*.

3. One main benefit following from the person-centered values of Black English is that of *clarity*. If your idea, your sentence, assumes the presence of at least two living and active people, you will make it understand-able because the motivation behind every sentence is the wish to say something real to somebody real.

As the weeks piled up, translation from Standard English into Black English or vice versa occupied a hefty part of our course work.

> Standard English (hereafter S.E.): "In considering the idea of study-ing Black English those questioned suggested—"
>
> (What's the subject? Where's the person? Is anybody alive in there, in that idea?)
>
> Black English (hereafter B.E.): "I been asking people what you think about somebody studying Black English and they answer me like this:"

But there were interesting limits. You cannot "translate" instances of Standard English preoccupied with abstraction or with nothing/nobody evidently alive, into Black English. That would warp the language into uses antithetical to the guiding perspective of its community of users. Rather you must first change those Standard English sentences, themselves, into ideas consistent with the person-centered assumptions of Black English.

Guidelines for Black English

1. Minimal number of words for every idea: This is the source for the aphoristic and/or poetic force of the language; eliminate every possible word.

2. Clarity: If the sentence is not clear, it's not Black English.

3. Eliminate use of the verb *to be* whenever possible. This leads to the deployment of more descriptive and therefore more precise verbs.

4. Use *be* or *been* only when you want to describe a chronic, ongoing state of things.
   He *be* at the office, by 9. (He is always at the office by 9.)
   He *been* with her since forever.

5. Zero copula: Always eliminate the verb *to be* whenever it would combine with another verb in Standard English.
   S.E.: She is going out with him.
   B.E.: She going out with him.

6. Eliminate *do* as in:
   S.E.: What do you think? What do you want?
   B.E.: What you think? What you want?

Rules number 3, 4, 5, and 6 provide for the use of the minimal number of verbs per idea and, therefore, greater accuracy in the choice of verb.

7. In general, if you wish to say something really positive, try to formulate the idea using emphatic negative structure.
   S.E.: He's fabulous.
   B.E.: He bad.

8. Use double or triple negatives for dramatic emphasis.
    S.E.: Tina Turner sings out of this world.
    B.E.: Ain nobody sing like Tina.

9. Never use the *–ed* suffix to indicate the past tense of a verb.
    S.E.: She closed the door.
    B.E.: She close the door. Or, she have close the door.

10. Regardless of intentional verb time, only use the third person singular, present indicative, for use of the verb *to have*, as an auxiliary.
    S.E.: He had his wallet then he lost it.
    B.E.: He have him wallet then he lose it.
    S.E.: He had seen that movie.
    B.E.: We seen that movie. Or, we have see that movie.

11. Observe a minimal inflection of verbs. Particularly, never change from the first person singular forms to the third person singular.
    S.E.: Present Tense Forms: He goes to the store.
    B.E.: He go to the store.
    S.E.: Past Tense Forms: He went to the store.
    B.E.: He go to the store. Or, he gone to the store. Or, he been to the store.

12. The possessive case scarcely ever appears in Black English. Never use an apostrophe ('s) construction. If you wander into a possessive case component of an idea, then keep logically consistent: *ours, his, theirs, mines.* But, most likely, if you bump into such a component, you have wandered outside the underlying world-view of Black English.
    S.E.: He will take their car tomorrow.
    B.E.: He taking they car tomorrow.

13. Plurality: Logical consistency, continued: If the modifier indicates plurality, then the noun remains in the singular case.
    S.E.: He ate twelve doughnuts.
    B.E.: He eat twelve doughnut.
    S.E.: She has many books.
    B.E.: She have many book.

14. Listen for, or invent, special Black English forms of the past tense, such as: "He losted it. That what she felted." If they are clear and readily understood, then use them.

15. Do not hesitate to play with words, sometimes inventing them: e.g., "astropotomous" means huge like a hippo plus astronomical and, therefore, signifies real big.

16. In Black English, unless you keenly want to underscore the past tense nature of an action, stay in the present tense and rely on the overall context of your ideas for the conveyance of time and sequence.

17. Never use the suffix *-ly* form of an adverb in Black English.
    S.E.: The rain came down rather quickly.
    B.E.: The rain come down pretty quick.

18. Never use the indefinite article *an* in Black English.
    S.E.: He wanted to ride an elephant.
    B.E.: He want to ride him a elephant.

19. Invarient syntax: in correct Black English it is possible to formulate an imperative, an interrogative, and simple declarative idea with the same syntax:
    B.E.: You going to the store?
         You going to the store.
         You going to the store!

Where was Willie Jordan? We'd reached the mid-term of the semester. Students had formulated Black English guidelines, by consensus, and they were now writing with remarkable beauty, purpose, and enjoyment.

I ain hardly speakin for everybody but myself so understan that.
—Kim Parks.

Samples from student writings:
    "Janie have a great big ole hole inside her. Tea Cake the only thing that fit that hole . . .
    "That pear tree beautiful to Janie, especial when bees fiddlin with the blossomin pear there growin large and lovely. But personal speakin, the love she get from starin at that tree ain the love what starin back at her in them relationship." (Monica Morris)
    "Love is a big theme in, *They Eye Was Watching God*. Love show people new corners inside theyself. It pull out good stuff and stuff back bad stuff . . . Joe worship the doing uh his own hand and need other people to worship him too. But he ain't think about Janie that she a

person and ought to live like anybody common do. Queen life not for Janie." (Monica Morris)

"In both life and writin, Black womens have varietous experience of love that be cold like a iceberg or fiery like a inferno. Passion got for the other partner involve, man or woman, seem as shallow, ankle-deep water or the most profoundest abyss." (Constance Evans)

"Family love another bond that ain't never break under no pressure." (Constance Evans)

"You know it really cold/When the friend you/Always get out the fire/Act like they don't know you/When you in the heat." (Constance Evans)

"Big classroom discussion bout love at this time. I never take no class where us have any long arguin for and against for two or three day. New to me and great. I find the class time talkin a million time more interestin than detail bout the book." (Kathy Esseks)

As these examples suggest, Black English no longer limited the students in any way. In fact, one of them, Philip Garfield, would shortly "translate" a pivotal scene from Ibsen's *Doll House*, as his final term paper:

> **Nora:** I didn't gived no shit. I thinked you a asshole back then, too, you make it so hard for me save mines husband life.
>
> **Krogstad:** Girl, it clear you ain't any idea what you done. You done exact what I once done, and I losed my reputation over it.
>
> **Nora:** You asks me believe you once act brave save you wife life?
>
> **Krogstad:** Law care less why you done it.
>
> **Nora:** Law must suck.
>
> **Krogstad:** Suck or no, if I wants, judge screw you wid dis paper.
>
> **Nora:** No way, man. (Philip Garfield)

But where was Willie? Compulsively punctual, and always thoroughly prepared with neatly typed compositions, he had disappeared. He failed to show up for our regularly scheduled conference, and I received neither a note nor a phone call of explanation. A whole week went by. I wondered if Willie had finally been captured by the extremely current happenings in South Africa: passage of a new constitution that did not enfranchise the Black majority, and militant Black South African reaction to that affront.

I wondered if he'd been hurt, somewhere. I wondered if the serious workload of weekly readings and writings had overwhelmed him and changed his mind about independent study. Where was Willie Jordan?

One week after the first conference that Willie missed, he called: "Hello, Professor Jordan? This is Willie. I'm sorry I wasn't there last week. But something has come up and I'm pretty upset. I'm sorry but I really can't deal right now."

I asked Willie to drop by my office and just let me see that he was okay. He agreed to do that. When I saw him I knew something hideous had happened. Something had hurt him and scared him to the marrow. He was all agitated and stammering and terse and incoherent. At last, his sadly jumbled account let me surmise, as follows: Brooklyn police had murdered his unarmed, twenty-five-year-old brother, Reggie Jordan. Neither Willie nor his elderly parents knew what to do about it. Nobody from the press was interested. His folks had no money. Police ran his family around and around, to no point. And Reggie was really dead. And Willie wanted to fight, but he felt helpless.

With Willie's permission I began to try to secure legal counsel for the Jordan family. Unfortunately, Black victims of police violence are truly numerous, while the resources available to prosecute their killers are truly scarce. A friend of mine at the Center for Constitutional Rights estimated that just the preparatory costs for bringing the cops into court normally approaches $180,000. Unless the execution of Reggie Jordan became a major community cause for organizing, and protest, his murder would simply become a statistical item.

Again, with Willie's permission, I contacted every newspaper and media person I could think of. But the William Bastone feature article in *The Village Voice* was the only result from that canvassing.

Again, with Willie's permission, I presented the case to my class in Black English. We had talked about the politics of language. We had talked about love and sex and child abuse and men and women. But the murder of Reggie Jordan broke like a hurricane across the room.

There are few "issues" as endemic to Black life as police violence. Most of the students knew and respected and liked Jordan. Many of them came from the very neighborhood where the murder had occurred. All of the students had known somebody close to them who had been killed by police, or had known frightening moments of gratuitous confrontation with the cops. They wanted to do everything at once to avenge death. Number One: They decided to compose personal statements of condolence to Willie Jordan and his family written in Black English. Number Two: They decided to compose individual messages to the police, in Black English. These should be prefaced by an explanatory paragraph composed by the entire group. Number Three: These individual messages, with their lead paragraph, should be sent to *Newsday*.

The morning after we agreed on these objectives, one of the young women students appeared with an unidentified visitor, who sat through the class, smiling in a peculiar, comfortable way.

Now we had to make more tactical decisions. Because we wanted the messages published, and because we thought it imperative that our outrage be known by the police, the tactical question was this: Should the opening group paragraph be written in Black English or Standard English?

I have seldom been privy to a discussion with so much heart at the dead heat of it. I will never forget the eloquence, the sudden haltings of speech, the fierce struggle against tears, the furious throwaway, and useless explosions that this question elicited.

That one question contained several others, each of them extraordinarily painful to even contemplate. How best to serve the memory of Reggie Jordan? Should we use the language of the killers—Standard English—in order to make our ideas acceptable to those controlling the killers? But wouldn't what we had to say be rejected, summarily, if we said it in our own language, the language of the victim, Reggie Jordan? But if we sought to express ourselves by abandoning our language, wouldn't that mean our suicide on top of Reggie's murder? But if we expressed ourselves in our own language, wouldn't that be suicidal to the wish to communicate with those who, evidently, did not give a damn about us/Reggie/police violence in the Black community?

At the end of one of the longest, most difficult hours of my own life, the students voted, unanimously, to preface their individual messages with a paragraph composed in the language of Reggie Jordan. "*At least we don't give up nothing else. At least we stick to the truth: Be who we been. And stay all the way with Reggie.*"

It was heartbreaking to proceed, from that point. Everyone in the room realized that our decision in favor of Black English had doomed our writings, even as the distinctive reality of our Black lives always has doomed our efforts to "be who we been" in this country.

I went to the blackboard and took down this paragraph, dictated by the class:

... YOU COPS!

WE THE BROTHER AND SISTER OF WILLIE JORDAN, A FELLOW STONY BROOK STUDENT WHO THE BROTHER OF THE DEAD REGGIE JORDAN. REGGIE, LIKE MANY BROTHER AND SISTER, HE A VICTIM OF BRUTAL RACIST POLICE, OCTOBER 25, 1984. US APPALL, FED UP, BECAUSE THAT ANOTHER SENSELESS DEATH WHAT OCCUR IN OUR COMMUNITY. THIS WHAT WE FEEL, THIS, FROM OUR HEART, FOR WE AIN'T STAYIN' SILENT NO MORE:

With the completion of this introduction, nobody said anything. I asked for comments. At this invitation, the unidentified visitor, a young Black man, ceaselessly smiling, raised his hand. He was, it so happened, a rookie cop. He had just joined the force in September and, he said, he thought he should clarify a few things. So he came forward and sprawled easily into a posture of barroom, or fireside, nostalgia:

"See," Officer Charles enlightened us, "most times when you out on the street and something come down, you do one of two things. Over-react or under-react. Now, if you under-react, then you can get yourself kilt. And if you over-react, then maybe you kill somebody. Fortunately, it's about nine times out of ten and you will over-react. So the brother got kilt. And I'm sorry about that, believe me. But what you have to understand is what kilt him: Over-reaction. That's all. Now you talk about Black people and white police, but see, now, I'm a cop myself. And (big smile) I'm Black. And just a couple months ago I was on the other side. But see it's the same for me. You a cop, you the ultimate authority: the Ultimate Authority. And you on the street, most of the time you can only do one of two things: over-react or under-react. That's all it is with the brother: Over-reaction. Didn't have nothing to do with race."

That morning Officer Charles had the good fortune to escape without being boiled alive. But barely. And I remember the pride of his smile when I read about the fate of Black policemen and other collaborators in South Africa. I remember him, and I remember the shock and palpable feeling of shame that filled the room. It was as though that foolish, and deadly, young man had just relieved himself of his foolish, and deadly, explanation, face to face with the grief of Reggie Jordan's father and Reggie

Jordan's mother. Class ended quietly. I copied the paragraph from the blackboard, collected the individual messages, and left to type them up.

Newsday rejected the piece.

The Village Voice could not find room in their "Letters" section to print the individual messages from the students to the police.

None of the tv news reporters picked up the story.

Nobody raised $180,000 to prosecute the murder of Reggie Jordan.

Reggie Jordan is really dead.

I asked Willie Jordan to write an essay pulling together everything important to him from that semester. He was still deeply beside himself with frustration and amazement and loss. This is what he wrote, unedited, and in its entirety:

> Throughout the course of this semester, I have been researching the effects of oppression and exploitation along racial lines in South Africa and its neighboring countries. I have become aware of South African police brutalization of native Africans beyond the extent of the law, even though the laws themselves are catalyst affliction upon Black men, women, and children. Many Africans die each year as a result of the deliberate use of police force to protect the white power structure.
>
> Social control agents in South Africa, such as policemen, are also used to force compliance among citizens through both overt and covert tactics. It is not uncommon to find bold-faced coercion and cold-blooded killings of Blacks by South African police for undetermined and/or inadequate reasons. Perhaps the truth is that the only reasons for this heinous treatment of Blacks rests in racial differences. We should also understand that what is conveyed through the media is not always accurate and may sometimes be construed as the tip of the iceberg at best.
>
> I recently received a painful reminder that racism, poverty, and the abuse of power are global problems which are by no means unique to South Africa. On October 25, 1984, at approximately 3:00 p.m., my brother, Mr. Reginald Jordan, was shot and killed by two New York City policemen from the 75th precinct in the East New York section of Brooklyn. His life ended at the age of twenty-five. Even up to this current point in time the Police Department has failed to provide my family, which consists of five brothers, eight sisters, and two parents, with a plausible reason for Reggie's death. Out of

the many stories that were given to my family by the Police Department, not one of them seems to hold water. In fact, I honestly believe that the Police Department's assessment of my brother's murder is nothing short of ABSOLUTE BULLSHIT, and thus far no evidence had been produced to alter perception of the situation.

Furthermore, I believe that one of three cases may have occurred in this incident. First, Reggie's death may have been the desired outcome of the police officer's action, in which case the killing was premeditated. Or, it was a case of mistaken identity, which clarifies the fact that the two officers who killed my brother and their commanding parties are all grossly incompetent. Or, both of the above cases are correct, i.e., Reggie's murderers intended to kill him and the Police Department behaved insubordinately.

Part of the argument of the officers who shot Reggie was that he had attacked one of them and took his gun. This was their major claim. They also said that only one of them had actually shot Reggie. The facts, however, speak for themselves. According to the Death Certificate and autopsy report, Reggie was shot eight times from point-blank range. The Doctor who performed the autopsy told me himself that two bullets entered the side of my brother's head, four bullets were sprayed into his back, and two bullets struck him in the back of his legs. It is obvious that unnecessary force was used by the police and that it is extremely difficult to shoot someone in his back when he is attacking or approaching you.

After experiencing a situation like this and researching South Africa, I believe that, to a large degree, justice may only exist as rhetoric. I find it difficult to talk of true justice when the oppression of my people both at home and abroad attests to the fact that inequality and injustice are serious problems whereby Blacks and Third World people are perpetually short-changed by society. Something has to be done about the way in which this world is set up. Although it is a difficult task, we do have the power to make a change.

Willie J. Jordan Jr.
EGL 487, Section 58, November 14, 1984

It is my privilege to dedicate this book to the future life of Willie J. Jordan Jr.
August 8, 1985

Notes

1. Black English aphorism crafted by Monica Morris, a Junior at S.U.N.Y. at Stony Brook, October, 1984.

2. *English Is Spreading, But What Is English*. A presentation by Professor S.N. Sridahr, Dept. of Linguistics, S.U.N.Y. at Stony Brook, April 9, 1985: Dean's Conversation Among the Disciplines.

3. Ibid.

4. *New York Times,* March 15, 1985, Section One, p. 14: Report on study by Linguistics at the University of Pennsylvania.

5. Alice Walker, *The Color Purple,* p. 11, Harvourt Brace, N.Y.

Persimmons

Li-Young Lee

In sixth grade Mrs. Walker
slapped the back of my head
and made me stand in the corner
for not knowing the difference
between *persimmon* and *precision*.
How to choose

persimmons. This is precision.
Ripe ones are soft and brown-spotted.
Sniff the bottoms. The sweet one
will be fragrant. How to eat:
put the knife away, lay down newspaper.
Peel the skin tenderly, not to tear the meat.
Chew the skin, suck it,
and swallow. Now, eat
the meat of the fruit,
so sweet,
all of it, to the heart.

Donna undresses, her stomach is white.
In the yard, dewy and shivering
with crickets, we lie naked,
face-up, face-down.
I teach her Chinese.
Crickets: *chiu chiu.* Dew: I've forgotten.
Naked: I've forgotten.
Ni, wo: you and me.
I part her legs,
remember to tell her
she is beautiful as the moon.

Other words
that got me into trouble were
fight and *fright, wren* and *yarn.*
Fight was what I did when I was frightened,
fright was what I felt when I was fighting.
Wrens are small, plain birds,
yarn is what one knits with.
Wrens are soft as yarn.
My mother made birds out of yarn.
I loved to watch her tie the stuff;
a bird, a rabbit, a wee man.

Mrs. Walker brought a persimmon to class
and cut it up
so everyone could taste
a *Chinese apple.* Knowing
it wasn't ripe or sweet, I didn't eat
but watched the other faces.

My mother said every persimmon has a sun
inside, something golden, glowing,
warm as my face.

Once, in the cellar, I found two wrapped in newspaper,
forgotten and not yet ripe.
I took them and set both on my bedroom windowsill,
where each morning a cardinal
sang, *The sun, the sun.*

Finally understanding
he was going blind,
my father sat up all one night
waiting for a song, a ghost.
I gave him the persimmons,
swelled, heavy as sadness,
and sweet as love.

This year, in the muddy lighting
of my parents' cellar, I rummage, looking
for something I lost.
My father sits on the tired, wooden stairs,
black cane between his knees,
hand over hand, gripping the handle.

He's so happy that I've come home.
I ask how his eyes are, a stupid question.
All gone, he answers.

Under some blankets, I find a box.
Inside the box I find three scrolls.
I sit beside him and untie
three paintings by my father:
Hibiscus leaf and a white flower.
Two cats preening.
Two persimmons, so full they want to drop from the cloth.

He raises both hands to touch the cloth,
asks, *Which is this?*

This is persimmons, Father.

Oh, the feel of the wolftail on the silk,
the strength, the tense
precision in the wrist.
I painted them hundreds of times
eyes closed. These I painted blind.
Some things never leave a person:
scent of the hair of one you love,
the texture of persimmons,
in your palm, the ripe weight.

The Transformation of Silence into Language and Action

Audre Lorde

I have come to believe over and over again that what is most important to me must be spoken, made verbal and shared, even at the risk of having it bruised or misunderstood. That the speaking profits me, beyond any other effect. I am standing here as a Black lesbian poet, and the meaning of all that waits upon the fact that I am still alive, and might not have been. Less than two months ago I was told by two doctors, one female and one male, that I would have to have breast surgery, and that there was a 60 to 80 percent chance that the tumor was malignant. Between that telling and the actual surgery, there was a three-week period of the agony of an involuntary reorganization of my entire life. The surgery was completed, and the growth was benign.

But within those three weeks, I was forced to look upon myself and my living with a harsh and urgent clarity that has left me still shaken but much stronger. This is a situation faced by many women, by some of you here today. Some of what I experienced during that time has helped elucidate for me much of what I feel concerning the transformation of silence into language and action.

In becoming forcibly and essentially aware of my mortality, and of what I wished and wanted for my life, however short it might be, priorities and omissions became strongly etched in a merciless light, and what I most regretted were my silences. Of what had I *ever* been afraid? To question or to speak as I believed could have meant pain, or death. But we all hurt in so many different ways, all the time, and pain will either change or end. Death, on the other hand, is the final silence. And that might be coming quickly, now, without regard for whether I had ever spoken what needed to be said, or had only betrayed myself into small silences, while I planned someday to speak, or waited for someone else's words. And I began to recognize a source of power within myself that comes from the knowledge that while it is most desirable not to be afraid, learning to put fear into a perspective gave me great strength.

I was going to die, if not sooner then later, whether or not I had ever spoken myself. My silences had not protected me. Your silence will not protect you. But for every real word spoken, for every attempt I had ever made to speak those truths for which I am still seeking, I had made contact with other women while we examined the words to fit a world in which we all believed, bridging our differences. And it was the concern and caring of all those women which gave me strength and enabled me to scrutinize the essentials of my living.

The women who sustained me through that period were Black and white, old and young, lesbian, bisexual, and heterosexual, and we all shared a war against the tyrannies of silence. They all gave me a strength and concern without which I could not have survived intact. Within those weeks of acute fear came the knowledge—within the war we are all waging with the forces of death, subtle and otherwise, conscious or not—I am not only a casualty, I am also a warrior.

What are the words you do not yet have? What do you need to say? What are the tyrannies you swallow day by day and attempt to make your own, until you will sicken and die of them, still in silence? Perhaps for some of you here today, I am the face of one of your fears. Because I am woman, because I am Black, because I am lesbian, because I am myself—a Black woman warrior poet doing my work—come to ask you, are you doing yours?

And of course I am afraid, because the transformation of silence into language and action is an act of self-revelation, and that always seems fraught with danger. But my daughter, when I told her of our topic and my difficulty with it, said, "Tell them about how you're never really a whole person if you remain silent, because there's always that one little piece inside you that wants to be spoken out, and if you keep ignoring it, it gets madder and madder and hotter and hotter, and if you don't speak it out one day it will just up and punch you in the mouth from the inside."

In the cause of silence, each of us draws the face of her own fear—fear of contempt, of censure, or some judgment, or recognition, of challenge, of annihilation. But most of all, I think, we fear the visibility without which we cannot truly live. Within this country where racial difference creates a constant, if unspoken, distortion of vision, Black women have on one hand always been highly visible, and so, on the other hand, have been rendered invisible through the depersonalization of racism. Even within the women's movement, we have had to fight, and still do, for that very visibility which also renders us most vulnerable, our Blackness. For to survive in the mouth of this dragon we call america, we have had to learn this first and most vital lesson—that we were never meant to survive. Not as human beings. And neither were most of you here today, Black or not. And that visibility which makes us most vulnerable is that which also is the source of our greatest strength. Because the machine will try to grind you into dust anyway, whether or not we speak. We can sit in our corners mute forever while our sisters and our selves are wasted, while our children are distorted and destroyed, while our earth is poisoned; we can sit in our safe corners mute as bottles, and we will still be no less afraid.

In my house this year we are celebrating the feast of Kwanza, the African-american festival of harvest which begins the day after Christmas and lasts for seven days. There are seven principles of Kwanza, one for each day. The first principle is Umoja, which means unity, the decision to strive for and maintain unity in self and community. The principle for yesterday, the second day, was Kujichagulia—self-determination—the decision to define ourselves, name ourselves, and speak for ourselves, instead of being defined and spoken for by others. Today is the third day of Kwanza, and the principle for today is Ujima—collective work and responsibility—the decision to build and maintain ourselves and our communities together and to recognize and solve our problems together.

Each of us is here now because in one way or another we share a commitment to language and to the power of language, and to the reclaiming of that language which has been made to work against us. In the transformation of silence into language and action, it is vitally necessary for each one of us to establish or examine her function in that transformation and to recognize her role as vital within that transformation.

For those of us who write, it is necessary to scrutinize not only the truth of what we speak, but the truth of that language by which we speak it. For others, it is to share and spread also those words that are meaningful to us. But primarily for us all, it is necessary to teach by living and speaking those truths which we believe and know beyond understanding. Because in this way alone we can survive, by taking part in a process of life that is creative and continuing, that is growth.

And it is never without fear—of visibility, of the harsh light of scrutiny and perhaps judgment, of pain, of death. But we have lived through all of those already, in silence, except death. And I remind myself all the time now that if I were to have been born mute, or had maintained an oath of silence my whole life long for safety, I would still have suffered, and I would still die. It is very good for establishing perspective.

And where the words of women are crying to be heard, we must each of us recognize our responsibility to seek those words out, to read them and share them and examine them in their pertinence to our lives. That we not hide behind the mockeries of separations that have been imposed upon us and which so often we accept as our own. For instance, "I can't possibly teach Black women's writing—their experience is so different from mine." Yet how many years have you spent teaching Plato and Shakespeare and Proust? Or another, "She's a white woman and what could she possibly have to say to me?" Or, "She's a lesbian, what would my husband say, or my chairman?" Or again, "This woman writes of her sons and I have no children." And all the other endless ways in which we rob ourselves of ourselves and each other.

We can learn to work and speak when we are afraid in the same way we have learned to work and speak when we are tired. For we have been socialized to respect fear more than our own needs for language and definition, and while we wait in silence for that final luxury of fearlessness, the weight of that silence will choke us.

The fact that we are here and that I speak these words is an attempt to break that silence and bridge some of those differences between us, for it is not difference which immobilizes us, but silence. And there are so many silences to be broken.

Coming into Language

Jimmy Santiago Baca

On weekend graveyard shifts at St. Joseph's Hospital I worked the emergency room, mopping up pools of blood and carting plastic bags stuffed with arms, legs, and hands to the outdoor incinerator. I enjoyed the quiet, away from the screams of shotgunned, knifed, and mangled kids writhing on gurneys outside the operating rooms. Ambulance sirens shrieked and squad car lights reddened the cool nights, flashing against the hospital walls: gray—red, gray—red. On slow nights I would lock the door of the administration office, search the reference library for a book on female anatomy and, with my feet propped on the desk, leaf through the illustrations, smoking my cigarette. I was seventeen.

One night my eye was caught by a familiar-looking word on the spine of a book. The title was *450 Years of Chicano History in Pictures*. On the cover were black-and-white photos: Padre Hidalgo exhorting Mexican peasants to revolt against the Spanish dictators; Anglo vigilantes hanging two Mexicans from a tree; a young Mexican woman with rifle and ammunition belts crisscrossing her breast; César Chávez and field-workers marching for fair wages; Chicano railroad workers laying creosote ties; Chicanas laboring at machines in textile factories; Chicanas picketing and hoisting boycott signs.

From the time I was seven, teachers had been punishing me for not knowing my lessons by making me stick my nose in a circle chalked on the blackboard. Ashamed of not understanding and fearful of asking questions, I dropped out of school in the ninth grade. At seventeen I still didn't know how to read, but those pictures confirmed my identity. I stole the book that night, stashing it for safety under the slop-sink until I got off work. Back at my boardinghouse, I showed the book to friends. All of us were amazed; this book told us we were alive. We, too, had defended ourselves with our fists against hostile Anglos, gasping for breath in fights with the policemen who outnumbered us. The book reflected back to us our struggle in a way that made us proud.

Most of my life I felt like a target in the crosshairs of a hunter's rifle. When strangers and outsiders questioned me I felt the hang-rope tighten around my neck and the trapdoor creak beneath my feet. There was nothing so humiliating as being unable to express myself, and my inarticulateness increased my sense of jeopardy, of being endangered. I felt intimidated and vulnerable, ridiculed and scorned. Behind a mask of humility, I seethed with mute rebellion.

Before I was eighteen, I was arrested on suspicion of murder after refusing to explain a deep cut on my forearm. With shocking speed I found myself handcuffed to a chain gang of inmates and bused to a holding facility to await trial. There I met men, prisoners, who read aloud to each other the works of Neruda, Paz, Sabines, Nemerov, and Hemingway. Never had I felt such freedom as in that dormitory. Listening to the words of these writers, I felt that invisible threat from without lessen—my sense of teetering on a rotting plank over swamp water where famished alligators clapped their horny snouts for my blood. While I listened to the words of the poets, the alligators slumbered powerless in their lairs. Their language was the magic that could liberate me from myself, transform me into another person, transport me to other places far away.

And when they closed the books, these Chicanos, and went into their own Chicano language, they made barrio life come alive for me in the fullness of its vitality. I began to learn my own language, the bilingual words and phrases explaining to me my place in the universe. Every day I felt like the paper boy taking delivery of the latest news of the day.

Months later I was released, as I had suspected I would be. I had been guilty of nothing but shattering the windshield of my girlfriend's car in a fit of rage.

Two years passed. I was twenty now, and behind bars again. The federal marshals had failed to provide convincing evidence to extradite me to Arizona on a drug charge, but still I was being held. They had ninety days to prove I was guilty. The only evidence against me was that my girlfriend had been at the scene of the crime with my driver's license in her purse. They had to come up with something else. But there was nothing else. Eventually they negotiated a deal with the actual drug dealer, who took the stand against me. When the judge hit me with a million-dollar bail, I emptied my pockets on his booking desk: twenty-six cents.

One night in my third month in the county jail, I was mopping the floor in front of the booking desk. Some detectives had kneed an old drunk and handcuffed him to the booking bars. His shrill screams raked my nerves like a hacksaw on bone, the desperate protest of his dignity against their inhumanity. But the detectives just laughed as he tried to rise and kicked him to his knees. When they went to the bathroom to pee and the desk attendant walked to the file cabinet to pull the arrest record, I shot my arm through the bars, grabbed one of the attendant's university textbooks, and tucked it in my overalls. It was the only way I had of protesting.

It was late when I returned to my cell. Under my blanket I switched on a pen flashlight and opened the thick book at random, scanning the pages. I could hear the jailer making his rounds on the other tiers. The jangle of his keys and the sharp click of his boot heels intensified my solitude. Slowly I enunciated the words . . . p-o-n-d, ri-pple. It scared me that I had been reduced to this to find comfort. I always had thought reading a waste of time, that nothing could be gained by it. Only by action, by moving out into the world and confronting and challenging the obstacles, could one learn anything worth knowing.

Even as I tried to convince myself that I was merely curious, I became so absorbed in how the sounds created music in me and happiness, I forgot where I was. Memories began to quiver in me, glowing with a strange but familiar intimacy in which I found refuge. For a while, a deep sadness overcame me, as if I had chanced on a long-lost friend and mourned the years of separation. But soon the heartache of having missed so much of life, that had numbed me since I was a child, gave way, as if a grave illness lifted itself from me and I was cured, innocently believing in the beauty of life again. I stumblingly repeated the author's name as I fell asleep, saying it over and over in the dark. Words-worth, Words-worth.

Before long my sister came to visit me, and I joked about taking her to a place called Kubla Khan and getting her a blind date with this *vato* named Coleridge who lived on the seacoast and was *malías* on morphine. When I asked her to make a trip into enemy territory to buy me a grammar book, she said she couldn't. Bookstores intimidated her, because she, too, could neither read nor write.

Days later, with a stub pencil I whittled sharp with my teeth, I propped a Red Chief notebook on my knees and wrote my first words. From that moment, a hunger for poetry possessed me.

Until then, I had felt as if I had been born into a raging ocean where I swam relentlessly, flailing my arms in hope of rescue, of reaching a shoreline I never sighted. Never solid ground beneath me, never a resting place. I had lived with only the desperate hope to stay afloat; that and nothing more.

But when, at last I wrote my first words on the page, I felt an island rising beneath my feet like the back of a whale. As more and more words emerged, I could finally rest: I had a place to stand for the first time in my life. The island grew, with each page, into a continent inhabited by people I knew and mapped with the life I lived.

I wrote about it all—about people I had loved or hated, about the brutalities and ecstasies of my life. And, for the first time, the child in me who had witnessed and endured unspeakable terrors cried out not just in impotent despair, but with the power of language. Suddenly, through language, through writing, my grief and my joy could be shared with anyone who would listen. And I could do this all alone; I could do it anywhere. I was no longer a captive of demons eating away at me, no longer a victim of other people's mockery and loathing that had made me clench my fist white with rage and grit my teeth to silence. Words now pleaded back with the bleak lucidity of hurt. They were wrong, those others, and now I could say it.

Through language I was free. I could respond, escape, indulge; embrace or reject earth or the cosmos. I was launched on an endless journey without boundaries or rules, in which I could salvage the floating fragments of my past, or be born anew in the spontaneous ignition of understanding some heretofore concealed aspect of myself. Each word steamed with the hot lava juices of my primordial making, and I crawled out of stanzas dripping with birth-blood, reborn and freed from the chaos of my life. The child in the dark room of my heart, who had never been able to find or reach the light switch, flicked it on now; and I found in the room a stranger, myself, who had waited so many years to speak again. My words struck in me lightning crackles of elation and thunderhead storms of grief.

When I had been in the county jail longer than anyone else, I was made a trustee. One morning, after a fist fight, I went to the unlocked and unoccupied office used for lawyer-client meetings, to think. The bare white room with its fluorescent tube lighting seemed to expose and illuminate my dark and worthless life. And yet, for the first time, I had something to lose—my chance to read, to write; a way to live with dignity and meaning, that had opened for me when I stole that scuffed, second-hand book about the Romantic poets. In prison, the abscess had been lanced.

"I will never do any work in this prison system as long as I am not allowed to get my G.E.D." That's what I told the reclassification panel. The captain flicked off the tape recorder. He looked at me hard and said, "You'll never walk outta here alive. Oh, you'll work, put a copper penny on that, you'll work."

After that interview I was confined to deadlock maximum security in a subterranean dungeon, with ground-level chicken-wired windows painted gray. Twenty-three hours a day I was in that cell. I kept sane by borrowing books from the other cons on the tier. Then, just before Christmas, I received a letter from Harry, a charity house samaritan who doled out hot soup to the homeless in Phoenix. He had picked my name from a list of cons who had no one to write to them. I wrote back asking for a grammar book, and a week later received one of Mary Baker Eddy's treatises on salvation and redemption, with Spanish and English on opposing pages. Pacing my cell all day and most of each night, I grappled with grammar until I was able to write a long true-romance confession for a con to send to his pen pal. He paid me with a pack of smokes. Soon I had a thriving barter business, exchanging my poems and letters for novels, commissary pencils, and writing tablets.

One day I tore two flaps from the cardboard box that held all my belongings and punctured holes along the edge of each flap and along the border of a ream of state-issue paper. After I had aligned them to form a spine, I threaded the holes with a shoestring, and sketched on the cover a hummingbird fluttering above a rose. This was my first journal.

Whole afternoons I wrote, unconscious of passing time or whether it was day or night. Sunbursts exploded from the lead tip of my pencil, words that grafted me into awareness of who I was; peeled back to a burning core of bleak terror, an embryo floating in the image of water, I cracked out of the shell wide-eyed and insane. Trees grew out of the palms of my hands, the threatening otherness of life dissolved, and I became one with the air and sky, the dirt and the iron and concrete. There was no longer any distinction between the other and I. Language made bridges of fire between me and everything I saw. I entered into the blade of grass, the basketball, the con's eye and child's soul.

At night I flew. I conversed with floating heads in my cell, and visited strange houses where lonely women brewed tea and rocked in wicker rocking chairs listening to sad Joni Mitchell songs.

Before long I was frayed like a rope carrying too much weight, that suddenly snaps. I quit talking. Bars, walls, steel bunk and floor bristled with millions of poem-making sparks. My face was no longer familiar to me. The only reality was the swirling cornucopia of images in my mind, the voices in the air. Mid-air a cactus blossom would appear, a snake-flame in blinding dance around it, stunning me like a guard's fist striking my neck from behind.

The prison administrators tried several tactics to get me to work. For six months, after the next monthly prison board review, they sent cons to my cell to hassle me. When the guard would open my cell door to let one of them in, I'd leap out and fight him—and get sent to thirty-day isolation. I did a lot of isolation time. But I honed my image-making talents in that sensory-deprived solitude. Finally they moved me to death row, and after that to "nut-run," the tier that housed the mentally disturbed.

As the months passed, I became more and more sluggish. My eyelids were heavy, I could no longer write or read. I slept all the time.

One day a guard took me out to the exercise field. For the first time in years I felt grass and earth under my feet. It was spring. The sun warmed my face as I sat on the bleachers watching the cons box and run, hit the handball, lift weights. Some of them stopped to ask how I was, but I found it impossible to utter a syllable. My tongue would not move, saliva drooled from the corners of my mouth. I had been so heavily medicated I could not summon the slightest gesture. Yet inside me a small voice cried out, I am fine! I am hurt now but I will come back! I am fine!

Back in my cell, for weeks I refused to eat. Styrofoam cups of urine and hot water were hurled at me. Other things happened. There were beatings, shock therapy, intimidation.

Later, I regained some clarity of mind. But there was a place in my heart where I had died. My life had compressed itself into an unbearable dread of being. The strain had been too much. I had stepped over that line where a human being has lost more than he can bear, where the pain is too intense, and he knows he is changed forever. I was now capable of killing, coldly and without feeling. I was empty, as I have never, before or since, known emptiness. I had no connection to this life.

But then, the encroaching darkness that began to envelop me forced me to re-form and give birth to myself again in the chaos. I withdrew even deeper into the world of language, cleaving the diamonds of verbs and nouns, plunging into the brilliant light of poetry's regenerative mystery. Words gave off rings of white energy, radar signals from powers beyond me that infused me with truth. I believed what I wrote, because I wrote what was true. My words did not come from books or textual formulas, but from a deep faith in the voice of my heart.

I had been steeped in self-loathing and rejected by everyone and everything—society, family, cons, God and demons. But now I had become as the burning ember floating in darkness that descends on a dry leaf and sets flame to forests. The word was the ember and the forest was my life.

I was born a poet one noon, gazing at weeds and creosoted grass at the base of a telephone pole outside my grilled cell window. The words I wrote then sailed me out of myself, and I was transported and metamorphosed into the images they made. From the dirty brown blades of grass came bolts of electrical light that jolted loose my old self; through the top of my head that self was released and reshaped in the clump of scrawny grass. Through language I became the grass, speaking its language and feeling its green feelings and black root sensations. Earth was my mother and I bathed in sunshine. Minuscule speckles of sunlight passed through my green skin and metabolized in my blood.

Writing bridged my divided life of prisoner and free man. I wrote of the emotional butchery of prisons, and of my acute gratitude for poetry. Where my blind doubt and spontaneous trust in life met, I discovered empathy and compassion. The power to express myself was a welcome storm rasping at tendril roots, flooding my soul's cracked dirt. Writing was water that cleansed the wound and fed the parched root of my heart.

I wrote to sublimate my rage, from a place where all hope is gone, from a madness of having been damaged too much, from a silence of killing rage. I wrote to avenge the betrayals of a lifetime, to purge the bitterness of injustice. I wrote with a deep groan of doom in my blood, bewildered and dumbstruck; from an indestructible love of life, to affirm breath and laughter and the abiding innocence of things. I wrote the way I wept, and danced, and made love.

THE WORK WE DO

Think back to your first job. Were you lucky enough to get it through a network of family or friends? Or did you pound the pavement, go from one fast-food joint to the next, filling out applications and sniffing the air for possibility? Do you recall the deadening numbness of those early—and even later—jobs, the need to keep a job, but the loathing you felt each time you stepped through the doors? For those of us lacking in education, training, skills, or opportunity, the kind of work we can get often is repetitive, mind-deadening, and sometimes physically brutal.

For those who labor in the agricultural fields, work is not only back-breaking, it also can undermine the possibility of social and educational opportunities for their migrant children. Francisco Jiménez paints an intimate portrait of the effects of migrant farmwork on a young Latino boy and his family in his story "The Circuit." Moving from one town to the next, the child finally finds a place for himself at a new school only to discover that the family is moving again.

Other times, the kind of work we do doesn't fit into our concept of a "work culture" in American society. For example, in Debra Busman's "Like the Wind," we meet an unusual entrepreneur, a young shoplifter who passes stolen goods along to needier friends. A wise soul in a young body, she states, "*Some*one's got to redistribute the wealth."

Turning to a more traditional line of work, Natasha Trethewey captures the working-class experience of a domestic household worker in "Domestic Work, 1937," a woman who holds "a wish for something better."

Diana García, in her poem "Cotton Rows, Cotton Blankets," also comments on agricultural practices when she describes cotton pickers who are unavoidably delayed, then, to make up time, are forced to work "through lunch without water" by a brutal labor contractor.

For her part, Lorna Dee Cervantes captures the deadening work of cannery workers—"peach fuzz reddening their lips and eyes—/I imagine them not speaking, dumbed/by the can's clamor"—in her poem "Cannery Town in August."

In contrast to agricultural and factory work, Chân Không describes the heroic efforts of Vietnamese social workers during the Tet Offensive. In the essay "In the War Zone," the social workers successfully appeal to the compassion of soldiers, both North and South Vietnamese, to save 11,000 civilians huddled on a campus for safety.

Diana García, in her essay "Camp Observations," conveys the relentless drudgery faced by field-workers even as they're surrounded by the San Joaquin Valley's natural beauty, and how this combination of forces results in lives that come "to us in the small details that remain when the major upheavals subside."

Finally, Gloria Anzaldúa, in her essay "now let us shift . . . the path of conocimiento . . . inner work, public acts," continues this question of how to make our work lives as meaningful as our personal lives. Anzaldúa writes, "Conocimiento es otro mode de conectar across colors and other differences to allies also trying to negotiate racial contradictions, survive the stresses and traumas of daily life, and develop a spiritual-imaginal-political vision together."

The Circuit

Francisco Jiménez

It was that time of year again. Ito, the strawberry sharecropper, did not smile. It was natural. The peak of the strawberry season was over and the last few days the workers, most of them braceros, were not picking as many boxes as they had during the months of June and July.

As the last days of August disappeared, so did the number of braceros. Sunday, only one—the best picker—came to work. I liked him. Sometimes we talked during our half-hour lunch break. That is how I found out he was from Jalisco, the same state in Mexico my family was from. That Sunday was the last time I saw him.

When the sun had tired and sunk behind the mountains, Ito signaled us that it was time to go home. "Ya esora," he yelled in his broken Spanish. Those were the words I waited for twelve hours a day, every day, seven days a week, week after week. And the thought of not hearing them again saddened me.

As we drove home Papá did not say a word. With both hands on the wheel, he stared at the dirt road. My older brother, Roberto, was also silent. He leaned his head back and closed his eyes. Once in a while he cleared from his throat the dust that blew in from outside.

Yes, it was that time of year. When I opened the front door to the shack, I stopped. Everything we owned was neatly packed in cardboard boxes. Suddenly I felt even more the weight of hours, days, weeks, and months of work. I sat down on a box. The thought of having to move to Fresno and knowing what was in store for me there brought tears to my eyes.

That night I could not sleep. I lay in bed thinking about how much I hated this move.

A little before five o'clock in the morning, Papá woke everyone up. A few minutes later, the yelling and screaming of my little brothers and sisters, for whom the move was a great adventure, broke the silence of dawn. Shortly, the barking of the dogs accompanied them.

While we packed the breakfast dishes, Papá went outside to start the "Carcanchita." That was the name Papá gave his old '38 black Plymouth. He bought it in a used-car lot in Santa Rosa in the winter of 1949. Papá was very proud of his little jalopy. He had a right to be proud of it. He spent a lot of time looking at other cars before buying this one. When he finally chose the "Carcanchita," he checked it thoroughly before driving it out of the car lot. He examined every inch of the car. He listened to the motor, tilting his head from side to side like a parrot, trying to detect any noises that spelled car trouble. After being satisfied with the looks and sounds of the car, Papá then insisted on knowing who the original owner was. He never did find out from the car salesman, but he bought the car anyway. Papá figured the original owner must have been an important man because behind the rear seat of the car he found a blue necktie.

Papá parked the car out in front and left the motor running. "Listo," he yelled. Without saying a word, Roberto and I began to carry the boxes out to the car. Roberto carried the two big boxes and I carried the two smaller ones. Papá then threw the mattress on top of the car roof and tied it with ropes to the front and rear bumpers.

Everything was packed except Mamá's pot. It was an old large galvanized pot she had picked up at an army surplus store in Santa María the year I was born. The pot had many dents and nicks, and the more dents and nicks it acquired, the more Mamá liked it. "Mi olla," she used to say proudly.

I held the front door open as Mamá carefully carried out her pot by both handles, making sure not to spill the cooked beans. When she got to the car, Papá reached out to help her with it. Roberto opened the rear car door and Papá gently placed it on the floor behind the front seat. All of us then climbed in. Papá sighed, wiped the sweat off his forehead with his sleeve, and said wearily: "Es todo."

As we drove away, I felt a lump in my throat. I turned around and looked at our little shack for the last time.

At sunset we drove into a labor camp near Fresno. Since Papá did not speak English, Mama asked the camp foreman if he needed any more workers. "We don't need no more," said the foreman, scratching his head. "Check with Sullivan down the road. Can't miss him. He lives in a big white house with a fence around it."

When we got there, Mamá walked up to the house. She went through a white gate, past a row of rose bushes, up the stairs to the front door. She rang the doorbell. The porch light went on and a tall husky man came out. They exchanged a few words. After the man went in, Mamá clasped her hands and hurried back to the car. "We have work! Mr. Sullivan said we can stay there the whole season," she said, gasping and pointing to an old garage near the stables.

The garage was worn out by the years. It had no windows. The walls, eaten by termites, strained to support the roof full of holes. The dirt floor, populated by earthworms, looked like a gray road map.

That night, by the light of a kerosene lamp, we unpacked and cleaned our new home. Roberto swept away the loose dirt, leaving the hard ground. Papá plugged the holes in the walls with old newspapers and tin can tops. Mamá fed my little brothers and sisters. Papá and Roberto then brought in the mattress and placed it on the far corner of the garage. "Mamá, you and the little ones sleep on the mattress. Roberto, Panchito, and I will sleep outside under the trees," Papá said.

Early next morning Mr. Sullivan showed us where his crop was, and after breakfast, Papá, Roberto, and I headed for the vineyard to pick.

Around nine o'clock the temperature had risen to almost one hundred degrees. I was completely soaked in sweat and my mouth felt as if I had been chewing on a handkerchief. I walked over to the end of the row, picked up the jug of water we had brought, and began drinking. "Don't drink too much; you'll get sick," Roberto shouted. No sooner had he said that than I felt sick to my stomach. I dropped to my knees and let the jug roll off my hands. I remained motionless with my eyes glued on the hot sandy ground. All I could hear was the drone of insects. Slowly I began to recover. I poured water over my face and neck and watched the dirty water run down my arms to the ground.

I still felt a little dizzy when we took a break to eat lunch. It was past two o'clock and we sat underneath a large walnut tree that was on the side of the road. While we ate, Papá jotted down the number of boxes we had picked. Roberto drew designs on the ground with a stick. Suddenly I noticed Papá's face turn pale as he looked down the road. "Here comes the school bus," he whispered loudly in alarm. Instinctively, Roberto and I ran and hid in the vineyards. We did not want to get in trouble for not going to school. The neatly dressed boys about my age got off. They carried books under their arms. After they crossed the street, the bus drove away. Roberto and I came out from hiding and joined Papá. "Tienen que tener cuidado," he warned us.

After lunch we went back to work. The sun kept beating down. The buzzing insects, the wet sweat, and the hot dry dust made the afternoon seem to last forever. Finally the mountains around the valley reached out and swallowed the sun. Within an hour it was too dark to continue picking. The vines blanketed the grapes, making it difficult to see the bunches. "Vámonos," said Papá, signaling to us that it was time to quit work. Papá then took out a pencil and began to figure out how much we had earned our first day. He wrote down numbers, crossed some out, wrote down some more. "Quince," he murmured.

When we arrived home, we took a cold shower underneath a water-hose. We then sat down to eat dinner around some wooden crates that served as a table. Mamá had cooked a special meal for us. We had rice and tortillas with "carne con chile," my favorite dish.

The next morning I could hardly move. My body ached all over. I felt little control over my arms and legs. This feeling went on every morning for days until my muscles finally got used to the work.

It was Monday, the first week of November. The grape season was over and I could now go to school. I woke up early that morning and lay in bed, looking at the stars and savoring the thought of not going to work and of starting sixth grade for the first time that year. Since I could not sleep, I decided to get up and join Papá and Roberto at breakfast. I sat at the table across from Roberto, but I kept my head down. I did not want to look up and face him. I knew he was sad. He was not going to school today. He was not going tomorrow, or next week, or next month. He would not go until the cotton season was over, and that was sometime in February. I rubbed my hands together and watched the dry, acid-stained skin fall to the floor in little rolls.

When Papá and Roberto left for work, I felt relief. I walked to the top of a small grade next to the shack and watched the "Carcanchita" disappear in the distance in a cloud of dust.

Two hours later, around eight o'clock, I stood by the side of the road waiting for school bus number twenty. When it arrived I climbed in. Everyone was busy either talking or yelling. I sat in an empty seat in the back.

When the bus stopped in front of the school, I felt very nervous. I looked out the bus window and saw boys and girls carrying books under their arms. I put my hands in my pant pockets and walked to the principal's office. When I entered, I heard a woman's voice say: "May I help you?" I was startled. I had not heard English for months. For a few seconds I remained speechless. I looked at the lady who waited for an answer. My first instinct was to answer her in Spanish, but I held back.

Finally, after struggling for English words, I managed to tell her that I wanted to enroll in the sixth grade. After answering many questions, I was led to the classroom.

Mr. Lema, the sixth grade teacher, greeted me and assigned me a desk. He then introduced me to the class. I was so nervous and scared at that moment when everyone's eyes were on me that I wished I were with Papá and Roberto picking cotton. After taking roll, Mr. Lema gave the class the assignment for the first hour. "The first thing we have to do this morning is finish reading the story we began yesterday," he said enthusiastically. He walked up to me, handed me an English book, and asked me to read. "We are on page 125," he said politely. When I heard this, I felt my blood rush to my head; I felt dizzy. "Would you like to read?" he asked hesitantly. I opened the book to page 125. My mouth was dry. My eyes began to water. I could not begin. "You can read later," Mr. Lema said understandingly.

For the rest of the reading period I kept getting angrier and angrier with myself. I should have read, I thought to myself.

During recess I went into the restroom and opened my English book to page 125. I began to read in a low voice, pretending I was in class. There were many words I did not know. I closed the book and headed back to the classroom.

Mr. Lema was sitting at his desk correcting papers. When I entered, he looked up at me and smiled. I felt better. I walked up to him and asked if he could help me with the new words. "Gladly," he said.

The rest of the month I spent my lunch hours working on English with Mr. Lema, my best friend at school.

One Friday during lunch hour Mr. Lema asked me to take a walk with him to the music room. "Do you like music?" he asked me as we entered the building.

"Yes, I like corridos," I answered. He then picked up a trumpet, blew on it, and handed it to me. The sound gave me goose bumps. I knew that sound. I had heard it in many corridos. "How would you like to learn how to play it?" he asked. He must have read my face because before I could answer, he added: "I'll teach you how to play it during our lunch hours."

That day I could hardly wait to get home to tell Papá and Mamá the great news. As I got off the bus, my little brothers and sisters ran up to meet me. They were yelling and screaming. I thought they were happy to see me, but when I opened the door to our shack, I saw that everything we owned was neatly packed in cardboard boxes.

Like the Wind

Debra Busman

Taylor's favorite job was stealing from Sears, working for her best friend Mario's uncle Enrique. Enrique had hated Sears ever since he'd gotten fired for pointing out to management that the blond workers seemed to be having way too much fun while the brown workers got all the shit jobs and early pink slips. So, Sears was the usual target of choice, although Pep Boys and Montgomery Wards were also fair game. Taylor stole bicycles, clothes, electronics, tools, watches, anything she could grab and ride or run away with.

She and Mario had figured out pretty quick that, as a white girl, Taylor wasn't followed around the stores by security cops like all her Mexican friends were. So they would separate before entering a store, Mario, Jesús and Ricky all going in one door and Taylor in the other, her hair combed, her pink blouse pressed. Once inside, Jesús and Mario would start a fight, or Ricky would "get lost" and start to cry for his mama, or they would "accidentally" knock down the five-foot-high pyramid of Valvoline 10-40 motor oil cans, anything to cause a distraction. Once personnel went running to see what the commotion was all about, Taylor stuffed something in her jacket or, when she was lucky, hopped on a ten-speed or Sting Ray bike and just rode right out the door. "*Like the wind*," Enrique would say. "That girl rides like the mother-fuckin' wind."

All she had to do was ride down the street until she saw Enrique's white van. He'd be standing outside by the rear of the vehicle. If all was clear, he'd open the back doors and help throw Taylor and the bike inside. If someone was after her, Enrique would leave the van doors shut, look away, and she'd know to keep on riding, ditch the bike, and start hopping fences. They never once got caught, although Taylor hopped a lot of fences.

Once inside the van, she and Enrique would circle around to the other side of the shopping center and pick up Mario, Jesús, and Ricky down by whatever gas station they'd checked out beforehand, usually a Chevron or a Union 76, cuz Ricky liked the little orange balls they gave away. The boys would all pile in and brag about what they'd done to attract security, and everyone would laugh, and Taylor would tell them how she got away, and then Enrique would say, "Damn you guys done good," and tousle their hair. Then, he'd light up a reefer for him and Mario to smoke, and sometimes Taylor took a hit, too.

Taylor had that job from the time she was seven until she turned eleven and Enrique got drafted. Four years. Just like her dad, she never called in sick, never missed a day of work. Enrique was an excellent boss. He taught Taylor lessons that would serve her throughout her life. Like never *act* like you're stealing when you're stealing. Act like you already own it, like it already belongs to you and somehow got placed on the shelf by mistake. "Ride that motherfuckin' bike like it's *yours,* chica," he used to tell Taylor, "not like you're stealing it from no goddamn pussy Sears store."

Sometimes, Taylor got to see Enrique himself in action. Once, when his grandmother needed a new refrigerator, he brought her home a brand-new Westinghouse double-door chrome handle with deluxe ice maker. First, he stole a pair of overalls from Sears that looked just like the ones the guys wore down at the Montgomery Wards warehouse. Then he sewed on a name tag—"Frankie," he laughed. "Es un buen nombre, no?" Taylor watched Enrique check out the appliance section of the Van Nuys Wards a couple of times and then damn if he didn't just walk right into the store and come out a few minutes later wheeling a huge, shiny refrigerator on a bright red dolly. Stole the dolly, too.

For years, the kids would try and get Enrique to tell them the story of how he stole his grandmother's refrigerator. He'd just laugh and say, "Ah sí, mi abuelita. We never did find out how el refrigerador de mi abuelita wound up at Montgomery Wards. Qué misterio!" he'd smile, his eyes crinkling up. "Pues," he'd continue, "once I knew the refrigerador was in the wrong place, I had to liberate it, no? Bring it back to my grandmother where it belonged. It's only right, you know. Es la verdad."

Enrique was shot two months after being shipped out to Nam. Killed by friendly fire while he was out taking a piss, two days after his battalion had finally gotten their ammo and were heading for the front lines. He never stopped talking to Taylor, though. Every time she stole a bike, she'd hear his voice whispering in her ear. "*Ride* that bike like the motherfuckin' wind," he'd tell her. "Ride it like it's yours." When she'd walk into a bookstore, Taylor could hear Enrique's voice get real low and fierce. "Yes, chica," she'd hear him say, "these books *belong* to you. Liberate one or two for me while you're at it," he'd ask her, "and remember to share them with los niños, okay? *Some*one's got to redistribute the wealth, eh mija?"

When Taylor got older, Enrique was still right there with helpful advice. "Look like you belong," he told her when she started stealing from the fancy department stores downtown, "especially if you don't." When her clothes got too shabby, he warned her, "Niña, te acuerdas, only the rich can afford to dress poor." In fact, it was Enrique's idea to start selling raggedy jeans to the hippies out in Griffith Park. Taylor and Mario collected worn-out Levi's and work shirts from all the neighbors, pulling them from the hands of the mothers who first wanted to sew up the tears in their son's brother's husband's work clothes. "No mama," Mario would say. "That's the whole point. You don't gotta sew this shit anymore. Taylor's gonna sell 'em to los hippies. They pay *more* money if the pants are torn. I *know* es muy loco, mama, pero es la verdad. Give them to me. You'll see."

Every Saturday, Taylor and Mario would take the bus down to Griffith Park and sell the raggedy clothes to the hippies at their love-ins and anti-war rallies. Taylor was dealing pot to them anyway, so it was pretty easy to set up shop. If fact, it was a great cover and explained any money Taylor might have on her if the cops rousted them. Mario stood out too much in the crowd, so he'd stay clean, lay low, and watch, ready to cover Taylor's back if necessary. Every weekend, they'd bring home more money, and every Monday the women in the neighborhood would go out and buy new jeans for their kids, new work shirts for their husbands.

"Only the rich can afford to dress poor," Mario said to Taylor one day as they watched the kids head off to school in their brand-new clothes. When she looked at him with surprise, he added, "Hey man, you don't think you're the only one he talks to, do you? That motherfucker's been yappin' inside my head ever since he got shot. That cholo talks more now than when he was alive."

Taylor laughed. "No kiddin'?" she asked. "He ever sing that stupid-ass Dylan song to you?"

"Oh man," Mario whined. "Only all the fucking time. Every time I even think about shaking somebody down or putting some of the hippie money in my own pocket, I gotta hear that guy singing, *to leeve out side the law, chu mus be ho-nest . . .*"

Taylor laughed at Mario's imitation of Enrique's rendering of Bob Dylan. She'd heard that refrain on more than one occasion herself. "Come on," she said, pushing Mario gently. "Let's go check out what those motherfuckers got on sale today down at Sears. Hey, *somebody's* got to redistribute the wealth, right, man?"

Domestic Work, 1937

Natasha Trethewey

All week she's cleaned
someone else's house,
stared down her own face
in the shine of copper-
bottomed pots, polished
wood, toilets she'd pull
the lid to—that look saying

Let's make a change, girl.

But Sunday mornings are hers—
church clothes starched
and hanging, a record spinning
on the console, the whole house
dancing. She raises the shades,
washes the rooms in light,
buckets of water, Octagon soap.

Cleanliness is next to godliness . . .

Windows and doors flung wide,
curtains two-stepping
forward and back, neck bones
bumping in the pot, a choir
of clothes clapping on the line.

Nearer my God to thee . . .

She beats time on the rugs,
blows dust from the broom
like dandelion spores, each one
a wish for something better.

Cotton Rows, Cotton Blankets

Diana García

Sprawled on the back of a flatbed truck
we cradled hoes, our minds parceling rows
of cotton to be chopped by noon. Dawn stuck
in the air. Blackbirds rang the willows.

Ahead, a horse trailer stretched across the road.
Braced by youth and lengths of summer breeze
we didn't give a damn. We'd be late, we joked,
stalled by a pregnant mare draped in sheets.

Later, backs to the sun, bandanas tied
to shade our brows, hands laced with tiny cuts;
later, when the labor contractor
worked us through lunch without water; our dried
tongues cursed that mare in cotton blankets
brought to foal in the outlines of summer.

Cannery Town in August

Lorna Dee Cervantes

All night it humps the air.
Speechless, the steam rises
from the cannery columns. I hear
the night bird rave about work
or lunch, or sing the swing shift
home. I listen, while bodyless
uniforms and spinach-specked shoes
drift in monochrome down the dark
moon-possessed streets. Women
who smell of whiskey and tomatoes,
peach fuzz reddening their lips and eyes—
I imagine them not speaking, dumbed
by the can's clamor and drop
to the trucks that wait, grunting
in their headlights below.
They spotlight those who walk
like a dream, with no one
waiting in the shadows
to palm them back to living.

In the War Zone

Chân Không

On July 5, 1967, I was on my motorbike en route to Binh Phuoc Village, when another social worker going in the opposite direction waved me down and told me that four SYSS workers—Tuan, Tho, Lanh, and Hy—had been murdered. Their bodies were still lying on the ground near the Binh Phuoc River. Ha Van Dinh, a novice monk, survived the murder attempt and was in the hospital.

My first thought was that someone should guard Ha Van Dinh, because as the only witness, he could be killed in the hospital. So right away I went to see him, and I helped move him to another hospital, where he registered under a false name. Dinh told me that the murderers had acted almost friendly as they led the five students to the riverbank. Dinh thought that they were about to get into a boat, when one of the men said rather suddenly, "Are you from the School of Youth for Social Service?" The students all said "Yes," and the man said, "I am sorry, but we have to kill you." Then they shot our five friends, one by one. Dinh fell into the water and survived, but the other four died immediately.

I went to the riverbank and saw the bodies of my beloved younger brothers, and I was close to despair. Thây Thanh Van arrived an hour later, and together we arranged for the bodies to be brought back to the school. We set the date for a funeral, and again, Thây Thanh Van asked me to write a eulogy for him to read.

Pro-communist Vietnamese told us, "You should cry out against the Americans! It was CIA agents who killed your friends!" Pro-American Vietnamese said, "You should speak out against the communists. It was they who killed your friends." Even among Buddhists, there was strong pressure for us to condemn the killers. But we knew that, according to the teaching of the Buddha, humans are not our enemies. Misunderstanding, hatred, jealousy, and confusion are our enemies. Still, it was hard to put that into words when confronted with the corpses of our four dear friends.

For three days and nights, I could hardly sleep. I dwelled in mindfulness, reciting gathas, mindfulness verses, as I did my everyday activities: "Washing my hands, I vow to have clean hands to embrace the path of love. I pray that the thoughts and deeds of those who killed my friends will be cleansed." During the third night, the murderer's words that Dinh had told me, "I am sorry, but we have to kill you," sprang into my mind, and I began to see that the message of understanding and love that Thây Thanh Van had delivered at the last funeral had reached even the killers. It was obvious that these men had been forced to kill our friends, for if they refused, they themselves could have been killed. In the speech I wrote for Thây Thanh Van, I thanked the murderers for saying that they were forced to kill. "That proved that you did not want to kill us, but for your own safety, you had to do it. We hope that one day you will help us in our work for peace." The funeral was held four days after the murders, and from then on, we received support everywhere we went. The number of workers in the SYSS increased quickly, and we had the full cooperation of monks and nuns throughout the country.

In January 1968, eight months after Nhat Chi Mai burned herself to death as a prayer for peace, the fighting continued fiercely. I knew that I had to do something to help my Dharma sister realize her dream of peace, so I drafted a petition calling upon the warring parties to prolong the cease-fire that was already scheduled for Têt, the Vietnamese New Year. I persuaded a number of prominent professors from Saigon University to sign it, and the professors asked their colleagues to sign. Eventually we had seventy-one signatures, more than one-third of the faculty, and we published the petition on January 16, 1968. Students in the peace movement also arranged for a Peace Festival to celebrate Têt and express their wish for a longer cease-fire. The North Vietnamese had declared a three-day cease-fire, but the South Vietnamese had declared only one day.

As it turned out, just a few hours after the cease-fire started, fierce battles broke out in provinces throughout the South. The National Liberation Front forced civilians in the countryside to walk alongside their guerrilla troops, thus forming a sea of people who were screaming, "Advance, advance!" Seeing such huge crowds, the South Vietnamese army panicked and called for the Americans to drop bombs, and hundreds of civilians were killed. Eighty-five percent of the homes in many provinces and cities were destroyed, including those in Ben Tre, my hometown. The guerrillas advanced into Ben Tre City, Hue City, and the Saigon suburbs, infiltrated into crowded slums, and shot at the planes, thus attracting more bombs and destruction.

Following the battle, there were dead bodies all over the streets of Saigon. When the Red Cross workers tried to collect them, they were shot at by the guerrillas. So I suggested to my colleagues at the SYSS that we gather the dead bodies and bury them. I knew that after three or four days, the stench would be unbearable and that diseases could spread. For four years, many Buddhist rescue committees had the experience of going into war zones to rescue the wounded, protected only by the Buddhist flag. In Vietnam the Buddhist flag was safer than the Red Cross flag, because both warring sides respected the Buddhists. But when I told Thây Thanh Van, "We need to go out and pick up dead bodies," he was silent for a while and then reminded me that we were a school for training social workers in rural development, not ambulance drivers or Red Cross workers. I was very disappointed, and silently I decided to do the work alone. I announced this privately to my Tiep Hien friends and a few SYSS coworkers.

Eventually other young monks, nuns, and laypersons joined me in that work. After a few days of gathering up the dead bodies, we went back to the SYSS, deeply touched by the frailty of human bodies. Men and women who were strong and beautiful when they were alive turned to rotten, smelly corpses in just a few days. The images of once joyful, vibrant faces of friends now dead and rotting stayed with me. I shared the experiences of my deep meditation on life and death with Thây Thanh Van, and he was inspired by this and joined us in our efforts to pick up and bury the many corpses.

It was an extraordinarily difficult task. There was an enormous gap between my idealistic perception and the reality of the situation. The bodies smelled horrible! At that time, there were no gloves, work clothes, or chemicals to neutralize the smell, so we put peanut oil on our noses—but that didn't help at all. That stench followed me for months so that the smell of anything organic brought back the nauseating smell of rotting corpses, and I could only eat plain, salted rice for several months. Thây Thanh Van may have been right when he said that we could not ask people to do such difficult work.

During the days of the Têt Offensive, when fighting went on in the streets of Saigon, people were asked not to leave their homes unless absolutely necessary. People were glued to their radios listening to the latest news. Suddenly I heard the Minister of Education on the radio calling "the seventy-one university professors who had signed a petition for peace on January 16, 1968," to come to the ministry "for an urgent national matter." Then the speaker read all seventy-one names, including mine, not just once, but every half hour. My family urged me not to go, fearing that I would be shot. We had just seen on television Colonel Nguyen Ngoc Loan shooting a guerrilla he had caught. I was very afraid, but I thought that since the petition had been my idea, I had to take full responsibility and go. If I didn't, it could be all the worse for the others.

Only twenty-one of us came to the Ministry of Education at the time announced on the radio. The minister told us that the National Police suspected we had plotted the Têt Offensive with the communists. He said he wanted to protect us, and that we only needed to retract our peace appeal and sign a new petition condemning the communists. Eighteen professors signed the new petition, hoping to avoid trouble during these tumultuous times. But Father Nguyen Ngoc Lan, Professor Chau Tam Luan, and I refused. We said that we could not sign the ministry's petition, because our students had heard our names mentioned every half hour on the governmental radio and now the same names on the radio again for signing the new petition. It would be clear that we had succumbed to the government's pressure to sign. We did, however, offer to draft another petition later, outside the ministry, condemning the violation of the Têt cease-fire. By refusing to sign the ministry's petition, I was certain I would go to jail. At that meeting, I told my colleagues, "The most important gift a teacher can give his students is dignity. We have always tried our best to be worthy of our students' trust. If we die under violence, our spirits will blossom in their hearts. But if we sign the petition offered by the government today, it means we have submitted to the government's threats. This is not what we want to teach the younger generation." After that meeting, we were all released, but I suspected the matter was not yet over.

When I returned home, I packed my toothbrush, pajamas, and a light sweater, so I would be ready to go to jail when the police came. But, instead, I received an invitation from the Minister of Education to come to his office. When I arrived, he said, "You have refused to retract your declaration. I am very busy, but the Chief of Police has asked me to settle this matter. If you still refuse to retract, I will have to inform the police, and you will be arrested immediately and relieved of your post at the university."

I breathed deeply and said in a very firm voice, "Sir, I came to you today because I know that you were once a professor, my elder brother in teaching. When you speak in such a threatening way, it is impossible for us to have real communication. So do what you want with me. Please send me to jail. If I allow you to coerce me as you suggest, I would be no better than Colonel Lieu, the cherished comrade of President Thieu, who, as soon as he was arrested by the communists in Ben Tre, called upon all South Vietnamese soldiers to join the side of the North."

With tears in my eyes, I continued more gently, "Sir, I am like a bamboo shoot among university teachers. I am young, but my spirit may grow strong and beautiful. I spoke out frankly about the situation of the country, not for my own sake, but for the sake of the nation, even though prison may await me as a result. I appeal to your conscience as an elder brother to help me grow in this attitude, not to bow before coercion. Don't force me to go against my conscience. If I agree to sign your petition under threat of violence, then tonight if unknown men enter my house with guns and force me to sign a petition saying, 'Long live Mao Tse Tung,' must I not also sign that? If I sign under the threat of guns against my conscience and belief, who will be at fault? Do you really want to teach me that way of coercion?"

He seemed embarrassed and his attitude changed immediately. He said that I had misunderstood him, that he only wanted to protect me. Then he let me go without signing anything, and the police never came to arrest me. Apparently he protected me from the police.

In May 1968, a Japanese Quaker friend, Masako Yamanouchi, came to my home in Saigon to tell me that bombs were dropping around the campus of the SYSS. Masako was a lovely, young woman who came to work voluntarily with us. As an Asian wearing a Vietnamese *ao dai*, she looked just like a Vietnamese woman. She learned and spoke Vietnamese too, so she was a unique foreign social worker who was accepted in our school. We couldn't accept American or European social workers into the SYSS, because we knew we would be labeled by the communists as CIA agents.

Masako said that our water pump motor was out of gasoline and that she was on her way to buy some. "Thousands of people are caught at the school campus," she told me. "The gunfire is very dangerous. The water pump has been working all day and night, and now we are out of water."

I immediately took some medicine and bandages, and I rode on my motorbike to the SYSS headquarters. When I arrived close to the campus, I was terrified to see and hear bombs exploding everywhere. One rocket fell on the field right in front of me, and another landed behind me as I rode along on my motorbike. I realized I could be killed at any moment. There was so much bombing, people did not know where to run. The bombs were destroying homes throughout the area, and thousands of local residents ran to our campus for refuge.

People were ushered into the meditation hall, then the classrooms, the library, the dining room, the kitchen, and finally the students' dormitory rooms, until all forty rooms of the main building were completely filled with people huddled closely, side by side. People continued to come, and we had to usher them into the bathrooms and eventually even into the hallways and closets. Nearly 11,000 people squeezed into every nook and cranny of the campus. To try to prevent bombs from being dropped on us, we raised the Buddhist flag from the highest point of the school building.

So many of the people were wounded that we used up our entire supply of bandages in less than two hours, and many girls then tore up their own dresses to make more. Most of us were not trained to be nurses, doctors, or surgeons, but we had to do the work anyway. One young SYSS worker, trained as a nurse, served as doctor, delivering ten babies over the next several days.

At one point, while I was bandaging a wounded man, a small boy started tugging on my dress and saying something to me. His request seemed less serious than the man's wound, so I asked him to wait, but he kept tugging at me. Half an hour later, someone cried, "Look!" and I saw the same little boy pulling the bleeding body of an old woman. The desperate look in his eyes pressed on me like a clamp squeezing my heart. Later, I learned that he was an orphan and the wounded woman was his grandmother. Imagine how desperate he was to save her!

There was so much shooting around the campus that it was impossible for us to go outside and bury the eight dead bodies that had been carried by relatives to our campus. We finally had to ask three male students to go just outside the main building and dig the graves. With bullets flying around their heads, they managed to dig three holes the first day and five the second.

At that time, there were only thirty-seven social workers at the school, organizing the care of almost 11,000 refugees. We invited a few hundred of those able to take responsibility for themselves to help us, and we divided into teams—one team to do the medical work, one for childcare, one to cook, one to distribute food, one to take care of water, one to clear the road, and one to clean the rooms and the bathrooms. In addition, we dug a number of holes outside to use as latrines. We let our water pump run twenty-four hours a day for three days, and when it ran out of fuel, Masako had to go out and find some more. Fortunately, a good mechanic among the refugees was able to fix the pump each time it broke, but during the hours it wasn't working, we had 11,000 people without water. We really came to appreciate such simple things as having water when you need it.

Each night, after the refugees went to sleep, we social workers had a meeting to discuss the problems that had come up that day. We had to figure out many things, such as how to transport the seriously wounded to the hospital. That entailed crossing the fire zone, but we decided to try. We chose the shortest path across the battlefield. The monks and nuns in their yellow robes walked at the head of the line holding Buddhist flags, and behind them, we carried five seriously wounded persons. Crossing the area of the least intense fighting, we arrived at an area where we could hire a van and bring them to the hospital in Saigon.

On the third day of the May offensive, with the sudden influx of refugees on our campus, there was a rumor that the campus would be bombed very soon and that everyone should move out immediately. Some people believed the rumor, some didn't, and an atmosphere of panic ensued. Many people wanted to run away, but outside, the shooting was everywhere. South Vietnamese troops and NLF guerrillas were fighting each other on all four sides of the campus. Thây Thanh Van knew he had to do something.

Four months later, he revealed to us what he had done. He crossed the fire zone by himself, without even a Buddhist flag, just wearing his humble brown monk's robe, and he walked to the largest post of the South Vietnamese army, where he asked to see the commanding officer. When he met the officer in charge, he told him, "I request one thing of you. Please instruct the planes not to bomb our campus. We have 11,000 war victims there who have already lost their homes and their relatives. They have only this refuge in the heart of the war area." I think no one could say "no" to this frail bodhisattva. He also said, "I request your permission to let me go to the communists and ask them also not to attack or enter our campus. Please, don't shoot me en route."

The Saigon officer answered, "I cannot guarantee that there will be no shooting, because if we stop shooting, the other side will think we have surrendered, and they will advance on us." So Thây Thanh Van suggested, "Please shoot into the sky or at the land, but not at me. If you do that, they will hear the noise of your bullets, and they will think that you are shooting at them. If you refrain from shooting at me, I will have the chance to negotiate for the safety of 11,000 people who suffer so much from the war."

Thây Thanh Van then crossed the fire zone again, and, as he did so, the South Vietnamese troops continued to shoot, but not at him. When he spoke to the communist side, he pleaded in the same way, "Please, do not send troops onto our campus or shoot at our campus. There are 11,000 people who suffer there." And they agreed.

When Thây Thanh Van came back, he didn't tell us what he had done. The few hundred persons who had already left returned when they found so much fighting and bombing right outside the campus. People were panicky, not knowing whether to leave the campus or stay. So Thây Thanh Van took a large megaphone to ask people to stay, but then he thought, What if I ask them to stay and then a bomb drops on the campus and they die? How could I live? So he put the megaphone down.

At that time, a number of villagers who had been assisting us reported that there were some NLF guerrillas posing as refugees, and they were planning to shoot at the American planes from our campus. We knew that if they did, the campus would probably be bombed. Because in Vietnam we respect our elders very much, we decided to ask the oldest persons among the refugees to go around and say to everyone, "We pray that those who have guns will not use them. If you know anyone who has a gun, please advise him to bury it, for the safety of 11,000 people." Finally, there was no trouble at all.

Everything was going well. We had been able to take the seriously wounded to the hospital, bury eight dead bodies, and deliver ten babies. The soldiers from both sides, although shooting at each other at the periphery of the campus, never tried to enter the campus directly. After eight days, when the battle finally ended, the countryside was in ruins. Thousands of houses had been destroyed, and thousands of trees were burned to the ground. But our campus remained intact, fresh, and green. The acacia trees continued to produce beautiful blossoms, and the thickets of yellow bamboo continued to shine brightly under the delicate green leaves.

That sumptuous, green campus in the midst of a large devastated area was the fruit of our collective work, but I could see that the wisdom and fearlessness of Thây Thanh Van played a particularly important role in its realization.

Those eight days were a turning experience for me. Seeing so much death and despair, I learned that we must resist war at any price. Once a war gets started, it has a momentum and intensity that are very hard to stop.

Camp Observations

Diana García

My poems and stories begin at five in the morning, any weekday morning between February and November in the middle of California's San Joaquín Valley. The old plastic-cased radio sputters. Two rooms away, I hear that radio crackle. We're on! All of us, every set of ears in that house, pretend not to hear the sweep of violin, the throaty brass, the 12-stringed guitars, the anonymous announcer cry, "KXAX, Radio Campesino." Miguel Aceves Mejía breaks into "La verdolaga"; we begin again.

Outside, if it's winter, tule fog blankets sky and ground. If it's summer, we'll be sizzling in 90-degree weather by 10 a.m. Inside, the radio sings, the coffee pot clatters, eggs sputter in a cast iron skillet. Practical sounds: the clump of work boots on the kitchen linoleum. Mexican sounds: *"¿Quieres papas? ¿Vas a querer un plátano en tu lonche?"*

Those of us not going out to the fields or out to the construction site slide down deeper in bed. We know we're next. We know the bacon and egg routine. If we say we're not hungry, we'll get stewed prunes. No problem: we eat the bacon and eggs.

When I write about the morning routine years later, I understand I must fill in where needed. Much of the literary space is devoid of images of the poor, the undocumented, and the migrant. Those who work in the fields or who live on the margins are invisible except perhaps to Wal-Mart shoppers. In response, I fill in with pieces about the lives of people I knew in the San Joaquín Valley, about lives like those of the people I know. Most of those people migrated from Durango and Chihuahua, from Arizona and the Imperial Valley. Others migrated from Louisiana and Arkansas, China, France, and Italy.

In the 1930s, we suffered a depression. The U.S. government responded with the Repatriation Act: thousands of Mexican migrant workers were shipped back home. At the California-Arizona border, posted guards even turned back dust-bowl migrants. Thankfully, both efforts were like turning the tide. In the 1940s, farmers demanded cheap labor to harvest the fields, and the Department of Agriculture implemented the Bracero Program. In the 1950s, the Second World War and Korea behind us, returning veterans demanded educations and better homes. They shouted slogans like "America for Americans." The U.S. government responded with Operation Wetback and sent braceros back where they came from.

This sentiment spreads like thick tule fog today. Ask the former San Diego mayor who commandeered the Light Up the Border forces at the San Diego–Tijuana border on irregular Friday nights. Ask the backers of Propositions 187 and 227 in California. Ask another former mayor, who declared, "Those Cubans are the worst kind of Mexicans there are!"

A man—I don't know his name; I've never met him—came to California in the '30s, a dust-bowl fugitive from Oklahoma. Anyway, that Oklahoma fugitive read a copy of my poem, "When Living Was a Labor Camp Called Montgomery," that my mother had given his daughter. He remembered Montgomery. He probably didn't know who Miguel Aceves Mejía was—my parents' favorite singer. The old man never cared (I could have written: never gave a fig) for mariachi music. But he remembered the camp. He knew thick summer days sorting boxes of dried figs. He knew the sticky fig honey on his hands and face, knew flies sticking to him like flypaper.

What he and the migrant workers in the camps shared were years of hard, hot days, cold, foggy nights. Dreams of buying a house someday. A house with a thick foundation. A house with a few good lines. You could remodel this house, enclose its California bungalow porch with smoked picture windows, replace the double-hung windows with sliding aluminum, tinker with the kitchen and the bath. I know lives like these. I was born in one of those camps, then raised in a house remodeled so many times I forget what is original. I write for all the people of the camps, both for those from the 1940s and for those in the 1990s who don't have a camp to call home.

An early mentor instructs me to write what I know. Much of what I know comes through experience but also through a life-long commitment to eavesdropping. For example, inspiration comes one summer afternoon while listening to my mother, her cousins, and all their husbands laugh about their teenaged days in Camp Montgomery. The occasion is a festive one: no funeral to attend. We are celebrating another aunt's and uncle's fiftieth wedding anniversary. I trace their voices and stories in the weeks and months that follow.

I write what I hear and see, the stories my dad, his friends and brothers, my godfather tell over six-packs of beer and plates piled with tacos. I listen to the aunts gossip in the kitchen, voices hushed as they recall some long-ago tragedy. The men howl at how they almost got swept up by la migra. The women weep for husbands killed by pesticides, nephews and nieces killed in a fire when the kerosene heater exploded. And always the guitars and songs, one uncle's clear baritone, my father's perfect harmony, the women listening for tones long forgotten.

I write what I eat and smell. Roasted jalapeños mixed with tomatoes canned last summer. Fresh flour tortillas rolled around chunks of roast beef. Refried beans oozing lard and jack cheese. Salsa, beef, cheese. The scent of Coty face powder and Emeraude cologne against a layer of Dixie Peach pomade. Peaches rotting beneath a mound of flies, the dry dust of the orchards in August.

Inspiration comes while teaching poetry workshops to children in San Diego's North County whose first language is Tarasco or Zapotec. These are children for whom Spanish is a second language, English a third. They could have been children of the camps if they had had camps to call home. They would love to call a camp like Montgomery or CPC home. Instead they climb out of canyons beneath some of the most exclusive neighborhoods in the county. Their parents walk them to their work sites, the strawberry and flower fields. They bathe their children's hands and faces in irrigation water. They send them to school an hour before the first bus comes to pick them up. The promise I made to myself, after listening to my family's stories and my students' stories, was to give voice to all those experiences.

As a child, I was my maternal grandmother's changuita, her pobrecita, the poor monkey she pitied because I could never be beautiful. I was so dark. Perhaps that's why I was one of her favorites. In my mid-thirties, a year before she died, I paid a visit to my grandmother. As I walked up the sidewalk to her house, she opened her screen door. She stared at me as if she didn't recognize me. When I kissed her cheek, she said, "But you've gotten so beautiful!" This woman loved me, but even she couldn't forget her conditioning: It is better to be light-skinned than dark. Much of my work confronts the trauma of being different. Poems of anger and reconciliation, they're my warning that I give good smile but watch out for my teeth.

The old orchards and fields are disappearing. The labor camp I knew best, Camp CPC—better known in the 1940s and '50s as Camp Bear Creek—is still there, the camp where my parents lived when I was born. Some of the cabins at Camp Montgomery remain, but the fig orchard disappeared in the late 1990s. The last time I drove past, fig trees were piled as if to build a funeral pyre. Their twisted trunks and gnarled branches reminded me of the old people from the camps, too old and arthritic to work in the fields. New houses multiply where fig trees once grew. Former pasture land now nurtures the newest University of California.

My writings are in response to Helene Cixous's exhortation to "write the body." They're also a reaction to marianismo, a devotion to the Virgin Mary that precludes any untoward behavior on the part of women, including women characters in fiction and poetry. For my models I call on María Luisa Bombal, Carmen Boullosa, Angeles Mastretta, Luisa Valenzuela, and Elena Poniatowska. I call on Sandra Cisneros, Ana Castillo, Pat Mora, and Denise Chávez. Their poems, novels, and short stories inspire me to write the lives of women who make their way out of the camps, women whose histories leave them ill-suited to succeed in the cities. You can't be too nice or too proper to succeed in the city, no husband, no education, no job experience. Just a couple of kids and a car that needs a new gasket.

In my work, I acknowledge how life comes to us in the small details that remain when the major upheavals subside. My work centers on the San Joaquín Valley's endless expanses—what Gaston Bachelard called "intimate immensity." As a child and a young woman, that immensity ended with the coastal range on one side, the Sierra Nevada foothills on the other. Later, home for me came to refer to the San Diego County landscape, a space scented with sage heavy as wet pillows, a scent so heavy you can touch it. This is what I touch when I write the space I call home.

from now let us shift . . . the path of
conocimiento . . . inner work, public acts

Gloria Anzaldúa

7. shifting realities . . . acting out the vision or spiritual activism

> The bridge will hold me up.
> —Gabrielle in *Xena, Warrior Princess*

You're three years old and standing by the kitchen table staring at the bright orange globe. You can almost taste its tart sweetness. You'll die if you don't have it. You reach for it but your arms are too short. Body quivering, you stretch again, willing yourself to reach the fruit. Your arms elongate until your small hands clasp the orange. You sense you're more than one body—each superimposed on the others like sheaths of corn. Years later after a few more experiences of bilocation, you describe it as a yoga of the body.[1] The ability to recognize and endow meaning to daily experience (spirituality) furthers the ability to shift and transform.

When and how does transformation happen? When a change occurs, your consciousness (awareness of your sense of self and your response to self, others, and surroundings) becomes cognizant that it has a point of view and the ability to act from choice. This knowing/knower is always with you, but is displaced by the ego and its perspective. This knower has several functions. You call the function that arouses the awareness that beneath individual separateness lies a deeper interrelatedness "la naguala."

When you shift attention from your customary point of view (the ego) to that of la naguala, and from there move your awareness to an inner-held representation of an experience, person, thing, or world, la naguala and the object observed merge. When you include the complexity of feeling two or more ways about a person/issue, when you empathize and try to see her circumstances from her position, you accommodate the other's perspective, achieving un conocimiento that allows you to shift toward a less defensive, more inclusive identity. When you relate to others not as parts, problems, or useful commodities, but from a connectionist view, compassion triggers transformation. This shift occurs when you give up investment in your point of view[2] and recognize the real situation free of projections—not filtered through your habitual defensive preoccupations. Moving back and forth from the situation to la naguala's view, you glean a new description of the world (reality)— a Toltec interpretation. When you're in the place between worldviews (nepantla), you're able to slip between realities to a neutral perception. A decision made in the in-between place becomes a turning point initiating psychological and spiritual transformations, making other kinds of experiences possible.

Core beliefs command the focus of your senses. By changing some of these convictions you change the mental/emotional channel (the reality). In the Coatlicue state, an intensely negative channel, you're caged in a private hell; you feel angry, fearful, hopeless, and depressed, blaming yourself as inadequate. In the more optimistic space cultivated by las nepantleras, you feel love, peace, happiness, and the desire to grow. Forgiving yourself and others, you connect with more aspects of yourself and others.

Orienting yourself to the environment and your relationship to it enables you to read and garner insight from whatever situation you find yourself in. This conocimiento gives you the flexibility to swing from your intense feelings to those of the other without being hijacked by either. When confronted with the other's fear, you note her emotional arousal, allow her feelings/words to enter your body, then you shift to the neutral place of la naguala. You detach so those feelings won't inhabit your body for long. You listen with respect,[3] attend to the other as a whole being, not an object, even when she opposes you. To avoid miscommunication you frequently check your understanding of the other's meaning, responding with, "Yes, I hear you. Let me repeat your words to make sure I'm reading you right." When an experience evokes similar feelings in both, you feel momentarily in sync. Like consciousness, conocimiento is about relatedness—to self, others, world.

When you're troubled, conocimiento prompts you to take a deep breath, shift your attention away from what's causing pain and fear, and call upon a power deeper and freer than that of your ego, such as la naguala y los espíritus, for guidance. Direction may also come from an inner impression, dream, meditation, I Ching, Tarot cards. You use these spiritual tools to deal with political and personal problems. Power comes from being in touch with your body, soul, and spirit, and letting their wisdom lead you.

By moving from a militarized zone to a roundtable, nepantleras acknowledge an unmapped common ground: the humanity of the other. We are the other, the other is us—a concept AnaLouise Keating calls "re(con)ceiving the other" (*Women*, 75–81). Honoring people's otherness, las nepantleras advocate a "nos/otras" position—an alliance between "us" and "others." In nos/otras, the "us" is divided in two, the slash in the middle representing the bridge—the best mutuality we can hope for at the moment. Las nepantleras envision a time when the bridge will no longer be needed—we'll have shifted to a seamless nosotras. This move requires a different way of thinking and relating to others; it requires that we act on our interconnectivity, a mode of connecting similar to hypertexts' multiple links—it includes diverse others and does not depend on traditional categories or sameness. It enacts a retribalization by recognizing that some members of a racial or ethnic group do not necessarily stay with the consciousness and conditioning of the group they're born into, but shift momentarily or permanently. For example, some whites embody a woman-of-color consciousness, and some people of color, a "white" consciousness.

Conocimiento of our interconnectivity encourages white women to examine and deconstruct racism and "whiteness." But perhaps, as Keating suggests, "white" women who are totally invested in this privileged identity can't be nepantleras: "I really think that 'whiteness' is a state of mind—dualistic, supremacist, separatist, hierarchical. . . . all the things we're working to transform; I'm still not sure how this concept of 'whiteness' as an oppressive/oppressing mindset corresponds to light-skinned bodies, but I do believe the two are not synonymous."[4]

This move to a roundtable—generated by such concepts as nos/otras and retribalization—incites women of color to speak out and eventually refuse the role of victim. Though most identify with their mestizaje, you wonder how much of a mestiza a person must become before racial categories dissolve and new ones develop, before committing to social concerns that move beyond personal group or nation, before an inclusive community forms. You wonder when others will, like las nepantleras, hand themselves to a larger vision, a less-defended identity.

This is your new vision, a story of how conocimiento manifests, but one with a flaw: it doesn't work with things that are insurmountable, or with all people at all times (we haven't evolved to that stage yet), and it doesn't always bring about immediate change. But it works with las nepantleras, boundary-crossers, thresholders who initiate others in rites of passage, activistas who, from a listening, receptive, spiritual stance, rise to their own visions and shift into acting them out, haciendo mundo nuevo (introducing change). Las nepantleras walk through fire on many bridges (not just the conference one) by turning the flames into a radiance of awareness that orients, guides, and supports those who cannot cross over on their own. Inhabiting the liminal spaces where change occurs, las nepantleras encourage others to ground themselves to their own bodies, and connect to their own internal resources, thus empowering themselves. Empowerment is the bodily feeling of being able to connect with inner voices/resources (images, symbols, beliefs, memories) during periods of stillness, silence, and deep listening or with kindred others in collective actions. This alchemy of connection provides the knowledge, strength, and energy to persist and be resilient in pursuing goals. Éste modo de capacitar comes from accepting your own authority to direct rather than letting others run you.

Not long ago your mother gave you un milagro, a tiny silver hand with a heart in its palm, never knowing that for years this image has resonated with your concept of el mundo zurdo amplified here into the model of conocimiento; la mano zurda with a heart in its palm is for engaging with self, others, world. The hand represents acting out and daily implementing an idea or vision, as opposed to merely theorizing about it. The heart es un corazón con razón, with intelligence, passion, and purpose, a "mind-full" heart with ears for listening, eyes for seeing, a mouth with tongue narrowing to a pen tip for speaking/writing. The left hand is not a fist pero una mano abierta raised with others in struggle, celebration, and song. Conocimiento es otro mode de conectar across colors and other differences to allies also trying to negotiate racial con-tradictions, survive the stresses and traumas of daily life, and develop a spiritual-imaginal-political vision together. Conocimiento shares a sense of affinity with all things and advocates mobilizing, organizing, sharing information, knowledge, insights, and resources with other groups.

Although all your cultures reject the idea that you can know the other, you believe that besides love, pain might open this closed pas-sage by reaching through the wound to connect. Wounds cause you to shift consciousness—they either open you to the greater reality normally blocked by your habitual point of view or else shut you down, pushing you out of your body and into desconocimiento. Like love, pain might trigger compassion—if you're tender with yourself, you can be tender to others. Using wounds as openings to become vulnerable and available (present) to others means staying in your body. Excessive dwelling on your wounds means leaving your body to live in your thoughts, where you re-enact your past hurts, a form of desconocimiento that gives energy to the past, where it's held ransom. As victim you don't have to take responsibility for making changes. But the cost of victimhood is that nothing in your life changes, especially not your attitudes, beliefs. Instead, why not use pain as a conduit to recognizing another's suffering, even that of the one who inflicted the pain? In all the great stories, says Jean Houston (105–6), wounding is the entrance to the sacred. Openings to the sacred can also be triggered by joyful experiences—for example meditation, epiphanies, communion with nature, sexual ecstasy, and desire—as in your childhood experience of reaching for the orange. Because most of you are wounded, negative emotions provide easier access to the sacred than do positive emotions.

You reflect on experiences that caused you, at critical points of transformation, to adopt spiritual activism. When you started traveling and doing speaking gigs, the harried, hectic, frenzied pace of the activist stressed you out, subjecting you to a pervasive form of modern violence that Thomas Merton attributes to the rush of continual doing. To deal with personal concerns while also confronting larger issues in the public arena, you began using spiritual tools to cope with racial and gender oppression and other modern maladies—not so much the seven deadly sins, but the small acts of deconocimientos: ignorance, frustrations, tendencies toward self-destructiveness, feelings of betrayal and powerlessness, and poverty of spirit and imagination. The spiritual practice of conocimiento: praying, breathing deeply, meditating, writing—dropping down into yourself, through the skin and muscles and tendons, down deep into the bones' marrow, where the soul is ballast—enabled you to defuse the negative energy of putdowns, complaints, excessive talk, verbal attacks, and other killers of the spirit. Spirituality became a port you moor to in all storms.

This work of spiritual activism and the contract of holistic alliances allows conflict to dissolve through reflective dialogue. It permits an expansive awareness that finds the best instead of the worst in the other, enabling to you to think of la otra in a compassionate way. Accepting the other as an equal in a joint endeavor, you respect and are fully present for her. You form an intimate connection that fosters the empowerment of both (nos/otras) to transform conflict into an opportunity to resolve an issue, to change negativities into strengths, and to heal the traumas of racism and other systemic desconocimientos. You look beyond the illusion of separate interests to a shared interest—you're in this together, no one's an isolated unit. You dedicate yourself, not to surface solutions that benefit only one group, but to a more informed service to humanity.

Relating to others by recognizing commonalities does not always serve you. The person/group with conflicting desires may continuously attack you no matter how understanding you are. Can you assume that all of us, Ku Klux Klan and holistic alliances members, are in it together just because we're all human? If consciousness is as fundamental to the universe as matter and energy, if consciousness is not local, not contained in separate vessels/bodies, but is like air and water, energy and matter, then we *are* all in it together.⁵ When one person steps into conocimiento, the whole of humanity witnesses that step and eventually steps into consciousness. It's like Rupert Sheldrake's concept of morphic resonance: when rats in a laboratory maze learn the way out, as time goes on rats in other mazes all over the world do it more and more quickly because of morphic resonance from previous members that have learned the hard way (Houston, 311). Before holistic alliances can happen, many people must yearn for a solution to our shared problems.

But sometimes you need to block the other from your body, mind, and soul. You need to ignore certain voices in order to respect yourself—as when in an abusive relationship. It's impossible to be open and respectful to all views and voices. Though las nepantleras witness as impartially as they can in order to prevent being imprisoned by the other's point of view, they acknowledge the need for psychological armor (picture un nopal) to protect their open vulnerable selves from negative forces while engaging in the world. For attempting the best possible outcome not just for her own group, but for the other—the enemy—the nepantlera runs the risk of being stoned for this heresy—a case of killing the messenger. She realizes that to make changes in society and transform the system, she must make time for her needs—the activist must survive burn-out. When the self is part of the vision, a strong sense of personal meaning helps in identity and culture construction. By developing and maintaining spiritual beliefs and values la nepantlera gives the group hope, purpose, identity.

You hear la Llorona/Cihuacóatl wailing. Your picture of her coiled serpent body with the head of a woman, shedding its skin, regenerating itself reminds you of the snake story in Genesis. A hunger to know and to build on your knowledge sweeps over you. You recommit to a regime of meditation, reflection, exercise. These everyday acts contain the sacred, lending meaning to your daily life.

Through the act of writing you call, like the ancient chamana, the scattered pieces of your soul back to your body. You commence the arduous task of rebuilding yourself, composing a story that more accurately expresses your new identity. You seek out allies, and together, begin building spiritual/political communities that struggle for personal growth and social justice. By compartiendo historias, ideas, las nepantleras forge bonds across race, gender, and other lines, thus creating a new tribalism. Éste quehacer—internal work coupled with commitment to struggle for social transformation—changes your relationship to your body, and, in turn, to other bodies and to the world. And when that happens, you change the world.

For you, writing is an archetypal journey home to the self, un proceso de crear puentes (bridges) to the next phase, next place, next culture, next reality. The thrust toward spiritual realization, health, freedom, and justice propels you to help rebuild the bridge to the world when you return "home." You realize that "home" is that bridge, the in-between place of nepantla and constant transition, the most unsafe of all spaces. You remove the old bridge from your back, and though afraid, allow diverse groups to collectively rebuild it, to buttress it with new steel plates, girders, cable bracing, and trusses. You distend this more inclusive Puente to unknown corners—you don't build bridges to safe and familiar territories, you have to risk making [un] mundo nuevo, have to risk the uncertainty of change. And nepantla is the only space where change happens. Change requires more than words on a page—it takes perseverance, creative ingenuity, and acts of love. In gratitude and in the spirit of your Mamagrande Ramona y Mamagrande Locha, despachas éstas palabras y imágenes as giveaways to the cosmos.

ritual ... prayer ... blessing ... for transformation

Every day you visit the sea, walk along Yemaya's glistening shores. You want her to know you, to sense your presence as you sense hers. You know deep down that she's not independent of humans, not indifferent, not set apart. At the lips del mar you begin your ritual/prayer: with the heel of your left foot you draw a circle in the sand, then walk its circumference, stand at the center, and voice your intention: to increase awareness of Spirit, recognize our interrelatedness, and work for transformation.

Then with feather, bone, incense, and water you attend the spirits'
     presence:
Spirit embodying yourself as rock, tree, bird, human, past, present, and
future,
     you of many names, diosas antiguas, ancestors,
          we embrace you as we would a lover.

You face **east,** feel the wind comb your hair, stretch your hands toward
the rising sun and its orange filaments, breathe its rays into your body,
on the outbreath send your soul up to el sol,[6] say:
     Aire, with each breath may we remember our interrelatedness
     see fibers of spirit extend out from our bodies
     creating us, creating sky, seaweed, serpent, y toda la gente.
     "El alma prende fuego,"[7] burns holes in the walls separating us
     renders them porous and passable, pierces through posturing and
          pretenses
     may we seek and attain wisdom.

Moving sunwise you turn to the **south:**
Fuego, inspire and energize us to do the necessary work, and to honor it
     as we walk through the flames of transformation.
          May we seize the arrogance to create outrageously
               soñar wildly—for the world becomes as we dream it.

Facing **west** you send your consciousness skimming over the waves toward
the horizon, seamless sea and sky. Slipping your hands into el ojo
     del agua
you speak to the spirit dwelling here en éste mar:
Agua, may we honor other people's feelings
     respect their anger, sadness, grief, joy as we do our own.
          Though we may tremble before uncertain futures
               may we meet illness, death, and adversity with strength
               may we dance in the face of our fears.

You pivot toward the **north,** squat, scoop sand into your hands:
Madre tierra, you who are our body, who bear us into life, swallow us in
     death
     forgive us for poisoning your lands, guide us to wiser ways of caring
          for you.

May we possess the steadfastness of trees
the quiet serenity of dawn
the brilliance of a flashing star
the fluidity of fish in our element
Earth, you who dream us, te damos las gracias.

Completing the circle, retornas al **centro**, look down to the **underworld**:
May the roaring force of our collective creativity
    heal the wounds of hate, ignorance, indifference
    dissolve the divisions creating chasms between us
    open our throats so we who fear speaking out raise our voices
        by our witnessing, find connections through our passions
        pay homage to those whose backs served as bridges.
        We remember our dead:
        Pat Parker, Audre Lorde, Toni Cade Bambara, Barbara
            Cameron, y tantas otras.

You raise your head to the **sky**:
May the words and the spirit of this book, our "giveaway" to the world,
    take root in our bodies, grow, sprout ears that listen
    May it harm no one, exclude none
        sabemos que podemos transformar este mundo
        filled with hunger, pain, and war
        into a sanctuary of beauty, redemption, and possibility
            may the fires of compassion ignite our hands
            sending energy out into the universe
            where it might best be of service
            may the love we share inspire others to act.

You walk back along the circle, erase the lines en la arena, leave a
    tortilla to symbolize
feeding the ancestors, feeding ourselves, and the nurturing shared in
    this book.
        Qué éste libro gather in our tribe—all our tribes—y alze nuestras
            voces en canto.
            Oh, Spirit—wind sun sea earth sky—inside us, all around us,
                enlivening all
            we honor tu presencia and celebrate the spirit of *this bridge*
                we call home.

We are ready for change.
Let us link hands and hearts
together find a path through the dark woods
　　step through the doorways between worlds
　　leaving huellas for others to follow,
　　build bridges, cross them with grace, and claim these puentes our
　　　"home"
　　　sí se puede, que asi sea, so be it, estamos listas, vámonos.

Now let us shift.

　　　　　　　　　　　　　　　　contigo,
　　　　　　　　　　　　　　　　gloria

Notes

1. *Interviews/Entrevistas*, 97. "'Yoga' means union of body with mind and spirit" (99).
2. Palmer; Keyes, especially her take on reframing.
3. The Latin term *respectus* comes from a verb meaning "to turn around to look back." It is the root of the word *respect*. You wonder if the word *perspective* comes from the same etymology.
4. According to AnaLouise in a comment she made while critiquing this essay.
5. Cognitive scientist and mathematician David Chalmer makes a similar point, claiming that consciousness is not confined to the individual brain and body or even to the present moment.
6. The charging of the sun is an ancient Mayan ritual.
7. Lhasa de Sela's (Mexican-American/Jewish) "El desierto."

Works Cited

Anzaldúa, Gloria E. In *Interviews/Entrevistas*. Ed. AnaLouise Keating. New York: Routledge, 2000.

Houston, Jean. *The Search for the Beloved: Journeys in Sacred Psychology*. Los Angeles: Jeremy P. Tarcher, 1987.

Keating, AnaLouise. *Women Reading Women Writing: Self-Invention in Paula Gunn Allen, Gloria Anzaldúa, and Audre Lorde*. Philadelphia: Temple University Press, 1996.

Keyes, Margaret Frings. *Emotions and the Enneagram: Working Through Your Shadow Life Script*. Muir Beach, CA: Molysdatur, 1992.

Palmer, Helen. *Enneagram: The Placement of Attention*. Credence Cassettes, 1994.

∽ 6 ∽

A Story About the Body

Environment, Illness, and Health

Writers have a long history of environmental activism. Who has not been influenced by Rachel Carson's classic book *Silent Spring*, first published in 1962 and currently in its 104th printing? Carson's breakthrough book alerted us to the environmental and human dangers of pesticides, and was a catalyst for revolutionary changes in laws affecting our air, land, and water.

Which writers have transformed your ideas about the environment? Perhaps it was Terry Tempest Williams's 1990 book *Refuge*, which made the connection between the deaths of her mother and grandmother from cancer and exposure to fallout from the U.S. government's nuclear weapons tests in the Nevada desert in the 1950s.

Perhaps it was Robert Bullard's 1997 edited volume *Unequal Protection: Environmental Justice and Communities of Color*, which documented and protested the locating of an unfair share of toxic hazards in communities of color. Or perhaps it was the 2006 film and book *An Inconvenient Truth*, about global warming and former U.S. Vice President Al Gore's fight to raise awareness and break our steady path toward destroying the planet.

Concerns about the environment have reached a top priority for many of us and, in particular, for writers. They use their writing as a way to resist the poisoning of the environment and of their/our bodies, and as a catalyst for change. The poems, short stories, and creative nonfiction pieces in part 6 are loosely centered around the body in its many forms as it moves through and affects or is affected by the environment.

David Mas Masumoto's "epitaph for a peach," for example, both laments our disconnection from the environment and evokes his deep connection to it. Martín Espada's "Federico's Ghost" takes the reader inside the devastation of farmworkers' experiences of being sprayed and poisoned by pesticides. Margo Tamez's "Addiction to the Dead" witnesses the effects of pesticides through the generations from the narrator's grandfather ("burned my grandfather's flesh and eyes") to herself ("me the lanky child/running through glossy fields") to her own unborn child ("You push to be born fully alive").

Rafael Albarran's "With Knees to the Ground" uses poem as prayer for the protection of those who must put themselves in danger to earn their living. Robert Hass's "A Story About the Body" carries the large complexities of health, gender, and body image within the grace of a haunting image. Paola Corso's surreal poem "Once I Was Told the Air Was Not for Breathing" embodies the death of twenty people poisoned by fumes from the zinc and iron works in Donora, near Pittsburgh, in the first known American deaths from air pollution. And Melissa Tuckey's poem "Ghost Fishing Louisiana" witnesses the fallout of "railroad cars full of poison." Aya de León's poem "Grito de Vieques" resists the devastation of U.S. policy on Vieques, Puerto Rico, and the U.S. Navy's use of the island as a bombing range and weapons-testing ground. Kate Gale's narrator in "Sphere" finds safety with "the goats/who were my only friends as a child."

This section also celebrates beauty, as in Gary Young's "Eating Wild Mushrooms," where he takes us under the trees, "when the earth releases/a little wheezing breath. . . ." Evelyn C. White's "Born to Beauty" witnesses the health care challenges faced by the narrator's mother in her working-class black community and honors her elegant ingenuity. Linda Hogan's "All My Relations" uses writing as ceremony in her narrative of the sweat lodge. "Ceremony . . . is part of a healing and restoration. It is the mending of a broken connection. . . ." "[W]ords create a relationship with other people, with animals, with the land. To have health, it is necessary to keep all these relations in mind." Ceremony, Hogan writes, provides a "vision of the earth that holds us within it, in compassionate relationship to and with our world," a fitting description of what the writers included in this section strive toward.

epitaph for a peach

David Mas Masumoto

The last of my Sun Crest peaches will be dug up. A bulldozer will be summoned to crawl into my fields, rip each tree from the earth, and toss it aside. The sounds of cracking limbs and splitting trunks will echo throughout the countryside. My orchard will topple easily, gobbled up by the power of the diesel engine and the fact that no one seems to want a peach variety with a wonderful taste.

Yes, wonderful. Sun Crest tastes like a peach is supposed to. As with many of the older varieties, the flesh is so juicy that it oozes down your chin. The nectar explodes in your mouth and the fragrance enchants your nose, a natural perfume that can never be captured.

Sun Crest is one of the last remaining truly juicy peaches. When you wash that treasure under a stream of cooling water, your fingertips instinctively search for the gushy side of the fruit. Your mouth waters in anticipation. You lean over the sink to make sure you don't drip on yourself. Then you sink your teeth into the flesh, and the juice trickles down your cheeks and dangles on your chin. This is a real bite, a primal act, a magical sensory celebration announcing that summer has arrived.

The experience of eating a Sun Crest peach automatically triggers a smile and a rush of summer memories. Eating a Sun Crest reminds us of the simple savory pleasures of life.

My dad planted our Sun Crest orchard twenty years ago, and those trees paid my college tuition. But now they are old and obsolete. Stricter and stricter quality standards coupled with declining demand cut deeply into production levels. Our original fifteen acres and 1,500 trees have been reduced to a patch of 350.

I'm told these peaches have a problem. When ripe, they turn an amber gold rather than the lipstick red that seduces the public. Every year the fruit brokers advise me to get rid of those old Sun Crests. "Better peaches have come along," they assure me. "Peaches that are fuller in color and can last for weeks in storage."

I have a recurring nightmare of cold-storage rooms lined with peaches that stay rock hard, the new science of fruit cryonics keeping peaches in suspended animation. There is no room there for my Sun Crests, all of them rejected with the phrase NO SHELF LIFE stamped in red across each box.

"Consumers love the new varieties," brokers advise. "They'll abandon your old Sun Crests."

My sales returns at the end of each growing season confirm their comments. Demand remains weak and I have to accept lower prices. But I can't give up. I often picture shoppers picking a Sun Crest out of one of my boxes, not knowing the hidden treasure that awaits them. When they bite into it they'll say, "Aah. *This* is a peach!"

I've been keeping those old peaches for years, rationalizing that it's worth hanging on to something that has meaning beyond mere monetary reward. But I'm scared. Scared because I can't sell my peaches; thousands of boxes sit in storage, blacklisted with a bad reputation. Boxes that have been paid for, fruit that cost me and my family, a year's labor wasted, unproductive and impotent.

Many family farmers with fruit varieties like Sun Crest peaches no longer calculate how much they earn but how much they owe. Can you imagine working an entire year and having your boss inform you that you owe him money? No matter what you believe, you can't farm for very long and only be rewarded with good-tasting peaches.

This year will witness not only the possible death of this peach but also the continuing slow extinction of the family farmer. A fruit variety is no longer valued and a way of life is in peril. My work remains unrewarded.

When I first started, I realized I would never make a fortune in farming, but I hoped I could be rich in other ways—and maybe, just maybe, my work would create some other kind of wealth in the process.

Part of me knows I'll survive. The family farmer is a tough species, and we will find ways to continue. But when I think of that Sun Crest orchard, it hurts to see a slice of my life ripped out, flavor lost along with meaning. Life will be different without Sun Crest peaches, and with the loss of variety, consumers will be the ultimate losers.

I envision my orchard yielding to the bulldozer and the trees tumbling without a fight. I imagine setting a match to them and listening to the crackle of dry leaves as the dead branches are engulfed by rising flames. I estimate the embers will last for days, glowing in the chill of the fall nights.

I'll plan on going out daily to watch the fire, my face and arms warmed by the heat of the burning wood. Later I'll plow the ashes back into the earth. The ground will be renewed, and I'll hope that my next orchard will become as rich. Are my Sun Crest peaches obsolete? This, it seems, is my epitaph for a peach.

Federico's Ghost

Martín Espada

The story is
that whole families of fruitpickers
still crept between the furrows
of the field at dusk,
when for reasons of whiskey or whatever
the cropduster plane sprayed anyway,
floating a pesticide drizzle
over the pickers
who thrashed like dark birds
in a glistening white net,
except for Federico,
a skinny boy who stood apart
in his own green row,
and, knowing the pilot
would not understand in Spanish
that he was the son of a whore,
instead jerked his arm
and thrust an obscene finger.

The pilot understood.
He circled the plane and sprayed again,
watching a fine gauze of poison
drift over the brown bodies
that cowered and scurried on the ground,
and aiming for Federico,
leaving the skin beneath his shirt
wet and blistered,
but still pumping his finger at the sky.

After Federico died,
rumors at the labor camp
told of tomatoes picked and smashed at night,
growers muttering of vandal children
or communists in camp,
first threatening to call Immigration,
then promising every Sunday off
if only the smashing of tomatoes would stop.

Still tomatoes were picked and squashed
in the dark,
and the old women in camp
said it was Federico,
laboring after sundown
to cool the burns on his arms,
flinging tomatoes
at the cropduster
that hummed like a mosquito
lost in his ear,
and kept his soul awake.

El Fantasma de Federico

Martín Espada

Cuentan que
familias enteras de peones
aún se arrastraban entre los surcos
de los campos al anochecer,
cuando a raíz de whiskey o lo que sea
el avión regador roció de todas maneras,
dejando flotar una llovizna pesticida
sobre los que piscaban,
retorciéndose como pájaros oscuros
en una blanca red reluciente,
todos menos Federico,
un flaco joven de pie aparte
en su propio surco verde,
que a sabiendas de que el piloto
no comprendería en español
lo que era un hijo de puta,
sacudió su brazo
y lo embistió con un dedazo obsceno.

El piloto comprendió.
Hizo girar el avión y regó de nuevo,
mirando la fina gasa de veneno
esparcirse por encima de los cuerpos morenos
que se refugiaron y arrastraron por el suelo,
y haciéndole blanco a Federico,
dejándole la piel mojada y ampollada
por debajo de la camisa,
aún embistiendo su dedo hacia el cielo.

Después de que murió Federico,
los chismes en el campamento de trabajo
hablaban de tomates piscados y aplastados de noche,
terratenientes murmullando de niños vándalos
o comunistas infiltrados,
primero amenazando con llamar a la Migra,
después prometiendo domingos sin trabajo
a cambio de que dejaran de machacar los tomates.

Pero los tomates seguían siendo piscados y aplastados
en la oscuridad,
y las ancianas del campamento
decían que era Federico,
trabajando después del anochecer
para calmar las quemaduras en sus brazos,
lanzándole tomates
al avión regador
que zumbaba como un mosquito
perdido en su oído,
manteniendo su alma despierta.

translated by Camilo Pérez-Bustillo and Martín Espada

Addiction to the Dead

Margo Tamez

I lift my body one leg then another over the
cold curve of the claw-foot tub
Like a walking stick with a colossal cocoon
attached
A beast and a mutant   I am this

Hooked on the steam of hot water I
Negotiate stretched skin a sore spine the
splitting of eminent birth

What do you want

Mammoth   a domemoon stomach
Carved by spidery trails   former
settlement

You in there   *baby*   think you're ready
for this

Sing soprano notes   sing sounds of upness
Says the midwife
She says go *ahead   smoke some marijuana   you*
see she's our *motherherb   sacred medicine*
not for foolery and selfishness   never to be
used in that way you know
She works deeply niece   can take care those
injuries
Bad mister   wrecks   he set   snaring you

This medicine   will   show you   the things
killing
All of us

⌒ ⌒

This is what's necessary   I sustain you
You are not ready for me   What is out here

Cruel minds separate small girls from girlhood
Fists pound your brother's brains through the
wall
Yellowdrunk eyes from a failed mind   lick
every pair of Breasts in the room
At home the smoke shop the wake the burial the
ceremony the Indian-taco stand—at Casa Blanca
Road

I'm done

⌒ ⌒

Just keep sleeping on my mucous pillow
And don't push on me

O   pouring bowls of light
I see the horrific truths
The most beautiful lie
Will never fool

Never fool
Never fool
The fool

⌒ ⌒

What will be the venting of this
Where will we be
How will the vault be lifted

A tinny sound   the drip of persistence
Water into water looking for its level
Always seeking level

No more a drip now a stream continuous motion
Unified atoms
Pearls cells   threads cries—O! Na'ii'ees! O!
Monster Slayer!   O! Child of the Water!   I've
been banished
For these wrecks I've made!   For these wrecked
decisions!
My mother stripped me down . . . refusing me to be
her daughter
For this choice . . . stepping out . . . with Owl Man,
dabbler in multiple choices, appropriator and
cultural tourist,
Frauding us all . . .

The house and early night are each black and
black

One a lonesome gaping mouth   the other a
safe place
To plan
The real fact of spirit leaving body

                    ∽ ∽

You push to be born fully alive
You press my addiction to the dead world
Birth me out a muse

                    ∽ ∽

Ancestors glide
Landing on the levee where DDT   petroleum
sulfur and
Sugar cane harvests
Burned my grandfather's   flesh and eyes

Emiliano
and fueled
My   mother's resistance   *Tseta' . . . all*
the pretty Chiricahua mothers chanting songs
of revenge . . . and redemption
Singing and singing songs of the mutilations
death marches   death camps   serial killing
gangs   necrophilia   genocides   mass graves
presidios   forts   railroads   chemical
warfare   nuclear war plantations   slave
labor   traffick   human bondage to the
wreckage of surviving . . .

Ancestors scold me   me the lanky child
running through glossy fields
Crabgrass Indian gum plants Johnson grass
Waxy from spraying   the continuous spraying
O freedom of the green revolution   O post-war
Stockpiles

O   fucking   inheritance of the
indigenous 'ethnic'
    poor

O   how   we've   been   *fucked*

        ∽ ∽

I go through the window opening after opening
Memory buried upon memory that's how this
appears

Skins   burst   unseam   and inside these is
me
A skinny dark girl with a dark brain and a
dark mind

Seeking the deja-vu   Zone of Time Flow
Outside of fear

O   no one   can see me   or see what is real
The invasive spray seeping
Follows me and flows my blood through decades

To my room and the ease of dark and sleep
Dreaming how I'll wage war on my raiders

O settlers of the empire
O land thieves
O scalpers of my grandfathers
O rapists of my foremothers
O traders of scalps and genitalia
O capitalists
O war mongers
O slave traders of my people

Books   stand like enemies
Rapists who'll conspire to kill the people

They wrestle me   I wrestle back   kicking
their spines
Splitting their tiny black seeds with my knife
the little Black letters ejaculate from
Their splintered and crushed chaff

My uterus stops   the surging jolt of *you*
kicking
You will not miscarry
Not one more
Not ever again

With Knees to the Ground

Rafael Albarran

Primer misterio:
Praise the farm workers
Rising to the noise of crickets
and the day's first train.
Y luego plantan, riegan,
piscan/cortan, empacan
hasta que el semai hace su último viaje.

Segundo misterio:
Beware the rancher spraying pesticides
up and down, left and right.
The women with *panoletas*
and the men in face masks
turn their heads away
from methyl bromide and DDT.

Tercer misterio:
Listen to the sick children
coughing and sneezing
throughout the night,
covered in their mothers' *rebosos*,
slowly digging
their own graves.
From stillborn to infertile,
syndromes to cancer.

Cuarto misterio:
Follow *la peregrinación de la gente.*
Harvesting the lettuce
back and forth,
Salinas to Huron to Yuma.
Shoved into labor camps,
like head lettuce in a box.

Quinto misterio:
Condemn the ignorance of the public,
never denied the right to water,
the right to a toilet
the right to a break
year after year.

Virgen inmaculada
Ruega por ellos . . .
Estrella del cielo
Ruega por ellos . . .
Salud de los enfermos
Ruega por ellos . . .
Puerto del cielo
Ruega por ellos . . .
Ruega por ellos . . .
Ruega por ellos . . .

A Story About the Body

Robert Hass

The young composer, working that summer at an artist's colony, had watched her for a week. She was Japanese, a painter, almost sixty, and he thought he was in love with her. He loved her work, and her work was like the way she moved her body, used her hands, looked at him directly when she made amused and considered answers to his questions. One night, walking back from a concert, they came to her door and she turned to him and said, "I think you would like to have me. I would like that too, but I must tell you that I have had a double mastectomy," and when he didn't understand, "I've lost both my breasts." The radiance that he had carried around in his belly and chest cavity—like music—withered very quickly, and he made himself look at her when he said, "I'm sorry. I don't think I could." He walked back to his own cabin through the pines, and in the morning he found a small blue bowl on the porch outside his door. It looked to be full of rose petals, but he found when he picked it up that the rose petals were on top; the rest of the bowl—she must have swept them from the corners of her studio—was full of dead bees.

Once I Was Told the Air Was Not for Breathing

Paola Corso

I held my breath and counted backwards
until my lungs began sucking in
my body instead of the air
that was not for breathing
if I were to be particular
about the particulates and I
could and I was and I had to
for myself and for the memory
of the twenty in the smog
who blued from asphyxiation,
waiting for a 130-pound tank of oxygen
strapped on somebody's back, lugged
from house to house in darkness,
puffing them up with a little purity
and then gone for another who was
just as particular about the particulates,
the sulfur, carbon monoxide, heavy
metal dust trapped in the river valley
and I imagined all this as my lungs
inhaled my face and neck and chest
then my stomach, legs, and feet
until I was all inside myself
and I took one look at my lungs
the sponge that was now a board

with no give no take
the color of an oil slick
the song of a worm
and I wanted out.

Author's Note: In October 1948, twenty people were killed from the smoke and fumes of the zinc and iron works in Donora, 28 miles south of Pittsburgh in the first known American deaths from air pollution. Source: *When Smoke Ran Like Water: Tales of Environmental Deception and the Battle Against Pollution*, by Devra Lee Davis (Basic Books, 2002).

Ghost Fishing Louisiana

Melissa Tuckey

> These people are in prison and there's poison loose.
> —Rev. Willie T. Snead, Sr., Mossville, Louisiana

It gets in your clothes it gets
in the way you talk

That's not an ambulance
that's the sun going down
in your rear view mirror

And the thunder late at night
railroad cars full of poison
bumping into one another

Sugar is refined here for sweet tea
flour bleached white
Men selling melons the size of heads

Gambling boats ghost fishing
on Lake Charles

Her house held the cancer
like fish in a locked box

Author's note: Written in response to an environmental justice
tour of Louisiana. In memory of Damu Smith (1952–2006).

Grito De Vieques

Aya de León

My name is Vieques.
I am Puerto Rican girl.
My stepfather is the United States.
He comes into my room at night to do his
business.

My names is Vieques.
I used to dream that Spain, my real father,
would come back and rescue me.
But he's gone for good.
I have only the faint and echoing voices of
Africana and Taina ancestors telling me that
I can survive this.

My name is Vieques.
When my body started to change, my stepfather
dressed me in a clingy, itchy dress.
"Smile," he told me. "Smile at the nice foreign
military man," and pushed me toward him.
The military man was not nice.
His skin was pasty. He breath smelled. I
couldn't understand his language.
He came into my room and did his business.

My name is Vieques.
Sometimes my stepfather sells me to whole
groups.
He calls them allied forces.

I fought back the best I could with chains and
live bodies and fishing boats.
It happened anyway.

My name is Vieques.
I am still fighting back.
I am bigger and stronger now.
I have put a church, an encampment, a struggle
up at my bedroom door.
My stepfather can't get in.
He has not been able to do his business for
months now, longer than I ever dreamed.

My name is Vieques.
Without the shock of constant bombardment,
the numbness is subsiding.
I look at my body and see the devastation.
Lagoons, like self-esteem, have dried up to nothingness.
My womb is wilting with radiation from illegally
used uranium ammunition.
Where my skin was once lush and soft, I am
scarred.
Old tanks, like cigarette burns, dot my flesh.
Unexploded bombs, like memories, may detonate
in the future
when chosen lovers touch me in the wrong spot
or without warning.

My name is Vieques.
The numbness is subsiding.

Tender shoots of grass push up toward the sky.
A lizard sneaks back to sun itself on a chunk of
shrapnel.
A butterfly alights on a rusted-out jet.
Fish slowly make their way back toward my
shores,
no longer reverberating with shockwaves of
violation.

My name is Vieques.
This is *my* body.
It may be worth eighty million dollars a year to
you, Yanqui,
but it is priceless to me.

My door is barred.
I have burned the clingy, itchy dress.
The encampment grows stronger.
The lizards, the grass, the fish, the butterflies
stand with me.
I'll never be the same,
but I'll never be yours again to do your dirty
business.

My name is Vieques
and I will be free.

Author's Note: Vieques, a small island that is part of Puerto Rico, has been under U.S. military occupation since 1941. During that time, the island and its occupants have been subjected to continuous U.S. military exercises with live ammunition, including radioactive material. In April 1999, two bombs missed their target and killed David Sanes-Rodriguez, a civilian security guard. This incident touched off the most recent wave of resistance in Vieques and throughout the Puerto Rican community at large.

Sphere

Kate Gale

You can't imagine the goats
who were my only friends as a child
how they tore at my underwear,
hitting their heads into my legs,
playfully throwing me into the air.
How their snores rattled the night.
How their milk tasted sweet
and thick and altogether wild.
How they followed me through the orchard
and up into the rocky fields above
and ate blueberries through the afternoon.
How at twilight I'd walk down,
a hand on two goats' backs
and they'd talk me all the way down.
How many times I was beaten
about the face and shoulders and back.
How the goat smell kept me
from properly experiencing food.
How I crept out to the goats in the night
and slept very well there
the goats licking my bruises as though I
were sacred and wounded and divine.

Eating Wild Mushrooms

Gary Young

After the rain, when the earth releases
a little wheezing breath and loosens
its brittle hold on the surface of things,

wild mushrooms appear under the trees,
against logs and along the rotting
boards behind the barn. I see them lift

the ground under the quince and spread
the scallions apart and rise, and open.
I have been shown by those who know

the slick-skinned Blewit, the Prince
like a man's head, and Satyr's Beard
with its yellow mange. But for the rest

I cultivate an ignorance and pick
puffballs a particular shade of beige,
toadstools with the prettiest caps

or purple, spongy stem. What I don't know
can't hurt me. What I do know
is that mushrooms rise from the dead

to die again, to enter the death
of whatever enters the earth. When I
pick an unfamiliar mushroom and eat it

the ground gives up for once and is cheated.
It is like kissing a stranger on the mouth.
It is knowing what you are and being forgiven.

All My Relations

Linda Hogan

It is a sunny, clear day outside, almost hot, and a slight breeze comes through the room from the front door. We sit at the table and talk. As is usual in an Indian household, food preparation began as soon as we arrived, and now there is the snap of potatoes frying in the black skillet, the sweet smell of white bread overwhelming even the grease, and the welcome black coffee. A wringer washer stands against the wall of the kitchen, and the counter space is taken up with dishes, pans, and boxes of food.

I am asked if I still read books and I admit that I do. Reading is not "traditional" and education has long been suspect in communities that were broken, in part, by that system, but we laugh at my confession because a television set plays in the next room.

In the living room there are two single beds. People from reservations, travelers needing help, are frequent guests here. The man who will put together the ceremony I have come to request sits on one, dozing. A girl takes him a plate of food. He eats. He is a man I have respected for many years, for his commitment to the people, for his intelligence, for his spiritual and political involvement in concerns vital to Indian people and nations. Next to him sits a girl eating potato chips, and from this room we hear the sounds of the freeway.

After eating and sitting, it is time for me to talk to him, to tell him why we have come here. I have brought him tobacco and he nods and listens as I tell him about the help we need.

I know this telling is the first part of the ceremony, my part in it. It is story, really, that finds its way into language, and story is at the very crux of healing, at the heart of every ceremony and ritual in the older America.

The ceremony itself includes not just our own prayers and stories of what brought us to it, but also includes the unspoken records of history, the mythic past, and all the other lives connected to ours, our families, nations, and all other creatures.

I am sent home to prepare. I tie fifty tobacco ties, green. This I do with Bull Durham tobacco, squares of cotton that are tied with twine and left strung together. These are called prayer ties. I spend the time preparing alone and in silence. Each tie has a prayer in it. I will also need wood for the fire, meat and bread for food.

On the day of the ceremony, we meet in the next town and leave my car in public parking. My daughters and I climb into the back seat. The man who will help us is drumming and singing in front of us. His wife drives and chats. He doesn't speak. He is moving between the worlds, beginning already to step over the boundaries of what we think, in daily and ordinary terms, is real and present. He is already feeling, hearing, knowing what else is there, that which is around us daily but too often unacknowledged, a larger life than our own. We pass billboards and little towns and gas stations. An eagle flies overhead. It is "a good sign," we all agree. We stop to watch it.

We stop again, later, at a convenience store to fill the gas tank and to buy soda. The leader still drums and is silent. He is going into the drum, going into the center, even as we drive west on the highway, even with our conversations about other people, family, work.

It is a hot balmy day, and by the time we reach the site where the ceremony is to take place, we are slow and sleepy with the brightness and warmth of the sun. Others are already there. The children are cooling off in the creek. A woman stirs the fire that lives inside a circle of black rocks, pots beside her, a jar of oil, a kettle, a can of coffee. The leaves of the trees are thick and green.

In the background, the sweat lodge structure stands. Birds are on it. It is still skeletal. A woman and man are beginning to place old rugs and blankets over the bent cottonwood frame. A great fire is already burning, and the lava stones that will be the source of heat for the sweat are being fired in it.

A few people sit outside on lawn chairs and cast-off couches that have the stuffing coming out. We sip coffee and talk about the food, about recent events. A man tells us that a friend gave him money for a new car. The creek sounds restful. Another man falls asleep. My young daughter splashes in the water. Heat waves rise up behind us from the fire that is preparing the stones. My tobacco ties are placed inside, on the framework of the lodge.

By late afternoon we are ready, one at a time, to enter the enclosure. The hot lava stones are placed inside. They remind us of earth's red and fiery core, and of the spark inside all life. After the flap, which serves as a door, is closed, water is poured over the stones and the hot steam rises around us. In a sweat lodge ceremony, the entire world is brought inside the enclosure. The soft odor of smoking cedar accompanies this arrival. It is all called in. The animals come from the warm and sunny distances. Water from dark lakes is there. Wind. Young, lithe willow branches bent overhead remember their lives rooted in ground, the sun their leaves took in. They remember that minerals and water rose up their trunks, and birds nested in their leaves, and that planets turned above their brief, slender lives. The thunderclouds travel in from far regions of earth. Wind arrives from the four directions. It has moved through caves and breathed through our bodies. It is the same air elk have inhaled, air that passed through the lungs of a grizzly bear. The sky is there, with all the stars whose lights we see long after the stars themselves have gone back to nothing. It is a place grown intense and holy. It is a place of immense community and of humbled solitude; we sit together in our aloneness and speak, one at a time, our deepest language of need, hope, loss, and survival. We remember that all things are connected.

Remembering this is the purpose of the ceremony. It is part of a healing and restoration. It is the mending of a broken connection between us and the rest. The participants in a ceremony say the words "All my relations" before and after we pray; those words create a relationship with other people, with animals, with the land. To have health it is necessary to keep all these relations in mind. The intention of a ceremony is to put a person back together by restructuring the human mind. This reorganization is accomplished by a kind of inner map, a geography of the human spirit and the rest of the world. We make whole our broken-off pieces of self and world. Within ourselves, we bring together the fragments of our lives in a sacred act of renewal, and we reestablish our connections with others. The ceremony is a point of return. It takes us toward the place of balance, our place in the community of all things. It is an event that sets us back upright. But it is not a finished thing. The real ceremony begins where the formal one ends, when we take up a new way, our minds and hearts filled with the vision of earth that holds us within it, in compassionate relationship to and with our world.

We speak. We sing. We swallow water and breathe smoke. By the end of the ceremony, it is as if skin contains land and birds. The places within us have become filled. As inside the enclosure of the lodge, the animals and ancestors move into the human body, into skin and blood. The land merges with us. The stones come to dwell inside the person. Gold rolling hills take up residence, their tall grasses blowing. The red light of canyons is there. The black skies of night that wheel above our heads come to live inside the skull. We who easily grow apart from the world are returned to the great store of life all around us, and there is the deepest sense of being at home here in this intimate kinship. There is no real aloneness. There is solitude and the nurturing silence that is relationship with ourselves, but even then we are part of something larger.

After a sweat lodge ceremony, the enclosure is abandoned. Quieter now, we prepare to drive home. We pack up the kettles, the coffeepot. The prayer ties are placed in nearby trees. Some of the other people prepare to go to work, go home, or cook a dinner. We drive. Everything returns to ordinary use. A spider weaves a web from one of the cottonwood poles to another. Crows sit inside the framework. It's evening. The crickets are singing. All my relations.

Born to Beauty

Evelyn C. White

As a black woman who came of age during the 1960s, I routinely heard impassioned paeans to Mother Africa. Delivered by dashiki-clad black activists in fiery poems, at theater events and during protest marches, the praise songs to the motherland countered degrading images of spear-chucking, wooly-haired "savages" then pervasive in Tarzan movies.

Civil-rights-era tributes to Africa as the birthplace of Nefertiti and other regal, sepia-hued women also helped to assuage the impact of black female stereotypes such as the slave Mammy or the pious church lady exemplified by "Mama" in the landmark Lorraine Hansberry play, *A Raisin in the Sun.*

And as strange as it sounds, Italian actress Sophia Loren, now in her early 70s, remains a prevailing force in my perceptions about black women and motherhood. The 2007 death of her husband, film producer Carlo Ponti, sparked youthful memories of her widely publicized attempts to bear children. For me, the loving care Loren received during her pregnancies set a standard that, by contrast, illuminated the challenges faced by my mother in our working-class black community. Refracted in the light of Sophia, my mother also taught me that comfort, elegance, and style can be cultivated by all.

Just like thousands of readers in the 1960s, I learned of Sophia Loren's arduous journey to motherhood from the pages of *Life* magazine. Then in my early teens, I was mesmerized by the magazine's beautifully photographed features in which the actress agonized over her inability to carry a child to term. I was awestruck when, in an effort to prevent a miscarriage, she confined herself to a luxury suite in a Swiss hotel. There, under the direction of a physician, she surrendered to a strict regimen of bed-rest. Nine months later, she and Ponti celebrated the birth of a son whose arrival made international headlines, as did the birth of their second child.

The global focus on the Loren-Ponti clan captured my attention because my mother Amanda, by the late 1960s, had also survived difficult pregnancies to give birth to five children. But there were no articles about her or the other neighborhood women who continued to cook, clean, braid hair, and change dirty diapers even as their expanding abdomens gave evidence of more children to come. Such was life in Gary, Indiana, my gritty, blue-collar hometown.

Ever inquisitive, I awaited the arrival of my siblings with a burning question: Why couldn't my mother luxuriate like Sophia? Upon closer inspection, I realized that she did.

Consider the egg-white facial. Skeptical of the "age-defying" properties of pricey department-store astringents and scrubs, my mother crafted many of her beauty supplies. Chief among them was a lather of whipped egg whites that she routinely applied to her face. Stiffened within minutes, the mixture created a tight facial mask that she'd remove with a warm cloth, leaving her skin silky smooth and aglow. Prompted by what she described as "hormonal changes," my mother increased her egg white treatments during pregnancy.

And long before Victoria's Secret propelled intimate apparel into the collective conscience, my mother and her friends claimed their right to elegant slips, robes, and negligees. This I know because I often accompanied my mother to the home of an acquaintance with whom she'd "ooh" and "aah" over neat piles of lacy lingerie. Her arms filled, my mother would later disperse the rose-, peach-, and lilac-colored undergarments among neighborhood women.

The items were "factory seconds" destined for discount warehouses. But all I saw was the gratitude in the eyes of my mom's expectant friends as they held the delicate fabrics against their swollen bellies. For me, the image rivals the famous movie scene in which a scantily clad Sophia Loren charms Marcello Mastroianni.

Not too long ago, I enjoyed a visit from a childhood friend. A high-powered salesman at an exclusive boutique, he noticed a framed photo of my mother. Taken shortly before her death, the image features my mom, beaming, as she stands next to a sunflower in our backyard. "I think Ms. Amanda is wearing a Pucci blouse," my friend declared, amazed. It was not lost on me that Emilio Pucci, a 1960s-era designer of bold, swirling prints, had been a favorite of Sophia Loren. Confident that my mother had never purchased a couture item, I smiled, in loving appreciation of her innate beauty, generosity, and style.

RELEASING THE DRAGONS

When the Prison Doors Are Opened

It has been said that the mark of a civilization can be judged by examining its prisons. What are we to make of the fact that the United States is now the world's leading jailor? According to the U.S. Department of Justice, as of June 2008, more than 2.3 million people were behind bars in this country—an increase of almost 20 percent just since 2000. This gives the United States an incarceration rate of 762 per 100,000 residents—the highest in the world, dwarfing those of other democracies like Great Britain (152 per 100,000), Canada (116), and Japan (63). Who are the people we are locking up? Increasingly, the rates of incarceration fall disproportionally on the poor and working class, on youth, and on men and women of color. According to the Sentencing Project, black men in the United States are 6.6 times more likely than white men to be incarcerated, imprisoned at a rate far higher than they were in South Africa under Apartheid.

In this part, we hear some of the voices from "inside," writers locked away from society, arguably the most silenced of all marginalized groups. And yet, they write. In "Mourning Exercise," Buddhist, writer, and death row inmate Jarvis Jay Masters portrays a tense moment in a San Quentin exercise yard, where men risk their lives to protect a raging, grief-stricken fellow inmate, refusing to leave his side, even as guardsmen's bullets rain down around them. Masters describes how the men, bodies on the line, sobbing, "were suddenly holding each other, not as hardened prisoners, but simply as human beings." Political prisoner Assata Shakur, currently in exile in Cuba, speaks of the life-affirming power of resistance in her poem "No One Can Stop the Rain." "You can lock up the grass," she writes. "Watch, the grass is beautiful./The guards try to mow it down, but it keeps on growing./The grass grows into a poem./The grass grows into a song."

The fierce insistence and reclamation of one's humanity is a powerful theme woven throughout these writings, as prisoners struggle to hold on to human decency in the most dehumanizing environments imaginable. Chris Abani, in his poem "Mango Chutney," writes of the brutality of prison guards lining up inmates for "sport" executions, acting as "Judge, jury, executioner . . . drunken/petty tyrant; lust, rude and unbridled." For the prisoner, "a simple lust—to live as long as I can." Katya Komisaruk, in her poem "They Are Searching," describes the daily indignity and resistance of a body search, asking "Do they think it is so easy to find?/Do they imagine I will surrender it,/simply because they force me to spread my legs/while they investigate?" In his poem "Letters Come to Prison," Jimmy Santiago Baca speaks of the incredible impact correspondence from the outside can have on inmates, how letters come "[f]rom the cold hands of guards," then "crash upward through/Layers of ice around our hearts."

In an excerpt from her own story "Cleansing the Doors of Perception," about coming from the outside to lead writing workshops with San Quentin inmates, Judith Tannenbaum shares some of the writers' struggles to claim humanity in an often brutal and dehumanizing environment. Elmo, one of the workshop participants, writes of "the grave in my heart/where I've buried the man/I used to be," and later speaks to the pain that comes with the vulnerability of speaking truth. Addressing Tannenbaum and other "visiting" writers who have the privilege to leave his locked-down world, Elmo writes, "It is always the same/For three hours/you or Phavia or Sharon or Scoop/manage to get close to me/only to be peeled away/like the bark from a young tree/leaving behind a little spot/bare and vulnerable/that does not want to see you go/but will die of exposure/long before you return."

In an excerpt from *Prison Writings: My Life Is My Sun Dance*, political prisoner Leonard Peltier reminds us that his own personal story cannot be told without going back through centuries of assault on indigenous peoples, back to the "holocaust . . . at Wounded Knee," and even further, to 1492, when the "Great Sorrow began." Dennis Brutus and Ethel Rosenberg also call upon us to remember our history, to challenge the silencing of "voices" that "threaten the structures/of seemingly safe respectable lives" (Brutus, "Sequence for Mumia Abu-Jamal"), to "[w]ork and build . . . a monument to . . . human worth" (Rosenberg, "If We Die"). In her poem "No Public Safety," Chrystos provides a trenchant critique on the implications of poverty, racism, and sexism, charging that "We like to take better care/of our papers   file cabinets   metal desks . . . / potted plants   posters of trees in Yosemite/than an old woman."

In her essay "To Be Led by Happiness," Alice Walker writes about being arrested at an anti-war demonstration where she and fellow activists made the conscious choice to face police intervention. Describing her arrest, alongside fellow writers Susan Griffin, Maxine Hong Kingston, and Amy Goodman, Walker says, "None of us could live with ourselves if we sat by and did nothing while a country filled with children, a lot of them disabled, homeless, and hungry, was blown to bits using money we need in the United States to build hospitals, housing, and schools."

In all these poems and stories, from the daily small moments of a rescued "pink Indian cotton shirt . . . tossed into a pile of orphaned clothes" in Judith Clark's poem "After My Arrest," and the simple acts of kindness and courage shown in Masters's story "Mourning Exercise," to Peltier's profound positioning of self within the larger community of tribe and ancestors, these writers remind us of the power of humanity, kindness, and justice. In his closing line, Peltier calls upon us all to challenge the inequity of incarceration, asking, "America, when will you live up to your own principles?"

Mourning Exercise

Jarvis Jay Masters

The day was just getting started when I went out to the exercise yard. I was one of the last prisoners to be let out, so I knew I wouldn't have a chance to play basketball. The teams would have already been picked, and they would go on playing with each other until the high-tower buzzer indicated that our three hours of exercise time were up.

It was exhilarating to be outside after three hot summer days cooped up in my single-man cell. My mood was expansive as I wandered about, talking to my fellow prisoners. Other men in the yard were lifting weights and gambling around the game table for push-ups.

An excellent day, I thought, to just hang out and take in some sun. I took off my T-shirt and leaned against the fence, watching everyone from the corner of the yard. There were the cheaters like Ace and Slick on the basketball court, and Billy and Sonny on the handball court. They were incredibly skillful. Many years of playing together had fine-tuned them like naturals. I watched them win game after game under the burning sun.

I was the first to see the prison chaplain approach the fence. The yard suddenly fell silent. I held my breath, hoping he wasn't headed my way. Most of us never saw the prison chaplain unless it was Christmas or we were about to receive some very bad news.

The chaplain walked along the fence, staring through his wire-frame glasses. He seemed like a messenger of death. I wanted to turn away and pretend I'd never seen this man of the cloth before. But like so many of my fellow prisoners I had: this very priest had brought me the news of the sudden deaths of my mother, brother, and sister.

He pressed his hands against the fence, his eyes searching intently for someone in the yard. I had nothing—no basketball to bounce, no handball to hit, no weights to lift—to distract me from my inner pleading, "Not me again!"

First relief, then sadness swept over me when I saw the chaplain trying to get Freddie's attention on the basketball court. "Hey, Freddie," he said. "Buddy, I have a bit of bad news for you. I need to speak to you—just for a minute, OK?" But Freddie only played harder. I watched fear pinch his eyes as he tried to concentrate. The other players upped the pace of the game as if to shield him from the chaplain's voice. This was their way of supporting their friend for as long as he needed to deny that the chaplain's news was for him.

I had known Freddie for many years in San Quentin. We were always on the same basketball team. Like me, he was thirty-two, but six foot, bulky and powerful, stronger than I was. He was serving a fifty-year-to-life sentence and could easily bench-press the heaviest bar, 450 pounds. No one else on the yard could lift as much as he could.

The chaplain remained poised at the fence, waiting patiently. I pondered the many phone calls he had received over the years from the outside world, informing him whose mother, son, or daughter had died. He had come to know that many prisoners are capable of shedding their hardened images, to break down and cry like any other human being.

I looked at Freddie. Neither his mind nor physical skills could forestall the tragedy awaiting him. He played aggressively, like a stranger to his teammates. But even they began to acknowledge what he had to do, and finally so did Freddie.

He walked over to the fence, and he and the chaplain stood together for a minute or two. Then Freddie stepped back, a slight smile on his face, and the basketball game resumed. I was shocked. The Freddie I knew couldn't possibly take this so well. The noise level on the yard picked up again.

Several minutes later Freddie glanced up at the two guardsmen in the gun tower. I didn't make much of it, until he turned and I could see that his eyes were filled with tears, just as tears had filled my own world when members of my family had died. He was fighting hard to stay strong, to keep the pain from showing, to resist his desire to cry in front of us, whose tears he had never seen.

Freddie didn't let himself cry. Instead, rage began rolling through him like a thunder cloud about to burst. His fists tightened and his body shook violently. "Damn, he's going to explode!" I thought.

Rattler, Ace, and Slick, who were standing on the court with him, had overheard the chaplain tell him his grandmother, his only family, had died from a heart attack. They realized that he was losing it, spinning off the scales of his sanity. They approached him, like courageous swimmers, venturing into the depths of the ocean to save a drowning comrade who had begun to panic.

Rattler reached his hand out to Freddie, only to be an answered with blows to his head. The tower guardsmen fired two warning shots in the air. "Freeze!" they ordered, but Freddie kept swinging violently at his friends. His rage was directed not against them, but against his own will to survive.

As his friends tried to back off, Freddie lunged at them pulling them down hard onto the asphalt. The guardsmen yelled another warning before pointing their rifles and firing into the yard. Pow! Pow! . . . Pow! Pow! . . . Pow! bullets punched deep holes into the asphalt, only inches away from the men scuffling on the ground. Pow! Pow!

"Don't shoot!" hollered Rattler. "Man, don't shoot. Can't you see there's something wrong with him?"

"Back away from him! Get off him!" a guard barked from the gun tower. The rifles were still pointed down; their next shots would not be aimed to miss.

"Hell, no!" shouted Rattler.

They had finally pinned Freddie to the ground and were struggling to keep him there.

"Man, can't you see something's wrong with him?" Rattler screamed, tears pouring down his face. "Can't you see he needs help? Hell, just shoot us, kill us all!"

Ace and Slick began to sob too as they held Freddie. They were suddenly holding each other, not as hardened prisoners, but simply as human beings. The entire exercise yard, all fifty or more of us, stared in amazement.

It was as humans first and men second that we all, including Freddie, returned to our cells that day.

No One Can Stop the Rain

Assata Shakur

Watch, the grass is growing.
Watch, but don't make it obvious.
Let your eyes roam casually, but watch!
In any prison yard, you can see it,—growing.
In the cracks, in the crevices, between the steel and the concrete,
    out of the dead gray dust, the bravest blades
    of grass shoot up, bold and full of life.
Watch, the grass is growing. It is growing through the cracks.
The guards say grass is against the law.
Grass is contraband in prison.
The guards say that the grass is insolent.
It is uppity grass, radical grass, runaway grass, militant
    grass, terrorist grass, they call it weeds.
Nasty weeds, nigga weeds, dirty spic, savage indian, wetback,
    pinko, commie weeds,—subversive!
And so the guards try to wipe out the grass.
They yank it from its roots.
They poison it with drugs.
They maul it.
They rake it.
Blades of grass have been found hanging in cells, covered
    with bruises, "apparent suicides."
The guards say that the "GRASS IS UNAUTHORIZED."
"DO NOT LET THE GRASS GROW."
We say, "DO NOT STEP ON THE GRASS."
You can spy on the grass.
You can lock up the grass.
You can mow it down, temporarily,
but you will never keep it from growing.

Watch, the grass is beautiful.
The guards try to mow it down, but it keeps on growing.
The grass grows into a poem.
The grass grows into a song.
The grass paints itself across the canvas of life.
And the picture is clear, and the lyrics are true,
    and haunting voices sing so sweet and strong,
    that the people hear the grass from far away.
And the people start to dance, and the people start to sing,
    and the song is freedom.
Watch! the grass is growing.

No Public Safety

Chrystos

for Anna Mae Peoples

I can't tell you how much
they want to lock her up
She sleeps in their building   It's trespassing   How would you
like to come to work in the morning & have to step over her
See how little she has   compared to you
Chronic Paranoid Schizophrenic they say
The law is ambiguous   Can she take care of herself
or not
Obviously not if she thinks the building for Public Safety
means just that
There are laws against the literal interpretation of words
She has been taken to Western State Hospital & observed
They say she hallucinates
Join the army   murder a lot of people you don't know   but don't
hallucinate   That's crazy
Incompetent to stand trial they say   Would you
let her live in your house   sleep on your porch
keep her bags in your garage   pitch a tipi for her on your lawn
What would the neighbors think
Better lock her up   We don't want to look at failure   scares us
isn't safe   They say for her to sleep alone in that building
why anything could happen to her
Let's keep the building warm & lit all night even after
the janitors go home   We like to take better care
of our papers   file cabinets   metal desks   plastic chairs

potted plants   posters of trees in Yosemite
than an old woman
Who does she think she is anyway   expecting us to help
to give her safety   Anyone who doesn't take care of themselves
should be locked up   we have lots of places for it
We're all terrified   not of growing old   but of being unable
to take care of ourselves
Would you rather sleep in the Public Safety Building
or be locked up on a back ward at Western State Hospital
the food   the drugs   regular & terrible
This is her second trial   Keep the lawyers off the streets
They can take care of themselves with a little help
from their wives who clean   buy groceries   take the suits
to the cleaners   change the bed   cook meals   raise
the children   & admire
Who admires Anna Mae Peoples besides me
What is shelter   the judge asks rhetorically
you won't catch HIM sleeping under bridges or begging
$40,230 buys a lot of shelter   a king size bed
hot massage shower   wall to wall carpeting or probably
oriental rugs   A long time ago Anna Mae Peoples
probably waxed judges' floors
Too old now her back hurts all the time
the cool floor of the Public Safety Building is all she asks
They want to label her gravely disabled
they think there's a very good chance they'll win
Nowhere in the six column article
is one word
that Anna Mae Peoples has to say

They Are Searching

Katya Komisaruk

The officer puts out his hand as I leave Building C.
I give him my jacket
and he checks the pockets.

The walk to my housing unit
is one hundred yards.
I keep my back straight, my head high.
Cameras, mounted on poles and walls
relay my progress to monitoring screens in Building A.
More guards watch through the mirrored windows of Building B,
as I approach.

At the door, another cop waits to explore my jacket again.
Finishing, she gestures with one hand,
indicating that I should turn my back to her.
Now I stand with feet apart,
arms stretched horizontally.
As she explores my thighs,
I stare into the distance,
demanding that my face stay
disinterested and undisturbed.

Do they think it is so easy to find?
Do they imagine I will surrender it,
simply because they force me to spread my legs
while they investigate?

Fools.
I've never hidden it.
I carry it openly all the time.
And their kind attentions simply make it larger.

Letters Come to Prison

Jimmy Santiago Baca

From the cold hands of guards
Flocks of white doves
Handed to us through the bars,
Our hands like nests hold them
As we unfold the wings
They crash upward through
Layers of ice around our hearts,
Cracking crisply
As we leave our shells
And fly over the waves of fresh words,
Gliding softly on top of the world
Flapping our wings for the lost horizon.

1976, Arizona State Prison–Florence
Florence, Arizona

If We Die

Ethel Rosenberg

You shall know, my sons, shall know
why we leave the song unsung,
the book unread, the work undone
to rest beneath the sod.

Mourn no more, my sons, no more
why the lies and smears were framed,
the tears we shed, the hurt we bore
to all shall be proclaimed.

Earth shall smile, my sons, shall smile
and green above our resting place,
the killing end, the world rejoice
in brotherhood and peace.

Work and build, my sons, and build
a monument to love and joy,
to human worth, to faith we kept
for you, my sons, for you.*

Ossining, NY, January 24, 1953

*Later changed to "for our sons and yours."

After My Arrest

Judith Clark

among the everyday
pieces lost
a bright pink Indian cotton shirt

    worn through months of
    nursing, quickly unbuttoned
    to bring the rooting baby to my breast
    her head in its
    soft, filmy folds

set adrift among the debris
of police searches, overturned lives
tossed into a pile of orphaned clothes
and taken to a tag sale

    where my friend,
    recognizing it,
    bought it
    to keep me close

and wore it one day
to bring my daughter for a visit,
greeting me cheerfully,
"Remember this?"

and I laughed,
scooping up my baby
to carry her into the

toy-filled playroom
where she rode me, her horsey
among the oversized stuffed animals
until visiting hours were over

when I stood at that great divide,
the visitor's exit gate,
and watched my shirt and my child
leave
with my friend

1996, Bedford Hills Correctional Facility
Bedford Hills, New York

Mango Chutney

Chris Abani

Plucking mangoes
Sport for guards, soldiers, policemen.

Drunk, home bound from shift-end
they stop at death row, choose casually,

lining us up against the wall scarred from
previous plucking, under that spreading tree.

Picking his teeth, Hassan, veteran of this
game, picks us off, shooting blindfolded.

Last rites, an unceremonious smoke
harsh, throat and lung burning.

Usually pure marijuana soaked in valium.
They aren't too good at moving targets.

Sometimes they tie us, binding to post.
Legs have a habit of giving out in the face of death,

knees kneading your shame into dust, your feet
muffling whimpers in the sand.

Tied there, you die in clockwork regularity
long before any shots are fired.

Guns spit, arcs of fire hit bodies,
jerking limbs drown in empty spaces.

Bullets dust your body apologetically; you slump
but hemp hugs tightly so only your head lolls

face hidden. Ropes cut fresh tribal marks onto
your body, weight pulling against them.

Untied, you crumble slowly to the floor, and leaves
fall in spirals to land on bloody corpses.

I never get used to the amount of
blood; bodies droop like so many flowers.

Eyes stare, bright and alive, into
another world. And death becomes some men.

Others wear it shamefully; others still, defiantly.
Their protest choking, suffocating.

Looking on, you notice small details.
His trousers are torn at the groin. He has a

lazy eye which gazes crookedly
into your mind.

His crime? Maybe he said no in the face of tyranny.
Maybe he murdered. The point? We will never know.

Walking over to the bodies, Hassan kicks them
hoping perhaps that they are not all dead.

The problem with mango plucking is the fruit
falls too quickly; and harvest season is over far too soon.

Spitting he bends down and cuts their throats
—to make doubly sure—vermin are tough and cunning.

Judge, jury, executioner—Hassan, drunken
petty tyrant; lust, rude and unbridled

by gun and 27 allocated rounds of ammo per week.
And for me a simple lust—to live as long as I can.

"Let's go," he shouts to his friends; amid
much laughter and back-slapping they leave.

"Who did they shoot tonight?" a cell mate asks.
"I don't care," I reply looking away, "as long as it's not me."

Daily epiphanies bloom as angels walk among us,
the few, the chosen.

Sequence for Mumia Abu-Jamal

Dennis Brutus

I

Some voices must be silenced
they threaten the structures
of seemingly safe respectable lives
their clear vibrations
may shatter the crystalline shelters
that encase us from reality
shielding us from unbearable truths

but some may choose not to be deaf
they beat with broken palms
against the smooth impenetrable glass
of lies and comfort and power
and beg to hear the piteous cries
rising from the smoke and fire:
some voices must not be silenced.

II

The smooth impenetrable glass
of indifference and uncaring
is cool and pleasant to the touch
like the stone heart of power
that conceals the rottenness within.

III

In the night
anger burns like fire
along the veins
in the brain
and at the core
of the anguished
unavailing heart.

IV

Red and orange and saffron
the fiery ghosts
rise in the night
to sear the dreaming brain
and blast the wakeful eyeballs
staring into the dark:
images of terror.

V

Red, bright red as blood
luminous with life
anger runs through the brain
anger against injustice
anger against pain
anger against impotence

And red, red as a rose
red as soft red velvet
red as a deep red rose
with shadows dark to black
red as poppies in sunlight
red as massed salvia

red as the blood of children
in the dust of Soweto
(come see the blood of children
in the streets of Soweto)

red as poppies in sunlight
with their fragile beauty
with their indestructible beauty
steadfast under battering rain
so strong, so red our courage:
we will not bow down
we will not submit to defeat
our courage will endure
our truth will survive.

VI: Postscript

When the blight of stillness advances
when songs and speech are silenced
when a light of life and laughter is gone,
the spirit still speaks and endures
like sparks that flash from silica—
tough stardust, common dust of the world.

from Cleansing the Doors of Perception

Judith Tannenbaum

"Just want you to see," Elmo smiled slyly, handing me a sheet of paper, "that I do know where Hikmet's coming from."

I looked down and read what Elmo said was the first poem he'd written after coming to prison:

Metamorphosis
Hostility
like a garden
grows
rising up
out of the grave in my heart
where I've buried the man
I used to be.

September's red and gold light had long ago burst into October flame; October's brief heat had cooled in November; then Thanksgiving, Chanukah, Christmas, the New Year. Week after week, on Monday nights after class, I watched my students disappear into that dark beyond Max Shack, and I wondered what seasons and holidays were to men who might spend their whole lives in prison; I pondered what each man might have buried in that grave in his heart.

Around the turn of the year, I discovered an article that had been published ten years before. In it, an Arizona prisoner, Michael Hogan, who'd served seven and one-half years on a fourteen-year sentence for big-time forgery, wrote:

One of the most common experiences in prison is the gradual numbing of emotion. You can't openly express rage or fear without putting yourself in a position where you are certain to kill, be killed, or spend a fantastic amount of time in the Hole.

So even though rage and fear are the "natural" emotions to feel in many prison situations, you suppress them, you "hold your mud," you stay "cool." Your wife leaves, your father dies, and there is nothing you can do in the cellblock. There is no acceptable outlet for your grief . . .

So you do not express your sorrow, your remorse, your grief. You are quiet and cool.

Your sense of alienation grows. As the years go by: Christmas without carols or children or presents, birthdays without a simple card, friends dying from overdose or stab wounds, no privacy, not one fucking minute alone, you cease to feel anything . . .

When people outside the gates of San Quentin heard words like Hogan's, they often sighed, "Give me a break! Where does this guy get off with his moaning? The ones who've ceased feeling are these creeps' victims; *they're* the ones not getting cards on their birthdays. Matter of fact, they have no more birthdays. These losers you want me to weep for *stole* all the birthdays."

Although I myself did weep for Elmo and Coties, Richard, Angel, Gabriel, Glenn, Leo, and Spoon, I understood why others might not. What I couldn't understand, though, was why these others weren't weeping for us all, for humankind.

They weren't weeping, I supposed, because more and more folks outside the gates of San Quentin didn't see my students—or others like them—*as* humankind. They saw them instead as animals who, therefore, deserved life in a cage.

Before I had walked into that Tehachapi classroom, the word "criminal" had been an abstraction—an image on a TV screen, a sensationalized headline, a statistic, a revolutionary hero in some radical rag. But when these men shook my hand, my skin against each large, sweaty, or insistent palm informed me that I touched an actual person. These handshakes served as the pinch to convince me that these were breathing human beings: one with his long, straight, black hair; one with his wild bush of an Afro; one in the back row wearing his prison-issue clothing as though he sat at some walnut conference table in a three-piece suit; and one whose eyes and lips seemed straight from a Mayan sculpture.

And now, at San Quentin, spending Monday nights as I did, I saw that even those of my students who had committed the gravest of crimes were not monsters, but human. I didn't see how we as a society could do any serious thinking about crime if we didn't acknowledge this basic fact.

Walking into and out of San Quentin, I thought: "Human beings have killed other human beings; human beings have locked human beings in cages for life. What does it mean to be human?"

A scene from the movie *Playing for Time* often came to my mind. In the film, a group of women are interned in a concentration camp. One of them refers to the Nazi guards as inhuman beasts. Vanessa Redgrave's character shakes her head: No, they're not beasts; they are human. That is the horror; that's what we have to face. Human beings have done this.

Of course, men at San Quentin knew the truth. As one of them put it, "I'm not a demon. I'm not a behemoth. I'm not a throwback or a Neanderthal. I'm a person." Over and over I heard men remind themselves that they were more than animals locked inside cages.

The injunction I heard repeated most often during my years at the prison was "Never call your cell home; it's not your home. If you come back to a cell that's been ransacked, be glad. Let it remind you: Never get too comfortable here."

"San Quentin is a blight on my drive home," someone wrote in a letter to Marin County's weekly, the *Pacific Sun*. "I don't want the view blocked." When my students heard "fighting words" such as these, they responded in a variety of ways that insisted that they be included in the "family of man." As Coties put it, sweetly, in a poem:

Say how ya doing
Outside world?
Do you remember me?
I'm that intricate part
Missing from the whole
The one y'all decided to forget.

Like Coties, I longed to be able to see "human," whole. I longed for a vision that would allow me to see each of my students next to each individual guard, each warden, each victim of crime, each politician, each voter who was convinced that more prisons was a solution. And me, too; I was part of this circle.

I sensed that what was required for such vision were William Blake's cleansed doors of perception, which allowed one to see "everything . . . as it is, infinite." In early 1986, I pinned a quote by the filmmaker Robert Bresson over my desk, and that tacked sheet of paper stayed within sight for the next three and one-half years: "Accustom the public to divining the whole of which they are given only part. Make people diviners. Make them desire it." I desired it.

As late summer became fall and turned into winter, I frequently thought of Hikmet's warning that too many years *looking* tough might actually *make* one tough. I assumed part of my job was to encourage my students to polish that jewel in the left side of their chests, and to avoid what Michael Hogan described as that "gradual numbing of emotion" that would eventually lead to cessation of feeling.

In his article, though, Hogan referred to his fellow prison poet, Paul Ashley, who had died from stab wounds inflicted out on that Arizona prison yard. Hogan wrote: "He let his guard down—something free-world poets, I'm told, do quite regularly but prison poets do only with a terrible sense of the risks involved."

Hogan ended his article by saying that he continued to write as a way to tell other prisoners: "There are choices you still can make. The Man can kill you but he can't stop you from feeling. Only you can do that. He can mess you up but he can't make you hate life or lose your sense of wonder. Only you can do that."

True, I thought, but Hogan—with his seven and one-half years served—had paid enough dues to deliver that message. As Elmo's post-Hikmet questions had forced me to notice, I was free to walk out of San Quentin and drive home each Monday night and, therefore, could not claim quite the same right.

How was I going to encourage my students to polish that jewel and always remember how little I knew about the risks in prison to a lustrous heart? "Do I contradict myself?" Walt Whitman wrote. "Very well then I contradict myself."

Six months at San Quentin had already made it quite clear that I'd do well to increase my capacity for living with such contradiction. Encouraged by words, as I tended to be, I papered the wall over my desk with more quotations. Near Bresson's injunction, I tacked F. Scott Fitzgerald's: "The test of a first-rate intelligence is the ability to hold two opposed ideas in the mind at the same time, and still retain the ability to function." Just to make sure I got the point, I added Keats's definition of negative capability: "when man is capable of being in uncertainties, Mysteries, doubts, without an irritable reaching after fact and reason."

When I left my desk Monday evenings to enter San Quentin, the concurrence of sensations brushing my body summoned the wisdom these writers urged. As I walked into the most maximum security prison in the state, I flashed my ID card and listened to the sound of gulls over the bay. I waited for the guard to swing the massive gate open, and felt a moist breeze against my cheek. I smelled the diesel from a bus bringing in orange-suited new guys, and looked out on the million-dollar view that letter writer resented the prison for blocking. And each week in class, I'd sit in a room with my students, men I admired and cared for, some of whom were also murderers.

∽ ∽

For months, Spoon had continued to sit silent. I knew nothing about him but his long, black body, his eyes hidden behind sunglasses, his immobile face. Spoon sat at the edge of Floyd's San Quentin poetry class, too, but Spoon made Floyd nervous. He didn't make me nervous. Although I would have liked to have been able to make him more comfortable, Spoon's perch at the room's farthest reach didn't particularly disturb me. If I weren't teaching this class, I'd probably be the one sitting at its edges.

Because he said nothing and showed us no poems, I couldn't tell what Spoon was getting from our class. But week after week he was there in his chair by the door, and I decided that, for the moment, what Spoon took from these Monday nights was his own business.

Then, one night in April, I asked the men to close their eyes and wait for a scene to appear from childhood. I asked them to notice the sensual details. If they found themselves in a room, what colors were its walls? Where was the furniture placed? What smells traveled in from the kitchen? What was their brother saying? What sounds could they hear from the streets?

For the first time, Spoon pulled his chair up to our table and wrote. After everyone had finished, Spoon handed me his poem, and I read the first written words of Spoon's that I'd seen:

I see the jack rabbit gracefully
attempting to flee from the slender
greyhound who is right on its
tail. He catches the rabbit and
packs it back and suddenly there's
another rabbit and there's rabbits
everywhere. He catches five or
six rabbits. But never catches his
breath so he has gotten caught along
with the rabbits and ceases to
exist.

My own earliest memory was of myself at age two and one-half standing in the house my parents and I were about to move into. My father was dismantling a crib and telling me that my baby brother had been born dead. It was September in Los Angeles and hot. The window behind my father faced south, and bright light surrounded his body. As I watched my father's hands and listened to his words, I suddenly experienced "myself" for the first time; for the first time I realized that I was contained in a body.

Before this, my experience must have been global. Even since that moment when awareness of self whooshed into my skin, I have continued to have trouble, as current jargon has it, with "boundaries." So, for example, in the spring of 1986, I often sat at some Bay Area poetry venue sensing my San Quentin students around me.

I'd be sitting upstairs at the Cafe Milano listening to Lucille Clifton, and I would hear Elmo praise those words she'd whittled to essence. At Cody's, I'd hover at the edge of a folding chair enjoying Laura Schiff's translations of the Romanian poet Nina Cassian, and suddenly Gabriel would laugh at a poem's ironic turn. When Irina Ratushinskaya—who had been a political prisoner in the Soviet Union—read at Black Oak, all my students crowded around me. We listened together in awe as Ratushinskaya spoke of how she'd written her poems with a sharpened matchstick onto a bar of soap. She memorized each line, then washed her hands, freeing the soap for recording the next poem.

I might feel my whole class accompany me to these readings around town, but I knew that, really, the men were back at San Quentin, most likely locked in their cells for the night. So each Monday I would speak about whoever I'd heard read during the previous week; I'd bring in sample poems; I'd rent videotaped poetry readings. Best of all, though, were actual guest artists. After Milosz, I asked Phavia Kujichagulia to visit our class.

I had first heard Phavia read in San Francisco in late 1985. She climbed the raised platform that served as a stage for that reading, resplendent in dreadlocks and cowry shells. I paid careful attention, sensing Phavia had something important to teach me.

By the time I heard Phavia read, I had been sharing poetry in various settings—public schools, community colleges, art centers, and now prison—for over ten years. From the beginning, I had felt passionately that each student's voice must be heard. I especially wanted to give airspace to the voices society most often shut out. I worried that some student might feel excluded or that her way was wrong, so I made sure to bring in material from as many different cultures, written in as many different styles, and in as great a variety of voices, as possible. I pleaded with students who asked for more rules, "Poetry isn't arithmetic; there isn't just one right answer."

In these years of teaching—first in Mendocino County and now in the Bay Area—I operated from a vague sense that art belongs to everyone and that the gift of creating is a human birthright. But my culturally democratic philosophy was instinctual; experience had not yet made me pay careful, articulate attention to what I naturally felt to be proper pedagogy. And though I sensed that the apparently objective technical information I could give students to help them with their writing in fact applied to only a small portion of world literature, I had spent most of my life in fairly homogenous communities and was not yet aware of the depth and dangers of artistic imperialism.

As a child, I attended schools in which the majority of students were Jewish. (One of the football cheers at Fairfax, my first high school, exhorted: "Abie, Izzie, Moishe, Sam/We're the boys who eat no ham./ Grab your *yarmulkes*, hold them tight./Come on, Fairfax, Fight, Fight, Fight!") When we lived on the northern California coast, there were a few children from Pomo, Chicano, African American, and Jewish backgrounds, but the vast majority of the student body at Point Arena Elementary was white and Christian.

Now my experience was changing. Teaching through California Poets in the Schools in the Bay Area, I visited classrooms where students had come from all over the planet. In one—not particularly unusual—Oakland elementary school, the children in the fifth grade class I shared poems with came (the children themselves, not their parents or grand-parents) from Nigeria, Ethiopia, Bulgaria, Poland, Mexico, El Salvador, Vietnam, Cambodia, Thailand, Laos, Korea, and China, as well as from a number of different cities in the United States.

The population of U.S. prisons was, increasingly, black and Latino. As Chris, a man soon to join our San Quentin class, would succinctly put it, prison was becoming "apartheid, American style."

So in 1985, I carefully watched Phavia on that makeshift stage, knowing I had a lot to learn about the richness of cultures my students—in public school and prison—had come from.

> *to catch*
>   *to catch*
>   *to catch*
>   *to catch, to . . .*

Phavia began with "Martial Arts," her poem honoring John Coltrane, Erik Dolphy, and other masters of jazz, or—as I first heard Phavia put it—African American classical music.

> *we found out how many Miles*
> *a Cannonball has to travel*
> *to catch*
>   *to catch*
>   *to catch*
> *a speeding Trane a*
> *Coltrane*
>   *quick like*
>   *exotic in flight . . .*

I often told my classes that long ago, what we call "poems" were not separate from song or dance. I knew this and said this, but watching Phavia on stage was the first time I saw for myself such a merging of melody, movement, and word.

Phavia's poems often used rhyme, a strong beat, and repetition. Often they had a message, clearly stated. I'd assumed, when any San Quentin student showed me a rhymed, didactic poem, that he was adopting the forms of English verse most of us had been taught in school. I thought that by bringing in examples of free verse, I was expanding my students' sense of poetry's possibilities. Image was at the center of most of the poems I brought to our class; awareness of, and ability to use, image was a great deal of the technical matter we dealt with.

But the brilliance of Phavia's performance made me step back and ask myself a few questions. Maybe my students had not been mimicking some out-of-date English verse, but instead were actively interested in poetic qualities to which I'd given short shrift. That very first night of class, for example, Manny said he was a musician, and that poems were like songs, right? Rhyme and rhythm and all? I'd nodded and talked about poetry's roots, but now I wondered if I'd cheated Manny. For I'd hardly mentioned "rhyme, rhythm, and all" in over six months of teaching. I'd never asked Manny to say more about what he meant by the notion of "song." He might have meant the ballads of the British tradition, the *corridos* of his own people, or poem/chants like Phavia's. Manny had long ago drifted away from our class, and now I'd never know because I'd never asked.

That room in San Francisco exploded in all sorts of pleasure and praising as Phavia finished her set. As usual, I felt Elmo, Coties, Gabriel, Spoon—the whole group—whistling, clapping, and stamping their feet at my side. This time the force of their felt presence urged me to approach Phavia and ask her if she'd consider visiting our class at San Quentin.

Most often Jim stayed at the prison on Monday nights until all Arts-in-Corrections classes began. The Monday night I drove Phavia to San Quentin, though, Jim wasn't there and Luis, Jim's prison boss, settled into our classroom to chat with Phavia and me until class began.

I hadn't yet met Luis, a short, squat Chicano with bouncing energy and a quick-paced verbal style. Luis was San Quentin's community resources manager, and his job was both to oversee special programs such as Arts-in-Corrections and to serve as a link to the larger Bay Area community.

Phavia talked of her twin daughters, Taiwo and Kehinde, and Luis said his wife had given birth to triplets but that one had died when three months old. Gemini was their sign, he told us, the sign of split birth.

Phavia asked if the babies were girls or boys. "Boys," Luis said, "three boys. Mexicans always have boys."

> *look*
> *know the strength of my beauty*
> *for i am woman*
> *wife*
> > *mother*
> > > *cook*
> > > *Queen of the Nile*
> *i am the epitome of love*
> *the perpetuation of life*
> *i am a well understood arrogance*
> *i am woman*

Phavia began, after my students had gathered.

> *just wide-eyed innocence*
> *of my ancestors*
> *sent me*
> > *woman*

"I was the ugliest baby," Phavia said in response to curiosity about her name.

The men clicked and groaned in disbelief.

"I was so ugly," Phavia continued, "my mama didn't think this baby was hers. But she was the only woman giving birth that night, so she had to accept the fact: Her baby was ugly.

"My father named me Phavia, 'black beauty,' hoping that naming would turn true."

One man after another called out that it had, it had, but Phavia had hardly been flirting.

"And Ku . . . Ju . . . How do you say it?"

"Kujichagulia. Sounds just like it's spelled. Sound out each syllable. *Kujichagulia:* self-determination. I gave myself that one."

I sat toward the back of the room, both caught in the spell Phavia had cast and also observing the nature of this particular magic. I saw men responding as men, appreciating a beautiful woman; I saw poets applauding a powerful sayer-of-poems; I saw incarcerated beings cut away from their roots, nourished by talk of ancestors and gifts from the Creator.

Of course I—woman with all those quotes on her wall—longed for moments exactly like this one, moments in which "the part we were given," as Bresson put it, "divined the whole." Bringing in guests from the outside world fed my own hunger and also seemed one appropriate thing I could do to nurture that jewel in the left side of each student's chest.

Over the next three and one-half years, close to three dozen guest artists would visit our class, many returning a number of times. "Poetry" is how we named what we shared, and, of course, our guests and my students did share poems. But when these guests chose to fully encounter the prisoners, when they were "real" as the men put it, poetry was simply the strong-enough vehicle for this meeting; *meeting* is what we essentially shared.

The moment always arrived—whether I was teaching alone or sharing the evening with a guest artist—when the officer would announce count had cleared and class was now over. We'd all gather our papers, walk up the stairs, and shake hands. I, alone or with a guest, would watch the men turn right on their way to the blocks. In that instant before turning left to walk out of the prison I felt, as more than one visitor put it, like Cinderella: Coaches and ball gowns turned back into pumpkins and rags.

One week I talked to my students about the sensation of severance I felt upstairs after class, and showed them a poem I was working on, trying to capture what I felt. The following Monday, Elmo handed me a poem of his own:

> *For three hours in that basement room*
> *we are cut off*
> *A million miles away*
> *from your daughter and your cat*
> *A hundred yards from death row.*

Elmo described the connection in "Disguised as a Poem" and then, the parting:

It is always the same
For three hours
you or Phavia or Sharon or Scoop
manage to get close to me
only to be peeled away
like the bark from a young tree
leaving behind a little spot
bare and vulnerable
that does not want to see you go
but will die of exposure
long before you return.

from Prison Writings

My Life Is My Sun Dance

Leonard Peltier

Chapter 9

My life is an Indian life. I'm a small part of a much larger story. If I ever have the years of freedom necessary to write another book, I'll appear in it only as a minor character. The personal specifics of my life are unimportant. Being an Indian, that's what's important. My autobiography is the story of my people, the Indian people of this Great Turtle Island. My life has meaning only in relation to them. It's insignificant in and of itself. Only when I identify with my people do I cease being a mere statistic, a meaningless number, and become a human being.

American Indians share a magnificent history—rich in its astounding diversity, its integrity, its spirituality, its ongoing unique culture and dynamic tradition. It's also rich, I'm saddened to say, in tragedy, deceit, and genocide. Our sovereignty, our nationhood, our very identity—along with our sacred lands—have been stolen from us in one of the great thefts of human history. And I am referring not just to the thefts of previous centuries but to the great thefts that are still being perpetrated upon us today, at this very moment. Our human rights as indigenous peoples are being violated every day of our lives—and by the very same people who loudly and sanctimoniously proclaim to other nations the moral necessity of such rights.

Over the centuries our sacred lands have been repeatedly and routinely stolen from us by the governments and peoples of the United States and Canada. They callously pushed us onto remote reservations on what they thought was worthless wasteland, trying to sweep us under the rug of history. But today, that so-called wasteland has surprisingly become enormously valuable as the relentless technology of white society continues its determined assault on Mother Earth. White society would now like to terminate us as peoples and push us off our reservations so they can steal our remaining mineral and oil resources. It's nothing new for them to steal from nonwhite peoples. When the oppressors succeed with their illegal thefts and depredations, it's called colonialism. When their efforts to colonize indigenous peoples are met with resistance or anything but abject surrender, it's called war. When the colonized peoples attempt to resist their oppression and defend themselves, we're called criminals.

I write this book to bring about a greater understanding of what being an Indian means, of who we are as human beings. We're not quaint curiosities or stereotypical figures in a movie, but ordinary—and, yes, at times, extraordinary—human beings. Just like you. We feel. We bleed. We are born. We die. We aren't stuffed dummies in front of a souvenir shop; we aren't sports mascots for teams like the Redskins or the Indians or the Braves or a thousand others who steal and distort and ridicule our likeness. Imagine if they called their teams the Washington Whiteskins or the Washington Blackskins! *Then* you'd see a protest! With all else that's been taken from us, we ask that you leave us our name, our self-respect, our sense of belonging to the great human family of which we are all part.

Our voice, our collective voice, our eagle's cry, is just beginning to be heard. We call out to all of humanity. Hear us!

Chapter 11

My own personal story can't be told, even in this abbreviated version, without going back long before my own birth on September 12, 1944, back to 1890 and to 1876 and to 1868 and to 1851 and, yes, all the way back through all the other calamitous dates in the relations between red men and white, back to that darkest day of all in human history: October 12, 1492, when our Great Sorrow began.

But, for our limited purposes in these pages, let's skip past all those earlier dates and settle here for beginning my story in 1890, that crucial and terrible year, the year when we and the Sacred Hoop of our Nation were finally broken.

Or so they thought.

Whenever I think of the holocaust that occurred at Wounded Knee, South Dakota, on December 29, 1890, I hear the voices of the children crying out from the cold and hunger and terror. I hear the wails and lamentations of the mothers weeping in agony for their dying babies.

The stories passed on to me by the Lakota Elders describe the incredible sufferings of Chief Big Foot and his starving followers as they fled through the vicious Dakota winter on their way to Pine Ridge that terrible December day, just two weeks after the utterly unprovoked murder of Sitting Bull, who was murdered through treachery like so many others of our people.

Big Foot's band, fleeing for their lives, didn't know why they were being targeted and killed; they were heading for refuge with Red Cloud's band at Pine Ridge. Ostensibly, claimed the government, they sent their troops to stop us from performing the Ghost Dance, a purely religious rite. This was just a pretext, of course; they're very good to this day at finding pretexts to attack us. The real reason behind their attack was that they wanted to run their railroads from the stolen Black Hills back to Chicago and the East, right through what was left of our lands, which the Fort Laramie Treaty of 1868 had solemnly promised to us for "as long as the grass grows and the rivers run."

When Big Foot's starving, freezing band saw the soldiers of the Seventh Cavalry, Custer's old unit, moving toward them through the deep snow, they figured the cavalry could only be there to help them, surely. Hadn't they been told that if they surrendered to the Indian Agency at Pine Ridge they would be cared for with food and medicine and shelter?

I can physically feel this very moment the misery and suffering that more than three hundred men, women, and children endured as they made their way through South Dakota blizzards, below-zero temperatures, and impenetrable snowdrifts. I can imagine the terror and the fear rushing through them as the soldiers opened fire on them the following morning—the echoes and roar of the Gatling guns mixed with booming cannons and the rattling sabers and the screams of the women and children.

As an Indian of Sioux blood I can hear those screams and feel the pain of those mothers, children, and old men as they are torn to pieces by the bullets and the flashing blood-tipped sabers, striking them again and again and again as they lay there defenseless. I relive every one of their deaths. I die with each one of them again and again.

Chief Big Foot's band had refused to fight the *wasichu* (white man), believing only peace could overcome the animosity between the people. Big Foot himself was an old man at the time, nearly dead of pneumonia. They surrendered to the cavalry, camped at Wounded Knee Creek, ate a meager meal—much like the final meal of the condemned before execution—slept a few hours, and then that next morning were promptly slaughtered, allegedly because one old Indian, probably deaf, had raised his rifle rather than surrender it to a soldier. Somehow the gun went off—or so the government claimed—and the Gatling guns and cannons up on the hill fired right down into the people. They even killed a few dozen of their own soldiers standing there.

Afterward, the proud butchers of the Seventh Cavalry were awarded twenty-six Medals of Honor for their heroics. White man's history books still call it a "battle," as if to give some dignity to what had none. It was a slaughter, pure and simple. A crime against all humanity, though there was no such phrase in those days.

The late James High Hawk, one of the few survivors of the Wounded Knee massacre, gave this eyewitness account:

> My mother was crying and trying to save and protect her small family, and I was myself just a little boy. A soldier came to where we were hiding and shot my mother and baby brother and myself as my mother pleaded for our lives. I was wounded and lay there for hours, until Oglalas [Lakotas] from Pine Ridge saved me.
>
> . . . This massacre is . . . the most disgraceful, cowardly, and treacherous killing ever staged by the United States Army. White people say the Indians are treacherous, but we are not. We love our families. We do not bother the white people, but they came here and killed us—women and children. We have the wounds to prove what they've done.

Yes, we have the wounds. And these atrocities against my people continue to this day, only now they're carried out with more sophisticated means than Gatling guns and cannons and sabers. There are subtler ways of killing. Call it death by statistics. Today, white man lets his statistics do the killing for him. Indian reservations in South Dakota have the highest rates of poverty and unemployment and the highest rates of infant mortality and teenage suicide, along with the lowest standard of living and the lowest life expectancy—barely forty years!—in the country. Those statistics amount to genocide. Genocide also disguises itself in the form of poor health facilities and wretched housing and inadequate schooling and rampant corruption. Our remaining lands, eyed by a thousand local schemers only too eager to stir up trouble and division on the reservation, continue to be sold off acre by acre to pay off tribal and individual debts. No square inch of our ever-shrinking territory seems beyond the greedy designs of those who would drive us into nonexistence.

The American Indian Movement through the years has sought every means possible to bring these crimes against humanity to the attention of the world, hoping that at least some of you would listen and search deep within yourselves for the humanity to demand that the U.S. government stop these crimes.

The destruction of our people must stop!

We are not statistics. We are the people from whom you took this land by force and blood and lies. We are the people to whom you promised to pay, in recompense for all this vast continent you stole, some small pitiful pittance to assure at least our bare survival. And we are the people from whom you now snatch away even that pittance, abandoning us and your own honor without a qualm, even launching military attacks on our women and children and Elders, and targeting—illegally even by your own self-serving laws—those of us, our remaining warriors, who would dare to stand up and try to defend them. You practice crimes against humanity at the same time that you piously speak to the rest of the world of human rights!

America, when will you live up to your own principles?

To Be Led by Happiness

(Re: March 8, 2003)

Alice Walker

I wrote this essay as a thank you to Medea Benjamin, an activist
hero, who invited me to participate in this event and later asked if I
would write an Op-Ed piece about it.

Not buying
War
Grief remains
Unsold

It started with Einstein. I had written a poem about his hair. It wasn't
just about his hair: I was thinking about his statement that World War
III might be fought with nuclear weapons but World War IV would be
fought with sticks and stones. I was walking down a gray, chilly street
near my home in Berkeley, thinking about the sadness of his eyes, the
sadness of our situation: about to invade and massively bomb Iraq, a
country inhabited by old people, orphans, women and children. Boys and
men. The children, half the country's population, under fifteen years of
age. I was thinking about my impending journey to Washington, D.C.,
to join a demonstration against the war; a city whose streets, during
slavery, were laid out by Benjamin Bennaker, a free African American
(father African, mother Irish-African) tobacco planter from Maryland.
I thought of the ancestors who, enslaved, built (eyes lowered, muscles
straining), the imposing symbols of freedom in Washington, including
the White House.

Though wanting to join the women of CODE PINK who had been
holding a vigil in front of the White House for four months, dressed in
pink to signify the feminine concern for the safety, especially, of children,

I was dreading the long lines at the airport, and the flight. I stopped at a light, thinking of how our experience now at airports, being searched and sometimes seized, bears a resemblance worth scrutinizing to what Palestinians, attempting to enter and leave their Israeli-restricted areas, go through. Reflecting on this, I rested my hand on a telephone pole before rather wearily crossing the street. A piece of paper near my hand fluttered in the wind. There, just above my head, was another quote from Einstein someone had stapled to a pole. *The problems we face today cannot be solved by the minds that created them.*

It was a pretty grim message, perhaps grimmer than the earlier one; still, I found myself beginning to smile. Here he was: an ancestor who knew, and said out loud, that if we keep going in the direction we're headed, the jig is up. On the other side of the street I thought: Whose mind has not been heard at all on the direction we must immediately turn? The Mind of the Grandmothers of the World. But that's another story.

Ten thousand women dressed in hot pink, cool pink, all shades of pink, marched and rallied in Washington, D.C., to celebrate March 8, International Women's Day, 2003. There were rousing speeches; there was music and dance. Enormous and magical puppets. There was laughter and solemnity. The march was led by several rows of small children chanting "One Two Three Four, We Don't Want Your Crummy War: Five Six Seven Eight, We Will Not Participate." They were followed by writers and artists and activists, including Susan Griffin, Maxine Hong Kingston, Rachel Bagby, Terry Tempest Williams, Medea Benjamin, Nina Utne, and me. Behind us the sea of pink stretched far as the eye could see.

At Lafayette Park, across from the White House, we paused. Twenty-five of us were chosen to enter the park (a number previously authorized); only to find admittance denied. After a brief huddle, squatting at the knees of a line of police, we moved forward. Several hours later, having sung "Peace Salaam Shalom" and "Give Peace a Chance" the entire time, we were arrested. And it is of that moment, that hour—because it took a long time—that I wish to speak, and of our time in a holding cell before being set free.

I had been arrested before. While protesting apartheid in South Africa; while attempting to block the shipment of weapons, by train, to Central America. Those were serious times, but this time felt different. This time felt like: *All the information is in.* If our species does not outgrow its tendency to fight wars, we can kiss all we have created, and ourselves, good-bye. To bring children into the world at all, given the state of things, seems not only thoughtless but cruel. And it was of the children I thought, partly because there, right across from us, as we sang in front of the White House, were huge photographs of dismembered fetuses held by an anti-abortion group whose leader began to harangue us through a bullhorn. He called us traitors and murderers and accused us of nagging.

Nagging. What century was he from? we thought.

That he could not make the connection between the gruesomely dismembered bodies in his photographs and those of children bombed in Iraq seemed unbelievable. As he shouted at us we sang: "Protect the women and the children of Iraq." Eventually, scowling, looking extremely churlish, he left.

Standing between my Irish American sister (Susan Griffin) and my Chinese American one (Maxine Hong Kingston), and with twenty-four other courageous women all around us; with Amy Goodman of *Democracy Now!* interviewing us for our communities across the world, and Kristin Michaels, a videographer, taping us, I felt the sweetest of all feelings: peace. The police began to gather their horses, their paddy wagons, their plastic handcuffs. We sang. Being women, we noticed and made much of the fact that a rainbow appeared suddenly in the sky.

Amy (who within minutes would be arrested herself) asked each of us how we felt about being arrested. Maxine said she felt it was the least she could do. I said I felt happier than I'd felt in years. Susan said her happiness went beyond happiness to joy. None of us could live with ourselves if we sat by and did nothing while a country filled with children, a lot of them disabled, homeless, and hungry, was blown to bits using money we need in the United States to build hospitals, housing, and schools.

The arrest went smoothly. I thought the police were considerate, human. Some of us tried to help them do their job by sticking our arms out in front of us but the handcuffs go behind, not in front. We sang in the paddy wagons, we sang later in the holding cells. We recited poetry to each other and told stories from our lives. And all the while, there was this sweetness. Even though the floor of the cell, where some of us had to sit, was cold, and even though the toilet wouldn't flush, I found Fannie Lou Hamer's voice coming out of my throat and led our cell in singing "This Little Light of Mine."

I realized that, at the root of the peace cradling me, was not only Einstein, and other ancestors who told us the truth, but especially Martin Luther King, Jr. I had followed him faithfully since I was in my teens; his fearless, persistent struggle against injustice mesmerized me. *Perfect love casts out fear*. That is what he had. And that, ultimately, is what the sea of pink symbolized. We were women and children who loved ourselves in our Iraqi form of women and children; loving ourselves as humans meant loving ourselves as all humans. We understood that whatever we did to stop war, we did it not for the "other" but for a collective us. The heart enjoys experiencing the liberating feeling of compassion; it expands and glows, as if beaming its own sun upon the world. That is the warmth our cooling emotional world so desperately needs to preserve its humanity. It is this savoring of the ecstatic nature of impersonal love that lets the peacemakers of the world do our job. It is this love whose inevitable companion is not only peace, but happiness, and, as Susan said, joy.

We are the ones we have been waiting for.

❧ 8 ❧

WAR AND OTHER FORMS
OF VIOLENCE

According to Anne Llewellyn Barstow, in her book, *War's Dirty Secret*, "In World War I, the ratio of military personnel killed to civilians was 8:1. In World War II, it was 1:1. In the many smaller wars since 1945, the ratio has been 1:8. This means that the victims of wars have changed: the great majority being civilians; they are mainly women, children, and the elderly" (p. 3).

Social action writers who seek models of how to write about war will not find writings about the supposed "glory" of war in this section. Rather, they will find writers witnessing the raw reality and tragedy of it and reaching for nonviolent ways of being in the world. What the writer will find here are social action stories and poems about war in its multiple embodiments. As feminist historian Bettina Aptheker says, "All forms of violence are interconnected; separately and together, they hold multiple systems of domination in place" (p. 5).

Writers will find no debate here about whether writing can affect social change. It can and it does. "Healing begins," Aptheker goes on to say, "when we shine some light, however initially feeble, upon that which has been hidden and silenced. With disclosure, cycles of violence may be stopped."

In this section, social action writers shine that light on the effects of war: in Iraq (Marc Harshman), in El Salvador (Carolyn Forché), in Vietnam (Daniel Cano), in Bunia, Africa (Khadijah Queen), and in Palestine (Mahmoud Darwish). They also expose the effects of slavery (Akasha Gloria Hull), of colonization in Puerto Rico (Esmeralda Santiago), of homelessness in New York City (Alicia Ostriker), and of the war against women's bodies and minds (June Jordan and Janice Mirikitani).

In Daniel Cano's story "Somewhere Outside Duc Pho," Peña, a Mexican American soldier in Vietnam, goes AWOL because "something was wrong . . . inside," "a feeling, like something that grabs at your stomach . . . feels like your insides are falling. . . ." Across continents and oceans, in Palestine "something" is also wrong, and Palestinian poet Mahmoud Darwish, in his poem "The House Murdered," evokes it, in both the demolition of houses by Israeli tanks and in the demolition of a people. "In each thing there's a being that aches . . . the memory of fingers, of a scent, of an image./And houses get murdered just as their residents get murdered."

Carolyn Forché's "The Colonel" witnesses the raw brutality of power and her encounter with a general in El Salvador during the human rights abuses of the 1970–80s civil war. In Iraq, in Marc Harshman's poem "Even the Tin Man Had a Heart," a grandfather wanders awake among the dead asking "who would tell . . . the names of these two/children, the names of all the children." Khadijah Queen's "blue helmets" embody multiple levels of violence in her poem "Peacekeeping in Bunia," the capital of the Ituri province in the Democratic Republic of the Congo, Africa.

The "something" is doubly wrong, when Hanako, a mother in Janice Mirikitani's story "Tomatoes" who was interned as a young girl with her parents in a "concentration camp located in the middle of the desert," later staves off an aggressor against her daughter, her "hoe high in the air, whacked like a sword. . . ."

"Something" is wrong when, according to statistics from the National Coalition for the Homeless, more than three million people make their homes on the streets in the United States, a third of them children. In Alicia Ostriker's excerpted poem "interlude: the avenue of the americas," the narrator reaches out to a homeless woman in New York City, "above the tongues of taxicabs." "[S]orrow," she says, "pressed into me like a hot iron."

Rigoberto González's poem witnesses the violence to the families of the village when the men leave. In his "In the Village of Missing Fathers," González says, "paper sorrow folds/into a boat, a bed into a holding cell/ for moans that bleed out of sleep."

Social action poems speak of resistance, of resilience, and of the healing that "begins when we shine some light." Akasha Hull recited her poem "These Bones, These Bones" at the Middle Passage Monument

Ceremony in March 1999 in New York City. "These African bones/that did not live/to tell their story," after which a gravestone was lowered to the floor of the Atlantic to honor "our ancestral spirits who perished." June Jordan, in her "Poem About My Rights," rejects the aggressors, the "battery assault and limitless/armies against whatever I want to do with my mind/and my body and my soul. . . ." She boldly reaffirms her "simple and daily and nightly self-determination."

These poems and stories break open the denial around the effects of war. As children's-rights activist Marion Wright Edelman says, "Even to put the names and the narratives together is to take the first step toward peace" (p. 190).

And, as Gloria Anzaldúa says in her essay "now let us shift . . . the path of conocimiento . . . inner work, public acts," in part 5, "Change requires more than words on a page—it takes perseverance, creative ingenuity, and acts of love."

Works Cited

Aptheker, Bettina. *Intimate Politics: How I Grew Up Red, Fought for Free Speech, and Became a Feminist Rebel.* Emeryville, CA: Seal Press, 2006.

Barstow, Anne Llewellyn. *War's Dirty Secret: Rape, Prostitution, and Other Crimes against Women.* Cleveland: The Pilgrim Press, 2000.

Edelman, Marion Wright. In *Speak Truth To Power: Human Rights Defenders Who Are Changing Our World.* Kerry Kennedy Cuomo and Eddie Adams; edited by Nan Richardson. New York: Crown Publishers, 2000.

National Coalition for the Homeless, Washington, D.C., 2002. www.nationalhomeless.org.

Somewhere Outside Duc Pho

Daniel Cano

The night we heard that our good friend Jesse Peña was missing, we decided to get a search party together and check the bars in Duc Pho, an old city in Vietnam's central highlands. We were in the rear area for a short rest before beginning the next operation, and we knew that under stress, sometimes guys who reached the limit and could not go on another day ended up AWOL, lost in the delirium of booze and chaos. But our orders came through and we were restricted to base camp, forced to disband our posse.

Two days later a long line of double-propped Chinook helicopters with 105 howitzers and nets full of ammunition dangling beneath them choppered us into the mountains, about a half hour outside our base camp. They lifted us to the top of a mountain that was scattered with light vegetation. Below and all around us, the jungle landscape was immense. Mountain ranges stretched in every direction.

We began knocking down trees, clearing away brush, unloading tools, equipment, packs, and ammunition. On our bare shoulders we lugged 55-pound projectiles into the ammo dump . . . long lines of shirtless men, bodies shining with sweat. The sledgehammers clanged against metal stakes and echoed as the gun crews dug in their howitzers. We filled and stacked hundreds of sandbags, which formed long crooked walls, some semi-circular, others round or rectangular—all protecting the battery just like the walls of a castle. And above the shouting voices, the striking metal, and the popping smoke grenades roared the engines of the helicopters as they landed, dropped their cargo, and quickly lifted away.

Once the battery was settled in, I took up my position on the outpost. There were three of us. We dug a four-foot deep bunker for ourselves and stacked three rows of sandbags around the front and sides, protection from incoming rounds and something we didn't like to think about: human assaults on our position.

One night, after a week of wind and cold, a trip flare erupted, lighting up the jungle in front of us. We waited, then saw a shadow move across the perimeter. Instinctively we threw hand grenades and set off the claymores. Later, from another outpost, a machine gun burst into a steady stream of fire. The howitzers exploded, sending bright lights into the sky. I gripped my rifle tightly and watched the shadowy tree line as the flares descended and a cold silence filled the air. As always the flares burned out. Once the darkness hit, again the world rumbled around us.

An explosion sent a blast of light across our field of vision, the ground vibrated, my ears buzzed . . . and moments later, my left arm felt warm. I slid my fingers over the wet skin and touched a hole of punctured flesh, just below the shoulder. I told the others that I was wounded, and they got on the field telephone and called for a medic. The firing stopped. The jungle reverted back to an eerie blackness. Doc Langley, the battery medic, walked me back to our small infirmary and gave me some antibiotics, bandaged my left arm, and told me to get some sleep.

The next morning I was choppered to the field hospital at Pleiku. Doc Langley, who was also a good friend, went with me to take care of the paperwork and refill his supply of Darvon. The doctors sewed me up and I slept the whole day.

When I woke up, Doc Langley was sitting on my bunk. I caught most of his talk, even though I felt dizzy from the anesthetic. He told me that Jesse Peña had been spotted. Some men from the Tiger Force, a reconnaissance outfit, had been on a listening post in the jungle. They'd been observing a squad of Vietcong. As the enemy moved along the trail, there, right in the middle of the VC column, they saw Peña, or a chubby Mexican-looking guy in American fatigues. The Tigers claimed that Peña carried an M-16 and walked right along with the VC squad, not like he was a prisoner but like he was a part of them.

When Doc Langley left, I sat up in my bunk. There was no way I could believe that Peña was in the jungle with the VC. It was just too ridiculous, and I knew that none of our friends would believe it either. I started to think about Peña and the last time any of the guys or I had seen him.

Peña was part of a small group of friends. There were about ten of us when everybody showed up, but usually five or six regulars. Since most of us were assigned to different units of the 101st Airborne Division, we'd split up during the operations, but always get back together when we were in the rear area. Each night, we would meet at an isolated spot somewhere in the brigade area—behind a sandbag wall or trash dump—for what we called our sessions. We would drink beer, joke, and talk about hometowns and friends.

Peña, who could hold our attention for what seemed like hours, hadn't said much that last night he was with us. He'd been a bit removed, sitting slightly in the shadows, and he refused to drink any beer. Still, he had smiled a lot, as if nothing was wrong, and had eaten a couple of cans of peaches and just watched and listened. Someone had asked if he was all right, and he'd just answered, "Yeah, I'm O.K." While it was still early in the evening, he got up and said that he was tired—carrying the radio during the last operation had kicked his ass. He straightened his fingers into a mock salute, touched the tip of his cap, and said, "Time to go."

"So early? How come?" Little Rod had asked.

"I'm getting short . . . only three months. Gotta save all my energy so when I get back home, I'll have everything ready for you guys. Sabes?" said Jesse, his words confusing us.

"Come on, have a beer," Little Rod persisted.

"Can't, gotta keep my mind clear. Me voy."

Jesse turned, walked into the darkness of the brigade area, and that was the last we saw of him.

Jesse Peña was short, rotund, and always smiling, like one of those happy little Buddha statues. Although overweight, he was handsome. There was a childlike quality about him, a certain innocence and purity that made him immediately likeable. Two large dimples, one on each chubby cheek, brought a glow to his face.

After each operation, we'd look forward to our sessions, so we could hear more of his jokes and stories. His humor wasn't slapstick or silly, but intelligent, and always with a point or moral. Sometimes he'd reminisce about family and friends back home in Texas, like his cousin Bernie who was so much against the war that he had traveled down to Eagle's Pass, Texas, pretended to be a bracero, and was picked up by the U.S. immigration. According to Jesse, Bernie, who was American and fluent in English, spoke only Spanish to the INS agents. He was deported and went to live with relatives in Piedras Negras. All this, Peña said, just to beat the draft. In this way, Bernie could say that he hadn't dodged the draft; it was the U.S. that had rejected him.

His stories led to questions and analyses, and all of us participated, pulling out every piece of information and insight that we could. Peña always seemed to have the right answers, but he was never overly egotistical. Always he came across as sincere and gracious.

I envied his ability to switch from English to Spanish in mid-sentence. His words moved with a natural musical rhythm, a blend of talk-laugh, where even tragic stories took on an element of lightness. He didn't present himself as an intellectual. His speech had a sophistication that didn't come with schooling but with breeding. Someplace in his family's background of poverty there must have been an honest appreciation of language.

And he loved his Texas. To hear him talk, one would think that San Antonio was San Francisco, New York, or Paris. In his mind, San Anto', as he called it, had culture and personality. When it came to music, no one could come close to the talents of Willie Nelson or Little Joe y La Familia. Those of us from California didn't even know who they were. He'd play their music on his little tape recorder, and we'd laugh and call him a goddamn cowboy, a redneck Mexican out of step with the times, and then we'd slip into arguing about our states and which was best, and how the city was better than the country . . . and on and on until we'd drained ourselves.

I placed my hands behind my head and looked at the wounded men around me. I didn't really see them, though, because I was thinking too much about Jesse Peña. It didn't make sense that he had suddenly shown up on his unit's duty roster as missing. Why would he go AWOL?

Three weeks later, the operation ended, the scab on my arm had hardened, and we were all back at our front area base camp. I wasn't the only one who'd heard the rumor. All of the guys knew about it. Big Rod, who was about six inches taller than Little Rod, knew some guys in the Tiger Force who confirmed the sighting.

Feeling superstitious about the whole thing, we decided to move the location of our next session. Two of the guys found an isolated spot near the edge of the brigade area. On one side it was separated from the rest of the brigade by a decaying sandbag wall about four feet high. Many of the bags were torn, but the heat and moisture of the tropical valley air had hardened the sand as if it were cement. Empty wooden ammo boxes, some broken and black with mildew, were scattered around the area. Twenty-five yards to our front was the jungle—not as thick as the field, but dense enough to hide someone or something. As the night moved in, the foliage darkened and the only protection from the wilderness beyond was a gun tower manned by two fellow paratroopers.

It didn't take long before the guys, and some interested new ones, started arriving. We discussed the possibilities that Jesse was either kidnapped or had deserted. Kidnap seemed impossible because our base camp was a fortress: guards securing the perimeter in gun towers, MPs patrolling in gun Jeeps, units posting watches throughout the night; it just didn't seem possible. Besides, I argued, what interest would the VC have in a PFC radio operator from San Antonio who only cared about getting home to his wife and child?

Alex Martínez, a surly Californian from the San Fernando Valley, stuck to the argument that Peña had just gone AWOL. "Old Peña split, man— just got tired of the shit. He's probably shacked up with some old lady downtown. Tiger Force probably saw some fat gook dressed in fatigues and thought it was him, man. He'll be back. Give him a few days."

We kicked the idea around. It wasn't absurd. We were reminded of Michael Oberson, a cook who had gone AWOL, changed his name, and lived with a Vietnamese waitress in Saigon for fourteen months. He'd gotten himself a job with an American insurance company and a nice apartment in the Chalon district. He finally turned himself in, and while he waited for his court martial, he was assigned to our unit. We remembered how he had laughed when he told us that the U.S. government subsidized a portion of the salaries of all the employees who worked for the insurance company. "So," he would say, "Uncle Sam was paying me to stay AWOL. How could I give it up?"

Danny Ríos argued that Jesse was too short. Nobody went AWOL with only three months left. It didn't make sense, any of it. Besides, he reminded us, Peña was so committed to his wife that he wouldn't even look at other women. Although he admitted he'd seen a change in Peña's personality over the past couple of months. Like everybody else, Danny took it as a mood swing. He shook his head, more confused than anything else.

Big Rod said that he suspected more. "I've been thinking, you know," Big Rod began. "Not too long ago Peña told me something was wrong . . . inside. I asked him like if it was his old lady or kid, but he said no, it wasn't like that. He said it was more of a feeling, like something that grabs at your stomach and twists and twists and doesn't let go. Not too much a pain, you know, more like a chunk of metal glued to your stomach, something that hangs and pulls until it feels like your insides are falling, and he said it wouldn't go away. Every day he woke up feeling like that."

After a few hours, many of the newer guys went back to their units. The night thickened and the five of us who were Peña's closest friends remained.

We sat in a circle. In the middle was a used C-ration can filled with lighted heat tablets that gave some relief from the darkness of the jungle—a darkness that loomed silently around us. Every once in a while, we heard the whispers of the perimeter guards who were positioned in the jungle . . . human alarms against a possible attack.

Little Rod, who was from Brownsville, Texas—"Right down in the corner of the goddamn country," he once told us—pulled out his Camels, slowly tapped the bottom of the pack, and placed a cigarette to his lips. He sat on an empty wood ammo crate and leaned back against the sandbag wall. After a long silence, Little Rod leaned over, stuck his cigarette into the heat tablet, and sucked on the tobacco until the tip swelled in an orange glow.

"I seen him start to change," said Little Rod, whose English was heavily accented. He wore his cap down low on his forehead so that the shadow from the brim buried his eyes.

"When Peña volunteered to carry the radio, I told him not to do it. He never saw much action—not until he started humping that radio. I saw how he kept laughing, real nervous, when he came to the sessions, but I saw that he was trying to hide it. I could tell, man, that he was scared, too, something in his eyes. He tried to not show it . . . but I seen it. I seen it."

"Sure he was scared, man," responded level-headed Danny Ríos, a Northern Californian who always tried to find a balance in every situation . . . a cause for every effect . . . a good reason for every tragedy. He wore his cap high on his head, like a star baseball player, so that his whole face was visible. He continued: "Peña didn't know what he was getting himself into. He said he wanted to see some action, said he was tired of filling sandbags and carrying ammo. Yep, he got his transfer all right, and I think he hated it out in the bush. That's Charlie's country. That's his backyard. You go messing around out there and you best be scared. Common sense, man . . . common sense."

Little Rod didn't turn to face Danny. He spoke, his back against the dirty sandbags and his voice came out of the darkness: a somber tone exploring, probing, "It ain't what I mean. Peña's a nice kinda guy, you know? He got his vieja and kid. Every time the priest comes out to the bush, Peña goes to communion. Something bad had to of happen to him. Maybe he learned that God ain't out there. Maybe he learned that God ain't here either. The first time he carried that radio was when his platoon went in to help out C Company. You remember, C Company got ambushed . . . bodies tore up into thousands of pieces. Peña smelt the burnt meat, bodies that belonged to his friends. He saw those dead, nasty eyes."

"So what are you saying?" argued Alex. "You believe it was Peña the Tiger Force saw out there, that Peña is out there fighting with the Cong, that death is going to make him run off with the gooks? It don't make sense, man, no sense at all."

Little Rod continued, "I remember one time his squad come in from the bush, must a been right after his transfer; he's carrying that radio. Remember, Ríos? You was there. We was set up someplace outside of Tuy Hoa.

"Rain come down in chorros. Everything was like a sponge. Peña come out of that jungle into our battery area . . . his eyes big . . . like two big ol' hard-boiled eggs. That ain't a regular scared. He's soaked, dirty, smelly, and he's talkin' a hundred miles an hour. You had to slow him down. Hundred miles an hour, ese. That ain't regular scared. Something happen to Peña, man. I seen it. That ain't no shit; I seen it."

"Little Rod's right. Peña was panicked. His face was stretched, his skin white . . . cold, like a ghost." Danny Ríos confirmed Rod's words. "He talked like a machine gun and moved with quick jerks. I felt sorry for him. His lieutenant let him stay with us a couple of hours. We made him some hot chocolate and warmed him up. He just kept talking, man. He couldn't stop. Two hours later, when his squad moved out, Peña went. No questions asked, didn't complain, didn't fight it; just like the other guys in the squad. He walked back into the bush like a zombie, and that jungle, with rain still coming down, swallowed him right up. They said they had to find cover before dark. Little Rod's right. That wasn't no regular scared. Hell, made me thank God I was in the artillery. But it's just common sense, man. Put a dude in a situation like that and . . . hey."

"Then it's still not logical. If he's scared," I asked, "why's he going to take off with the Cong? He wouldn't even know how to find them. And if he did, they'd probably shoot him first. Alex is right, man. It doesn't make sense."

"Yup. Don't fucking sound like Peña to me," Alex said, the light shining against his square jaw and pitted skin. "He's probably in town right now, hung over and wanting to come back."

Finally, Big Rod, who was like a brother to Peña, went through jump school with him, and had met his family while they were both on leave in San Antonio, spoke up, his voice more serious than I'd ever heard:

"I think he went. I think he took off into that jungle and went with them. I don't know how he did it, why, or where he went, but he's out there looking for something . . . maybe looking for us . . . maybe looking for hisself. Remember his last words, 'I'll have everything ready for you guys.' He was trying to tell us something."

∽ ∽

The battery commanders from A and B batteries called each of us in to find out what they could. It was clear that they thought Jesse was AWOL and somewhere in Duc Pho. That's what most of the guys in the brigade thought, too. Jesse would come back, get court martialed, and that would be the end of it. But Jesse had never been in trouble before. He was the one who kept us out of trouble, making sure we'd get back to camp after a crazy day in town or calming us down after a run-in with an NCO or officer.

A month passed before a new rumor started. We were still operating somewhere outside of Duc Pho. A squad of grunts had made contact with a group of VC. They swore that a guy who looked like a Mexican, wearing GI camouflaged fatigues, had been walking point for the communists. It was no mistaken identity. One of the guys said he stared right into the pointman's eyes and that the Mexican just looked at him and smiled. Guns and grenades started going off, but Peña and his squad slipped back into the jungle.

Everybody in the brigade was talking about it. The guys who saw Jesse swore that it was "a Mexican-American" they'd seen out there. "The guy looked me right in the eyes. He coulda' shot me if he wanted. I was froze shitless" were the words of one grunt. It was strange how the words flew and the story built, but then, after a short time, the story transformed itself into a legend.

The story of an American leading a Vietcong squad was not uncommon. Everyone had heard it one time or another during his tour. Usually, the American was blond, tall, and thin. No one who told the story had ever seen the guy. The story was always distanced by two or three narrators, and it was more of a fable or myth, our own type of antiwar protest, I guess. What made this thing about Jesse so different was that the guys reporting it claimed personally to have seen him. Still, not many guys really believed it, except Big Rod, Little Rod, and the grunts who said they'd seen Jesse.

"Things are so crazy 'round this place guys'll make up anything fer 'musement," said Josh Spenser, an Oklahoman, who added, "I just don't know, man. I just don't know."

Two weeks passed before the next sighting. "Saw Peña, man. The guys who were now reporting the sightings started using his name, as if they personally knew him. One evening, when we were in the front area base camp, Big Rod, Little Rod, Alex, and I walked across the brigade area to talk to one of the soldiers who said he'd seen Jesse.

At first he didn't believe we were Jesse's friends. The guy didn't trust anybody because, as he put it, guys were saying that he was making the whole thing up, but after we explained our relationship to Jesse, he began to talk.

"It's the shits, man. Captain tol' me he didn't want me spreadin' no rumors," his voice lowered, "but I saw 'em. Big as shit, I saw."

The guy's name was Conklin. He seemed wired, like he was high on speed, sincere . . . yet nervous. He told us his story like someone who had been trying to convince people that he'd seen a UFO. Conklin said that he and his squad were on an ambush. They had the whole thing set up by nightfall: claymores out, good cover, M-16s, grenades, and an M-60 at the ready. He said that it was quiet out there, no noise, no animal sounds, nothing. But, as he told it, the VC never showed.

Since there had been no contact, the choppers came out to pick them up the next morning. He described how he bent down low and made his way out to retrieve the claymores. He disconnected the cap, and squatting down low, started to wrap the wire around the curved, green device. As he wrapped, he kept his eyes on the trail, looking both ways and also checking the jungle to his front. And then he saw Peña. Just like that, Conklin said, using Jesse's last name.

"Peña," pronouncing it Peenya, "was down in the bush, a Thompson submachine gun pointed right at me. I was gonna reach for my rifle but he just nods, cool-like, slow . . . and I know he means for me to not go for it so's I jes' set there and stare at him, and all he does is stare back. I couldn't talk, man. I couldn't yell. It was like . . . like one of them nightmares where you feel suffocated and can't nobody help you. Then he moves back, real slow-like, still squatting, like gooks do, an' then I see two other gooks, one on each side of him. He stands up and the gooks stand up and they move backward into the brush, just like that, fuckin'-A, man, and he's gone."

"What's he look like?" asked Alex.

"Got on gook clothes, man. Pajamas—a black top and black bottoms, cut off just above the knees . . . light complexion, 'bout like you," he says pointing to Big Rod. "I guess he's close to 5'7" or 8", not too tall . . . probably 145 or 150 pounds."

"Peña's closer to 175, maybe 180," Alex tells Conklin.

"Not no more he ain't. Guy I saw wasn't no 180. And when he smiled, he made me feel O.K., you know. Even though I was scared and he could'a blown a hole through me, still . . . made me feel like . . . O.K. Maybe had something to do with those dimples. Big mothers . . . one on each cheek."

Big Rod and I looked at each other.

"Kinda made him look like a kid. But he wasn't bullshitting, man. It wasn't no joke. If I'd a gone for my weapon, he'd a blowed my ass clean away. I can't figure it out, man. Gone, just like that . . . disappeared with those gooks right into the jungle. And nobody else seen it, only me."

Three months had passed since Jesse disappeared. His ETS date came and went. Maybe we expected a miracle, as if Jesse was going to walk into the base camp, say "hi," and tell us about his days with the VC as he packed his bags and prepared to catch a hop to Cam Ranh Bay where he'd DEROS home. But nothing. It was just another day; besides, by this time we were in Phan Rhang, our rear area base camp, and a long way from where Peña had last been seen.

That night, the night of Peña's ETS, we held a "session," more of a funeral, over by the training course, which was at the perimeter of the brigade area. Even some of the nonbelievers showed up.

We met in front of the mess hall, one of many in the brigade area. It was located on a hill at the east end of the base camp, where we could look out over the entire airborne complex.

The sun had descended and the work day completed. We could see GIs slowly walking the dirt roads, some going to the Enlisted Men's or Officers' Clubs, others to the USO, and still others strolling as if they were out for an evening in some country town. In an hour or so it would be dark and carefully rationed lights would bring a different life to the area. There would be drinking and card games, laughter and yells, tales about families and girlfriends, stories of heroics in the field with a few guys displaying the macabre trophies. Some guys would listen to records in their tents and wonder what their buddies back home were doing. At the USO, they'd be talking to the donut dollies, playing Monopoly, Scrabble, dominoes, and other games, while in their minds they'd be making love to the American women who sat at the opposite side of the game boards.

We turned away and headed toward the obstacle course. A range of jungle-covered mountains formed the camp's eastern perimeter.

We followed a dirt trail down a hill and gathered in a clearing that was used for a map-reading course. It was off-limits at night, so we had to be quiet.

As the two Rods and I approached, we saw that Alex and Danny, with C-ration cans and heat tablets, had designed a church-like atmosphere. The small blue flames, much like candles, were spread out in a circle to our front, lifting the darkness so that our faces were barely recognizable. The jungle surrounded us with a heaviness that leaned more toward enigma than fear. After a short while, the shuffling of feet along the trail stopped, the whispering voices were silent, and about twenty of us sat on logs formed into a semi-circle.

Big Rod said that there would be no drinking, not yet, anyway. Doc Langley handed him a stack of joints. Big Rod passed them around and said to light up. Not everyone liked to smoke, but this night they all breathed in the stinging herb. It didn't take long for the weed to take effect. The jungle moved in closer. The trees came down over our heads like thick spiderwebs and the plants weighed against our backs. The joints moved around the circle until the air and smoke mingled into a kind of anesthetized gas.

Big Rod pulled a paper from his pocket, unfolded it, and began to read. It was from Margaret, Peña's wife. The army had told her that Jesse was listed as AWOL because it couldn't be determined when he officially had been lost. In her letter, which made Big Rod pause many times as he read, she wanted to know what happened to her husband. She trusted that Rod would tell her the truth since it seemed nobody else would. Was Jesse dead? That's what she really wanted to know.

"Please answer soon," were her last words. Rod wanted to know how he should respond, then, frustrated, he gave me the letter. He said that since I was the one with some college, I should answer.

Johnny Sabia, an infantryman from Sevilla, New Mexico, and a guy who didn't come around much, said that we shouldn't be moping but that we should be celebrating. "Write her," he said to me. "Tell her the truth. Her old man split. The dude's the only one with any balls. I don't know how, but this guy Peña understands that everything here means nothing. I've never met the guy, but I've been thinking about him and

I've heard the stories. Everybody's talking about him. I heard that Peña lives in San Antonio, in some rat hole that he can't afford to buy because the bank won't lend him the money. I heard that in the summer when it hits a hundred, him and his neighbors fry like goddamn chickens because they can't afford air conditioning. So now they send him here to fight for his country! What a joke, man."

None of us ever talked about it. Peña never talked about it. Sabia was the first one who raised the issue. All we wanted to do was fight the war, get to the rear area, drink, joke, and never think about why we were here or what the truth was about our lives back home.

An argument started. Someone said that whatever we have it's better than what other people have. Even if we work in the fields in the states, it's better than working the fields in Mexico. An angry voice said, "Bullshit! We don't live in Mexico. We live in the U.S. Our parents worked to make the U.S. what it is; our fathers fought and died in WWII. We got rights just like anybody else."

Someone else wanted to know how come we get the worst duties. Whether it's pulling the shittiest hours on guard duty or going into dangerous situations, if there's a Chicano around, he's the one who gets it.

"Because we don't say shit, man. Whatever they want to push on us, we just take it. Like pendejos . . . we do whatever nobody else wants to do. We don't want to be crybabies. Well, maybe we should start crying."

"That's right," someone else said. "Gonzales got himself shot up because nobody else wanted to take their turn at the point. He walked the point for his squad almost every operation. What good did it do? He's dead now. Pobre Gonzales, man; talk about poor, he showed me a picture of his family who lived in someplace called Livingston, in Califas. His house looked like a damn chicken coop."

Then Alex stood up. He told how he was raised in the middle-class San Fernando Valley and remembered teachers who insulted him in front of his Anglo classmates, but only now, tonight, did he understand that it was because he was Mexican. Lamely, he said, "It never hit me. I just thought I was the only fuck-up in that school. There were a lot of white dudes who screwed up, but I don't ever remember the teachers jumping on them like they jumped on me."

Johnny Sabia talked some more, about tennis clubs built over fields where the townspeople of Sevilla had once grown corn and vegetables, about schoolhouses with holes in the roofs, streets still unpaved in 1967, primitive electrical systems for lighting. And he and others went on and on until they worked themselves into a fury.

Someone pulled out the beer. As the alcohol hit, the voices got louder and belligerent. Before long, the whiskey bottles started to make the rounds and nobody was talking about Peña any longer. Everyone talked about their friends back home, their girlfriends, or good places to find prostitutes in Phan Rhang. The session was over. Somebody kicked out the heat tabs, and the jungle, once again, distanced itself from us.

We marched over to the Enlisted Men's Club, toasted Jesse Peña several times, honoring him and wishing him well, and drank until they threw us out. Then we staggered along the roads, falling into ditches, staring at the stars splattered against the sky, and vomiting as we worked our way back to our units. We finally found our bunks and sank into a dizzying sleep.

The next morning when we woke up, most of us were hung over. We went through our usual routines, cleaning weapons and resupplying our units. A few days later, we flew out in C-130 transport planes to the next operation, somewhere outside of Chu Lai. There were a few rumors that Peña was still traveling with the VC, but no one would swear to the sightings. His memory became painful for those of us who knew him. When I left Vietnam, the new guys joining the Division heard about the Mexican who ran off to join the VC, and they kept the story alive, building on Peña's adventures. One squad reported that they saw his dead body after the ambush of a VC unit, but nobody believed that story either.

Tomatoes

Janice Mirikitani

"We have to read *The Red Badge of Courage*."
"We all had to read it."
"But all heroes are not men."
—Dialogue with my daughter

Hanako loved her garden. She and her young daughter lived with her parents on a farm planted in the stretch of fields near Gilroy. Her husband died during the war. He was a hero. Received medals and letters of commendation for valor in battle, for defending his country, for saving fellow soldiers in his regiment.

Hanako had delivered to her an American flag and his medal after she and her parents got out of the concentration camp located in the middle of the desert.

When they returned to her parent's farm, the house had to be repaired and rebuilt and the land was dried, cracked like weathered skin.

Hanako would look out over the wide flat expanse of the valley. In the dry season it reminded her of the camp desert where the heat would shimmer up and if you looked long enough you thought you could see someone approaching. She'd do that a lot, dreaming her husband would be running toward her. She'd shade her eyes and watch as the sun pulsated, conjuring up the man with the strong warm hands that would go up her neck and through her hair and pull her face close to him. The heat from the ground would travel through her body and she would weep from the barrenness of knowing he would never be coming back.

Lisa looked like him, his squarish jaw, his deep black eyes, the smile lines in her cheek.

Mommy, I want red flowers.

Hanako set about to soften her earth, make her garden. She wielded her hoe like a sword, breaking hard crusts of dirt. Lisa would bring out the hose and buckets to help moisten the ground, playing in the water, muddy pools created by Hanako's shovel. She planted bright geraniums that grew sturdily in dry climate next to her tomato vines.

The Haufmanns, who lived four acres away, came over the day they returned to the farm, talked about the hard times they had during the war and difficulties in keeping up their own land. They just couldn't afford to water anyone else's crops even with the extra money and the furniture, china, tractor, seedlings, livestock they were given by Hanako's parents before their hasty departure to the camps. Mr. Haufmann kicked the dirt as he commented that Hanako didn't look any the worse for wear. He eyed her breasts under her white cotton blouse, and admired how Lisa had grown into a fine young girl with slender hips like her mommy and so sorry
to hear about the husband.

Hanako answered politely
      the war is over and done.
      We've come back to start our life again
      like planting new seeds and hoping they'll
      grow stronger.

Mr. Haufmann would frequently visit if he'd see Hanako and Lisa in their resurrected garden, weeding, pulling the dandelion from her tender tomato vines, her sweet peas with their thin, delicate stalks climbing the stakes she had hammered into the ground in neat rows, the robust thick stubs of kale, and Lisa's geraniums brightly red in the heat.
      Kinda delicate, aren't you, doing
      all this work? Skin's going to shrivel
      in this mean sun. Work's too heavy for little girls.

Hanako would stand up straight and speak politely, softly,
      there are many things we must learn
      to do without
      and find the strength
      to do ourselves.

Lisa, tending her flowers, ran up to Mr. Haufmann, who lifted her high in the air, her skirt flying above her panties. Mr. Haufmann laughing, flinging her up again and again, until Hanako would tell Lisa to finish her watering chores, her eyes turning black and silent as she whacked at the heads of dandelion weeds with her hoe.

The heat rose early that day, its fingers clutching the rows of dirt. Hanako from the kitchen window did not see Lisa in the garden, watering as she usually did. She went immediately outside, looking, instinctively picked up her hoe and walked through the shimmering heat.

Hanako started toward the Haufmann farm when she saw Lisa running toward her with a paper bag.

> Mommy. Mommy. Mr. Haufmann
> gave me pears and figs. They're ripe
> and sweet. He let me climb and pick
> them myself. He's so strong, let me
> stand on his shoulders so I could reach
> the top branches.

Hanako's knuckles turned white on the handle of the hoe, told Lisa she was not to play at the Haufmanns' again, returned to her garden and sprayed for insects.

Mr. Haufmann appeared in the waves of heat that afternoon, wiping off his face with the back of his hand. Hanako's sweat ran down her back, popped above her mouth. Haufmann red-faced, smiling

> Tomatoes looking good and juicy.
> Got a lotta nice young buds gonna pop soon, too.
> Heat's good for them I guess.

Hanako with her hoe turned the soil gently,

> How's your wife? Haven't seen her for awhile.

Wetting his lips

> O, that old mare's too tired to
> walk even this distance. Just sits at the
> radio and knits. Damn knitting gets on
> my nerves.

Hanako's hoe, turning, turning

> And your sons. Are they doing well?

Haufmann's hard laugh

> Too good for farming. Both in college,
> and don't hardly write or call. Busy
> chasing women and getting into trouble.
> Ha. Rascals they are. Men will be men.

Hanako's hoe fiercely cutting near the tomato vines

> You are fortunate to have healthy children.

Hanako's hoe high in the air, whacked like a sword through a ripe tomato, juices springing up, smearing the soil

There's nothing we won't do
to insure their happiness, is there?
her voice low and glinting now like her blade as she whacked off the head
of another tomato, smearing the handle red. Haufmann's eyes, fading
lights of blue, blinked as he stepped backward. Hanako's voice now like
the edge of sharp knives almost whispering
We see so much of ourselves
mirrored in our children
except more . . .
Whack. Hanako's hoe now fiercely slicing, thudding, crushing the ripened
crop of tomatoes as the blade smeared red, the handle now slippery with
juices and pink seeds
I have no bitterness Mr. Haufmann
not about the war, nor the losses.
She thought of her husband's final moments.
Did he suffer long. What were his thoughts . . .
the humiliation of those camps.
Did he remember her and their chubby Lisa waving from
the wire fence as he left them for the war?
the work or this heat
or the loneliness.
Only the regret
that my husband
The memory of smile lines in his cheek,
his warm hands stroking Lisa's hair,
quieting her in his rocking arms.
cannot see the growing,
budding, living hope
Lisa came running to her mother's side, speechless at the devastation,
the red mass of crushed tomatoes, her eyes wide and instantly older,
seeing Haufmann wilting
shriveled in sweat and the wrinkles
of his wet shirt.
He, wordless, slumped
to escape
into the waves of heat.
Mother. I'm so glad
you saved my geraniums.

These Bones, These Bones

Akasha Gloria Hull

for TCB

Long black bones
waving like angry spears
under an ocean of years and water
clamoring fronds uprising
in the cold and tropical sea

Grandmother bones
Father bones
Baby bones thrown overboard
Those who leaped
who fell in the fight
They who saw the future
        and ran screaming into time
The rot which could not go
        unburied
The troubled spirits swept clean
        away by the avenging storm
Lovers who held each other's hand
        and went down singing

These African bones
that did not live
to tell their story
are troubling the waters
are asking the bone
        of their bone

their present flesh
the black bones
redbones
half-white bones
bleached bones
brown bones
their bones
colored forever
in the dyes of history
about the unpoured libations
the monuments which do not rise
not even in our imaginations
are wondering how we came
to this place of forgetfulness
with not even a pile of stones
to mark the sacred plot

Author's note: "TCB" stands for "Toni Cade Bambara" and for
"Taking Care of Business." I recited this poem at the Middle Passage
Monument Ceremony on July 3, 1999, in New York City, after which
a gravestone was lowered to the floor of the Atlantic Ocean, 427
kilometers off New York harbor. Given the long-standing absence
of such markers, our books, paintings, and other forms of artistic
expression, and all our acts of creative living and struggle, have historically been the surviving monuments to our ancestral spirits who
perished during the infamous Middle Passage.

Poem About My Rights

June Jordan

Even tonight and I need to take a walk and clear
my head about this poem about why I can't
go out without changing my clothes my shoes
my body posture my gender identity my age
my status as a woman alone in the evening/
alone on the streets/alone not being the point/
the point being that I can't do what I want
to do with my own body because I am the wrong
sex the wrong age the wrong skin and
suppose it was not here in the city but down on the beach/
or far into the woods and I wanted to go
there by myself thinking about God/or thinking
about children or thinking about the world/all of it
disclosed by the stars and the silence:
I could not go and I could not think and I could not
stay there
alone
as I need to be
alone because I can't do what I want to do with my own
body and
who in the hell set things up
like this
and in France they say if the guy penetrates
but does not ejaculate then he did not rape me
and if after stabbing him if after screams if
after begging the bastard and if even after smashing
a hammer to his head if even after that if he
and his buddies fuck me after that

then I consented and there was
no rape because finally you understand finally
they fucked me over because I was wrong I was
wrong again to be me being me where I was/wrong
to be who I am
which is exactly like South Africa
penetrating into Namibia penetrating into
Angola and does that mean I mean how do you know if
Pretoria ejaculates what will the evidence look like the
proof of the monster jackboot ejaculation on Blackland
and if
after Namibia and if after Angola and if after Zimbabwe
and if after all of my kinsmen and women resist even to
self-immolation of the villages and if after that
we lose nevertheless what will the big boys say will they
claim my consent:
Do You Follow Me: We are the wrong people of
the wrong skin on the wrong continent and what
in the hell is everybody being reasonable about
and according to the *Times* this week
back in 1966 the C.I.A. decided that they had this problem
and the problem was a man named Nkrumah so they
killed him and before that it was Patrice Lumumba
and before that it was my father on the campus
of my Ivy League school and my father afraid
to walk into the cafeteria because he said he
was wrong the wrong age the wrong skin the wrong
gender identity and he was paying my tuition and
before that
it was my father saying I was wrong saying that
I should have been a boy because he wanted one/a
boy and that I should have been lighter skinned and
that I should have had straighter hair and that
I should not be so boy crazy but instead I should
just be one/a boy and before that
it was my mother pleading plastic surgery for
my nose and braces for my teeth and telling me
to let the books loose to let them loose in other
words

I am very familiar with the problems of the C.I.A.
and the problems of South Africa and the problems
of Exxon Corporation and the problems of white
America in general and the problems of the teachers
and the preachers and the F.B.I. and the social
workers and my particular Mom and Dad/I am very
familiar with the problems because the problems
turn out to be
me
I am the history of rape
I am the history of the rejection of who I am
I am the history of the terrorized incarceration of
my self
am the history of battery assault and limitless
armies against whatever I want to do with my mind
and my body and my soul and
whether it's about walking out at night
or whether it's about the love that I feel or
whether it's about the sanctity of my vagina or
the sanctity of my national boundaries
or the sanctity of my leaders or the sanctity
of each and every desire
that I know from my personal and idiosyncratic
and indisputably single and singular heart
I have been raped
be-
cause I have been wrong the wrong sex the wrong age
the wrong skin the wrong nose the wrong hair the
wrong need the wrong dream the wrong geographic
the wrong sartorial I
I have been the meaning of rape
I have been the problem everyone seeks to
eliminate by forced
penetration with or without the evidence of slime and/
but let this be unmistakable this poem
is not consent I do not consent
to my mother to my father to the teachers to
the F.B.I. to South Africa to Bedford-Stuy

to Park Avenue to American Airlines to the hardon
idlers on the corners to the sneaky creeps in
cars
I am not wrong: Wrong is not my name
My name is my own my own my own
and I can't tell you who the hell set things up like this
but I can tell you that from now on my resistance
my simple and daily and nightly self-determination
may very well cost you your life

Peacekeeping in Bunia

Khadijah Queen

Only costs $5, a bottle of water,
a job, a blow, a rip
somewhere quiet.
Or $1, $3, nothing,
a slap, a kick, a knife to reddened eyes
made to memorize foreign pornos.
In a truck, on a bus, in a house
by the trees, in the mud, in the weeds—
quiet
if you're 13,
quiet if your grandmother
sells you,
quiet your baby sister
watching, quiet if she's next,
quiet, quiet
blue helmets
spilling on the side of the road.

In the Village of Missing Fathers

Rigoberto González

Children run without shoes
because no bottles have been
broken there and no one knows how
to climb a tree or fly a kite. When the sheets
wave on the line they chirp and sing
and so no reason for feral birds.
No reason for clouds or sky.

When it rains the women never say
it's coming down, they point to the ground
and say it came. No angels hover
because no one wants flight
or things that float without water.
Newspaper boats on the puddle
are the only mystery: they refuse

to sink despite the heavy dream
of travel. They remain mute despite
the casing of words and the memory
of the grief the women poured onto the page
when they read about their sons' and husbands'
fates. Each article an obituary, each word
dressed for burial, each page an insult

even to the blue canaries that refuse
to plop their droppings there. And so
in the village of missing fathers, the tricks
of transformation: paper sorrow folds

into a boat, a bed into a holding cell
for moans that bleed out of sleep, a house
thins out into a ghost with the smell of Sunday

cologne, with the texture of a scratch
on the arm, with the sound of a throat
clearing after the triumph of uttered
pleasure. And the women watch their children
smear their laughter like paste on
any surface, hoping that something
worth keeping will stick. What wonder,

this collection of objects plucked and kept
in an empty matchbox: a leaf that sprung
out of rock, a bug that constricts
into the pellet of a goat, a lock of black hair
tied with red ribbon rescued from the kindling
bucket. And the boys gather around at dusk
to fantasize about its origin: a beauty from

some other village, no doubt, perhaps
a dancer who can point to the ceiling
with her toe while standing on the other
foot, perhaps a princess who wears silver
to bed and who sips tea made from flakes
of gold, perhaps a lady whose gown
cascades with light, whose hands only need

the strength to lift an ivory comb.
But certainly not any woman from here,
the village of missing fathers, where women
have traded their silks for meats, their kisses
for bolts on the doors, the curves
of their hips for a place to carve out
the names of the dead. The boys have caught

glimpses of such scarred tissue, and it
shamed them into never watching anyone else's
mother disrobe again. Not while they soak

their bony bodies in the bath and rise
one shade darker. Not while they slip
from one black cloak into another,
the momentary flash of flesh a sad

accident, like a foot falling on
the only daisy left standing after the cow
stampede. And certainly never at night
while their mothers lie in the hollow
of the mattress and roll their torsos
in the final trace of musk that must have
overwhelmed them once, when they were

wives. O delicious weight of passion,
O terrible tickle, O precious probe.
The women are becoming brittle without it.
The boys are growing anxious with it.
The walls of every house are threatening
to collapse from the negligence of it.
But no, beloved ones, never worry,

the sad architecture of abandonment
will always stand. The broken world
spins this way: a woman runs afraid
out to the street at midnight and the moon
stops her by stepping on her braid
and all the other women come to clothe her
with shadow. The town priestess prays for her

until the woman understands that muscle
crushed to bone will take the place of touch.
And the woman hardens her resolve.
And the woman snaps her body like a jigsaw
piece back into the hole she made
when she tore out of her home, just another
wound to mend, just another

episode of melancholia mentioned over
chamomile, forgotten by the time

the tea cups freeze to yawns inside
the cradle of the sink. The children
tip their heads against the pillows
and look as fragile, as if their skulls
could crumble with the furious tap

of after-hour angst, when the trap
invites the rodent to a suicide, when
the needle point trembles for its fix,
when the widow dresses hang themselves,
exhausted from the weight of stones.
If the children were awake they'd find
their mothers drifting in the air like errant

moths looking for a flower that blossoms
without light. They might even call them
beautiful if not for the oils that scurry down
their legs like piss. And if the women
were awake, they'd give each tiny lake
of blood beneath their feet a name.
But the broken world shows mercy

and each morning every person rises
none the wiser. The boys, fingering
their pockets stuffed with marbles, catch
the fleeting scent of something—*pudenda*
if they had the word, but they haven't
had it, so they run out to the road
to draw a circle on the dirt, a hole

dug in the center, an inverted nipple.
They play their game, pretending
that the aches inside their throats
are not their voices getting thicker.
If they begin to sound like grown-ups
they begin to die. That's life
in the village without handsome

men: suddenly they wear the shoes
that lose their way. Some say
they journey North to waste
their days as kitchen slaves. Some say
they trade their organs for quick pay,
and that their shame means begging
on the city streets for gauze or cotton,

stitches or thread, to heal their surgeries
and stand upright again without
rattling like coins inside a cup.
And some believe they're seized
by soldier's fury and off they run to war
on foreign lands so dry the wind sucks out
the fluids in their faces. If they regret

their choice they cannot spit. And if they
yearn for what they left behind
they cannot cry. And if they scratch their cheeks
in sleep, dreaming that they're clawing
on the buttocks of their wives they cannot
bleed. Whatever path they take, whatever
headlines speak above the rumors, no one

knows for sure, though the silence
of their vanishing comes certainly. So too
succumbing to the deadness of the air.
In this village, and many others like it,
no one talks about the missing. Not a word
about the hat clinging to the only hook
in the wall, embedded question mark

not seen since—

Not a word about the pair of slippers
hibernating like two polar bears beneath
the sofa since—

Not a word about the extra chair
that sits fasting at the table losing
weight each season since—

If the picket fences stand like crosses
never mention it. If the yellow ribbons
cut the circulation off the trees
don't point it out. Find the fallen fruit
scattered like landmines on the ground
and eat it before it explodes, before
it betrays widow and orphan with its truth:

the men are never ever coming home.

from interlude

the avenue of the americas

Alicia Ostriker

Above the tongues of taxicabs, the horns and buyers
the teeth of buildings grin at each other, the institutions
of media medicine publishing fashion

know how to
bite through human flesh
like hinged aluminum traps chopping the necks

of beavers, or like logging rigs, those saws
that go through a hundred-year-old
redwood in about three minutes

take out a thousand acres
of virgin oregon forest
annually because loggers need jobs

intellectuals need the special sections
of the *New York Times* stacked
on driveways

each rosy dawn, the Japanese need
the splinters these pines and spruces
finally get turned into

everybody needs what they can get
and more. Yesterday walking
between fifty-third and fifty-second

on the avenue of the americas at twilight on my way
to a good restaurant with good friends I passed
three beggars wrapped in plastic. Why not say

beggars?
Why invent novelty phrases like "the homeless"
as if our situation were modern and special

instead of ancient and normal,
the problem of greed and selfishness?
The beggars turned toward me

I put money in the woman's cup
though I didn't like her facial sores
her drowned eyes bobbed to the surface

as if they believed for a second
something new was about to happen
but nothing was

so the eyes sank rapidly back
like crabs into sand, and sorrow
pressed into me like a hot iron

after which I hurried through the hurrying crowd,
sky overhead primrose and lilac, skyscrapers
uncanny mirrors filled with cloud bouquets

to overtake my friends who had strolled ahead
chatting so as not to be embarrassed
by the sight of charity

the rotting odor of need

Even the Tin Man Had a Heart

Marc Harshman

I was not at home but wandering a demolition site,
        the air acrid with sulfuric shreds of headlines.
"We will not listen, we will not listen, we will not listen."
        I heard the chant in English and it seemed wrong.
        I heard the chant and wondered if it was the latest pop
            and it seemed wrong.
It seemed wrong because I was not in the States or Britain or Canada, but
        I was in a very hot place and it was called Hell, it was called
        the Middle East, it was called Iraq.
And I didn't know what I was doing there but it was here and gone.
It was a waste place doubly damned. It was a land full of craters
        bombed twice.

And an old man, he was a grandfather, wandered the wasted street,
        and there was a little boy uplifted into the arms of a naked tree
        and he just hung there, limp, a narrow branch skewered into
            him,
            entering below his collar bone and exiting his back just under
            his right
shoulder, and this had not yet killed him, and his sister, it was, lay face
        down, neatly,
in the sand, perfectly intact, it would seem, but how long could she
        breathe and eat sand?
I wondered in my daze, in my dream, and only the old man seemed
        awake,

And he asked me what to call this, asked who would tell their names,
    the names of these two
children, the names of all the children and the names of the old men
    like himself who
now hold in their hands in place of memory only a broken heart, broken
pieces of a heart no oil can ever fix.

The House Murdered

Mahmoud Darwish

In one minute, the whole life of a house ends. The house murdered is
also mass murder, even if vacant of its residents. It is a mass grave
for the basic elements needed to construct a building for meaning, or
for an insignificant poem in a time of war. The house, murdered, is
the amputation of things from their relations and from the names of
emotions, and it is tragedy's need to guide eloquence to contemplate
the life of a thing. In each thing there's a being that aches . . .
the memory of fingers, of a scent, of an image. And houses get
murdered just as their residents get murdered. And as the memory of
things get murdered—wood, stone, glass, iron, cement—they all scatter
in fragments like beings. And cotton, silk, linen, notepads, books, all
are torn like words whose owners were not given time to speak. And
the plates, spoons, toys, records, faucets, pipes, door handles, and the
fridge, the washer, the vases, jars of olives and pickles, and canned
foods, all break as their owners broke. And the two whites, salt and
sugar, are pulverized, and also the spices, the matchboxes, the pills
and oral contraceptives, elixirs, garlic braids, onions, tomatoes, dried
okra, rice and lentils, as happens with the residents. And the lease
contract, the marriage and birth certificates, the utility bills, identity
cards, passports, love letters, all torn to shreds like the hearts of their
owners. And the pictures fly, the toothbrushes, hair combs, make-up
accessories, shoes, underwear, sheets, towels, like family secrets hung
in public, in ruin. All these things are the memories of people who were
emptied of things, and the memories of things that were emptied of people . . .
all end in one minute. Our things die like us, but they don't get buried with us.

Translated by Fady Joudah

The Colonel

Carolyn Forché

What you have heard is true. I was in his house. His wife carried a tray of coffee and sugar. His daughter filed her nails, his son went out for the night. There were daily papers, pet dogs, a pistol on the cushion beside him. The moon swung bare on its black cord over the house. On the television was a cop show. It was in English. Broken bottles were embedded in the walls around the house to scoop the kneecaps from a man's legs or cut his hands to lace. On the windows there were gratings like those in liquor stores. We had dinner, rack of lamb, good wine, a gold bell was on the table for calling the maid. The maid brought green mangoes, salt, a type of bread. I was asked how I enjoyed the country. There was a brief commercial in Spanish. His wife took everything away. There was some talk then of how difficult it had become to govern. The parrot said hello on the terrace. The colonel told it to shut up, and pushed himself from the table. My friend said to me with his eyes: say nothing. The colonel returned with a sack used to bring groceries home. He spilled many human ears on the table. They were like dried peach halves. There is no other way to say this. He took one of them in his hands, shook it in our faces, dropped it into a water glass. It came alive there. I am tired of fooling around he said. As for the rights of anyone, tell your people they can go fuck themselves. He swept the ears to the floor with his arm and held the last of his wine in the air. Something for your poetry, no? he said. Some of the ears on the floor caught this scrap of his voice. Some of the ears on the floor were pressed to the ground.

from The American Invasion of Macún

Esmeralda Santiago

Lo que no mata, engorda.

What doesn't kill you, makes you fat.

Pollito, chicken
Gallina, hen
Lápiz, pencil
y Pluma, pen.
Ventana, window
Puerta, door
Maestra, teacher
y Piso, floor.

Miss Jiménez stood in front of the class as we sang and, with her ruler, pointed at the chicks scratching the dirt outside the classroom, at the hen leading them, at the pencil on Juanita's desk, at the pen on her own desk, at the window that looked out into the playground, at the door leading to the yard, at herself, and at the shiny tile floor. We sang along, pointing as she did with our sharpened pencils, rubber end out.

"*¡Muy bien!*" She pulled down the map rolled into a tube at the front of the room. In English she told us, "Now gwee estody about de Jun-ited Estates gee-o-graphee."

It was the daily English class. Miss Jiménez, the second- and third-grade teacher, was new to the school in Macún. She looked like a grown-up doll, with high rounded cheekbones, a freckled *café con leche* complexion, black lashes, black curly hair pulled into a bun at the nape of her neck, and the prettiest legs in the whole *barrio*. Doña Ana said Miss Jiménez had the most beautiful legs she'd ever seen, and the next day, while Miss Jiménez wrote the multiplication table on the blackboard, I stared at them.

She wore skirts to just below the knees, but from there down, her legs were shaped like chicken drumsticks, rounded and full at the top, narrow at the bottom. She had long straight hair on her legs, which everyone said made them even prettier, and small feet encased in plain brown shoes with a low square heel. That night I wished on a star that someday my scrawny legs would fill out into that lovely shape and that the hair on them would be as long and straight and black.

Miss Jiménez came to Macún at the same time as the community center. She told us that starting the following week, we were all to go to the *centro comunal* before school to get breakfast, provided by the Estado Libre Asociado, or Free Associated State, which was the official name for Puerto Rico in the Estados Unidos, or in English, the Jun-ited Estates of America. Our parents, Miss Jiménez told us, should come to a meeting that Saturday, where experts from San Juan and the Jun-ited Estates would teach our mothers all about proper nutrition and hygiene, so that we would grow up as tall and strong as Dick, Jane, and Sally, the *Americanitos* in our primers.

"And Mami," I said as I sipped my afternoon *café con leche*, "Miss Jiménez said the experts will give us free food and toothbrushes and things . . . and we can get breakfast every day except Sunday . . ."

"Calm down," she told me. "We'll go, don't worry."

On Saturday morning the yard in front of the *centro comunal* filled with parents and their children. You could tell the experts from San Juan from the ones that came from the Junited Estates because the *Americanos* wore ties with their white shirts and tugged at their collars and wiped their foreheads with crumpled handkerchiefs. They hadn't planned for children, and the men from San Juan convinced a few older girls to watch the little ones outside so that the meeting could proceed with the least amount of disruption. Small children refused to leave their mothers' sides and screeched the minute one of the white-shirted men came near them. Some women sat on the folding chairs at the rear of the room nursing, a cloth draped over their baby's face so that the experts would not be upset at the sight of a bare breast. There were no fathers. Most of them worked seven days a week, and anyway, children and food were woman's work.

"Negi, take the kids outside and keep them busy until this is over."

"But Mami . . ."

"Do as I say."

She pressed her way to a chair in the middle of the room and sat facing the experts. I hoisted Edna on my shoulder and grabbed Alicia's hand. Delsa pushed Norma out in front of her. They ran into the yard and within minutes had blended into a group of children their age. Héctor found a boy to chase him around a tree, and Alicia crawled to a sand puddle where she and other toddlers smeared one another with the fine red dirt. I sat at the door, Edna on my lap, and tried to keep one eye on my sisters and brother and another on what went on inside.

The experts had colorful charts on portable easels. They introduced each other to the group, thanked the Estado Libre Asociado for the privilege of being there, and then took turns speaking. The first expert opened a large suitcase. Inside there was a huge set of teeth with pink gums.

"*Ay Dios Santo, qué cosa tan fea*," said a woman as she crossed herself. The mothers laughed and mumbled among themselves that yes, it was ugly. The expert stretched his lips into a smile and pulled a large toothbrush from under the table. He used ornate Spanish words that we assumed were scientific talk for teeth, gums, and tongue. With his giant brush, he polished each tooth on the model, pointing out the proper path of the bristles on the teeth.

"If I have to spend that much time on my teeth," a woman whispered loud enough for everyone to hear, "I won't get anything done around the house." The room buzzed with giggles, and the expert again spread his lips, took a breath, and continued his demonstration.

"At the conclusion of the meeting," he said, "you will each receive a toothbrush and a tube of paste for every member of your family."

"*¿Hasta pa' los mellaos?*" a woman in the back of the room asked, and everyone laughed.

"If they have no teeth, it's too late for them, isn't it?" the expert said through his own clenched teeth. The mothers shrieked with laughter, and the expert sat down so that an *Americano* with red hair and thick glasses could tell us about food.

He wiped his forehead and upper lip as he pulled up the cloth covering one of the easels to reveal a colorful chart of the major food groups.

"*La buena* nutrition is *muy importante para los niños.*" In heavily accented, hard to understand Castilian Spanish he described the necessity of eating portions of each of the foods on his chart every day. There were carrots and broccoli, iceberg lettuce, apples, pears, and peaches. The bread was sliced into a perfect square, unlike the long loaves Papi brought home from a bakery in San Juan, or the round *pan de manteca* Mami bought at Vitín's store. There was no rice on the chart, no beans, no salted codfish. There were big white eggs, not at all like the small round ones our hens gave us. There was a tall glass of milk, but no coffee. There were wedges of yellow cheese, but no balls of cheese like the white *queso del país* wrapped in banana leaves and sold in bakeries all over Puerto Rico. There were bananas but no plantains, potatoes but no *batatas*, cereal flakes but no oatmeal, bacon but no sausages.

"But, *señor*," said Doña Lola from the back of the room, "none of the fruits or vegetables on your chart grow in Puerto Rico."

"Then you must substitute our recommendations with your native foods."

"Is an apple the same as a mango?" asked Cirila, whose yard was shaded by mango trees.

"*Sí,*" said the expert, "a mango can be substituted for an apple."

"What about breadfruit?"

"I'm not sure . . ." The *Americano* looked at an expert from San Juan who stood up, pulled the front of his *guayabera* down over his ample stomach, and spoke in a voice as deep and resonant as a radio announcer's.

"Breadfruit," he said, "would be equivalent to potatoes."

"Even the ones with seeds?" asked Dona Lola, who roasted them on the coals of her *fogón*.

"Well, I believe so," he said, "but it is best not to make substitutions for the recommended foods. That would throw the whole thing off."

He sat down and stared at the ceiling, his hands crossed under his belly as if he had to hold it up. The mothers asked each other where they could get carrots and broccoli, iceberg lettuce, apples, peaches, or pears.

"At the conclusion of the meeting," the *Americano* said, "you will all receive a sack full of groceries with samples from the major food groups." He flipped the chart closed and moved his chair near the window, amid the hum of women asking one another what he'd just said.

The next expert uncovered another easel on which there was a picture of a big black bug. A child screamed, and a woman got the hiccups.

"This," the expert said scratching the top of his head, "is the magnified image of a head louse."

Following him, another *Americano* who spoke good Spanish discussed intestinal parasites. He told all the mothers to boil their water several times and to wash their hands frequently.

"Children love to put their hands in their mouths," he said, making it sound like fun, "but each time they do, they run the risk of infection."

He flipped the chart to show an enlargement of a dirty hand, the tips of the fingernails encrusted with dirt.

"Ugh! That's disgusting!" whispered Mami to the woman next to her. I curled my fingers inside my palms.

"When children play outside," the expert continued, "their hands pick up dirt, and with it, hundreds of microscopic parasites that enter their bodies through their mouths to live and thrive in their intestinal tract."

He flipped the chart again. A long flat snake curled from the corner at the top of the chart to the opposite corner at the bottom. Mami shivered and rubbed her arms to keep the goose bumps down.

"This," the *Americano* said, "is a tapeworm, and it is not uncommon in this part of the world."

Mami had joked many times that the reason I was so skinny was that I had a *solitaria*, a tapeworm, in my belly. But I don't think she ever knew what a tapeworm looked like, nor did I. I imagined something like the earthworms that crawled out of the ground when it rained, but never anything so ugly as the snake on the chart, its flat body like a deck of cards strung together.

"Tapeworms," the expert continued, "can reach lengths of nine feet." I rubbed my belly, trying to imagine how long nine feet was and whether I had that much room in me. Just thinking about it made my insides itchy.

When they finished their speeches, the experts had all the mothers line up and come to the side of the room, where each was given samples according to the number of people in their household. Mami got two sacks of groceries, so Delsa had to carry Edna all the way home while I dragged one of the bags full of cans, jars, and bright cartons.

At home Mami gave each of us a toothbrush and told us we were to clean our teeth every morning and every evening. She set a tube of paste and a cup by the door, next to Papi's shaving things. Then she emptied the bags.

"I don't understand why they didn't just give us a sack of rice and a bag of beans. It would keep this family fed for a month."

She took out a five-pound tin of peanut butter, two boxes of corn-flakes, cans of fruit cocktail, peaches in heavy syrup, beets, and tuna fish, jars of grape jelly and pickles and put everything on a high shelf.

"We'll save this," she said, "so that we can eat like *Americanos cuando el hambre apriete*." She kept them there for a long time but took them down one by one so that, as she promised, we ate like Americans when hunger cramped our bellies.

∽ 9 ∽

WAGING PEACE/LOVE
AS REVOLUTION

The poems and stories in this part manifest multiple visions of a possible future, one centered on and emerging from love, compassion, and peace. They demonstrate the need for writers not solely to witness social injustice but also to imagine, to write at the edge, to transport their images of an alternative world. Social action writers are at the heart of this creation.

With war and violence pandemic and in multiple forms, urgency finds the words. Thich Nhat Hanh, in his poem "Call Me By My True Names," envisions a way to peace through compassion and through modeling nonviolent conflict resolution. "To educate people for peace, we can use words or we can speak with our lives. . . . We can be peace ourselves, and we can make peace with our friends and even with our so-called enemies."

Sonia Sanchez demonstrates the integration of compassion and imagination in her poem as prayer, "Litany," in which she calls the names of her heroes and gathers them to her and to her audience in order to honor their work for justice in the world. She read this poem to a jazz beat and with the African "click," on opening night at the inaugural Split This Rock gathering of activist poets in Washington, D.C., in March 2008. It is published here for the first time. Frances Payne Adler, in her poem "Matriot," creates a new definition of national defense, one of compassion that guarantees health, education, and shelter for everyone as a basic right. She is working on getting the word into the dictionary.

Linda Lopez, in her poem "Luna Llena," transforms the great loss of a brother in Iraq, into a testimony of great love. Elliot Ruchowitz-Roberts's poem "Revolution," written for the marriage of lesbian friends, celebrates "love as revolution's heart," where "Love's gravity sweeps me/Into this revolution so we become brother and sisters." Langston Hughes's story "Thank you, M'am" demonstrates compassion as an alternative way to respond to an act of violence. Becky Birtha, in her story "Route 23: 10th and Bigler to Bethlehem Pike," witnesses a mother's fierce love for her children and her act of revolution to keep them warm.

Sharon Olds, in "Late Poem to My Father," reaches past anger and toward healing in understanding an abusive father. "Suddenly I thought of you/as a child in that house. . . ." And Palestinian-American poet Naomi Shihab Nye witnesses the surreality of war in "Lunch in Nablus City Park," a poem about the Palestinian-Israeli war. "What makes a man with a gun seem bigger/than a man with almonds?" she asks. "How can there be war/and the next day eating. . . ." And it is her second poem, "Kindness," that walks the map of "the deepest thing inside."

William Stafford, a poet beloved for his kindness and for his commitment as a conscientious objector, pays honor to peace "At the Un-National Monument along the Canadian Border," "where the battle did not happen." South African poet Dennis Brutus, who has seen and lived so much as an activist against apartheid and as a prisoner at Robben Island, reflects on the current times and calls for the courage to create peace in his poem "shadow-patterns of leaves." In his poem "Allegory," physician and poet Rafael Campo writes about the day when healing comes, when "AIDS was cured," creating a surreal lens through which to envision the past and possible future.

Adrienne Rich, in an excerpt of her essay, "Arts of the Possible," examines the place of poetry and writing in the movement for social change. She writes of her concerns as a poet and as a citizen in a time of "increasingly cruel legislation" (p. 157) and "capitalism's drive to disenfranchise and dehumanize." In her "belief that language can be a vital instrument in combating unreality and lies," and that language is a "liberatory current," Rich calls on writers to come together in a collective "creative space, a liberatory political movement" (p. 153). "We're not simply trapped in the present," she says. "We're living through a certain part of history that needs us to live it and make it and write it. . . . We have to keep on asking the questions . . . the ones beginning *Why . . . ? What if . . . ? . . .* They are the imagination's questions."

Thank You, M'am

Langston Hughes

She was a large woman with a large purse that had everything in it but a hammer and nails. It had a long strap, and she carried it slung across her shoulder. It was about eleven o'clock at night, dark, and she was walking alone, when a boy ran up behind her and tried to snatch her purse. The strap broke with the sudden single tug the boy gave it from behind. But the boy's weight and the weight of the purse combined caused him to lose his balance. Instead of taking off full blast as he had hoped, the boy fell on his back on the sidewalk and his legs flew up. The large woman simply turned around and kicked him right square in his blue-jeaned sitter. Then she reached down, picked the boy up by his shirt front, and shook him until his teeth rattled.

After that the woman said, "Pick up my pocketbook, boy, and give it here."

She still held him tightly. But she bent down enough to permit him to stoop and pick up her purse. Then she said, "Now ain't you ashamed of yourself?"

Firmly gripped by his shirt front, the boy said, "Yes'm."

The woman said, "What did you want to do it for?"

The boy said, "I didn't aim to."

She said, "You a lie!"

By that time two or three people passed, stopped, turned to look, and some stood watching.

"If I turn you loose, will you run?" asked the woman.

"Yes'm," said the boy.

"Then I won't turn you loose," said the woman. She did not release him.

"Lady, I'm sorry," whispered the boy.

"Um-hum! Your face is dirty. I got a great mind to wash your face for you. Ain't you got nobody home to tell you to wash your face?"

"No'm," said the boy.

"Then it will get washed this evening," said the large woman, starting up the street, dragging the frightened boy behind her.

He looked as if he were fourteen or fifteen, frail and willow-wild, in tennis shoes and blue jeans.

The woman said, "You ought to be my son. I would teach you right from wrong. Least I can do right now is to wash your face. Are you hungry?"

"No'm," said the being-dragged boy. "I just want you to turn me loose."

"Was I bothering *you* when I turned that corner?" asked the woman.

"No'm."

"But you put yourself in contact with *me*," said the woman. "If you think that that contact is not going to last awhile, you got another thought coming. When I get through with you, sir, you are going to remember Mrs. Luella Bates Washington Jones."

Sweat popped out on the boy's face and he began to struggle. Mrs. Jones stopped, jerked him around in front of her, put a half nelson about his neck, and continued to drag him up the street. When she got to her door, she dragged the boy inside, down a hall, and into a large kitchenette-furnished room at the rear of the house. She switched on the light and left the door open. The boy could hear other roomers laughing and talking in the large house. Some of their doors were open, too, so he knew he and the woman were not alone. The woman still had him by the neck in the middle of her room.

She said, "What is your name?"

"Roger," answered the boy.

"Then, Roger, you go to that sink and wash your face," said the woman, whereupon she turned him loose—at last. Roger looked at the door— looked at the woman—looked at the door—*and went to the sink.*

"Let the water run until it gets warm," she said. "Here's a clean towel."

"You gonna take me to jail?" asked the boy, bending over the sink.

"Not with that face, I would not take you nowhere," said the woman. "Here I am trying to get home to cook me a bite to eat, and you snatch my pocketbook! Maybe you ain't been to your supper either, late as it be. Have you?"

"There's nobody home at my house," said the boy.

"Then we'll eat," said the woman. "I believe you're hungry—or been hungry—to try to snatch my pocketbook!"

"I want a pair of blue suede shoes," said the boy.

"Well, you didn't have to snatch *my* pocketbook to get some suede shoes," said Mrs. Luella Bates Washington Jones. "You could of asked me."

"M'am?"

The water dripping from his face, the boy looked at her. There was a long pause. A very long pause. After he had dried his face, and not knowing what else to do, dried it again, the boy turned around, wondering what next. The door was open. He could make a dash for it down the hall. He could run, run, run, *run!*

The woman was sitting on the daybed. After a while she said, "I were young once and I wanted things I could not get."

There was another long pause. The boy's mouth opened. Then he frowned, not knowing he frowned.

The woman said, "Um-hum! You thought I was going to say *but*, didn't you? You thought I was going to say, *but I didn't snatch people's pocketbooks*. Well, I wasn't going to say that." Pause. Silence. "I have done things, too, which I would not tell you, son—neither tell God, if He didn't already know. Everybody's got something in common. So you set down while I fix us something to eat. You might run that comb through your hair so you will look presentable."

In another corner of the room behind a screen was a gas plate and an icebox. Mrs. Jones got up and went behind the screen. The woman did not watch the boy to see if he was going to run now, nor did she watch her purse, which she left behind her on the daybed. But the boy took care to sit on the far side of the room, away from the purse, where he thought she could easily see him out of the corner of her eye if she wanted to. He did not trust the woman *not* to trust him. And he did not want to be mistrusted now.

"Do you need somebody to go to the store," asked the boy, "maybe to get some milk or something?"

"Don't believe I do," said the woman, "unless you just want sweet milk yourself. I was going to make cocoa out of this canned milk I got here."

"That will be fine," said the boy.

She heated some lima beans and ham she had in the icebox, made the cocoa, and set the table. The woman did not ask the boy anything about where he lived, or his folks, or anything else that would embarrass him. Instead, as they ate, she told him about her job in a hotel beauty shop that stayed open late, what the work was like, and how all kinds of women came in and out, blonds, redheads, and Spanish. Then she cut him a half of her ten-cent cake.

"Eat some more, son," she said.

When they were finished eating, she got up and said, "Now here, take this ten dollars and buy yourself some blue suede shoes. And next time, do not make the mistake of latching onto *my* pocketbook *nor nobody else's*—because shoes got by devilish ways will burn your feet. I got to get my rest now. But from here on in, son, I hope you will behave yourself."

She led him down the hall to the front door and opened it. "Good night! Behave yourself boy!" she said, looking out into the street as he went down the steps.

The boy wanted to say something other than, "Thank you, M'am," to Mrs. Luella Bates Washington Jones, but although his lips moved, he couldn't even say that as he turned at the foot of the barren stoop and looked up at the large woman in the door. Then she shut the door.

Call Me by My True Names

Thich Nhat Hanh

In 1976, I wrote a poem about a twelve-year-old girl, one of the boat people crossing the Gulf of Siam, who was raped by a sea pirate and threw herself into the sea; the pirate, who was born in a remote village along the coast in Thailand; and me. I was not on the boat—in fact, I was thousands of miles away—but because I was mindful, I knew what was going on in the Gulf.

I was angry when I received the news of her death, but I learned after meditating for several hours that I could not just take sides against the pirate. I saw that if I had been born in his village and brought up under the same conditions, I would be exactly like him. Taking sides is too easy. Out of my suffering, I wrote this poem, entitled "Please Call Me by My True Names." I have many names, and when you call me by any of them, I have to say, "Yes."

> Don't say that I will depart tomorrow—
> even today I am still arriving.
>
> Look deeply: every second I am arriving
> to be a bud on a spring branch,
> to be a tiny bird, with still fragile wings,
> learning to sing in my new nest,
> to be a caterpillar in the heart of a flower,
> to be a jewel hiding itself in a stone.
>
> I am still arriving, in order to laugh and to cry,
> in order to fear and to hope,
> the rhythm of my heart is the birth and death
> of every living creature.

I am a mayfly metamorphosing
on the surface of the river.
And I am the bird,
that swoops down to swallow the mayfly.

I am a frog swimming happily
in the clear water of a pond,
and I am the grass-snake
that silently feeds itself on the frog.

I am the child in Uganda, all skin and bones,
my legs as thin as bamboo sticks.
And I am the arms merchant,
selling deadly weapons to Uganda.

I am the twelve-year-old girl,
refugee on a small boat,
who throws herself into the ocean
after being raped by a sea pirate.
And I am the pirate,
my heart not yet capable
of seeing and loving.

I am a member of the politburo,
with plenty of power in my hands,
and I am the man who has to pay
his "debt of blood" to my people,
dying slowly in a forced-labor camp.

My joy is like spring, so warm
that it makes flowers bloom all over the Earth.
My pain is like a river of tears,
so vast that it fills all four oceans.

Please call me by my true names,
so I can hear all my cries and laughter at once,
so I can see that my joy and pain are one.

Please call me by my true names,
so I can wake up
and open the door of my heart,
the door of compassion.

We think we need an enemy. Governments work hard to get us to be afraid and to hate so we will rally behind them. If we do not have a real enemy, they will invent one in order to mobilize us. Recently I went to Russia with some American and European friends, and we found that the Russian people are wonderful. For so many years the American government told their people that Russia was "an evil empire."

It is not correct to believe that the world's situation is in the hands of the government and that if the President would only have the correct policies, there would be peace. Our daily lives have the most to do with the situation of the world. If we can change our daily lives, we can change our governments and we can change the world. Our presidents and our governments are us. They reflect our lifestyle and our way of thinking. The way we hold a cup of tea, pick up a newspaper, and even use toilet paper have to do with peace.

As a novice in a Buddhist monastery, I was taught to be aware of each thing I did throughout the day, and for more than fifty years, I have been practicing this. When I started, I thought this kind of practice was only for beginners, that advanced people did more important things, but now I know that the practice of mindfulness is for everyone. Meditation is to see into our own nature and wake up. If we are not aware of what is going on in ourselves and in the world, how can we see into our own nature and wake up? Are we really awake when we drink our tea, read our newspaper, or use the toilet?

Our society makes it difficult for us to be awake. There are so many distractions. We know that 40,000 children in the Third World die of hunger every day, but we keep forgetting. Our society makes us forgetful. That is why we need practice to help us be mindful. I know a number of friends who refrain from eating dinner two times each week in order to remember the situation in the Third World.

One day I asked a young Vietnamese refugee who was eating a bowl of rice whether children in his country eat rice of such high quality. He said no, because he knows the situation. He experienced hunger in Vietnam—there were times when he ate only dried potatoes, while he longed for a bowl of rice. In France, he has been eating rice for a year, and he is already beginning to forget. But when I asked him, he remembered. I could not ask the same question to a French or American child, because they have not had the experience of hunger. It is difficult for people in the West to understand the situation in the Third World. It seems to have nothing to do with their situation. I told the Vietnamese boy that the rice he was eating in France came from Thailand, and that most Thai children do not have rice of such high quality, because the best rice is set aside for export to Japan and the West in exchange for foreign currency.

In Vietnam we have a delicious banana called *chuôi già*, but the children and adults in Vietnam do not have the right to eat these bananas because they are all for export. In return, Vietnam gets guns in order to kill ourselves and our brothers. Some of us practice this exercise of mindfulness: We sponsor a child in the Third World and get news from him or her, thus keeping in touch with the reality outside. We try many ways to be awake, but our society still keeps us forgetful. Meditation is to help us remember.

There are other ways to nourish awareness. One thirteen-year-old Dutch boy visited our retreat center and joined us for a silent lunch. It was the first time he had eaten in silence, and he was embarrassed. Afterwards, I asked him if he had felt uncomfortable, and he said yes. I explained that the reason we eat in silence is to be in touch with the food and the presence of each other. If we talk a lot, we cannot enjoy these things. I asked him if there was some time when he turned off the TV in order to enjoy his dinner more, and he said yes. Later in the day, I invited him to join us for another silent meal, and he enjoyed it very much. Society bombards us with so many noises that we have lost our taste for silence. Every time we have a few minutes, we turn on the TV or make a phone call. We do not know how to be ourselves without something to distract us. So, the first thing we need to do is to return to ourselves and reorganize our daily lives so that we are not just victims of society and other people.

To educate people for peace, we can use words or we can speak with our lives. If we are not peaceful, if we are not feeling well in our skin, we cannot demonstrate real peace, and we cannot raise our children well either. To take good care of our children means to take good care of ourselves, to be aware of our situation. Please sit down with your child and, together, contemplate the little flowers that grow among the grasses. Breathing in and out, smiling together—that is real peace education. When we can learn to appreciate these small, beautiful things, we will not have to search for anything else. We can be peace ourselves, and we can make peace with our friends and even with our so-called enemies.

Litany

Sonia Sanchez

I call on living and ago resisters:

Rosa Parks, Jo Ann Gibson Robinson, Octavia Butler, John Lewis (click), Dorothy Cotton, Charlayne Hunter-Gault, John Conyers, Gloria Richardson, June Jordan (click), Cynthia McKinney, Mary McLeod Bethune, A. Philip Randolph, Herbert and Fay Aptheker, Adam Clayton Powell, Geronimo (click), Geronimo Pratt (click), Thelonious Monk (click, click), Marian Wright Edelman, Toni Cade Bambara, Toni Morrison, Kay Boyle, Barbara Lee, Barbara Deming, Anne Braden, Maria Stewart, Charles Houston, William Hastings, Shirley Chisholm, Angela Davis (click), Mary Church Terrell, Sojourner Truth, Katherine Dunham, Bill and Camille Cosby, Elizabeth Catlett (click), Rev. Calvin Butts, Maurice Bishop, Nat Turner, Medgar Evers, Maya Angelou, Oprah Winfrey, Cornell West, Tavis Smiley, John Coltrane (click), Shirley Graham Du Bois, W.E.B. Du Bois, Jean Hutson, Mr. Michaux, Richard Moore, C.L.R. James, Gandhi, Grace and James Boggs, Nicolás Guillén, Michel and Geneviève Fabre, Beverly and Walter Lomax, Mumia, Pablo Neruda, Gwendolyn Brooks, Amina and Amiri Baraka, Askia Toure, Lucille Clifton, The Last Poets, Bessie Smith (click), Haki Madhubuti, Dorothy Day, Fidel, Tupac, Rakim, Assata, Talib Kweli, The Roots, Yuri Kochiyama (click), Billie Holiday, Margaret Tayor-Burroughs, Mos Def, Dead Prez, Common, Ida Wells-Barnett, Betty Carter, Mfundi Ella Baker (click), Father Paul Washington, Dave Richardson, Dwight Evans, Marian Taşcău, Cherelle Parker, Martín Espada, Myrlie Evers-Williams, Dr. Dorothy Height, Henry Hampton, Bob Marley (click), the Rosenbergs, Howard Zinn, Kenneth Clark, Sonny Rollins, Asa Hilliard, Zaid Shakur, Lorraine Hansberry, Zora Neale Hurston, Louise Meriwether, Dennis Brutus, Tom Joyner, Nikki Giovanni, Kathleen Cleaver, Simon Ortiz, Jayne Cortez, Dolores Huerta, Chris Hani, Willie Kgositsile, Oliver Tambo, Aaron McGruder, Miles Davis, César Chávez, Kimiko Hahn,

Odetta (click), Sweet Honey in the Rock, Bernice Reagon, Vinie Burrows, Fannie Lou Hamer, Victoria Gray, Annie Devine, Walter Rodney (click), Thurgood Marshall, Charles Caldwell, Afeni Shakur-Davis, Audre Lorde, John Bracey, Sitting Bull, Lolita Lebrón, Byllye Avery, Luisa Moreno, José Martí, Diop, Vito Marcantonio, David Walker, Margaret Walker, Alice Walker, Maxine Greene, Gloria Steinem, Nkrumah, Robert Sobukwe, Dinah Washington, Abbey Lincoln, Oscar Brown, Jr., Ray Charles, William Wills Brown, Sterling Brown, John Brown (click), Bertolt Brecht, Dada and Mama Sisulu, Martin Delaney, Louis Burnham, Nelson Mandela, Winnie Mandela, Viola Plummer, KRS-One, Max Roach, Ella Fitzgerald, Sarah Vaughn, Dr. T.R.M. Howard (click), Charlene Mitchell, Lauryn Hill, Erykah Badu, Ursula Rucker, Cecil Gray, Toshi Reagon, Julian Bond, Charlie Cobb, Harry Belafonte, Danny Glover, Duke Ellington, Abraham Heschel, Ruby Doris, Mickey, James and Andy, Emmett Till, Bob Marley, Bessie Head, Frantz Fanon, Walter Mosley, Michael Weaver, Linton Kwesi Johnson, St. Clair Bourne, Ethel Hedgeman Lyle, Archbishop Tutu, John Henrik Clarke, Bob Moses, John Killens, Queen Mother Moore (click), Septima Clark, Es'kia Mphahlele, Bobby Sands, Patrick Hill, James Baldwin, Grace Paley, Allen Ginsberg, Paul Blackburn, Anne Waldman, Barbara Ann Teer, Eugene Redmond, George Lamming, John Hope Franklin, Sekou Sundiata, Ruby Dee, Ossie Davis, Art Tatum (click), Pam Africa, Ramona Africa, Langston Hughes, Chinua Achebe, Esther and Jim Jackson, Benjamin Davis, William Patterson, Toussaint, Dessalines, Sandino (click), Harriet Tubman, Vincent and Rosemary Harding, Monroe Trotter, Edward Said, Charlie Parker, Dick Gregory, Dizzy Gillespie, Marcus Garvey (click), Paul Robeson (click), Albert Einstein (click), Lumumba, Kwame Ture, Chuck D., Frederick Douglass, Coretta Scott King, Johnnetta Cole, Cabral, Richard Pryor, Sun Ra, Chairman Mao, Nina Simone, Joy Harjo, Njeri and Ngũgĩ wa Thiong'o, Adrienne Rich, Margaret Randall, Stephen Biko, Herman Ferguson, Betty Shabazz, Assata Shakur, Julia Wright, Richard Wright, Bishop Cámara, Leonard Peltier, Bayard Rustin, Grannies for Peace, Howard Thurman, Walt Whitman, Thich Nhat Hanh, Jose Martí, Michelle Obama, Barack Obama, Martin Luther King, Malcolm (click)(click)(click).

Sonia Sanchez read this poem, to a jazz beat and with the African "click," on opening night at the inaugural Split This Rock gathering of activist poets in Washington, D.C., March 2008.

Matriot

Frances Payne Adler

Helen Vandevere, born 1904

Matriot (ma´-tri–at) *noun* 1. One who loves his or her country.
2. One who loves and protects the people of his or her country.
3. One who perceives national defense as health, education, and
shelter for all people in his or her country, and the world.
(FPA, 1991)

There's not much that's important at my age
except making the world a better place.
What would *I* do?
I say we damn well better
get out on the streets again.
Everyone has to put their hand to the wheel
and get out and get off their butt
like in the sixties. We had compassion then,
and we've lost it. It breaks my heart.
I've lived through two depressions,
two of them. Everyone at that time
was just sick about the way things were,
just like now, only it's worse now.
I see things falling apart—
People, living on the streets.
Children, beaten in their homes.
Sick people without health care.
Imagine this, in a country
that spends so much on the war machine.

I'd spend the money on health instead.
I'd see that children are born healthy
and make sure they stayed that way.
All children no matter what age.
I'd clean the air, the water. I'd take away
all that polluting shit they put on vegetables.
I'd promote the use of sun, sea, and wind
for natural energy. I'd save the forests,
especially the redwoods. I'd ban firearms.
I'd take away every nuclear device man to man.
No more wars, ever. *Now* we're talking health.
How are we going to pay for all this?
No one ever says we don't have enough
money to go to war. No one ever says
we don't have money for national defense.
This is national defense.

1992

Luna Llena

Linda Lopez

On a full moon, slowly breathing,
I dreamt my brother left Iraq,
deserted the dunes
the way his own father deserted him,
fled with the moon and
vowed through tears, I forgive you father.

On a full moon, ojos cerrados.
I dreamt my brother left Iraq.
Howling his sanity,
he followed ancestral voices in the wind,
and absorbed each hissing voice
hoping they emptied his full stomach
to feed a starving Iraqi mouth.

On a full moon, bleeding heart,
I dreamt my brother was a killer.
Execution-style was his favorite,
killing in my name every time he shot.
Feeling the soft face of his son, In Lak Ech,
he vowed through the same tears of his father,
forgive me, mijo, I killed tonight.

On a full moon, boca abierta, hand in heart,
I dreamt I told my brother,
Hermano,
Peace to the ground you walk on,
Peace to your fearless heart,
Peace to the fire in your voice,
Peace to the next time la luna llena rises,
who so gently pieces us together.

In Lak Ech: Nahuatl translation for "you are a reflection of me."

Revolution

Elliot Ruchowitz-Roberts

for Mickey and Kathy
in celebration of your marriage on February 16, 2004

I had thought revolution's core was rage and hatred,
Robed in ideals pristine and unattainable, like freedom,
Or dictatorship of the proletariat, or all power to the people, but
       never,
Until now, have I known love as revolution's heart,
And such joy. Yours is not a revolt but a revolving,
An axial turning, the way the earth revolves on its axis;
An orbital turning, earth revolving around sun
And moon around earth. Love's gravity sweeps me
Into this revolution so we have become brother and sisters.
Sisters, you are writing and rewriting history, for is not love,
Hidden and much maligned, at the heart of all revolution?
Your love turns our world on its axis; now we can
See you, bathed in light, entire—no dark side of the moon
Any longer. And so, dear sisters, here's to love that makes
       history;
To revolutions that bring such joy to our hearts;
To acts that dispel darkness; to revolving planets and moons
And all your act has set in motion: a spinning
In my own heart and these whirling words, testament
To this tangible freedom of spirit, this dictatorship of the heart,
This power to all people who open themselves to love.

Late Poem to My Father

Sharon Olds

Suddenly I thought of you
as a child in that house, the unlit rooms
and the hot fireplace with the man in front of it,
silent. You moved through the heavy air
in your physical beauty, a boy of seven,
helpless, smart, there were things the man
did near you, and he was your father,
the mold by which you were made. Down in the
cellar, the barrels of sweet apples,
picked at their peak from the tree, rotted and
rotted, and past the cellar door
the creek ran and ran, and something was
not given to you, or something was
taken from you that you were born with, so that
even at 30 and 40 you set the
oily medicine to your lips
every night, the poison to help you
drop down unconscious. I always thought the
point was what you did to us
as a grown man, but then I remembered that
child being formed in front of the fire, the
tiny bones inside his soul
twisted in greenstick fractures, the small
tendons that hold the heart in place
snapped. And what they did to you
you did not do to me. When I love you now,
I like to think I am giving my love
directly to that boy in the fiery room,
as if it could reach him in time.

Lunch in Nablus City Park

Naomi Shihab Nye

When you lunch in a town which has recently known war
under a calm slate sky mirroring none of it,
certain words feel impossible in the mouth.
Casualty: too casual, it must be changed.
A short man stacks mounds of pita bread
on each end of the table, muttering
something about more to come.
Plump birds landing on park benches
surely had their eyes closed recently,
must have seen nothing of weapons or blockades.
When the woman across from you whispers
I don't think we can take it anymore
and you say there are people praying for her
in the mountains of Himalaya and she says
Lady, it is not enough, then what?

A plate of cigar-shaped meatballs, dish of tomato,
friends dipping bread—
I will not marry till there is true love, says one,
throwing back her cascade of perfumed hair.
He says the University of Texas seems remote to him
as Mars, and last month he stayed in his house
for 26 days. He will not leave, he refuses to leave.
In the market they are selling
men's shoes with air vents, a beggar displays
the giant scab of leg he must drag from alley to alley,
and students gather to discuss what constitutes
genuine protest.

In summers, this cafe is full.
Today only our table sends laughter into the trees.
What cannot be answered checkers the tablecloth
between the squares of white and red.
Where do the souls of hills hide
when there is shooting in the valleys?
What makes a man with a gun seem bigger
than a man with almonds? How can there be war
and the next day eating, a man stacking plates
on the curl of his arm, a table of people
toasting one another in languages of grace:
For you who came so far;
For you who held out, wearing a black scarf
to signify grief;
For you who believe true love can find you
amidst this atlas of tears linking one town
to its own memory of mortar,
when it was still a dream to be built
and people moved here, believing,
and someone with sky and birds in his heart
said this would be a good place for a park.

Kindness

Naomi Shihab Nye

Before you know what kindness really is
you must lose things,
feel the future dissolve in a moment
like salt in a weakened broth.
What you held in your hand,
what you counted and carefully saved,
all this must go so you know
how desolate the landscape can be
between the regions of kindness.
How you ride and ride
thinking the bus will never stop,
the passengers eating maize and chicken
will stare out the window forever.

Before you learn the tender gravity of kindness,
you must travel where the Indian in a white poncho
lies dead by the side of the road.
You must see how this could be you,
how he too was someone
who journeyed through the night with plans
and the simple breath that kept him alive.

Before you know kindness as the deepest thing inside,
you must know sorrow as the other deepest thing.
You must wake up with sorrow.
You must speak to it till your voice
catches the thread of all sorrows
and you see the size of the cloth.

Then it is only kindness that makes any sense anymore,
only kindness that ties your shoes
and sends you out into the day to mail letters and
    purchase bread,
only kindness that raises its head
from the crowd of the world to say
It is I you have been looking for,
and then goes with you everywhere
like a shadow or a friend.

Colombia

At the Un-National Monument along the Canadian Border

William Stafford

This is the field where the battle did not happen,
where the unknown soldier did not die.
This is the field where grass joined hands,
where no monument stands,
and the only heroic thing is the sky.

Birds fly here without any sound,
unfolding their wings across the open.
No people killed—or were killed—on this ground
hallowed by neglect and an air so tame
that people celebrate it by forgetting its name.

shadow-patterns of leaves

Dennis Brutus

shadow-patterns of leaves
on a window-shade
moving gently in a breeze

suddenly I am seized with sadness—
perhaps for the first time—
this is the world I must leave ere long

this is the loveliness I must lose

oh, craven, will you not act?
save, I beg you, our world,
find courage to challenge terror

6/24/08; durban s a

Allegory

Rafael Campo

Outside somewhere, beneath an atmosphere
So pure and new each breath is musical
And silent, mouth-watering, without taste,
So full of butterflies one can't imagine
Because it hurts to be so free, out there

There was a hospital where AIDS was cured
With Chinese cucumbers and royal jelly,
With herbal medicines, vaccines, colostrum.
I went there in a submarine, through space
It seemed, and I was armed with nuclear

ICBMs. I read *The New York Times*,
That's how relaxed and skeptical I was;
I sat upon the floor, my back against
The gleaming missiles. Strangely, no one else
But me was on the submarine, except

The President, whom I'd confined beneath
The lowest deck, inside somewhere where air
Was scarce and hardly breathable. One can't
Imagine what it's like to see a world
Like theirs from such a distance for the first

Time: God, was it beautiful, butterflies
And silent musical wind, the hospital
Where no one paid. I tried to give them small
Pox, missiles, blankets; they looked at me
Like I was crazy, and they asked me why

The President had been incarcerated.
There's no explaining of morality
To savages, I thought. And though it hurt
To leave, to conquer them and take with me
The royal jelly and colostrum, when I aimed

My missiles at their hospital I felt
Much better. Munching on a cucumber,
The light of the explosion brightening
My face, I couldn't help the tears, I was
So sad and happy, all at once, again.

Route 23

10th and Bigler to Bethlehem Pike

Becky Birtha

Ain't no reason for you to be gaping at me. I pay my taxes, just like everybody else. And it just don't make no sense. The mayor and all them city council men sitting up in all them little offices over in City Hall, ain't never been cold in they life. And me and my little ones freezing to death up on Thirteenth Street.

Last time I was down to City Hall to try and talk to one of them men, heat just pouring out the radiator in that office. I had to yell at Kamitra and Junie not to touch it, scared they was gonna burn theyself. Man I'm talking to done took off his jacket and drape it over the back of his chair. Wiping his forehead off with his hanky, talking bout, "No, Miz Moses, we can't do nothing for you. Not a thing. Not as long as you living in a privately-own residence and you not in the public housing. . . ."

I'm thinking how they only use them offices in the day time. Ain't nobody in em at night. And my babies is sleeping in the kitchen, ever since the oil run out two weeks ago and they ain't deliver no more. Landlord claim he outta town.

Hasan, my baby here, he don't hardly even know what warm is. He so little he can't remember last summer. All the others done had colds all winter. Noses ain't stopped running since last October. And Kleenex just one more thing I can't afford to buy em. Scuse me a minute.

—I know, Junie. I see it. Yeah, I see the swings. Can't get off and play today. Too cold out there. Maybe so, honey. Maybe tomorrow, if the sun come out. Lamont, let your sister have a turn to sit by the window now.—

Don't you be thinking I'm homeless, cause I ain't. You ever see a bag lady with all these kids? These here shopping bags is just a temporary measure. Like I said, I live up on Thirteenth Street. Seventeen hundred block. North. Top floor. You don't believe me you go look. My name on the mailbox: Leona Mae Moses. And all the rest of the stuff belong to us is right where we left it. The kids is got other clothes, and we got beds and dishes and all the same stuff you got in your house. We ain't planning to make this no permanent way of life. Just till this cold spell break.

—Cherise, honey, would you get the baby bottle out that bag you got up there? Right next to that box of Pampers. And you and Lamont gonna have to get off and get some more milk. Next time we come up to the A & P. Junie, get your hands away from that buzzer. We ain't there yet. We got to go all the way up to Chestnut Hill, and then turn around and come back down. Anyway, it's Kamitra turn to ring the bell this time.—

Ain't nobody got no call to stare at me like I'm some kinda freak. My kids got the same rights as other people kids. They got a right to spend the night someplace warm and dry. Got a right to get some sleep at night. Last night, along about eleven o'clock, when the man on the radio say the temperature gone down to fifteen below, he didn't have to tell me nothing. The pipes is froze, and the wind lifting the curtains right up at the windows in my kitchen. And my little girl crying, "Mama, I'm cold." Air so icy I can see a little cloud come out her mouth, every time she cry.

—Kamitra, sugar, don't sing so loud. Mama trying to talk. Anyway, other people on here besides us. They don't want to be bother listen to all that racket.—

You got kids? Well, think a minute what you would do if you was in my place. Last night I'm trying so hard to think what to do, feel like my head gonna split wide open. Nobody in my building ain't got no more heat than we do. I don't know no neighbors got space enough for all of us. They be sleep anyway. All my people still down south.

Kamitra crying done waked up the others, too. Then all of em crying they cold. I ain't crazy yet, but I like to went crazy last night trying to think what I'm gonna do. I just kept thinking theys got to be some place in this great big city that I can carry these children to, where it's warm, where it stay warm, even in the middle of the night. And then it come to me.

"Mama, where we going?" the kids is all asking. I just tell em to hush and go get they blankets and towels and sweaters and stuff. Comb everybody hair and dress em real warm. Start packing up some food to last us for a couple days. "Mama, what we gonna do? Where we taking all this stuff?" And Junie, he tickle me. Say, "Mama, we can't go no place. It's dark outside."

I just hush em all up and hustle em down to the corner. Little ones start crying again, cause even with all them layers on, they ain't warm enough for no fifteen below. Lamont done lost his gloves last week, and Cherise just got one a my scarf wrap around her head, cause it ain't enough hats to go round. Ain't a one of em got boots. Cherise still asking me where we going, while we standing at the corner, waiting. I tell em, "Mama got a surprise for you all. We taking a trip. We going on a nice, long ride."

—Get outta that bag, Kamitra. You can't have no more crackers. Mama gonna fix you some tuna fish for supper, pretty soon. What's the matter Junie? You gotta pee? You sure? Well then, sit still. Lamont, next time we come up to our corner, I want you to take him in to the bathroom, anyway. It don't hurt to try.—

I guess that explain howcome we here. We intend to stay here, too, right where we at, up till the weather break. Or the oil come. Whatever happen first. It ain't no laws against it. I pay my taxes to keep these things running, just like everybody else. And I done paid our fare. The ones under six rides for free, just like the sign say. I got enough quarters here to last us a long time.

My kids is clean—all got washed up at the library just this morning. And look how nice and well-behave they is. I ain't got nothing to be ashamed of.

I hope your curiosity satisfied, cause I really ain't got no more to say. This car big enough for all of us. You better find something else to gawk at. Better look on out the window, make sure you ain't miss your stop.

—Cherise, sugar, we at the end of the line again. Go up there and put these quarters in the man box. No, Junie. This trolley gonna keep running all night long. Time just come for the man to turn the thing around. We ain't getting off. This trip ain't over yet.

from Arts of the Possible

Adrienne Rich

Against a background and foreground of crisis, of technology dazzling in means and maniacally violent in substance, among declarations of resignation and predictions of social chaos, I have from time to time—I know I'm not alone in this—felt almost unbearable foreboding, a terrifying loss of gravity, and furious grief. I'm a writer in a country where native-born fascistic tendencies, allied to the practices of "free" marketing, have been trying to eviscerate language of meaning. I have often felt doubly cut off: that I cannot effectively be heard, and that those voices I need most to hear are being cut off from me. Any writer has necessary questions as to whether her words deserve to stand, whether his are worth reading. But it's also been a question, for me, of feeling that almost everything that has fertilized and sustained my work is in danger. I have known that this is, in fact, the very material I have to work with: it is not "in spite of the times" that I will write, but I will try to write, in both senses, *out of my time.*

(There is a 1973 painting by Dorothea Tanning in which the arm of the woman painter literally breaks through the canvas: we don't see the brush, we see the arm up to the wrist, and the gash in the material. That, viscerally, depicts what it means to me, to try to write *out of one's time.*)

I have stayed connected with activism and with people whose phoenix politics are reborn continually out of the nest charred by hostility and lying. I have talked long with other friends. I have searched for words—my own and those of other writers. I've been drawn to those writers, in so many world locations, who have felt the need to question the very activity their lives had been shaped around: to interrogate the value of the written word in the face of many kinds of danger, enormous human needs. I wasn't looking for easy reassurances but rather for evidence that others, in other societies, also had to struggle with that question.

Whatever her or his social identity, the writer is, by the nature of the act of writing, someone who strives for communication and connection, someone who searches, through language, to keep alive the conversation with what Octavio Paz has called "the lost community." Even if what's written feels like a note thrust into a bottle to be thrown into the sea. The Palestinian poet Mahmoud Darwish writes of the incapacity of poetry to find a linguistic equivalent to conditions such as the 1982 Israeli shelling of Beirut: *We are now not to describe, as much as we are to be described. We're being born totally, or else dying totally.* In his remarkable prose-meditation on that war, he also says, *Yet I want to break into song. . . . I want to find a language that transforms language itself into steel for the spirit—a language to use against these sparkling silver insects, these jets. I want to sing. I want a language that I can lean on and that can lean on me, that asks me to bear witness and that I can ask to bear witness, to what power there is in us to overcome this cosmic isolation.*

Darwish writes from the heart of a military massacre. The Caribbean-Canadian poet Dionne Brand writes from colonial diaspora: *I've had moments when the life of my people has been so overwhelming to bear that poetry seemed useless, and I cannot say that there is any moment when I do not think that now.* Yet finally, she admits, like Darwish: *Poetry is here, just here. Something wrestling with how we live, something dangerous, something honest.*

I've gone back many times to Eduardo Galeano's essay "In Defense of the Word," in which he says:

> I do not share the attitude of those writers who claim for themselves divine privileges not granted to ordinary mortals, nor of those who beat their breasts and rend their clothes as they clamor for public pardon for having lived a life devoted to serving a useless vocation. Neither so godly, nor so contemptible. . . .
>
> The prevailing social order perverts or annihilates the creative capacity of the immense majority of people and reduces the possibility of creation—an age-old response to human anguish and the certainty of death—to its professional exercise by a handful of specialists. How many "specialists" are we in Latin America? For whom do we write, whom do we reach? Where is our real public? (Let us mistrust applause. At times we are congratulated by those who consider us innocuous.)

To claim that literature on its own is going to change reality would be an act of madness or arrogance. It seems to me no less foolish to deny that it can aid in making this change.

Galeano's "defense" was written after his magazine, *Crisis*, was closed down by the Argentine government. As a writer in exile, he has continued to interrogate the place of the written word, of literature, in a political order that forbids literacy and creative expression to so many; that denies the value of literature as a vehicle for social change even as it fears its power. Like Nadine Gordimer in South Africa, he knows that censorship can assume many faces, from the shutting down of magazines and the banning of books by some writers, to the imprisonment and torture of others, to the structural censorship produced by utterly unequal educational opportunities and by restricted access to the means of distribution—both features of North American society that have become more and more pronounced over the past two decades.

I question the "free" market's devotion to freedom of expression. Let's bear in mind that when threats of violence came down against the publication and selling of Salman Rushdie's *Satanic Verses*, the chain bookstores took it off their shelves, while independent booksellers continued to stock it. The various small, independent presses in this country, which have had an integral relationship with the independent booksellers, are walking a difficult and risky edge as costs rise, support funding dwindles, and corporate distribution becomes more monolithic. The survival of a great diversity of books, and of work by writers far less internationally notable than Rushdie, depends on diverse interests having the means to make such books available.

It also means a non-elite but educated audience, a population who are literate, who read and talk to each other, who may be factory workers or bakers or bank tellers or paramedicals or plumbers or computer consultants or farmworkers, whose first language may be Croatian or Tagalog or Spanish or Vietnamese but who are given to critical thinking, who care about art, an intelligentsia beyond intellectual specialists.

I have encountered a bracingly hard self-questioning and self-criticism in politically embattled writers, along with their belief that language can be a vital instrument in combating unreality and lies. I have been grateful for their clarity, whether as to Latin America, South Africa, the Caribbean, North America, or the Middle East, about the systems that abuse and waste the majority of human lives. Overall, there is the conviction—and these are writers of poetry, fiction, travel, fantasy—that the writer's freedom to communicate can't be severed from universal public education and universal public access to the word.

Universal public education has two possible—and contradictory—missions. One is the development of a literate, articulate, and well-informed citizenry so that the democratic process can continue to evolve and the promise of radical equality can be brought closer to realization. The other is the perpetuation of a class system dividing an elite, nominally "gifted" few, tracked from an early age, from a very large underclass essentially to be written off as alienated from language and science, from poetry and politics, from history and hope, an underclass to be funneled—whatever its dreams and hopes—toward low-wage temporary jobs. The second is the direction our society has taken. The results are devastating in terms of the betrayal of a generation of youth. The loss to the whole society is incalculable.

But to take the other direction, to choose an imaginative, highly developed educational system that would serve all citizens at every age—a vast, shared, public schooling in which each of us felt a stake, as with public roads, there when needed, ready when you choose to use them—this would mean changing almost everything else.

It would mean refusing, categorically, the shallow premises of official pieties and banalities. As Jonathan Kozol writes in a "Memo to President Clinton":

> You have spoken at times of the need to put computers into ghetto schools, to set up zones of enterprise in ghetto neighborhoods, and to crack down more aggressively on crime in ghetto streets. Yet you have never asked the nation to consider whether ghetto schools and the ghetto itself represent abhorrent, morally offensive institutions. Is the ghetto . . . to be accepted as a permanent cancer on the body of American democracy? Is its existence never to be challenged? Is its persistence never to be questioned? Is it the moral agenda of our President to do no more than speak about more comely versions of apartheid, of entrepreneurial segregation . . . ?

Well, but of course, voices are saying, we're now seeing the worst of breakaway capitalism, even one or two millionaires are wondering if things haven't gone far enough. Perhaps the thing can be restructured, reinvented? After all, it's all we've got, the only system we in this country have ever known! Without capitalism's lure of high stakes and risk, its glamour of individual power, how could we have conceived, designed, developed the astonishing technological fireworks of the end of this century—this technology with the power to generate ever more swiftly obsolescent products for consumption, ever more wondrous connections among the well connected?

Other voices speak of a technology that can redeem or rescue us. Some who are part of this pyrotechnic moment see it as illuminating enormous possibilities—in education, for one instance. Yet how will this come about without consistent mentoring and monitoring by nontechnical, nonprofit-oriented interests? And where will such mentoring come from? whose power will validate it?

Is technology, rather than democracy, our destiny? Who, what groups, give it direction and purpose? To whom does it really belong? What should be its content? With spectacular advances in medical technology, why not free universal health care? If computers in every ghetto school, why ghettos at all? and why not classroom teachers who are well trained and well paid? If national defense is the issue, why not, as poet-activist Frances Payne Adler suggests, a "national defense" budget that defends the people through affordable health, education, and shelter for everyone? *Why should such minimal social needs be so threatening?* Technology—magnificent, but merely a means after all—will not of itself resolve questions like these.

We need to begin changing the questions. To become less afraid to ask the still-unanswered questions posed by Marxism, socialism, and communism. Not to interrogate old, corrupt hierarchical systems, but to ask anew, for our own time: What constitutes ownership? What is work? How can people be assured of a just share in the products of their precious human exertions? How can we move from a production system in which human labor is merely a disposable means to a process that depends on and expands connective relationships, mutual respect, the dignity of work, the fullest possible development of the human subject? How much inequality will we go on tolerating in the world's richest and most powerful nation? What, anyway, is social wealth? Is it only to be defined as private ownership? What does the much abused and trampled word *revolution* mean to us? How can revolutions be prevented from locking in on themselves? How can women and men together imagine "revolution in permanence," continually unfolding through time?

And if we are writers writing first of all from our own desire and need, if this is irresistible work for us, if in writing we experience certain kinds of power and freedom that may be unavailable to us in other ways—surely it would follow that we would want to make that kind of forming, shaping, naming, telling, accessible for anyone who can use it. It would seem only natural for writers to care passionately about literacy, public education, public libraries, public opportunities in all the arts. But more: if we care about the freedom of the word, about language as a liberatory current, if we care about the imagination, we will care about economic justice.

For the pull and suck of Capital's project tend toward reducing, not expanding, overall human intelligence, wit, expressiveness, creative rebellion. If free enterprise is to be totalizingly free, a value in and for itself, it can have no stake in other realms of value. It may pay lip service to charitable works, but its drive is toward what works for the accumulation of wealth; this is a monomaniacal system. Certainly it cannot enrich the realm of the social imagination, least of all the imagination of solidarity and cooperative human endeavor, the unfulfilled imagination of radical equality.

In a poem written in the early 1970s in Argentina, just as the political ground was shifting to a right-wing consolidation, military government, torture, disappearances and massacres, the poet Juan Gelman reflects on delusions of political compromise. The poem is called "Clarities":

> who has seen the dove marry the hawk
> mistrust affection the exploited the exploiter? false
> are such unspeakable marriages
> disasters are born of such marriages discord sadness
>
> how long can the house of such a marriage last?
>   wouldn't
> the least breeze grind it down destroy it the sky crush it
>   to ruins? oh, my country!
>
> sad! enraged! beautiful! oh my country facing the firing
>   squad!
> stained with revolutionary blood!

the parrots the color of mitre
that go clucking in almost every tree
and courting on every branch
are they more alone? less alone? lonely? for

who has seen the butcher marry the tender calf
tenderness marry capitalism? false
are such unspeakable marriages
disasters are born of such marriages discord sadness
        clarities such as

the day itself spinning in the iron cupola
above this poem

I have talked at some length about capitalism's drive to disenfranchise and dehumanize, to invade the very zones of feeling and relationship we deal with as writers—which Marx described long ago—because those processes still need to be described as doing what they still do. I have spoken from the perspective of a writer and a longtime teacher, trying to grasp the ill winds and the sharp veerings of her time—a human being who thinks of herself as an artist, and then must ask herself what that means.

I want to end by saying this to you: We're not simply trapped in the present. We are not caged within a narrowing corridor at "the end of history." Nor do any of us have to windsurf on the currents of a system that depends on the betrayal of so many others. We do have choices. We're living through a certain part of history that needs us to live it and make it and write it. We can make that history with many others, people we will never know. Or, we can live in default, under protest perhaps, but neutered in our senses and in our sympathies.

We have to keep on asking the questions still being defined as nonquestions—the ones beginning *Why . . . ? What if . . . ?* We will be told these are childish, naive, "pre-postmodern" questions. They are the imagination's questions.

Many of you in this audience are professional intellectuals, or studying to become so, or are otherwise engaged in the activities of a public university. Writers and intellectuals can name, we can describe, we can depict, we can witness—without sacrificing craft, nuance, or beauty. Above all, and at our best, we may sometimes help question the questions.

Let us try to do this, if we do it, without grandiosity. Let's recognize too, without false humility, the limits of the zone in which we work. Writing and teaching are kinds of work, and the relative creative freedom of the writer or teacher depends on the conditions of human labor overall and everywhere.

For what are we, anyway, at our best, but one small, persistent cluster in a greater ferment of human activity—still and forever turning toward, tuned for, the possible, the unrealized and irrepressible design?

1997

Works Cited

"We are now not to describe . . ." Mahmoud Darwish. *Memory for Forgetfulness: August, Beirut, 1982* (Berkeley: University of California Press, 1995), pp. 65, 52.

"I've had moments when the life of my people . . ." Dionne Brand. *Bread out of Stone: Recollections, Sex, Recognitions, Race, Dreaming, Politics* (Toronto: Coach House Press, 1994), pp. 182–83.

"I do not share the attitude of those writers . . ." Eduardo Galeano. "In Defense of the Word," in *Days and Nights of Love and War*, trans. Judith Brister (New York: Monthly Review Press, 1983), pp. 191, 185, 192.

"You have spoken at times of the need . . ." Jonathan Kozol. "Two Nations, Eternally Unequal" *Tikkun* 12, no. 1 (1996), p. 14.

"who has seen the dove marry the hawk . . ." Juan Gelman. "Clarities," in *Unthinkable Tenderness: Selected Poems*, ed. and trans. Joan Lindgren (Berkeley: University of California Press, 1997), p. 12.

Talking, Teaching, and Imagining

Social Action Writing

One of the important steps along the road to becoming a social action writer is to find writers whose work you admire, immerse yourself in their work, and read everything they have ever written. And read interviews of them as well—how did they come to do this work, why do they do it, what has been the effect of their work, how do they sustain themselves to do it? So in this last part, we provide some sample interviews with and essays by just a few of the many social action writers.

Characteristics of social action writing that make it a strong political tool:

June Jordan: Over the years of teaching poetry, I have found that when students get to the place where they're writing whatever is disturbing for them, something happens that empowers them in a way that means they'll never be the same. You can never silence them again. (Quoted in Olander, Renee. "An Interview with June Jordan," *AWP Chronicle* Vol. 27, February 1995.)

Martín Espada: Vivid, specific images. What people often resist in political speech is the rhetoric, the didacticism, the polemics. They don't want to be lectured; they don't want to be scolded. And I don't blame them. . . . Poetry, if it's done well, speaks in the language of the senses, in the language of the image.

Toi Derricotte: If we don't recognize anger, if we don't allow for it, if we're not ready, if we don't, in fact, welcome it as a creative force, then I think we're going to end up blaming and dividing people even more.

Sam Hamill: What poetry does above all else is develop sensibility. And that's what makes poetry so dangerous. That's why poetry is so good at undermining governments.

Miguel Algarín: The importance of the Slam, in fact the importance of poetry at the Cafe, is rooted in its capacity to draw in audiences. . . . The time has finally arrived when poetry as an interlacing art is being heard from again. It informs, it motivates, it challenges, and it makes for pleasure. It is entertaining. It is a live form of recreation. It couldn't have been said twenty years ago; not even the Beats managed to take poetry out of the coffeehouses. Yet now it is on television, on radio, in the movie houses, and in numberless clubs around the country where live performances of the poem have taken root.

Role of the social action writer:

Carolyn Forché: [T]o learn about the limitations of my understanding. Because I wasn't equipped to see or analyze the world. My perceptions were very distorted. . . . I would notice things in very general terms. . . . So I had to be *taught* to look and to remember and to think about what I was seeing.

Arundhati Roy: [F]iction is truth. I think fiction is the truest thing there ever was. My whole effort now is to remove that distinction. The writer is the midwife of understanding. It's very important for me to tell politics like a story, to make it real, to draw a link between a man with his child and what fruit he had in the village he lived in before he was kicked out, and how that relates to Mr. Wolfensohn at the World Bank.

Sam Hamill: It's difficult to put your own bare ass out on the limb every time you sit down to write a poem. But that's really sort of the ideal. Because if we don't discover something about ourselves and our world in the making of a poem, chances are it's not going to be a very good poem. So what I'm saying is that a lot of our best poets could be better poets if they wrote less and risked more in what they do.

Tips on how to sustain activism, balance:

Martín Espada: I could not be a political activist without a sense of humor and without a sense of joy. Those are the basic elements of hope, and without hope there is no movement to change things for the better.

As you read these interviews/essays and this book, listen to what you know through your body. Read with your mind AND with your body. Which are the passages that cause a fist to form in your stomach, the hair to bristle on your arms? At which words does you body respond? At which lines do you stop paying attention? It could be that the line *before* you stopped paying attention has caught you, won't let you go. Go back and re-read it. It has some importance for you. You may not even know why. Write it down, date it, ponder it. Sometimes our minds are so filled with what we're supposed to think, supposed to be, that the clutter keeps us from the important illuminations. Trust your body's reaction. Your body knows.

Building Nicole's Mama

Patricia Smith

for the 6th grade class of Lillie C. Evans School,
Liberty City, Miami

I am astonished at their mouthful names—
Lakinishia, Fumilayo, Chevellanie, Delayo—
their ragged rebellions and lip-glossed pouts,
and all those pants drooped as drapery.
I rejoice when they kiss my face, whisper wet
and urgent in my ear, make me their obsession
because I have brought them poetry.

They shout me raw, bruise my wrists with pulling,
and brashly claim me as mama as they
cradle my head in their little laps,
waiting for new words to grow in my mouth.

You.
You.
You.
Angry, jubilant, weeping poets—we are all
saviors, reluctant hosannas in the limelight,
but you knew that, didn't you? Then let us
bless this sixth grade class—40 nappy heads,
40 cracking voices, and all of them
raise their hands when I ask. They have all seen
the Reaper, grim in his heavy robe,
pushing the button for the dead project elevator,
begging for a break at the corner pawn shop,
cackling wildly in the back pew of the Baptist church.

I ask the death question and forty fists
punch the air, *me!, me!* And O'Neal,
matchstick crack child, watched his mother's
body become a claw, and 9-year-old Tiko Jefferson,
barely big enough to lift the gun, fired a bullet
into his own throat after Mama bended his back
with a lead pipe. Tamika cried into a sofa pillow
when Daddy blasted Mama into the north wall
of their cluttered one-room apartment,
Donya's cousin gone in a drive-by. Dark window,
click, click, gone, says Donya, her tiny finger
a barrel, the thumb a hammer. I am shocked
by their losses—and yet when I read a poem
about my own hard-eyed teenager, Jeffery asks

He is dead yet?

It cannot be comprehended,
my 18-year-old still pushing and pulling
his own breath. And those 40 faces pity me,
knowing that I will soon be as they are,
numb to our bloodied histories,
favoring the Reaper with a thumbs-up and a wink,
hearing the question and shouting *me, me,*
Miss Smith, I know somebody dead!

Can poetry hurt us? they ask me before
snuggling inside my words to sleep.
I love you, Nicole says, Nicole wearing my face,
pimples peppering her nose, and she is as black
as angels are. Nicole's braids clipped, their ends
kissed with match flame to seal them,
and *can you teach me to write a poem about my mother?*
I mean, you write about your daddy and he dead,
can you teach me to remember my mama?

A teacher tells me this is the first time Nicole
has admitted that her mother is gone,
murdered by slim silver needles and a stranger

rifling through her blood, the virus pushing
her skeleton through for Nicole to see.
And now this child with rusty knees
and mismatched shoes sees poetry as her scream
and asks me for the words to build her mother again.
Replacing the voice.
Stitching on the lost flesh.

So poets,
as we pick up our pens,
as we flirt and sin and rejoice behind microphones—
remember Nicole.
She knows that we are here now,
and she is an empty vessel waiting to be filled.

And she is waiting.
And she
is
waiting.
And she waits.

from Activism in Academia

A Social Action Writing Program

Frances Payne Adler

Try telling yourself
you are not accountable
to the life of your tribe
the breath of your planet . . .
—Adrienne Rich, "North American Time"

My work is rooted in the notion
that art can provoke social change.
—Willie Birch, "Knowing Our History, Teaching Our Culture"

You are the soothsayer with quill and torch.
Write with your tongues on fire.
—Gloria Anzaldúa, "Speaking in Tongues"

Witnessing is especially necessary
when the reality of a lived experience
is denied by the culture at large,
the culture to which the witness is brought.
—Judith McDaniel, "Sanctuary"

I think that the job of poetry, its political job,
is to refresh the idea of justice, which is going
dead in us all the time.
—Robert Hass, "An Interview with Robert Hass"

"The life of the tribe." "Tongues on fire." "Witnessing." "Social change." Writers' voices, invoking justice and peace. The Creative Writing and Social Action Program at California State University Monterey Bay (CSUMB) honors and teaches this kind of writing. We come by it honestly, as my mother used to say. It is in sync with our origins as a university. Since 1994, we have transformed CSUMB from a military base into an educational one. With the guns gone, we brought out the books and committed ourselves to "diversity, particularly low-income, working-class, and historically underserved students." We regard social action writing as an act of critical inquiry, the domain of academia. Social action writing teaches students to break silences, to witness their lives, to be engaged members of their communities, to bring together craft and critical inquiry.

∽ ∽

Evolution of a Vision for a Creative Writing Program Committed to Social Action

Though I could not have known it, for thirteen years before coming to CSUMB in 1996, everything I was doing was training me for this work. Let me begin with a story. It is 1986, and I am about to teach my first creative writing class. I have spent years learning the craft, and I am here to teach students how to write poetry and fiction—rhythm and meter, metaphor and simile, how to create characters, how to develop setting and plot. I am set, right?

"What shall I write about?" a student asks. "I have nothing to write about, nothing ever happens in my life." This is a central question, asked by many students in the class. Students are moving toward writing well-crafted poems and stories, but anemic ones. I try every writing exercise I know, yet students are still not inside their work. Many words, many pages, and they are silent within their words. Where is the passion, the energy in their writing, where is the "*duende*," as Federico García Lorca said, when "the blood burns like powdered glass" (1973: 93).

The nothing-ever-happens-in-my-life student becomes my teacher. After several visits to my office, she writes a story about her two brothers she has lost to suicide within the past year. All this is going on in her life at the same time she is saying she has nothing to write about. OK, I get it. Hear: nothing she is *allowed* to write about, talk about, reveal.

She brings me her story. "Do I have to read it to the class?" she asks. "It is a secret, I'm not supposed to tell." Such a large pain, and she is not allowed to tell. In how many ways has she been silenced? In whose interest is it for her to be silent? What would be the cost of breaking her silence? What might have happened had she broken her silence earlier?

Writers who had assisted me years earlier in my feminist awakening, in my own writing breakthroughs, flood through me; their voices enter the classroom and take a seat. Adrienne Rich: "What if I tell you, you are not different/it's the family albums that lie" (1984a: 323). Muriel Rukeyser: "Write what burns in you, what you can't forget" (1987: 203). "Your silence will not protect you," Audre Lorde (1984a: 41). "Of what had I *ever* been afraid?" again Audre Lorde (1984a: 41). "The will to power . . . is the will to write," Henry Louis Gates (1991: 4). Voices move from my own writing desk to the classroom. I use my own path to help students come to their full voices. It feels, at this time, somehow dangerous, not "legitimate creative writing pedagogy."

Theory about rhythm and meter, imagery and objective correlatives, that is what I had learned in graduate school, this is how to teach creative writing. Yes, and this method is not enough to peel away the constructed silencings; this method does not begin to deal with the gender, class, and race issues that bind the tongue. I see that a different kind of theory is needed. While I am inventing—with my students in the English department—a way to teach creative writing that is holistic, that feels right, that breaks silences, I also begin to teach women's literature in the Women's Studies Department. Feminist pedagogy cross-pollinates and reinforces my creative writing pedagogy. I am teaching Rich and Lorde and Rukeyser in both my literature classes and my creative writing classes. Essays and poems about undoing silences, peeling away the censors, witnessing. Judith McDaniel's voice enters: "Witnessing is especially necessary when the reality of a lived experience is denied by the culture at large, the culture to which the witness is brought" (1987: 128). Gloria Anzaldúa: "You are the truthsayer with quill and torch. Write with your tongues on fire" (1987: 73).

Carmen, a student in my creative writing class who is from the Imperial Valley, reads McDaniel and Anzaldúa and writes, at last, about her father picking grapes, years in the fields, dying of cancer. "The pesticides scratch, poison his lungs/clog his breath," she writes; for years she has held her anger, knowing without knowing until she reads the environmental reports, her voice now sharp as steel.

Years later, in 1993, I will hear Toni Morrison say on PBS radio, after she has received the Nobel Prize in Literature, "The master narrative is the story as written by the master. It's telling us who has value and who has not." I will think of Carmen, and so many other students, and my own experiences as a woman. But in the mid-eighties, I have not yet heard the term "master narrative," though I am certainly living in one.

I am listening to my body, outrage streaming through me at the silences I recognize around me. I am a new teacher and I have a pedagogical challenge here. I worry this may not be the "right" way to teach creative writing, and I do it anyway. I title the class "Woman As Witness," and I bring feminist theory into my pedagogy. "Poetry is not a luxury," Audre Lorde said. "Poetry is the way we help give name to the nameless so it can be thought" (1984b: 37). Students are lit up by retrieving lost voices, writing them, reading them to each other. Sandra MacPherson's voice enters: "Your story can help someone else to live" (1986: 30). Students are breaking long-held silences and are not struck dead by lightning. They are claiming what they know to be true, their wisdom, their perceptions, their authority. It spills over into their public lives. They become aware of another overlay of silence they have been keeping about what's going on in the world around them, concern they have had about the environment, war, homelessness, work conditions. The collaboration continues: the voices of writers speaking their process of coming to voice, students writing their lived experiences, reading them to their colleagues in the workshop, voices churning the classroom.

∽ ∽

As faculty, in an early part-time position in the Women's Studies Department at San Diego State University, I am told by our Chair, "Fran, you can't bring your activism into the classroom." I am collaborating again with photographer Kira Carrillo Corser. We are producing our second exhibition about lack of access to prenatal care. Six hundred women a month are being turned away from prenatal clinics, women who wanted to have their babies. We are opening in the State Capitol Building in Sacramento, and I am writing a letter to a state senator, inviting her to the opening. I am writing on department stationery. "Fran," my Chair says, "you must keep your activism and your teaching separate." She is a colleague and a friend. She is looking out for me, mentoring me about the ways of academia, what's done, what's not done.

∽ ∽

I've come to know that maintaining the status quo is in itself a form of activism.

Imagine my surprise when I see an ad in the *Chronicle*, posted by the new California State University Monterey Bay. They want someone committed to community building and social justice, yes, that's me, someone ready to pitch in and build a new university from scratch. They are looking for a poet who wants to join them in transforming the Fort Ord military base into a university. I interview for the position, do a workshop, challenge the silences, call in writers' voices. They join me in the classroom, collaborate with me to assist students to uncloak their silences.

In the workshop, students write, bend their heads over their note-pads, their faces flushed. And after class, there's Paulo, walking over to me, his eyes shy as lamps. He wants to talk. He is a songwriter, plays the guitar, has been writing songs for years. He has songs he sings for friends, for family, and he has songs he sings for no one. Angry songs. And he wants to show them to me. Would he sing one, I ask? He looks around, motions me to come outside. He leans against a quiet wall and sings his pain, his grandfather's crossing from Mexico, how he is beaten, robbed, left for dead, and he is not dead, he is angry. It is a story his *abuelo* has told him so very many years ago, *don't tell your abuela I told you, mijo*, the night air colluding in our secrecy. This is a song he has sung for no one. Audre Lorde is with us between the buildings: "Of what has he ever been afraid?" Why is he singing his song now, I ask. "The will to power is the will to write," he says, passing Gates's voice back to me.

This experience with Paulo reinforces that this is where I want to be. And then, to my surprise and joy, they ask me to come teach students how to do social action writing. They offer me the job and I grab it. No more explaining to my colleagues about the need for commitment to community involvement, interdisciplinarity, social action, and ethical reflection. I can just hear them saying, to *what*?

So five years ago, I arrive on the shores of this former military base in Monterey Bay. Fort Ord? Not any more. When I arrive, an on-line library is being set up, replacing the artillery vault. The survival training center? Parachutes and cyanide pills gone. It is going to be a child care center.

∽ ∽

I am in love with a vision that, at last, matches mine. Let me tell you about this place. I am hired in 1996. Thirteen founding faculty have arrived the year before me. The story goes that these founding faculty members are sitting down around a table in a light-filled room at Teatro Campesino in San Juan Bautista, and the president asks them to imagine what the university would look like "if the purpose of the university were learning." Their task is to design such a university. So they lean into each others' lit-up faces and ask themselves another question: "What knowledge, skills, and values do our students need to have in order to lead successful and meaningful lives in the twenty-first century?"

Can you imagine such a blank canvas? I call the founding faculty "interdisciplinary creators/artists of education." I call them bold, committed to diversity, to our students. They collaborate and come up with 13 skills, values, and funds of knowledge: Students need to be bilingual. They need to know their own and each others' histories, literatures, and cultures. They need to be able to ethically communicate across cultures. They need to know how to read and write critically and creatively. To produce a work of art, to express themselves creatively in the service of transforming culture. To participate democratically in their own government, to be involved citizens in their own communities, and to do service learning. They need to be scientifically sophisticated and value the earth. They need to know math. They need to be technologically literate. And they need to know how to be vibrantly healthy. These become our university learning requirements to graduate, known at other universities as general education requirements.

With these skills, our students can re-imagine and re-invent their worlds. About thirty percent of our students are Latina/o / Chicano/a, from Salinas, Castroville, Watsonville, Hollister, some from farmworking families. And African American students, some from former Fort Ord military families. Many other students from working-class families, first in their families to go to college. Many are returning students. My job? To create the Creative Writing and Social Action Program. I tell you, I have been guided to this place.

Establishing the Creative Writing and Social Action Program

I design the Creative Writing and Social Action Program out of the threads of my own years of experience with collaboration and social action—a program committed to activism and that other taboo word "compassion." The program is housed within an interdisciplinary new humanities institute, rather than in a traditional English Department. In collaboration with my colleagues in the Program and in the Institute, we define social action writing to be, yes, a form of critical inquiry, and an act of social responsibility. It is writing that witnesses, that breaks silences, that transforms lives. And the way we've housed the program within an integrated humanities context, is, I believe, the first creative writing program of its kind in the country. When Kira Carrillo Corser and I researched homelessness, we had to go across campus to the political science, women's studies, and history departments.

Creative writing faculty help our students to break silences and fine-tune the craft of writing poems, stories, memoirs, and life stories. Other Institute faculty assist them to build an integrated humanities foundation for their social action writing. Students learn their own and others' history, how to research it, how to analyze it, how to make it. They do oral histories, research and retrieve and write lost family stories. They come to understand and critique the cultural forces that have shaped and formed them. They learn multicultural literary analysis, feed their knowledge of diverse cultures through narratives. They acquire ethical communication skills, crucial to creative writers who write life stories in the form of poetry and fiction. They learn cross-cultural communication skills in which they explore power relations, become aware of their privileges and prejudices, developing keen self-reflection and relational skills. Through service learning, they collaborate with community organizations and develop heightened sensitivity to issues of race, class, and gender. They also learn to visually represent their ideas and images with new media technology, so that they can more effectively invite audiences into their poems and stories.

Social action writing students become involved in the community. To what public issue will the creative writing student respond? What are the ethical issues involved? With what other discipline will the student combine her or his creative writing? Environmental or health issues? Or one of the arts, music, or photography?

When Julie Bliss, one of our first creative writing graduates, wanted to research and retrieve her lost Choctaw heritage in the form of poems and photographs, she studied Native American literature and culture. She learned how to research Choctaw history from our cultural historian. In the National Archives, she met roadblocks, but moved beyond them by doing oral histories of her own family, retrieving lost papers and photographs. Moving across space and time, Julie found a woman in

Missouri who knew someone, who knew someone, who knew her lost relatives. And she wrote poems and took photographs and produced an exhibition titled "Choctaw: Stories of My Heritage Told for the First Time." The images in her poems and in the sepia photographs of her great-great grandmother Mary Garner Cole invoke in the viewer the desire to reach out and touch the wrought-iron gate at the cemetery, the imprint of her great-great grandmother's face in ashes in her hands, the palpable braid of hair, a leather thong wrapped around it. Listen to an excerpt from her poem "Ashes to Life" (1998).

> I see yarn spooled around her finger
> she weaves it through itself
> into the shawl I have only seen
> in decaying photographs
> I carry pictures in ashes
> of Mary who is swollen in death
> who is reborn in my palm

Julie seamlessly integrated the research of her Choctaw history and culture into her poems and photographs, demonstrating the tenacity it takes to grapple with this challenging subject. She built on earlier questions posed by her mother and grandmother, and went on to investigate and find answers to some of these questions. She moved past roadblocks to find some of her lost heritage, and successfully embodied one of her Choctaw ancestors in her poems and photographs.

Adrian Andrade wrote about six generations of his family, from the fields to the classroom. He studied Chicano history and culture, and researched his family's origins as Mexican landowners whose land was taken from them, coming to California as farmworkers, generation after generation. Finally, his mother said, "No, you children will go to school, you will not work the fields." When Adrian graduated, second in his family to go to college, the room was filled with four generations of his family, hearing his/their stories, breaking silences, adding their experiences to Chicana/o history.

A central thread at CSUMB is service learning, where our creative writing students integrate their writing and art with community need. In response to the 1998 welfare reform laws, social action writing students collaborated on an interdisciplinary, cross-cultural project, involving research, creative writing, community involvement, and service learning. The project, which resulted in a book titled *Education as Emancipation: Women on Welfare Speak Out*, was a collaboration between our Program and the EOPS/CARE Program at a local community college, Monterey Peninsula College. A colleague at MPC told me that she wanted "a book that cherishes my students. I'm tired of the way they are being misrepresented in the papers." Her students, single mothers receiving welfare assistance, were seeking college degrees and self-sufficiency. They were being cut off after just two years in college, and would not be able to go on to a four-year university and complete their degree, turn their economic lives around.

Our social action writing students researched welfare reform, interviewed the students at MPC, got to know them over several months, took their photographs, wrote stories and poems. For example, Erin Silvas collaborated with Antoinette "Toni" Fernandez, who was studying at the community college to become a nurse. Below is an excerpt from their poem "Were You There" (1998: 21):

Were you there mumbling *welfare bitch* while I paid for milk and bread
       with food stamps
Were you there in the pediatrician's office staring at the corrugated glass
       reading *We do not serve MediCal patients*
       Are you there now when my sons lie at my sides
       watching the rain against my bedroom window
       Or when my oldest son asks, *Mom, why are we on welfare?*
       Are you there to explain why Michael can't join the soccer team

       Are you there at the end of the month when there is
             no money for PG&E
             or peanut butter . . .
No
I am there
       alone with my two sons
       sitting at the pine kitchen table doing homework
I am there doing A.B.C.'s and Arithmetic
I am there on the mauve carpet that covers the tile floor
       studying my medical books
I am there
       a mother, a teacher, a student

The book focused on lived experiences and perspectives of women on welfare, placing the women most affected by welfare reform at the center of the public discussion. The book was presented by students and faculty at three statewide university conferences on welfare reform, at the Associated Writing Programs national conference, and at conferences in Peru, Hungary, and Russia.

Oh. One more story, this one about when we brought the "Matriot's Dream: Health Care For All" exhibition to CSUMB. At the opening, a donor in the community offered us funding to bring the show to Washington, D.C. This was 1997 and I was sitting in my office and writing a letter to Hillary Clinton inviting her to attend. You can be sure I called my Dean to ask her what she thought about my putting the letter on department stationery.

"Why are you asking me?" she asked.

"Just wanted to check that it's OK to mix my teaching and my activism."

"Fran," she said, "you are community-building, and on a national level. This is what we hired you to do. If you aren't doing it, you aren't doing your job. Of course use our letterhead."

Here in the earthquake territory of California, the stories are coming up. We teach students to become aware of their silences, to understand how and in whose interest their silences were constructed, and to break those silences. We teach them to research and retrieve their lost family stories, the stories of their communities. To learn the craft to powerfully write these experiences. And when that seismic-something shifts, when they claim their voices, they are transformed, they claim their power, claim social justice for themselves, and that leads, at CSUMB, to engagement in social justice in the community.

∞ ∞

Conclusion

We are living in a time when it is no longer sustainable to be silent, and when a different future *is* possible. It is amazing to me the level of disrespect and violence—a violence of commission and omission—that we have accepted, and in which we have colluded with our silence. How many million women, men, and children live on the streets? The homeless rate in Milwaukee has gone up 30 percent since welfare was repealed in Wisconsin. Forty-three million people now have no health insurance. Every three minutes a woman is diagnosed with breast cancer; every twelve minutes, a woman dies of breast cancer. Every six minutes, a woman is raped; every eighteen seconds, a wife or a child is beaten. One in four of our African-American young men are in prison. We drink toxic water, breathe toxic air, and ingest poisons in our food. These are just some of the unacceptable facts that are part of our everyday lives. And what part, we are asking more often these days, does this disrespect play in our policies abroad?

If we, as writers, are asking our creative writing students to ask the tough questions in their poems and in their stories, to critique our worlds, we had better also be providing them with the tools to envision and create new ones.

∽ ∽

Starting A Creative Writing and Social Action Program at Your University

We have often been asked how to start a creative writing and social action program at an already-existing university. One of the first steps is to collaborate. Put out a call around the university for faculty across the disciplines who are interested in social action. Meet regularly. Check out other creative writing programs that are working in the community: June Jordan's "Poetry For the People" Program at Berkeley; the MFA in Creative Writing programs at Chicago State University, at the University of Alaska at Fairbanks, and at Arizona State University; the New School at NYU; Writers Corps; and many other around the country. Use ideas from these programs to model one that suits your own university. Design common goals. Connect with the service learning community across the country. They are a growing and wonderful resource for experiential education, community involvement, and social justice learning.

Finally, hold your own university accountable for its mission statement. You'll find it in the university catalogue. You might be surprised to find some useful language for social action, language committed to quality education, to diversity, to ethical beliefs. (If there's no language about commitment to diversity, there will surely be something about quality education. In the twenty-first century, you can't have quality education without multicultural competency.) These mission statements are seldom at the center of a university's curriculum. Discuss your mission statement at your newly formed social action faculty group in the light of your social action goals. What transformation might be possible if you held your university accountable to its own published commitments?

Creative Writing and Social Action Program
California State University Monterey Bay
100 Campus Center, HCOM-Bldg. 2
Seaside, CA 93955-8001
(831) 582-3889
http://hcom.csumb.edu/createwriting

Works Cited

Anzaldúa, Gloria. "Speaking in Tongues," in *Borderlands/La Frontera: The New Mestiza*. San Francisco: Spinsters/Aunt Lute Press, 1987.

Birch, Willie. "Knowing Our History, Teaching Our Culture," *Re-Imaging America: The Arts of Social Change*. Philadelphia: New Society Publishers, 1990: 138.

Bliss, Julie. "Ashes To Life," in her exhibit Choctaw: Stories of My Heritage Told for the First Time. Capstone Institute for Human Communication, California State University Monterey Bay, Seaside, CA, Spring 1998.

Gates, Henry Louis. "Introduction: On Bearing Witness," in *Bearing Witness: Selections from African American Autobiography in the Twentieth Century*. New York: Pantheon, 1991: 4.

Hass, Robert. "An Interview with Robert Hass," *Mother Jones* 22 (March/April), 1997.

Lorca, Federico García. "Theory and Function of the *Duende*," in *The Poetics of the New American Poetry*. Eds. Donald Allen and Warren Tallman. New York: Grove Press, 1973: 93.

Lorde, Audre. "The Transformation of Silence into Language and Action," in *Sister Outsider*. Freedom, CA: The Crossing Press. 1984a: 37, 41.

Lorde, Audre. "Poetry Is No Luxury," in *Sister Outsider*. Freedom, CA: Crossing Press. 1984b: 36–39.

MacPherson, Sandra. "Secrets: Beginning To Write Them Out" *Field*. Oberlin, OH: Oberlin College, Spring 1986: 30.

McDaniel, Judith. "Sanctuary," in *Sanctuary: A Journey*. Ithaca, NY: Firebrand, 1987: 123–48.

Morrison, Toni. PBS radio interview after winning Nobel Prize in Literature, 1993.

Rich, Adrienne. "In the Wake of Home," in *Fact of a Doorframe: Poems Selected and New 1950–1984.* New York: W.W. Norton, 1984a: 323.

Rich, Adrienne. "North American Time," in *Fact of a Doorframe: Poems Selected and New 1950–1984.* New York: W.W. Norton, 1984b: 325.

Rukeyser, Muriel. *The Collected Poems.* NY: McGraw-Hill, 1987: 203.

Silvas, Erin. "Were You There," in *Education As Emancipation: Women on Welfare Speak Out.* Seaside/Monterey, CA: Creative Writing and Social Action Program, California State University Monterey Bay, and EOPS/CARE Program, Monterey Peninsula College, May 1998: 20–21.

Baring/Bearing Anger

Race in the Creative Writing Classroom

Toi Derricotte

A few weeks ago I got angry at a student in one of my creative writing classes who complained that I was talking too much about race. She said there were people in the class who were tired of hearing about it. I have heard that complaint from white students before and, in the past, I have been patient, tried to listen, and tried to clarify my purposes in a more tolerant manner. This time, however, I found myself tired and lashing out: "If you don't like it, you don't have to stay." She looked devastated. I thought about calling her that night and apologizing, but I didn't. It isn't that I didn't feel sorry for her pain, and it wasn't that I felt completely justified; however, I wanted to give us both time to think, and I wanted her to consider the seriousness of what I was trying to do. Sometimes anger can get one's attention.

That night I anguished about my behavior, but I'm sure I didn't feel the vulnerability that my student must have felt. Because of the dynamics of power, I am in a totally different position now in the classroom as a black professor than I was as a black student. I don't look black and, in fact, for many years, being the only black student in a traditional graduate English literature department, I never spoke about my race. Partly I didn't speak about it because there didn't seem to be an appropriate time, and partly it was because I felt, never having read a black author all the way through high school, college, and graduate school, that revealing my race might somehow endanger my fragile ambition to be a writer. Once I had asked a professor why we hadn't read any black writers in his class. "We don't go down that low," he had explained. I was too shocked to ask him what he meant. How would his opinion of my papers have changed if I had revealed I was black, or even if I had questioned him about his statement? I thought for a long time about going back to talk to him, but I didn't. It wasn't just that I thought my professors regarded the writings of blacks as inferior; the damage was even more corrosive—I thought that many of them felt black people themselves were incapable, either because of our minds, experiences, or language, of writing "real" literature.

The next day I called my student and we met for coffee. She told me how afraid she had been that she would lose our relationship. She had studied with me for three semesters and I had always been supportive. This was the first time she had seen me angry. I assured her that my anger had passed quickly. But I wanted her to know that, given the history of racism, at least as far as I was concerned, no relationship between blacks and whites will be genuine unless it can bear and bare anger—that bearing and baring anger is the real test of whether a relationship can last.

One of the writing assignments I give new writing students is based on a quote by Red Smith: "There is nothing to writing; all you have to do is sit down and open up a vein." We talk about the pain of revealing ourselves, of getting out what is inside. Later I may ask students to write a letter of unfinished business to someone from their past. Often the first important poems we write, our "breakthrough" poems, are angry. There's something about anger that motivates, that gets us over our "stuckness," over our fear. Often poems seem to burst out whole from some storeroom in the body or mind as if they had been just sitting around waiting for years. But there is a danger in anger for black students. White students often write "breakthrough" poems about their childhood. Often called "brave" by the other poets in the class, these poems are frequently painful reassessments of their parents. Black students, however, often don't go back to childhood. They have clear angers that are more weighty right here in the present. There is always a "last straw." Writing about the past is not threatening to others in the class, but writing about what is happening in the classroom here and now is. For the black writer breaking silence, breaking restraint is a frightening step. The person who was the catalyst for the angry poem, unaware of the long history of oppression and internalized rage, takes it as a personal insult. Some students side with the white student, some with the black, but most students remain silent, afraid to go in either direction. In any event, the black student may lose a few of his or her best supporters, people who can tolerate poems about race as long as they don't make anybody feel too uncomfortable. I have had people give me "gifts" after reading a poem of mine, quotations from the Bible or other calming and inspirational words suggesting ways to find love and inner peace. As Cornelius Eady says, presenting one's emotional truth is difficult enough. But unlike white writers, black writers are also expected to solve the problems they present in their work.

We would like to say that when people start talking, suddenly everything gets better, but in reality this does not happen. There's a very dangerous moment when feelings, real feelings, start to emerge. The reactions of white students to the writings of the one or two writers of color in my undergraduate and graduate writing classes vary, but often an entirely different state of receptivity is in effect. White students describe their typical reaction as one of feeling isolated, excluded, of being bombarded by experiences and words they don't understand. They have described a feeling of distance from the poems, feeling defensive and determined not to be made to feel guilty, responsible, or ashamed. Some students say that they listen in spite of these difficulties because it helps them to understand what it means to be black. An easy way out of seriously examining a poem may be to romanticize it, to say it must be "a black thing."

A student complained that he was tired of reading books by black writers and having "the race thing rubbed in my face." A black student asked him: How many books have you read? Four or six? The black student said that he had read thousands of books by white writers and felt it unjust that his writing was read through so many layers. When he picks up a book, he never expects a white writer, for example, to educate him about what it means to be white.

Hayes Davis, a student in my senior seminar, wrote this poem in response to that conversation.

Black Writers

I don't really give a rat's ass
if you're tired of reading black poets,
but I do, really, and I couldn't help
but think, if I want to write
for this class any more, I have to
start editing myself a little now,
and I'm angry about that
and I'm not going to let
you edit me through myself,

or are you really tired of me?
Are you tired of me, or Huie, or Cassandra,
are you tired of Toi?
Why the fuck are you in the class,
or are we acceptable black poets,
or were you thinking there wouldn't
be any black poets in the class?
Are we not really black poets?
Poets that happen to be black
ya know, but not really like black, ya know?

Race is a scary subject. Discussions about it in a diverse community
are fraught with dangers. People walk on eggs. My husband uses flip
charts when he makes presentations in the corporate world. Being the
only black person in the room most of the time, he feels people hear him
better when they aren't looking at his face. But we as writers are told to
reveal ourselves.

Michele Elliot wrote very sparingly during her two years as a graduate
student, and what she wrote she was careful about sharing. Though she
had shared little in class, she had made many comments to me about her
discomfort as one of two black students in the class, of her sadness that
classmates—even people she respected and liked—lacked understanding
of the most basic aspects of racism and made comments about her poems
that completely missed the boat. Finally, something in class triggered a
wild and unruly poem and the release of many years of anger.

Perhaps you will dismiss me as absurd, inflexible,
acting difficult as an unruly child. Maybe you will
never feel the colonization of your own mind, notice
the weight of its chains. You're defensive and you
don't even realize it. You're asking me questions
you've already created the answers for, formed
hypotheses, collected data, and published the results.
What would happen if the world split open and you
were forced to face the scared, uncomfortable you,
the unlistened to, unrecognizable you, unable to put
your feet down, orient yourself. The rules are gone,
no walls to hide behind, left on the plantation without a gun. The gaps are too big to bridge. In it you

can hear the violence of your own words, see the
consequences. Language has left you alone, lonely.
You're without an agenda, a place to be. Everything
is at stake, raw and unbearable.

For Ms. Eliot the most violent and revengeful fantasy she could imagine was for the tables to be turned, for the one who has privilege to walk the line between worlds, to see with double vision from the eyes of the "other." A white woman in one of my classes, Kristen Herbert, wrote a collection of poems titled *White Space* in which she interrupted the normal lines of the poem with cut-outs, so that you could open up the flaps and read what was underneath, what was inside the white space. Whiteness has to be examined, addressed, not taken as "normal." White people have to develop a double consciousness, too, a part in which they see themselves as "other." We are all wounded by racism, but for some of us those wounds are anesthetized. When we begin to feel it, we're awake.

I want to talk about anger, about how important it is as a part of the process of coming to one's voice, about how it is inevitable in a diverse classroom. I want to talk about how powerful it is, how dangerous it is, how mysterious, about how suddenly real feelings start to emerge. If we don't recognize anger, if we don't allow for it, if we're not ready, if we don't, in fact, welcome it as a creative force, then I think we're going to end up blaming and dividing people even more. We hesitate to allow it to happen, though anger is a part of life. (So often "life" is not allowed in the classroom.)

At the same time that we move toward clarity about our differences, it is also possible to move toward clarity about what makes us human, the same. The edges of the workshop are ragged. But I have seen a few black and white students bare and bear their own raw truths.

from Poetry into the Twenty-First Century

The Democratization of Verse

Miguel Algarín

[W]e at the Nuyorican Poets Cafe . . . open our doors to the multi-ethnic, formally poetic world that comes to us to read, to hear, to be heard. On any night that the doors open for our mock-Olympic poetry Slams, the magic is in the playfulness of the occasion and the absolute seriousness with which the poets and the audience interact. This is interactive art. If we wanted to make a parallel to the video world, we could call the Slam "Prime Time Interactive Literature."

The Grand Slam starts with our host, Bob Holman, reading his Dis-Claimer: "We disdain/competition and its ally war/and are fighting for our lives/and the spinning/of poetry's cocoon of action/in your dailiness. We refuse/to meld the contradictions but/will always walk the razor/for your love. 'The best poet/always loses.'" . . . Here we are in the realm of literate humor, with no discerning of "high" and "low," all in the service of bringing a new audience to poetry via a form of entertainment meant to tune up fresh ears to a use of language as art that has been considered dead by many. And after an hour or so of nonstop poetry, our host nods to the deejay in the booth and the room goes into a frenzy of dance, beer, wine, tea, and coffee, and that's called the Break. Winners go from the Grand Slam to the Nationals, which in 1993 featured poets from twenty-four cities.

The modern Slam is the creation of Marc Smith, who continues his weekly bare-knuckles events at the Green Mill in Chicago. The idea for the Slam grows out of ancient traditions of competitive and/or linked rhymes between orators—from the Greek mythological tale of Apollo and

Marsyas to the African griots, from the *Sanjūrokunin sen*, or imaginary poetry team competitions, of tenth-century Japanese court poet Fujiwara no Kinto to the African-American "dozens." It is a tradition that still exists very actively on the island of Puerto Rico, where El Trovador improvises in the plaza, spontaneously pulling into the verse the life of the folks in the small town, the tragedies that have occurred in their families, the gossip that surrounds their private lives, and the celebratory passages that talk about births, deaths, weddings, and baptisms. All of this is compacted into ten-syllable lines with end rhymes. . . . This tradition of El Trovador coming to perform to the audience for their approval or being punished by their disapproval is totally alive at the Nuyorican Poets Cafe.

So, it is Grand Slam night. . . . Regie Cabico . . . enters the room like a bullet, a young gay Filipino talking rhapsodically about the "fresh golden fleeces" and the "nine inches" of fun that he desires. Cabico is a dynamo of metaphors spun out of an extraordinarily sensitive blend of gay audacity and Filipino sensibility. By the time that Regie explains "orgasms are onomatopoeia," the crowd is wild, screaming, shouting, talking back to him, involved in his poetic process. Poet and listeners have become one. The room is now the Temple of Poetry. Here we do not exalt it, we bring it down home. We do not lavish praises on the sensibility of the poet, we imbibe him. And then after we've embraced the poet's daring, we proceed to give him a numerological value. If it seems illogical, it is. If it seems irreverent, it is. If it seems funny, raucous, and vaudevillian, that too it is. And the grade that Regie is given is a 29. Regie's delivery has been masterful, controlled, and intense. The excitement builds.

Anne Elliott . . . has a classic Northern European look. . . . Her projection is melodic, though her verse is a muscular line of thought woven delicately and interlaced with musical accents. She is "the all-new Gregorian chant," as Holman has just characterized her from the stage. The audience has felt at one with his characterization, and indeed it is in sync with what we now begin to hear. Someone from the audience exclaims, "We are in the intestines of a dark devil!" This judgment is anonymous, it is impossible to identify who among the 250 people present has said it, yet it goes directly to the heart of the matter. The silent attention that is being given to her contrasts intensely with the reactive, interactive world that Regie Cabico had created. At the Nuyorican Poets Cafe we work by contrasts, and here we are at the extreme of two poetic poles. Elliott is given a 27.4. The audience reacts with an enveloping round of applause, signaling to her a deep appreciation of the mastery with which she's spun the melodic verse and the excitement she created, as if we were in the midst of a sustained passion.

The importance of the Slam, in fact the importance of poetry at the Cafe, is rooted in its capacity to draw in audiences ranging from our immediate working-class neighbors out for a beer and some fun to serious poetry lovers willing to engage the new poets the Cafe features to the artists themselves, who seek both exposure of their poems and exposure to other poets. The interrelationship between what has been heretofore thought of as a highbrow art and its appeal to a mass public has become a very important polemic, i.e., poetry seems to want to move into daily American life. The poem, the poet, and the audience grow in a deepening relationship that has become ever more public, ever more popular, and ever more engaging. No matter which way it is seen, it is remarkable to look out into the Nuyorican Poets Cafe Slam on a Wednesday night or on a Friday night and see young couples sitting, holding hands, embracing, and spending an evening out on the town in a poets' cafe for no other reason than that it is fun to be here, in this space, involved in this intensely interactive relationship between the poet expressing and the listener absorbing and actively responding. The time has finally arrived when poetry as an interlacing art is being heard from again. It informs, it motivates, it challenges, and it makes for pleasure. It is entertaining. It is a live form of recreation. It couldn't have been said twenty years ago; not even the Beats managed to take poetry out of the coffeehouses. Yet now it is on television, on radio, in the movie houses, and in numberless clubs around the country where live performances of the poem have taken root.

At the center of this movement is "the Largest Stage in the World." On any given night the master of ceremonies at the Nuyorican Poets Cafe can look out into the audience and spot the voices that have grown in the room and that have become recognized and beloved by the audience. So when Holman spots Sekou Sundiata in the room and calls him up to perform, the audience is enthusiastic and expectant that Sundiata will deliver a moment of intense pleasure and significant content. If poetry has become a pastime, it is a recreation that actively demands an involvement from the audience to grow, an audience that will seek inside themselves spaces which are unfamiliar to the ordinary ways in which we in the United States find pleasure. When Sekou steps up to the mike, we are suddenly inside a performance that is elevating the discourse in the room: Space, a character from Sundiata's play *The Circle Unbroken Is a Hard*

Bop, begins to unravel his disjointed view of the world, and we in turn are made familiar with a personage we often run into in the subways and in the streets of the city. Space is a brilliant mind gone awry, having lost all connection to sequential thought. He splatters himself onto the sidewalk, into walls, onto the subway tracks in brilliant metaphoric effusions about how the CIA is taking over his mind, and about his masturbation in the name of Marilyn Monroe. Space's poem is a brilliant insight into what it means to be black, and a self-mocking assault on the audience and the fear that he, Space, can cause in his disjointed world.

Sekou's recital is a great lesson in self-discipline. Inside the play, Space spreads disruptively all over the stage, but before the audience on a Slam night, Space the character is contained inside the poet, and only the words are performed. If the listener has seen the dramatic rendition and contrasts that to this performance, an enormous lesson will have been learned about the theatricalization of poetry, the reason why poetry and theater are so intertwined, and why both are entering into the twenty-first century alive and well at the Nuyorican Poets Cafe.

Keenness, spontaneity, and trusting the moment are very important for the ceremonial master in the Nuyorican Poets Cafe. In keeping with the great commitment that the poets at the Cafe have made to writing the verse on the page and then lifting off the page into performing action, Holman's eyes survey the crowd, now spotting other poets who have grown in the room. Reg E. Gaines, who entered the room only ten minutes before, is caught and called up to center stage. When Gaines acquires control of the mike, we are in a very special place. Here is an African-American man who has discovered his poetic roots in the voice and sentiments of the Nuyorican poets. Reg E.'s command of Lucky Cien-Fuegos's and Miguel Piñero's poems is astounding. He can, from memory, recite some of their most important poems from the mid-seventies. To recite in two languages is an exciting phenomenon, since it implies that the performer is capable of blending a Spanish verb with an object in English and delivering an impact that excites and arouses the listener.

The fearlessness with which young African-American poets are now confronting languages other than English and involving themselves in the exploration of self-expression in other forms of speech is new and probably the most welcome sign of a new internationalism alive in the young African-American poets. Tracie Morris and Reg E. Gaines do not just make an easy nod to multilingual expression—they are daring in their willingness to stand before live audiences and speak in Spanish.

They speak their feelings in Spanish. When Tracie Morris begins her "Morenita" poem, we are soothingly involved and seduced in her bilingual sensual quest for love and precise definitions in relationships. Nuyorican language is no longer the property of Puerto Ricans speaking in a blend of English and Spanish; it is now more like one of the dialects at the edges of the Roman Empire, which were once called vulgar but are now the Spanish, Italian, and Portuguese of modern Europe.

Now, this is the very heart of the matter. They are both attempting complex intense communications in the Spanish language and are fearless about accents or mispronunciation. They are intent on diving into the endless possibility of multilingual expressiveness. This is new and exciting, and it shows enormous promise for the African-American poetic voice in the Western Hemisphere. Gone are the days when English would remain the only means of expression for North American artists. It is clear that today alternate systems of speech are growing increasingly popular and creatively alluring. Spanish has been present on the North American continent since the very beginning of the Columbian occupation. It is not about to disappear and in fact it will continue to grow in importance as the economic relationship between the Southern and the Northern hemispheres begins to equalize.

∞ ∞

The poetics that binds these poets is alive and being invented as they themselves evolve as poets and thinkers about their art and their craft. The media coverage that has engulfed these poets has been so plentiful that it is now possible to cull from the endless articles a sense of the poetics that is being created in midair from one article to the other as these poets are made to think about content, quality, and craft. In *Newsweek*, Kevin Powell says, "poetry is the quickest way to express what you see and feel," yet Paul Beatty seems worried about the hoopla that may dull the critical edge that poetry should have: "The real hook of poetry is that it turns things inside out, and I'm not sure all this trendiness measures with that." Beatty is expressing a very important reservation, but it is a reservation that is not just pertinent to these poets; it is a reservation that is pertinent to anything today in America, where trends are devoured like ice-cream cones, in seconds. It is clear that Beatty is worried about permanence and continuity.

Allen Ginsberg recently praised Beatty for "his very smooth, good, sophisticated, syncopated ear." He has also read Beatty's poems as "microchips bursting with information." Ginsberg has once again encapsulated the poetic moment, since it is true that Beatty is a condenser and a fine filtering voice for the experience of the late twentieth century. So that by the time that Evelyn McDonnell in the *Village Voice* describes him as perhaps "the first poet to transcribe the language of the telecommunications age onto paper," we have finally come the full circle round, and we have reached what is probably the best description of the poetics of the first decade of the twenty-first century.

from Poetry in Motion

An Interview with Carolyn Forché

Carolyn Forché's verse scans the contemporary landscape—
from the private to the public, from the self to El Salvador

Jonathan Cott

Perhaps no one better exemplifies the power and excellence of contemporary poetry than Carolyn Forché, who is not only one of the most affecting younger poets in America, but also one of the best poets writing anywhere in the world today. Born in Detroit in 1950, Forché won the Yale Series of Younger Poets Award in 1975 for her first book, *Gathering the Tribes* (New Haven: Yale University Press, 1976) . . . Her second book, *The Country between Us* (Harper & Row, 1981), was chosen as the Lamont Selection of the Academy of American Poets, and has elicited enormous praise from such writers as Denise Levertov, Margaret Atwood, and Jacobo Timerman. It has also sold about 17,000 copies to date, making it that rarest of things—a poetry best seller.

∽ ∽

The Country between Us has undoubtedly gained its unusually large readership because of its opening section—a series of eight overwhelming, harrowing poems about El Salvador, where Forché spent two years, on and off, as a human-rights investigator, political journalist, and sympathizer of the victims of what Walt Whitman called the "real war" that "never gets in the books." But in her poems, Forché is a witness not only to the cruelties of the Salvadoran (and, more generally, the Central

American) civil war, but to the lack of attention, compassion, and commitment of those of us who, as she writes in "Return," were "born to an island of greed/and grace where you have this sense/of yourself as apart from others."

As she concludes in "Ourselves or Nothing," the final poem of her book:

In the mass graves, a woman's hand
caged in the ribs of her child,
a single stone in Spain beneath olives,
in Germany the silent windy fields,
in the Soviet Union where the snow
is scarred with wire, in Salvador
where the blood will never soak
into the ground, everywhere and always
go after that which is lost.
There is a cyclone fence between
ourselves and the slaughter and behind it
we hover in a calm protected world like
netted fish, exactly like netted fish.
It is either the beginning or the end
of the world, and the choice is ourselves
or nothing.

ᔕ ᔕ

Q: Your epigraph to the first section of your second book, *The Country Between Us*, is by the Spanish poet Antonio Machado, and it says: "Walker, there is no road/You make your road as you walk." Your own poems, of course, mirror your own path—one that has taken you on all kinds of open roads. You seem to be a voracious traveler.

Carolyn Forché: If I indulge myself, I could say that there's been a sort of ongoing pattern or mysterious and compelling force in my life. But when I think about the reasons for my traveling, I could also say that my grandmother Anna was a wanderer, and that my aunt once told me that in every generation in my family there's been a woman who hasn't been able to settle in one place. And they all thought I was the one; they decided that "Carolyn goes off because she's Anna, she's got that restless thing in her." Also, when I traveled to the American Southwest, I was getting over the death of a friend, and I went there to wander around and was literally taken in by an older Indian couple in a pueblo in northern New Mexico. They gave me meals, and gradually I was taught a little Tewa, and one thing led to another. And always, wherever I would go, this seemed to happen.

I had very difficult, sad times in my early adulthood, and I thought, "Well, I'm not responsible for what has happened to me, but I *am* responsible for my responses. So I have to respond well or else I'll become deranged or whatever." Then, midway through my twenties, it occurred to me that I was also responsible for what happened to me, that I had a certain amount of choice, and that the ways in which I tended could determine events. So when I first felt the urge to translate the Salvadoran poet Claribel Alegría, who lives in exile in Mallorca, I realized that I was ignorant of the reality out of which her poems were written. Going to stay with her in Mallorca was not going to Latin America, but many writers who have fled Latin America for various reasons travel to visit her. I met women there who were tortured, one in an Argentine prison. And I became very depressed. I thought maybe I had island fever. Claribel would sit with a drink every afternoon and wait for the mail to come, blank-eyed, sad, unreachable. I couldn't speak to her. She would search through the mail for news of her friends or relatives, and then an hour later she would suddenly be all cheery and dressed and ready to engage in the evening. But these moments haunted me.

I kept working on the translations, but I left very saddened. And then I came back to California and began working very intensely for Amnesty International—I was writing my letters dutifully and all that—and one day, up pulls this dusty, white jeep into my driveway, and out gets this guy with two little girls and knocks on my door. Now, I had heard about this man, Leonel Gomez Vides—I'd heard about him in Spain; there were legends about him. He introduced himself to me, but I was properly terrified about Latin American strangers who purported to be this or that. But he had the two little girls with him, so I trusted him and let him into the house. I sat him down at the kitchen table and pointed to photographs I had taken in Spain and asked him to identify various people. He was amused and said that someone was so-and-so and someone else was the husband of so-and-so, and so on. "That's very good," he told me. "Now," he said, "how would you like to do something for Central America, since you've translated these poems and obviously have an interest?" I knew that he was associated with many humanitarian projects in El Salvador, and I thought I would be the lady in white working in the orphanage for one year who pats the little bottoms! I pictured myself that way, rather heroically. I had a Guggenheim fellowship to write poetry, so I had the year free, and I said yes, I'd like to go.

So he went out to the truck, got a roll of white butcher paper and about twenty pencils, and he smoothed the paper out on the table and began to diagram and doodle and make little drawings about the Salvadoran military and the American embassy and the various components of the Salvadoran society and economic and political structures. He did this for seventy-two hours straight, with many cups of coffee, and then he would test me. He'd say, "Okay, you are this colonel and this happens and there's possibly going to be a coup, what do you do?" He made me think of every component in this scenario. And he said, "Look, you have a dead Jesuit priest and a dead parish priest, you have forty nuns and priests expelled from the country or arrested, this is the situation, and I want you to come to Salvador to learn about it, because our country is your country's next Vietnam."

Now, my ex-husband had gone to Vietnam, as had my next-door neighbor and most of my friends in school and brothers and boyfriends and husbands of friends—they all went off to the war because we were of the class that *went* to Vietnam. We used to listen to those songs in high school—about the Green Berets and about pinning silver wings on my son's chest. We literally used to cry because our friends were there and we thought they would die. But I was a *greaser*, we thought this war was right, we were very patriotic. It didn't occur *not* to be until I went to the university, and I was the only one among my circle of friends who did go. . . . So I *had* to know about El Salvador. And here this man was offering me an opportunity to understand something, and also he promised me that, in an odd way, I would be able to make a contribution. So how could I not agree? I knew that I was ignorant about the situation there, and that it would be a worse ignorance to refuse this offer. But most of my friends at the time thought I was absolutely crazy to go.

Q: The poet Robert Bly recently spoke of our not being conscious of what we were (and are) doing in El Salvador. "We did it in Vietnam," he said, "and ever since have refused to become conscious of it. It is said that a dream will repeat itself until you understand it, until you become conscious of what's there." And I have the sense that making things conscious is exactly what you've been trying to do in poetry.

Carolyn Forché: For me, it's a process of understanding, a process that has not been completed and that probably can't be completed. But it certainly was startling for me to learn not only about Central America in a very immediate way, but also to learn about the limitations of my understanding. Because I wasn't equipped to see or analyze the world. My perceptions were very distorted—and I'm even talking about visual perception. I would notice things in very general terms, but there were certain things I would fail to see.

I would always marvel at the wealthy women in the suburbs of San Salvador—women playing canasta all day—and I spent many hours talking to them. They did not *see* poverty, it didn't exist for them. First of all, they never went outside the capital city, but even in the city they could go through a street in a car and not see the mother who has made a nest in rubber tires for her babies. What they saw was an assembly of colors of delight, of baskets and jugs on the heads of women. Yet they were being as accurate as they could possibly be in their descriptions.

Now, as to what *I* didn't see: I was once driving past rows of cotton fields—all I could see on either side of the highway for miles was cotton fields, and it was dusty and hot, and I was rolling along thinking about something in my usual way, which is the way that has been nurtured in this country. But I didn't see *between* the rows, where there were women and children, emaciated, in a stupor because pesticide planes had swept over and dropped chemicals all over them, and they were coughing and lethargic from those poisonous clouds . . . and also they were living in the middle of these fields because they had no place else to go, underneath sheet-plastic tarps that were no protection against the pesticides. The children had no clothing and were swollen-bellied and suffering from the second- and third-degree malnutrition that I had been taught to recognize in my work at the hospital. There they were, and I hadn't seen them. I had only seen cotton and soil between cotton plants, and a hot sky. I saw the thing endlessly and aesthetically; I saw it in a certain spatial way. So I had to be *taught* to look and to remember and to think about what I was seeing.

Q: What you're saying reminds me of John Keats' notion that "poetry must work out its own salvation in a man: It cannot be matured by law and precept, but by sensation and watchfulness in itself. . . ."

Carolyn Forché: Yes, I certainly don't mean to be programmatic in my writing, or ever to be strident or polemical. I don't want to argue a position; rather, I want to present in language the re-creation of a moment. Any judgment, any expression, even a most carefully rendered eyewitness testimony is viewed as political if you locate that testimony in an area associated with turmoil; whereas you can describe something in an area that's not so associated, and it will be considered something else. I tried not to write about El Salvador in poetry, because I thought it might be better to do so in journalistic articles. But I couldn't—the poems just came.

∽ ∽

Q: It must have been terrifying to confront the violent realities of El Salvador.

Carolyn Forché: I was very close to Monsignor Oscar Romero just before he was killed. And I had a very, very close brush with death. I was with a young defecting member of the Christian Democratic party, and we confronted a death squad that had three machine guns trained on our windshield. They had enough time to kill us, but this young man had a sort of uncanny quickness of reflexes, and he managed to throw the car into reverse and floor it and get back through a walled gate. But though it was split-second, I had enough time to see the machine guns. There's no reason why I'm here. Functionally, it was a fluke.

Q: Did you ever feel that you had come too close to the edge?

Carolyn Forché: I could have, but I didn't lose my sanity even briefly. I became very lucid, but I knew what was going to happen. And I felt more and more powerless to do anything about it, because no one would listen to me. I began to realize that it wouldn't matter if they did. I had to experience the full impact of this horror, that this is indeed what happened in Vietnam . . . and that I couldn't stop it. And that I was going to have to see it almost like someone whose eyelids are held open and you can't stop looking at something. And it was very hard to get through that period.

One of the things that's very heartening is that I met a whole network of people—many of them journalists—who never went off the path, who got involved during the Vietnam period for whatever reasons, who didn't go and climb the corporate ladder, who have maintained that their work be subservient to their conscience.

Q: Walt Whitman wrote: "The attitude of great poets is to cheer up slaves and horrify despots."

Carolyn Forché: That's an interesting view. I don't want to think of everyone who's been horrified as a despot, because a lot of people who've been horrified are very good-hearted and well-intentioned, especially the young ones. They come and they say, "What should we do?" They think that to write in an engaged way means you have to go to exotic climes. People don't want to learn about what is in their own immediate sphere. And this is understandable, isn't it, because of all the duplicity. "What should we do?" "That's not the beginning," I have to say. "Set off now and find *out* what you should do. The answer is not the beginning. The answer is maybe at the end, if you're very lucky."

An Interview with Sam Hamill

Anne-Marie Cusac

"This is where I come to hide," says Sam Hamill as he pulls the car into the grove of fir and cedar surrounding the house and studio he built himself. But he is not hiding. He has scheduled his *Progressive* interview hard upon his return from New York City, where, during a blizzard, he and poets Galway Kinnell, Sharon Olds, Martín Espada, and others read to a large and enthusiastic audience at Lincoln Center.

It is a late February day near Port Townsend, Washington, and Hamill has had little chance to retreat from public attention since mid-January, when he received a note from Laura Bush requesting his presence at a White House symposium on Langston Hughes, Emily Dickinson, and Walt Whitman.

Hamill responded with an e-mail to friends. It read, in part: "When I picked up my mail and saw the letter marked 'The White House,' I felt no joy. Rather, I was overcome by a kind of nausea. . . . Only the day before I had read a lengthy report on the President's proposed 'Shock and Awe' attack on Iraq, calling for saturation bombing that would be like the firebombing of Dresden or Tokyo, killing countless innocent civilians. The only legitimate response to such a morally bankrupt and unconscionable idea is to reconstitute a Poets Against the War movement like the one organized to speak out against the war in Vietnam." Hamill called upon all poets "to speak up for the conscience of our country" by submitting poems for "an anthology of protest."

Within thirty-six hours, the submissions of poems to Hamill's project had overwhelmed his e-mail account. The First Lady heard of the poets' plans and canceled the symposium.

On February 12, the day the White House symposium was supposed to happen, poets participated in more than 135 readings and events around the country denouncing Bush's war moves against Iraq. By that date, Hamill's new Web site (www.poetsagainstthewar.org) had published more than 6,000 poems.

At first glance, Hamill might seem a surprising person to cause an uproar. The esteemed editor, translator, essayist, and poet is, by his own admission, reclusive. But his life of contemplation and dedication to poetry prepared him more than adequately for his confrontation with the U.S. government.

Among many other things, he is the translator of Lu Chi's *Wen Fu: The Art of Writing*, a book that stresses the importance of calling things by their right name, a Confucian idea that applies as much to political rulers as it does to emotional states or descriptions of the natural world.

Hamill is a founding editor of Copper Canyon Press, which is known for its independence, as well as for its accurate and graceful translations. The Copper Canyon list includes such poets as Olga Broumas, Hayden Carruth, Cyrus Cassells, Odysseas Elytis, Carolyn Kizer, Thomas McGrath, Cesare Pavese, Kenneth Rexroth, and Eleanor Wilner.

An avowed pacifist, Hamill opens his book *A Poet's Work* with a quote from the Albert Camus essay "Neither Victims nor Executioners," which he says changed his life. "All I ask is that, in the midst of a murderous world, we agree to reflect on murder and to make a choice," Camus writes. "After that, we can distinguish those who accept the consequences of being murderers themselves or the accomplices of murderers, and those who refuse to do so with all their force and being."

Q: Why did your call for a new Poets Against the War movement elicit such support?

Sam Hamill: It was almost as if they were waiting breathlessly for someone to step forward and say, "Enough is enough." We became a chorus. Last week, the poems were coming in at one per minute. We have twenty-five editors downloading and formatting poems. We're well over 11,000 poems already, and we'll publish an anthology of probably about 225 pages of theoretically the best.

Q: Who inspired you to do this?

Hamill: The spirit of Denise Levertov, and listening to Galway Kinnell and Philip Levine and Etheridge Knight and June Jordan during the 1960s. That made me decide when I received the invitation to the White House that I simply couldn't just say no thank you and pretend that it was OK.

Poets should speak out against what we see as the assault against our Constitution and the warmongering that's going on. I'm perfectly willing to lay down my life for my Constitution, but I am not willing to take a life for it or any other reason because I think killing people is counterproductive.

I'm basically a poetry scholar, and I'm happier here in my studio with my row of Chinese dictionaries than I am, frankly, at Lincoln Center, although it was one of those lifetime moments, as they say.

Q: Can you describe what the Poets Against the War movement was like during Vietnam?

Hamill: Well, I can remember, I think it was 1967, sitting in the First Unitarian Church in Isla Vista, Santa Barbara, and seeing Phil Levine come out on the little stage. He sat on the edge and said, "You know, sometimes it's hard not to hate my country for the way I feel, at times, but I won't let that happen." And then he read, "They Feed They Lion," this incredibly powerful, incantatory poem that was inspired in part by the burning of Detroit in 1967 and the riots that followed. And then Galway Kinnell came out with that wonderful big, breathy, hollow voice of his and read, for the first time in public, "The Bear." That poem impressed me so much that I memorized it. I used it for years when I taught in prisons. It's a powerful extended metaphor for what the writing life is really all about. It's a uniquely powerful poem about self-transformation, and that's what we're asking, really, beyond even our objection to the war. We're asking people to look at themselves and think about what might be possible with a little self-transformation.

Each of us as poets, as decent suffering human beings, has to find a way to run our lives that is compassionate toward one another and toward our environment. Because if we don't, we are going to be committing suicide at a very large level. We're certainly not perfect, and we're not probably even better than anybody else, except that perhaps we are given to certain kinds of contemplation that provide a valuable balance to the knee-jerk reactionary behavior of most of our newspapers and political leaders. Poets are great doubters.

What poetry does above all else is develop sensibility. And that's what makes poetry so dangerous. That's why poetry is so good at undermining governments and so bad at building them. There's nothing harder to organize than a group of poets.

The only thing we all agree on, virtually every poet in this country, is that this Administration is really frightening, and we want something done about it.

Bush is using language that's a mirror image of the language of Osama bin Laden when he says, "We have God on our side. This is the struggle of good against evil." Isn't that exactly what bin Laden said? Bush the born-again Christian, bin Laden the born-again Muslim, and they're both convinced that they have God on their side, and they're both willing to kill countless numbers of innocent people to assert their rightness. Very dangerous, very dangerous.

Q: You've described yourself as anti-religious.

Hamill: Yes, yes. I am anti-religious.

Q: And why is that?

Hamill: Most of the ugly wars in history have been wars of religion. And there's nothing more dangerous than someone with religious certitude who creates consequences in the world that to me are simply inexcusable.

Q: You seem to be contrasting religious certitude with what you said about poets as doubters. Is that right?

Hamill: Yes. Well, we poets don't tend to be certain a lot. Much of our art is made out of our own uncertainty. And there is a not-knowingness, I think, that leads us back to suffering humanity with a more compassionate vision than most of our politicians have.

Q: In your essays, you write that poetry saved your life. I was wondering if you could explain what you mean.

Hamill: I was a violent, self-destructive teenager, who was adopted right at the end of World War II. I was lied to and abused by my parents. I hated life in Utah. I resented the Mormon Church, its sense of superiority and its certitude. I escaped through the Beat writers and discovered poetry and have devoted my entire life to the practice of poetry in varying ways. Poetry gave me a reason for being. And I'm not exaggerating when I say that. My ethics, my sense of morality, my work ethic, my sense of compassion for suffering humanity, all of that comes directly out of the practice of poetry, as does my Buddhist practice. Poetry is a very important element in the history of Buddhism in general and in Zen in particular. It was really Zen that motivated me to change the way I perceive the world.

It's not, I'm a poet who practices Zen. And it's not, I'm somebody who practices Zen who writes poetry. There's no separation for me. Sometimes people come up and they get infatuated with some little brief imagistic poem or something, and they say, "Oh, I really like your Zen poems." And I say, "Which ones are not Zen poems?"

Poetry teaches us things that cannot be learned in prose, such as certain kinds of irony or the importance of the unsaid. The most important element of any poem is the part that is left unsaid. So the poetry frames the experience that lies beyond naming.

Q: Did you have a political awakening, or have you always felt the way you do?

Hamill: I would say that my great political awakening was really born on Okinawa, reading Albert Camus: the "Neither Victims nor Executioners" essay and *The Rebel*. I was an eighteen-year-old kid. I hated myself. I hated my life. I thought nobody wanted me. All I'd ever heard my entire life in my family was, "Nobody wanted you, and we took you in." When you get that into your head at a tender age, you really feel like you are an unlovable human being, and then you behave like one. That's exactly what I had done. It took me many years to deal with my own violence and find my own niche.

Kenneth Rexroth took me under his wing for a brief period. I was fifteen years old, and I was smoking a lot of heroin and trying to be cool, man, and I really loved poetry. And Kenneth convinced me that destroying myself was not really the best possible solution, and that I needed to look at the world's literature, and not just my own life, in order to be hip, if you will. So he had a huge influence on what became of me thereafter.

I got interested in Zen when I was a teenage beatnik on the streets of San Francisco. And it was my interest in Zen, in part, that got me into the Marine Corps, because that was a ticket to Asia. So I spent a couple of years on Okinawa and began reading and thinking about how I wanted to go about conducting my life.

Q: I looked back at your translation of Lu Chi's *Wen Fu: The Art of Writing*. You make the observation that he lived in some ways a dangerous life by writing and naming things. What is the position of today's American poets in relation to that life?

Hamill: Well, I think a lot of American poets are swimming-pool Soviets. A lot of them have taken the comfortable, self-protective route too often. I know that I certainly have. That's easy to do. It's difficult: to put your own bare ass out on the limb every time you sit down to write a poem. But that's really sort of the ideal. Because if we don't discover something about ourselves and our world in the making of a poem chances are it's not going to be a very good poem. So what I'm saying is that a lot of our best poets could be better poets if they wrote less and risked more in what they do.

That said, I'll say that this is probably the best time for poetry since the T'ang dynasty. All the rest of the world is going to school on American poetry in the twentieth century, from Ezra Pound to W. S. Merwin, and for very good reason. We have soaked up influence in the last century like a sponge. It's cross-pollination, first law of biology, that the more variety you have the more health you have.

Q: Can you talk a little bit about translation as a discipline?

Hamill: One of the things I love about translation is it obliterates the self. When I'm trying to figure out what Tu Fu has to say, I have to kind of impersonate Tu Fu. I have to take on, if you will, his voice and his skin in English, and I have to try to get as deeply into the poem as possible. I'm not trying to make an equivalent poem in English, which can't be done because our language can't accommodate the kind of metaphors within metaphors the Chinese written language can, and often does, contain. For instance, there's a mat outside my door with a Chinese character on it. You can read that as two characters: a roof and a woman under it. If you combine those two characters, that's the character for harmony or for peace. If you put that same roof out there, and put two women under it, you get the character for disharmony. That's a visual linguistic pun. Well, it's hard for us to do anything equivalent like that in our language, so what I have to do is find other ways of putting the turn on this line or the edge on that image. You can't just do a word-for-word because they don't exist. We don't have a word for two women under one roof. So you have to find other ways of making it literary and of being true to the sensibility, if you will, of the original, as much as possible.

The oldest cliché in the world is about "what's lost in translation," but you don't very often read much intelligent about what's gained by translation, and the answer is everything. Our language is a compendium of translation.

Q: What is the proper role of poetry in our society?

Hamill: That's one of those questions that would just love to have a pat answer. You know, poetry's job is to make us feel good. Poetry exists to allow us to express our innermost feelings. There isn't one role for poetry in society. There are many roles for poetry. I wrote a poem to seduce my wife. I wrote a poem when I asked her to marry me. Poetry got me laid. Poetry got me married. I wrote a number of poems about Kah Tai lagoon, when Safeway was building that huge, ugly store down there where I used to love to watch the birds nest. That political poem, or environmental poem, was unsuccessful because Safeway built there anyway. And yet the poem has something to say today, as it did then. And I speak here only of my own poems. The agenda for every poet has to be different because most of us write from direct human experience in the world.

It would be nice if all the Republicans could put poetry in a little box and put the box under the bed and sit on it, but they can't. And neither can the left insist that poetry must do this or must do that. I've heard a lot of people quoting Auden famously that "poetry makes nothing happen," but none of the people who were quoting it seemed to have understood the irony of what he was saying. If you think for one second that Auden believed that poetry makes nothing happen in a real, literal way, then you're a damn fool.

Q: What do you say to members of the rightwing media who are saying that the poets organizing against the war are behaving badly or that they're looking foolish?

Hamill: I haven't seen any poet in this country behave nearly as rudely as Newt Gingrich or Bill O'Reilly. I'm not asking these people to approve of everyone's manners. I don't feel obliged to defend the manners of every poet who submits a poem to my Web site. That's not my job. My job is to provide them with an opportunity to speak from the heart. If there's not much in the heart and if the mouth is running wild, that's not my problem. Of course, there are some people who behave rudely. Allen

Ginsberg used to like to get up in public and take his clothes off. I don't do that, but I liked Allen Ginsberg. He was a nice guy [laughter].

When these idiot right-wingers start complaining about poetry being political, I'm fond of reciting Sappho to them, who excluded men from her world. Why does she exclude them? Mostly because of their warmongering.

Q: Is there a particular bit of Sappho you quote?

Hamill: There's a fragment that goes, "Some say the most beautiful thing in the world is a great cavalry riding down over the hill. / Others say it's a vast infantry on the march. / But I say the most beautiful thing is the beloved." How political can you get?

An Interview with Arundhati Roy

David Barsamian

There is a high-stakes drama playing out in India these days, and the novelist Arundhati Roy is one of its most visible actors. Multinational companies, in collusion with much of India's upper class, are lining up to turn the country into one big franchise. Roy puts it this way: "Is globalization about 'the eradication of world poverty,' or is it a mutant variety of colonialism, remote controlled and digitally operated?"

Roy, forty-one, is the author of *The God of Small Things* (Random House, 1997), which won the Booker Prize, sold six million copies, and has been translated into forty languages. Set in a village in the southwestern state of Kerala, the novel is filled with autobiographical elements. Roy grew up in Kerala's Syrian Christian community, which makes up 20 percent of the population. She laughs when she says, "Kerala is home to four of the world's great religions: Hinduism, Islam, Christianity, and Marxism." For many years, Kerala has had a Marxist-led government, but she hastens to add that party leaders are Brahmins and that caste still plays a strong role.

The success of Roy's novel has brought lucrative offers from Hollywood, which she takes impish delight in spurning. "I wrote a stubbornly visual but unfilmable book," she says, adding that she told her agent to make the studios grovel and then tell them no. In Kerala, the book has become a sensation. "People don't know how to deal with it," she says. "They want to embrace me and say that this is 'our girl,' and yet they don't want to address what the book is about, which is caste. They have to find ways of filtering it out. They have to say it's a book about children."

Roy lives in New Delhi, where she first went to become an architect. But she's not working as an architect or even a novelist these days. She's thrown herself into political activism. In the central and western states of Madhya Pradesh, Maharashtra, and Gujarat, a series of dams threatens the homes and livelihoods of tens of millions. A huge, grassroots organization, the Narmada Bachao Andolan (NBA), has arisen to resist these dams, and Roy has joined it. Not only did she give her Booker Prize money (about $30,000) to the group, she has also protested many times with it, even getting arrested.

She skillfully uses her celebrity status and her considerable writing gifts for this effort, as well as in the cause of nuclear disarmament. Her devastating essay on dams, "The Greater Common Good," and her searing denunciation of India's nuclear testing, "The End of Imagination," have literally kindled bonfires. The upper class didn't appreciate her critique of development, and the nationalists abhorred her for questioning India's nuclear arsenal. (These two essays comprise her latest book, *The Cost of Living*, [Modern Library, 1999].)

By now, Roy is used to criticism. "Each time I step out, I hear the snicker-snack of knives being sharpened," she told one Indian magazine. "But that's good. It keeps me sharp."

Her most recent essay is called "Power Politics." In it, she takes on Enron, the Houston-based energy corporation that is a large financial backer of George W. Bush. In India, Enron is trying to take over Maharashtra's energy sector. The scale of what is happening, she says, makes California's power woes look like child's play.

On a cold, mid-February afternoon, Roy gave the annual Eqbal Ahmad lecture at Hampshire College in Amherst, Massachusetts, before a huge crowd. It was a powerful, political talk, and afterward she was besieged by a long line of mostly young South Asian women, many of whom are studying at one of the five colleges in the Amherst area. She donated her lecture fee to earthquake relief in Gujarat.

The next morning, I interviewed her in the back seat of a car taking her from Amherst to Logan Airport in Boston. The two-hour drive went by in a flash.

Q: You grew up in Kerala. What's the status of women there?

Arundhati Roy: Women from Kerala work throughout India and the world earning money to send back home. And yet they'll pay a dowry to get married, and they'll have the most bizarrely subservient relationships with their husbands. I grew up in a little village in Kerala. It was a nightmare for me. All I wanted to do was to escape, to get out, to never have to marry somebody there. Of course, they were not dying to marry me [laughs]. I was the worst thing a girl could be: thin, black, and clever.

Q: Your mother was an unconventional woman.

Roy: She married a Bengali Hindu and, what's worse, then divorced him, which meant that everyone was confirmed in their opinion that it was such a terrible thing to do in the first place. In Kerala, everyone has what is called a *tharawaad* [lineage]. If you don't have a father, you don't have a tharawaad. You're a person without an address. That's what they call you. I grew up in Ayemenem, the village in which *The God of Small Things* is set. Given the way things have turned out, it's easy for me to say that I thank God that I had none of the conditioning that a normal, middle class Indian girl would have. I had no father, no presence of this man telling us that he would look after us and beat us occasionally in exchange. I didn't have a caste, and I didn't have a class, and I had no religion, no traditional blinkers, no traditional lenses on my spectacles, which are very hard to shrug off. I sometimes think I was perhaps the only girl in India whose mother said, "Whatever you do, don't get married" [laughs]. For me, when I see a bride, it gives me a rash. I find them ghoulish, almost. I find it so frightening to see this totally decorated, bejeweled creature who, as I wrote in *The God of Small Things*, is "polishing firewood."

Q: Tell me a little more about your mother.

Roy: She is like someone who strayed off the set of a Fellini film. She's completely nuts. But to have seen a woman who never needed a man, it's such a wonderful thing, to know that that's a possibility, not to suffer. We used to get all this hate mail. Though my mother runs a school and it's phenomenally successful—people book their children in it before they are born—they don't know what to do with her, or with me. The problem is that we are both women who are unconventional in their terms. The least we could have done was to be unhappy. But we aren't, and that's what bothers people.

By the way, my mother is very well known in Kerala because in 1986 she won a public interest litigation case challenging the Syrian Christian inheritance law that said a woman can inherit one-fourth of her father's property or 5,000 rupees, whichever is less. The Supreme Court actually handed down a verdict that gave women equal inheritance retroactive to 1956. But few women take advantage of this right. And the churches have gone so far as to teach fathers to write wills that disinherit their daughters. It's a very strange kind of oppression that happens there.

Q: Since you wrote your novel, you've produced some remarkable political essays. What was that transition like?

Roy: It's only to people in the outside world, who got to know me after *The God of Small Things*, that it seems like a transition. In fact, I'd written political essays before I wrote the novel. I wrote a series of essays called "The Great Indian Rape Trick" about a woman named Phoolan Devi, and the way the film *Bandit Queen* exploited her, and whether or not somebody should have the right to restage the rape of a living woman without her consent. There are issues I've been involved with for a while.

I don't see a great difference between *The God of Small Things* and my works of nonfiction. As I keep saying, fiction is truth. I think fiction is the truest thing there ever was. My whole effort now is to remove that distinction. The writer is the midwife of understanding. It's very important for me to tell politics like a story, to make it real, to draw a link between a man with his child and what fruit he had in the village he lived in before he was kicked out, and how that relates to Mr. Wolfensohn at the World Bank. That's what I want to do. *The God of Small Things* is a book where you connect the very smallest things to the very biggest: whether it's the dent that a baby spider makes on the surface of water or the quality of the moonlight on a river or how history and politics intrude into your life, your house, your bedroom.

Q: Estha, one of the main characters in your novel, is walking "along the banks of the river that smelled of shit and pesticides bought by World Bank loans." The World Bank scheme for the Narmada River Valley envisioned the construction of more than 3,000 dams. The bank has since withdrawn from the project, and the government of India has taken it over. Tell me about the Narmada Bachao Andolan, the NBA.

Roy: When I first met people from the NBA, they told me, "We knew that you would be against the dams and the World Bank when we read *The God of Small Things*." The remarkable thing about the NBA is that it is a cross-section of India. It is a coalition of Adivasis [India's indigenous people], upper-caste big farmers, the Dalits [formerly known as Untouchables], and the middle class. It's a forging of links between the urban and the rural, between the farmers and the fishermen and the writers and the painters. That's what gives it its phenomenal strength, and it's what a lot of people criticize it for in India, saying, you know, these middle class protesters! That makes me furious. The middle class urban engineers are the people who came up with this project! You can't expect the critique to be just Adivasi. You isolate them like that, and it's so easy to crush them. In many ways, people try to delegitimize the involvement of the middle class, saying, how can you speak on behalf of these people? No one is speaking on behalf of anyone. The point is that the NBA is a fantastic example of people linking hands across caste and class. It is the biggest, finest, most magnificent resistance movement since the independence struggle.

Q: One protest you were involved in last year took place at a village on the banks of the Narmada at the site of one of the proposed dams. You were among many who were arrested there. What was that like?

Roy: It was absolutely fantastic. I was in a village called Sulgaon. All night, all over the valley, people started arriving, by tractor, by motorcar, by foot. By three in the morning there were about 5,000 of us. We started walking in the dark to the dam site. The police already knew that the dam site would be captured, but they didn't know from where the people would come. There's a huge area of devastation there. So we walked in the dark. It was amazing. Five thousand people, mostly villagers, but also people from the cities—lawyers, architects, journalists—walking through these byways and crossing streams in absolute silence. There was not a person that lit a *bidi* or coughed or cleared their throats. Occasionally, a whole group of women would sit down and pee and then keep walking. Finally, at dawn, we arrived and took over the dam site. For hours, the police surrounded us. Then there was a baton charge. They arrested thousands of people, including me. The jails were full.

Q: You say that the government of India is "hell-bent on completing the project." What's driving it?

Roy: There are many things. First of all, you have to understand that the myth of big dams is something that's sold to us from the time we're three years old in every school textbook. Nehru said, "Dams are the temples of modern India." So they're like some kind of huge, wet national flags. Before the NBA, it was like, the dam will serve you breakfast in bed, it will get your daughter married and cure your jaundice. People have to understand that they're just monuments to political corruption, and they derive from very undemocratic political institutions. You just centralize natural resources, snatch them away from people, and then you decide who you're going to give them to.

The first dam that was built in the Narmada was the Bargi, completed in 1990. They said it would displace 70,000 people and submerge 101 villages. One day, without warning, the government filled the reservoir, and 114,000 people were displaced and 162 villages were submerged. People were driven from their homes when the waters rose. All they could do was run up the hill with their cattle and children. Ten years later, that dam irrigates 5 percent of the land that they said it would. It irrigates less land than it submerged. They haven't built canals. Because for contractors and politicians, just building the dam in itself is a lot of money.

Q: What happens to those who are displaced?

Roy: Nobody knows. When I was writing "The Greater Common Good," what shocked me more than the figures that do exist are the figures that don't exist. The Indian government does not have any estimate of how many people have been displaced by big dams. I think that's not just a failure of the state, but a failure of the intellectual community. The reason that there aren't these figures is because most of the people that are displaced are again the non-people, the Adivasis and the Dalits. I did a sanity check based on a study of fifty-four dams done by the Indian Institute of Public Administration. According to that study, just reservoir-displaced, which is only one kind of displacement, came to an average of something like 44,000 people per dam. Let's assume that these fifty-four dams are the bigger of the big dams. Let's quarter this average. We know that India has had 3,600 big dams built in the last fifty years. So just a sanity check says that it's thirty-three million people displaced. They all just migrate to the cities. And there, again, they are non-citizens, living in slums. They are subject to being kicked out at any minute, any time the housewives of New Delhi's upscale areas decide that all these slum people are dangerous.

Q: You've compared this uprooting to a kind of garbage disposal.

Roy: It's exactly like that. The Indian government has managed to turn the concept of nonviolence on its head. Nonviolent resistance and nonviolent governance. Unlike, say, China or Turkey or Indonesia, India doesn't mow down its people. It doesn't kill people who are refusing to move. It just waits it out. It continues to do what it has to do and ignores the consequences. Because of the caste system, because of the fact that there is no social link between those who make the decisions and those who suffer the decisions, it just goes ahead and does what it wants. The people also assume that this is their lot, their karma, what was written. It's quite an efficient way of doing things. Therefore, India has a very good reputation in the world as a democracy, as a government that cares, that has just got too much on its hands, whereas, in fact, it's actually creating the problems.

Q: But you say about your own politics that you're "not an anti-development junkie or a proselytizer for the eternal upholding of custom and tradition."

Roy: How can I be? As a woman who grew up in a village in India, I've spent my whole life fighting tradition. There's no way that I want to be a traditional Indian housewife. So I'm not talking about being anti-development. I'm talking about the politics of development, of how do you break down this completely centralized, undemocratic process of decision making? How do you make sure that it's decentralized and that people have power over their lives and their natural resources? Today, the Indian government is trying to present privatization as the alternative to the state, to public enterprise. But privatization is only a further evolution of the centralized state, where the state says that they have the right to give the entire power production in Maharashtra to Enron. They don't have the right. The infrastructure of the public sector in India has been built up over the last fifty years with public money. They don't have the right to sell it to Enron. They cannot do that. Three-quarters of our country lives on the edge of the market economy. You can't tell them that only those who can afford water can have it.

Q: Still, I sense some optimism on your part about what you call the "inherent anarchy" of India to resist the tide of globalization.

Roy: The only thing worth globalizing is dissent, but I don't know whether to be optimistic or not. When I'm outside the cities I do feel optimistic. There is such grandeur in India and so much beauty. I don't know whether they can kill it. I want to think they can't. I don't think that there is anything as beautiful as a sari. Can you kill it? Can you corporatize a sari? Why should multinationals be allowed to come in and try to patent basmati rice? People prefer to eat *roti* and *idlis* and *dosas* rather than McDonald's burgers. Just before I came to the United States, I went to a market in Delhi. There was a whole plate of different kinds of *dal*, lentils. Tears came to my eyes. Today, that's all it takes to make you cry, to look at all the kinds of dal and rice that there are, and to think that they don't want this to exist.

Q: Talk about the material you covered in "The End of Imagination" concerning the nuclear testing on the subcontinent.

Roy: It's so frightening, the nationalism in the air. I'm terrified by it. It can be used to do anything. I know that a world in which countries are stockpiling nuclear weapons and using them in the ways that India and Pakistan and America do to oppress others and to deceive their own people is a dangerous world. The nuclear tests were a way to shore up our flagging self-esteem. India is still flinching from a cultural insult, still looking for its identity. It's about all that.

Q: You said that the jeering young Hindu men celebrating the nuclear test were the same as the ones who were thrilled with the destruction of the Babri mosque.

Roy: Indian intellectuals today feel radical when they condemn fundamentalism, but not many people are talking about the links between privatization, globalization, and fundamentalism. Globalization suits the Indian elite to a T. Fundamentalism doesn't. It's also a class problem. When people stop some film from being shot or burn a book, it's not just that they are saying, this is against Indian culture. They are also saying, you Westernized, elite, English-speaking people are having too much of a good time. It's a very interesting phenomenon. I think it has to be addressed together, not separately. The religious right-wingism is directly linked to globalization and to privatization. When India is talking about selling its entire power sector to foreign multinationals, when the political climate gets too hot and uncomfortable, the government will immediately start saying, should we build a Hindu temple on the site of the Babri mosque? Everyone will go baying off in that direction. It's a game. That's something we have to understand. With one hand, you're selling the country out to Western multinationals. And with the other, you want to defend your borders with nuclear bombs. It's such an irony! You're saying that the world is a global village, but then you want to spend *crores* of rupees on building nuclear weapons.

Q: You use a metaphor of two truck convoys. One is very large, with many people going off into the darkness. The other is much smaller and is going into the light of the promised land. Explain what you mean.

Roy: India lives in several centuries at the same time. Every night outside my house I pass a road gang of emaciated laborers digging a trench to lay fiber-optic cables to speed up our digital revolution. They work by the light of a few candles. That is what is happening in India today. The convoy that melts into the darkness and disappears doesn't have a voice. It doesn't exist on TV. It doesn't have a place in the national newspapers. And so it doesn't exist. Those who are in the small convoy on their way to this glittering destination at the top of the world have completely lost the ability to see the other one. So in Delhi the cars are getting bigger and sleeker, the hotels are getting posher, the gates are getting higher, and the guards are no longer the old *chowkidars*, the watchmen, but they are fellows with guns. And yet the poor are packed into every crevice like lice in the city. People don't see that anymore. It's as if you shine a light very brightly in one place, the darkness deepens around. They don't want to know what's happening. The people who are getting rich can't imagine that the world is not a better place.

Q: You made a decision, or the decision was made for you, to identify with, or to be part of, that large convoy.

Roy: I can't be a part of the large convoy because it's not a choice that you can make. The fact that I'm an educated person means that I can't be on that convoy. I don't want to be on it. I don't want to be a victim. I don't want to disappear into the darkness. I am an artist and a writer, and I do think that one always places oneself in the picture to see where one fits. I left home when I was sixteen and lived in places where it was very easy for me to have fallen the other way. I could have been on the large convoy because I was a woman and I was alone. In India, that's not a joke. I could have ended up very, very badly. I'm lucky that I didn't.

I think my eyes were knocked open and they don't close. I sometimes wish I could close them and look away. I don't always want to be doing this kind of work. I don't want to be haunted by it. Because of who I am and what place I have now in India, I'm petitioned all the time to get involved. It's exhausting and very difficult to have to say, "Look, I'm only one person. I can't do everything." I know that I don't want to be worn to the bone where I lose my sense of humor. But once you've seen certain things, you can't un-see them, and seeing nothing is as political an act as seeing something.

Q: Are you thinking about writing any new fiction?

Roy: I need fiction like you need to eat or exercise, but right now it's so difficult. At the moment, I don't know how to manage my life. I don't know how I'll ever be able to make the space to say, "I'm writing a book now, and I'm not going to be able to do x or y." I would love to.

Q: You feel a sense of responsibility to these silent voices that are calling out to you.

Roy: No, I don't feel responsibility because that's such a boring word.

Q: You're in a privileged position. You are a celebrity within India and also outside.

Roy: But I never do anything because I'm a celebrity, as a rule. I do what I do as a citizen. I stand by what I write and follow through on what I write. It's very easy for me to begin to believe the publicity about myself, whether for or against. It can give you an absurd idea of yourself. I know that there's a fine balance between accepting your own power with grace and misusing it. And I don't ever want to portray myself as a representative of the voiceless. I'm scared of that.

But one of the reasons some people get so angry with me is because I have the space now that a lot of others who think like me don't. It was a mistake maybe for so many people to have opened their hearts to *The God of Small Things*. Because a lot of dams and bombs slipped in along with it.

Poet Illuminates the Politics of Outrage

An Interview with Martín Espada

Margaria Fichtner

Poet Martín Espada—6-foot-4 and 270 pounds—is a big man with a big message.

"My father was a political activist in the Puerto Rican community in New York, and so I was influenced by what I saw and heard all around me," Espada says from his office at the University of Massachusetts, Amherst, where he teaches a variety of Latino-lit courses and creative writing. "I'd been going to demonstrations since I was small. I remember one I went to when I was nine. It was for safe streets, nothing more controversial than that, but it revolved around the killing of a man in my neighborhood who had been murdered by junkies, kicked to death in the street. My father was one of the organizers of a massive demonstration that marched to the site of the murder. We were carrying candles in memory of this man who was a short-order cook with ten kids. But it happened that people in the buildings saw us, and they poured into the streets with their candles. It was a rainy night. I saw hundreds of candles become thousands of candles as we marched in the dark and the rain. I was transformed forever by that. How could you not be changed by such an environment?"

By fifteen, Espada had taken pen in hand, already stoking the fury and outrage that enflame many of his poems today. And as a former legal services lawyer (as well, as a one-time bouncer, factory worker, and desk clerk), he combines his poetic vision "with what I think of as a journalist's eye. That is to say, I know which kinds of experiences will make a good poem. It's something cultivated over time. I sometimes keep things I see or hear in my head for years." The candlelight demonstration simmered for three decades before it finally spilled out as "The Moon Shatters on Alabama Avenue." Typically, Espada's sixth collection, *A Mayan Astronomer in Hell's Kitchen* (W.W. Norton) is wide-ranging in subject and tone, encompassing the mundane (parking meters, his wife's earrings, the clot of burned rice in the bottom of a cooking pot) as well as the universal (slavery, bigotry, civil war). It also includes "Another Nameless Prostitute Says the Man Is Innocent," Espada's now-famous poem about Mumia Abu-Jamal, the radical journalist condemned to death in the 1981 slaying of a police officer in Philadelphia. The poem was commissioned by National Public Radio's *All Things Considered* program, which then, in a decision that raised a censorship storm, refused to air it.

"I learned some hard lessons there," Espada says. "But the fact is, . . . the poem got into so many places it wouldn't have gone otherwise. It's just remarkable how it boomeranged and had the opposite effect they desired." Espada comes to South Florida on Thursday to read for Broward Community College's Writes of Spring celebration.

Q: You're known, it's fair to say, as an angry poet, but there are funny poems in this new collection, too. How does someone who has pledged a lot of his life to trying to correct injustice keep a piece of himself compartmentalized for transcendence or redemption or joy?

A: I could not be a political activist without a sense of humor and without a sense of joy. Those are the basic elements of hope, and without hope there is no movement to change things for the better. . . . I begin with this observation: I'm silly. I'm just goofy. I like to laugh, and I like to make other people laugh. I couldn't consciously use humor as a political tool if I didn't find things innately funny. Political satire lowers the defenses. It makes people relax, makes them trust you. It opens their ears.

Q: What makes poetry such a good political tool?

A: Because it speaks, hopefully, in vivid, specific images. What people often resist in political speech is the rhetoric, the didacticism, the polemics. They don't want to be lectured; they don't want to be scolded. And I don't blame them. . . . Poetry, if it's done well, speaks in the language of the senses, in the language of the image. . . . If I can ground my poem in the image and get people to see and hear what I mean, to taste and touch what I mean, then the political idea will be much more moving and effective.

Q: The first poem in the collection is about your last name, the Spanish word for "sword" or "swordsman," but it's also about history. Why is the role of the poet not only to record history but also to challenge it?

A: That poem is all about looking at the hidden histories of African slaves or the indigenous peoples of the Caribbean, the Taínos, who resisted the Spanish conquest and rule. That still remains a largely untold story, and I can tell it through the prism of my own family. It's there for me. I obviously have roots in three distinct people. We come from the Spanish conquerors, but I also have Taíno blood and African blood. All that is contained in one identity, and that paradox is the essence, I think, of Latino identity. The blood of the conqueror and the blood of the conquered run in the same veins. If you saw my name only as referring to the conquerors, it would be pretty depressing, a terrible inheritance. But I've also inherited the sword of the rebel, the sword of the African slave or the Taíno who fought back.

Imagine the Angels of Bread

Martín Espada

This is the year that squatters evict landlords,
gazing like admirals from the rail
of the roofdeck
or levitating hands in praise
of steam in the shower;
this is the year
that shawled refugees deport judges
who stare at the floor
and their swollen feet
as files are stamped
with their destination;
this is the year that police revolvers,
stove-hot, blister the fingers
of raging cops,
and nightsticks splinter
in their palms;
this is the year
that dark-skinned men
lynched a century ago
return to sip coffee quietly
with the apologizing descendants
of their executioners.

This is the year that those
who swim the border's undertow
and shiver in boxcars
are greeted with trumpets and drums
at the first railroad crossing
on the other side;
this is the year that the hands

pulling tomatoes from the vine
uproot the deed to the earth that sprouts the vine,
the hands canning tomatoes
are named in the will
that owns the bedlam of the cannery;
this is the year that the eyes
stinging from the poison that purifies toilets
awaken at last to the sight
of a rooster-loud hillside,
pilgrimage of immigrant birth;
this is the year that cockroaches
become extinct, that no doctor
finds a roach embedded
in the ear of an infant;
this is the year that the food stamps
of adolescent mothers
are auctioned like gold doubloons,
and no coin is given to buy machetes
for the next bouquet of severed heads
in coffee plantation country.

If the abolition of slave-manacles
began as a vision of hands without manacles,
then this is the year;
if the shutdown of extermination camps
began as imagination of a land
without barbed wire or the crematorium,
then this is the year;
if every rebellion begins with the idea
that conquerors on horseback
are not many-legged gods, that they too drown
if plunged in the river,
then this is the year.

So may every humiliated mouth,
teeth like desecrated headstones,
fill with the angels of bread.

Imagina los Ángeles de Pan

Martín Espada

Este es el año cuando los desamparados
echan a los terratenientes,
mirando como almirantes desde el barandal del balcón
o levantando manos en alabanza
del vapor de la regadera;
este es el año
cuando refugiados en rebozos deportan a los jueces
que miran fijamente al piso
y a sus pies hinchados
al ver sus expedientes estampados
con su destino;
este es el año cuando los revólveres de policía,
calientes como estufas, ampollan los dedos
de policías iracundos,
y sus macanas se hacen astillas
en la palma de sus manos;
este es el año
cuando hombres de piel oscura
linchados hace un siglo
vuelven para saborear calladamente un café
con la descendencia arrepentida
de sus verdugos.

Este es el año cuando los que nadan
la resaca de la frontera
y tiemblan en los furgones
son saludados por trompetas y tambores
en el primer cruce del ferrocarril
del otro lado;
este es el año cuando las manos

que cosechan los frutos de la tomatera
arrancan los títulos a la tierra que la hace brotar,
cuando las manos que enlatan tomates
son nombradas en el testamento
del dueño de la enlatadora caótica;
este es el año cuando los ojos
que arden por el veneno que purifica los inodoros
se despiertan por fin a la visión
de un monte lleno de gallos estrepitosos,
peregrinaje del nacimiento inmigrante;
este es el año de la extinción
de las cucarachas, cuando ningún médico
encuentra una enterrada
en el oído de un infante;
este es el año cuando los cupones de alimento
de madres adolescentes
se subastan como doblones de oro,
y no se da ninguna moneda para comprar machetes
para el próximo ramillete de cabezas decapitadas
entre los cafetales.

Si la abolición de los grilletes del esclavo
se inició con una visión de manos sin grilletes,
entonces este es el año;
si el cierre de los campamentos del exterminio
se inició con la imaginación de una tierra
sin alambre de púas y sin crematorio,
entonces este es el año;
si cada rebelión se inicia con la idea
de que los conquistadores a caballo
no son dioses de piernas múltiples, que ellos también
se ahogan si son sumergidos en el río,
entonces este es el año.

Y que cada boca humillada,
sus dientes como lápidas profanadas,
se llene con los ángeles de pan.

Translation by Camilo Pérez-Bustillo and the author

Source Credits

1. Breaking Silence/The Politics of Voice

Busman, Debra, "You Gotta Be Ready for Some Serious Truth to Be Spoken." *Social Justice: Pedagogies for Social Change* 29(4):150–52. Copyright © 2002. www.socialjusticejournal.org. Reprinted by permission of the author.

Mirikitani, Janice, "Breaking Silence." From *Shedding Silence*, by Janice Mirikitani (Berkeley, California: Celestial Arts). Copyright © 1987 by Janice Mirikitani. Reprinted by permission of Ten Speed Press. www.tenspeed.com.

Rich, Adrienne, "Frame." From *The Fact of a Doorframe: Selected Poems 1950–2001*, by Adrienne Rich. Copyright © 2002, 1981 by Adrienne Rich. Reprinted by permission of the author and W.W. Norton & Company, Inc.

Abani, Chris, "Ode to Joy." From *Kalakuta Republic*, by Chris Abani. Copyright © 2000. Reprinted by permission of Saqi Books.

McCarriston, Linda, "A Castle in Lynn." From *Eva-Mary* (pp. 16–17), by Linda McCarriston. Copyright © 1991. Reprinted by permission of TriQuarterly Books/Northwestern University Press (Evanston, Illinois).

Kelly, Tracy, "My Coming Out." Printed by permission of the author.

Anzaldúa, Gloria, "Speaking in Tongues: A Letter to Third World Women Writers." From *This Bridge Called My Back: Writings by Radical Women of Color*, eds. Cherríe Moraga and Gloria Anzaldúa (New York: Kitchen Table Press, pp. 165–74). Copyright © 1983 The Gloria E. Anzaldúa Literary Trust. Reprinted by permission of the Gloria Anzaldúa Estate, AnaLouise Keating and Kit Quan, co-trustees.

Gates, Henry Louis, Jr., "Introduction: On Bearing Witness." From *Bearing Witness: Selections from African-American Autobiography in the Twentieth Century* (pp. 3–9). Copyright © 1991 by Henry Louis Gates, Jr. Reprinted by permission of the author.

2. Where I Come From

Soto, Gary, "The Jacket." From *The Effect of Knut Hamsun on a Fresno Boy: Recollections and Short Essays*, by Gary Soto. Copyright © 1983, 2000 by Gary Soto. Reprinted by permission of Persea Books, Inc. (New York).

Bloom, Jacob, "Singing." Printed by permission of the author.

Queen, Khadijah, "The New Reb." First published in *Poet's Canvas* (www .poetscanvas.org), Issue 20, Fall 2002. Reprinted by permission of the author.

Torres, Viana Enedina, "There Ain't No Starbucks in the East Side." Printed by permission of the author.

Shenoda, Matthew, "Where We Come From." From *Somewhere Else*. Copyright © 2005 by Matthew Shenoda. Reprinted by permission of Coffee House Press (Minneapolis, Minnesota), www.coffeehousepress.org.

Hamer, Forrest, "Goldsboro narrative #5: Elders the grandchildren of slaves." From *Call and Response*, by Forrest Hamer. Copyright © 1995. Reprinted by permission of the author and Alice James Books.

Herrera, Juan Felipe, "The Return of Jake Condor." From *Avatars of Kali: Parables, Mitologías, and Mandala Poems*, unpublished. Copyright © 2008 by Juan Felipe Herrera. Reprinted by permission of the author.

Blaeser, Kimberly, "Apprenticed to Justice." From *Apprenticed to Justice* (Salt Publishing, www.saltpublishing.com). Copyright © 2007 by Kimberly Blaeser. Reprinted by permission of the author.

Salisbury, Ralph, "A Fancy Dancer, Ascending Among Mountain Flowers." From *Blind Pumper at the Well* (Cambridge Earthworks Series). Copyright © 2008 by Ralph Salisbury. Reprinted by permission of the author.

Dixon, Amy Samala, "Chicken Blood." Printed by permission of the author.

Gonzalez, Ray, "Peace Grove." From *Memory Fever* (Tucson: University of Arizona Press, pp. 73–81) Copyright © 1993 by Ray Gonzalez. Reprinted by permission of the author.

Walker, Alice, "Beauty: When the Other Dancer Is the Self." From *In Search of Our Mothers' Gardens: Womanist Prose*. Copyright © 1983 by Alice Walker. Reprinted by permission of Houghton Mifflin Harcourt Publishing Company.

3. Writing Race, Class, Gender, and Resistance

Bambara, Toni Cade, "The Lesson." From *Gorilla My Love*, by Toni Cade Bambara. Copyright © 1972 by Toni Cade Bambara. Reprinted by permission of Random House, Inc.

Busman, Debra, "like a woman." Copyright © 2007. Originally published in *The Los Angeles Review* No. 4: 69–71. Reprinted by permission of the author.

Sundiata, Sekou, "Blink Your Eyes." From *The Language of Life: A Festival of Poets*, ed. Bill Moyers (New York: Broadway Books, 1995): 396–98. Reprinted by permission of Maurine D. Knighton, Administratrix, Estate of Robert Feaster.

Chin, Marilyn, "Blues on Yellow." From *Rhapsody in Plain Yellow*, by Marilyn Chin. Copyright © 2002 by Marilyn Chin. Reprinted by permission of W.W. Norton & Company, Inc.

García, Diana, "Las Rubias." From *When Living Was a Labor Camp*. Copyright © 2000 by Diana García. Reprinted by permission of the University of Arizona Press.

Clifton, Lucille, "poem to my uterus." From *Quilting: Poems 1987–1990*, by Lucille Clifton. Copyright © 1991 by Lucille Clifton. Reprinted by permission of BOA Editions, Ltd. www.boaeditions.org.

Ellis, Kelly Norman, "Daddy Blues." From *Tougaloo Blues*, by Kelly Norman Ellis. Copyright © 2003 by Kelly Norman Ellis. Reprinted by permission of Third World Press, Inc. (Chicago, Illinois).

Pratt, Minnie Bruce, "Standing in the Elevator." *The Progressive* 71(1): 30. Copyright © 2007. Reprinted by permission of *The Progressive* (409 E. Main St., Madison, WI 53703), www.progressive.org.

Divakaruni, Chitra Banerjee, "The Brides Come to Yuba City." From *Black Candle: Poems about Women from India, Pakistan, and Bangladesh*, by Chitra Banerjee Divakaruni. Copyright © 2000, 1991. Reprinted by permission of Calyx.

Kincaid, Jamaica, "Girl." From *At the Bottom of the River, by Jamaica Kincaid*. Copyright © 1983 by Jamaica Kincaid. Reprinted by permission of Farrar, Straus and Giroux, LLC.

Gildner, Gary, "First Practice." From *Blue Like the Heavens: New and Selected Poems*, by Gary Gildner. Copyright © 1984. Reprinted by permission of the University of Pittsburgh Press.

Mecca, Tommi Avicolli, "He Defies You Still: The Memoirs of a Sissy." From *Reconstructing Gender: A Multicultural Anthology*, 3rd ed. (Blacklick, Ohio: McGraw-Hill College) Copyright © 2003. Originally published in *Radical Teacher* #24. Reprinted by permission of the author.

Knapp, Zachary, "Terreno." Originally published in *Reflections on Community-Based Writing Instruction*, Spring 2000, Goucher College. Reprinted by permission of the author.

Adler, Frances Payne, "The Fear That Doesn't." From *The Making of a Matriot: Poetry and Prose 1991–2003* by Frances Payne Adler (Los Angeles: Red Hen Press): 37–38. Copyright © 2003 Frances Payne Adler. Originally published in *The Progressive* (Madison, Wisconsin), May 1997. Reprinted by permission of the author.

Dalton, Harlon. "White Skin Privilege" (excerpt). From *Racial Healing: Confronting the Fear between Blacks and Whites*, by Harlon L. Dalton. Copyright © 1995 by Harlon L. Dalton. Reprinted by permission of the author and Doubleday, a division of Random House, Inc.

4. Coming into Language

Yamamoto DeSoto, Hisaye, "Wilshire Bus." From *Seventeen Syllables and Other Stories*. Copyright © 1988 by Hisaye Yamamoto DeSoto. Reprinted by permission of Rutgers University Press.

Chrystos. "Not Editable." From *Making Face, Making Soul : Haciendo Caras*, ed. Gloria Anzaldúa. Copyright © 1990 by Chrystos. Reprinted by permission of Aunt Lute Books. www.auntlute.com.

Jordan, June, "Nobody Mean More to Me Than You / And the Future Life of Willie Jordan." From *On Call: Political Essays*, by June Jordan (South End Press, 1985): 123–39. Copyright © 2005 June Jordan Literary Estate Trust. Reprinted by permission. www.junejordan.com.

Lee, Li-Young, "Persimmons." From *Rose*, by Li-Young Lee. Copyright © 1986 by Li-Young Lee. Reprinted by permission of BOA Editions, Ltd. www.boaeditions.org.

Lorde, Audre, "The Transformation of Silence into Language and Action." From *The Cancer Journals* (pp. 16–22), by Audre Lorde. Copyright © 1980 by Audre Lorde. Reprinted by permission of Aunt Lute Books. www.auntlute.com.

Baca, Jimmy Santiago, "Coming into Language." From *Working in the Dark: Reflections of a Poet in the Barrio* (pp. 3–11). Copyright © 1994. Reprinted by permission of Red Crane Books/Museum of New Mexico Press.

5. The Work We Do

Jiménez, Francisco, "The Circuit." From *The Circuit* (pp. 73–82), by Francisco Jiménez. Copyright 1997 by Francisco Jiménez. Reprinted by permission of the author.

Busman, Debra, "Like the Wind." Originally published in *580 Split*, Issue 1: 55–58. Reprinted by permission of the author.

Trethewey, Natasha, "Domestic Work, 1937." From *Domestic Work*. Copyright © 2000 by Natasha Trethewey. Reprinted by permission of Graywolf Press (Saint Paul, Minnesota) and the author.

García, Diana, "Cotton Rows, Cotton Blankets." From *When Living Was a Labor Camp*, by Diana García. Copyright © 2000 by Diana García. Reprinted by permission of the author and the University of Arizona Press.

Cervantes, Lorna Dee, "Cannery Town in August." From *Emplumada*, by Lorna Dee Cervantes. Copyright © 1982. Reprinted by permission of the University of Pittsburgh Press.

Không, Chân, "In the War Zone." From *Learning True Love: How I Learned and Practiced Social Change in Vietnam*, by Sister Chân Không. Copyright © 1993. Reprinted by permission of Parallax Press (Berkeley, California), www.parallax.org.

García, Diana, "Camp Observations." An earlier version appeared in *When Living Was a Labor Camp*, by Diana García. Copyright © 2000 by Diana García. Reprinted by permission of the author and the University of Arizona Press.

Anzaldúa, Gloria, "now let us shift . . . the path of conocimiento . . . inner work, public acts" (excerpt). From *This Bridge We Call Home: Radical Visions for Transformation*, eds. Gloria E. Anzaldúa and AnaLouise Keating (New York: Routledge, 2002). Reprinted by permission of the Gloria Anzaldúa Estate, AnaLouise Keating and Kit Quan, co-trustees.

6. A Story About the Body: Environment, Illness, and Health

Masumoto, David Mas, "epitaph for a peach." Prologue from *Epitaph for a Peach: Four Seasons on My Family Farm* (pp. ix–xii), by David Mas Masumoto. Copyright © 1995 by David Mas Masumoto. Reprinted by permission of HarperCollins Publishers.

Espada, Martín, "Federico's Ghost" and "El Fantasma de Federico." From *Poetry Like Bread, ed. Martín Espada. (Willimantic, Connecticut: Curbstone Press)*: 144. Copyright © 1994, 2000–2001. Reprinted by permission of the author.

Tamez, Margo, "Addiction to the Dead." An earlier version appeared in *Raven Eye*, by Margo Tamez (University of Arizona Press, 2007). Reprinted by permission of the author.

Albarran, Rafael, "With Knees to the Ground." Printed by permission of the author.

Hass, Robert, "A Story About the Body." From *Human Wishes* (p. 32), by Robert Hass. Copyright © 1989 by Robert Hass. Reprinted by permission of HarperCollins Publishers.

Corso, Paola, "Once I Was Told the Air Was Not for Breathing." *The Progressive* 68(6): 41. Reprinted by permission of *The Progressive* (409 E. Main St., Madison, WI 53703), www.progressive.org.

Tuckey, Melissa, "Ghost Fishing Louisiana." From *Rope As Witness* (Columbus, Ohio: Puddinghouse Publications, 2007). Originally published in *Cincinnati Poetry Review*. Reprinted by permission of the author.

de León, Aya, "Grito de Vieques" (Burning Bush Publications: People Before Profit Poetry Prize). Copyright © 2000 by Aya de León. Reprinted by permission of the author.

Gale, Kate, "Sphere." From *Mating Season* (Tupelo Press). Copyright © 2004 by Kate Gale. Reprinted by permission of the author.

Young, Gary, "Eating Wild Mushrooms." From *The Dream of a Moral Life* (Providence, Rhode Island: Copper Beech Press): 13. Copyright © 1990 by Gary Young. Reprinted by permission of the author.

Hogan, Linda, "All My Relations." From *Dwellings: A Spiritual History of the Living World*, by Linda Hogan. Copyright © 1995 by Linda Hogan. Reprinted by permission of W.W. Norton & Company, Inc.

White, Evelyn C., "Born To Beauty." Copyright © 2008. Printed by permission of the author.

7. Releasing the Dragons: When the Prison Doors Are Opened

Masters, Jarvis Jay, "Mourning Exercise." From *Finding Freedom: Writings from Death Row* (Junction City, Califoria: Padma Publishing): 79–82. Copyright © 1997 by Jarvis Jay Masters. Reprinted by permission of Padma Publishing.

Shakur, Assata, "No One Can Stop the Rain." From *Hauling Up the Morning: An Anthology of Prison Writings*, eds. Tim Blunk, Raymond Luc Levasseur, and the editors of Jacobin Books. Copyright © 1990 by Assata Shakur. Reprinted by permission of Red Sea Press (Trenton, New Jersey).

Chrystos, "No Public Safety." From *Not Vanishing* (Vancouver: Press Gang): 26–27. Copyright © 1988 by Chrystos. Reprinted by permission of the author.

Komisaruk, Katya, "They Are Searching." From *Hauling Up the Morning: An Anthology of Prison Writings* (pp. 32–33), eds. Tim Blunk, Raymond Luc Levasseur, and the editors of Jacobin Books. Copyright © 1990 by Katya Komisaruk. Reprinted by permission of Red Sea Press (Trenton, New Jersey).

Baca, Jimmy Santiago, "Letters Come to Prison." From *Doing Time: 25 Years of Prison Writing* (p. 50), ed. Bell Gale Chevigny. Copyright © Jimmy Santiago Baca. Reprinted by permission of Arcade Publishing (New York, New York).

Rosenberg, Ethel, "If We Die." From *Hauling Up the Morning: An Anthology of Prison Writings* (p. 223), eds. Tim Blunk, Raymond Luc Levasseur, and the editors of Jacobin Books. Copyright © 1990. Reprinted by permission of Red Sea Press (Trenton, New Jersey).

Clark, Judith, "After My Arrest." From *Doing Time: 25 Years of Prison Writings*, ed. Bell Gale Chevigny. Copyright © Judith Clark. Reprinted by permission of Arcade Publishing (New York, New York).

Abani, Chris, "Mango Chutney." From *Kalakuta Republic* (pp. 71–73), by Chris Abani. Copyright © 2000. Reprinted by permission of Saqi Books.

Brutus, Dennis, "Sequence for Mumia Abu-Jamal." From *In Defense of Mumia*, eds. S. E. Anderson and Tony Medina (New York: Writers and Readers Publishing). Copyright © 1996. Reprinted by permission of the author.

Tannenbaum, Judith, "Cleansing the Doors of Perception" (excerpt). From *Disguised As a Poem: My Years Teaching Poetry at San Quentin*, by Judith Tannenbaum. Copyright © 2000 (Hanover, New Hampshire: University Press of New England): 26–46. Reprinted by permission.

Peltier, Leonard, "*Prison Writings: My Life Is My Sun Dance*" (excerpt). From *Prison Writings: My Life Is My Sun Dance*, ed. Harvey Arden (New York: St. Martin's Press). Copyright © 2000. Reprinted by permission of St. Martin's Press.

Walker, Alice, "To Be Led by Happiness (Re: March 8, 2003)." Copyright © 2006 by Alice Walker. This piece originally appeared in *We Are the Ones We Have Been Waiting For: Inner Light in a Time of Darkness*, by Alice Walker. Reprinted by permission of The New Press. www.thenewpress.com.

8. War and Other Forms of Violence

Cano, Daniel, "Somewhere Outside Duc Pho." Originally published in *Pieces of the Heart: New Chicano Fiction*, ed. Gary Soto (Chronicle Books): 24–37. Copyright © 1993 by Daniel Cano. Reprinted by permission of the author.

Mirikitani, Janice, "Tomatoes." From *Shedding Silence* (pp. 37–42), by Janice Mirikitani. Copyright © 1987 by Janice Mirikitani. Reprinted by permission of Celestial Arts (Berkeley, California). www.tenspeed.com.

Hull, Akasha Gloria, "These Bones, These Bones." From *Soul Talk*, by Akasha Gloria Hull. Copyright © 2001. Reprinted by permission of Inner Traditions/Bear & Co. (Rochester, Vermont 05767) www.InnerTraditions.com.

Jordan, June, "Poem About My Rights." From *Naming Our Destiny* (pp. 102–5), by June Jordan. Copyright © 2005 by the June Jordan Literary Estate Trust. Reprinted by permission. www.junejordan.com.

Queen, Khadijah, "Peacekeeping in Bunia." Reprinted by permission of the author.

González, Rigoberto, "In the Village of Missing Fathers." Printed by permission of the author.

Ostriker, Alicia, "interlude: the avenue of the americas" (excerpt). From *the volcano sequence* (University of Pittsburgh Press): 93–94. Copyright © 2002. Reprinted by permission of the author.

Harshman, Marc, "Even the Tin Man Had a Heart." *The Progressive* 67(9):34. Copyright © 2003. Reprinted by permission of *The Progressive* (409 E. Main St., Madison, WI 53703), www.progressive.org.

Darwish, Mahmoud, "The House Murdered." *The Progressive* 70(11):40. Copyright © 2006. Reprinted by permission of *The Progressive* (409 E. Main St., Madison, WI 53703), www.progressive.org.

Forché, Carolyn, "The Colonel." From *The Country between Us* (p. 16), by Carolyn Forché. Copyright © 1981 by Carolyn Forché. Originally published in *Women's International Resource Exchange*. Reprinted by permission of HarperCollins Publishers.

Santiago, Esmeralda, "The American Invasion of Macún" (excerpt). From *When I Was Puerto Rican* (pp. 61–68), by Esmeralda Santiago. Copyright © 1993. Reprinted by permission of Da Capo Press, a member of Perseus Books Group.

9. Waging Peace/Love as Revolution

Hughes, Langston, "Thank You, M'am." From *Short Stories*, by Langston Hughes. Copyright © 1996 by Ramona Bass and Arnold Rampersad. Reprinted by permission of Hill and Wang, a division of Farrar, Straus & Geroux, LLC.

Hanh, Thich Nhat, "Call Me by My True Names." From *Love in Action: Writings on Nonviolent Social Change*, by Thich Nhat Hanh. Copyright © 1993 by Thich Nhat Hanh. Reprinted by permission of Parallax Press (Berkeley, California). www.parallax.org.

Sanchez, Sonia, "Litany." Copyright © 2008 by Sonia Sanchez. Reprinted by permission of the author.

Adler, Frances Payne, "Matriot." From *The Making of a Matriot*, by Frances Payne Adler. Copyright © 2003 (Los Angeles: Red Hen Press): 33. Originally published in the *San Diego Tribune*, December 1993. Reprinted by permission of the author.

Lopez, Linda, "Luna Llena." Printed by permission of the author.

Ruchowitz-Roberts, Elliot, "Revolution." Printed by permission of the author.

Olds, Sharon, "Late Poem to My Father." From *The Gold Cell* (p. 40), by Sharon Olds. Copyright © 1987 by Sharon Olds. Reprinted by permission of the author and Alfred A. Knopf, a division of Random House, Inc.

Nye, Naomi Shihab, "Lunch in Nablus City Park" and "Kindness." From *Words Under the Words: Selected Poems*, by Naomi Shihab Nye. Copyright © 1995. Reprinted by permission of Far Corner Books (Portland, Oregon).

Stafford, William, "At the Un-National Monument along the Canadian Border." From *The Way It Is: New and Selected Poems*. Copyright © 1975, 1998 by the Estate of William Stafford. Reprinted by permission of Graywolf Press (Saint Paul, Minnesota).

Brutus, Dennis, "shadow-patterns of leaves." Reprinted by permission of the author.

Campo, Rafael, "Allegory." From *The Other Man Was Me*, by Rafael Campo. Copyright © 1994 by Arte Público Press, University of Houston. Reprinted by permission of Arte Público Press.

Birtha, Becky, "Route 23: 10th and Bigler to Bethlehem Pike." From *Lovers' Choice* (pp. 63–66), by Becky Birtha. Copyright © 1987. Reprinted by permission of Seal Press, a member of Perseus Books Group.

Rich, Adrienne, "Arts of the Possible" (excerpt). From *Arts of the Possible: Essays and Conversations*, by Adrienne Rich. Copyright © 2001 by Adrienne Rich. Reprinted by permission of the author and W.W. Norton & Company, Inc. The poem "Clarities," by Juan Gelman, which appears in this piece, was published in his book *Unthinkable Tenderness* (1997) and is reprinted by permission of the University of California Press.

10. Talking, Teaching, and Imagining: Social Action Writing

Smith, Patricia, "Building Nicole's Mama." From *Teahouse of the Almighty*, by Patricia Smith (Coffeehouse Press): 1–3. Copyright © 2006. Reprinted by permission of the author.

Adler, Frances Payne, "Activism in Academia: A Social Action Writing Program" (excerpt). From *Social Justice: Pedagogies for Social Change* (San Francisco) 29(4): 136–49. Copyright © 2002. www.socialjusticejournal.org. Reprinted by permission of the author.

Derricotte, Toi, "Baring/Bearing Anger: Race in the Creative Writing Classroom." From *AWP Chronicle* (Fairfax, Virginia), October–November 1995: 13–14. Reprinted by permission of the author.

Algarín, Miguel, "Poetry into the Twenty-first Century: The Democratization of Verse" (excerpt). From "Sidewalk of High Art, Introduction, Part III," in *Aloud: Voices from the Nuyorican Poets Café* (New York: Henry Holt & Co.): 14–23. Copyright © 1994 by Miguel Algarín. Reprinted by permission of the author.

Cott, Jonathan, "Poetry in Motion: An Interview with Carolyn Forché" (excerpt). *Rolling Stone College Papers* (New York): 81–87, 110–11. Copyright © 1983. Reprinted by permission of the author.

Cusac, Anne-Marie, "An Interview with Sam Hamill." *The Progressive* 67(4): 35–39. Copyright © 2003. Reprinted by permission of *The Progressive* (409 E. Main St., Madison, WI 53703), www.progressive.org.

Barsamian, David, "An Interview with Arundhati Roy." *The Progressive* (Madison, Wisconsin) April 2001: 33–39. Reprinted by permission of the author.

Fichtner, Margaria, "Poet Illuminates the Politics of Outrage: An Interview with Martín Espada." *Miami Herald*, April 1, 2001. Reprinted by permission of The Herald Printing and Publishing Co. and McClatchy Interactive West.

Espada, Martín. "Imagine the Angels of Bread" and "Imagina los Ángeles de Pan." From *Poetry Like Bread*, trans. Camilo Pez-Bustillo and Martín Espada (Willimantic, Conn.: Curbstone Press): ix–xiv. Copyright © 1996. Reprinted by permission of the author.

About the Editors

Frances Payne Adler has published political poetry for 25 years, collaborated with a photographer to bring activist art exhibitions into state and federal capitol buildings, and founded the Creative Writing and Social Action Program at California State University Monterey Bay. She is the author of five books: two books of poetry, *Making of a Matriot* (Red Hen, 2003) and *Raising the Tents* (Calyx, 1993); and three poetry-photography books and exhibitions with photographer Kira Carrillo Corser. The exhibitions, advocating for the homeless and for health care reform, have been shown in the Cannon and Rayburn Buildings in Washington, D.C., and in state capitol buildings across the country. Adler's poems and prose have also been published in *Poetry International*, *The Progressive*, *The Congressional Record*, *Calyx*, and *Women's Review of Books*, among others. Awards include an NEA Regional Award and a California State Senate Award for Artistic and Social Collaboration.

Debra Busman writes fiction and creative nonfiction and has been an activist all of her life, beginning *in utero* at marches and protests with her labor union mother. A community organizer and member of the National Coalition Building Institute, Busman has fought for decades for free speech, civil rights, and prison justice. She then became an activist writer and co-director of the Creative Writing and Social Action Program at CSU Monterey Bay, and coordinator of the Division of Humanities and Communication's Service Learning Program. Her stories have been published in *The LA Review*, *Chinquapin*, *Women's Studies Quarterly*, and *580 Split*. Her essay "You Gotta Be Ready for Some Truth" was published in *Social Justice Journal: Pedagogies for Social Change*. Busman received her MFA from Mills College. She was awarded an Astrea Foundation Award for fiction in 2003.

Diana García's first book of poetry, *When Living Was a Labor Camp* (University of Arizona Press, 2000), was awarded an American Book Award by the Before Columbus Foundation. Her work has been published in *Touching the Fire: 15 Poets of Today's Latino Renaissance* (Anchor/Doubleday, 1998), *El Coro: A Chorus of Latino and Latina Poetry* (University of Massachusetts, 1997), *Latino Boom: An Anthology of U.S. Latino Literature* (Pearson Longman, 2005), and *Pieces of the Heart: New Chicano Fiction* (Chronicle Books, 1993), among others. García was a founding member of the San Diego/Tijuana Border Voices Project and founder and former director of the Central Connecticut Poetry in the Schools Project. She has also taught in the California Poets in the Schools program. A native of California's San Joaquin Valley, she was born in Camp CPC, a migrant farmworker labor camp. At different times in her life, she has been a single mother on welfare, a secretary, a personnel manager, and a sentencing consultant to defense attorneys. García is an associate professor and co-director of the Creative Writing and Social Action Program at CSU Monterey Bay.

About the Contributors

Chris Abani published his first novel in his native Nigeria at the age of sixteen. Because his writings spoke against the Nigerian government, he was imprisoned, tortured, and eventually placed on death row. After escaping, Abani has lived in the United States since 1999. He is the author of many books of poetry and prose, most recently *Song for Night* (Akashic, 2007). Abani is a professor at the University of California, Riverside.

Rafael Albarran studied social action writing at California State University Monterey Bay. He currently attends law school and clerks for a Santa Cruz/Monterey County workers' compensation law firm. His interest is disability benefits for agricultural workers.

Miguel Algarín started the Nuyorican Poets' Cafe in 1971 in his living room on the Lower East Side of New York City. The Nuyorican Poets Cafe is now a successful nonprofit that sponsors literary and visual art. Algarín has written several books of poetry and prose, as well as plays, and has edited and contributed to multiple anthologies. Algarín is Professor Emeritus at Rutgers University.

Gloria Anzaldúa contributed to and edited anthologies that deal with race, feminism, and sexual identity, including *This Bridge Called My Back: Writings by Radical Women of Color* (co-edited with Cherríe Moraga, Kitchen Table, 1983). She also wrote several books, including *Borderlands/La Frontera: The New Mestiza* (Spinsters/Aunt Lute, 1987), which uses poetry and prose to discuss being a feminist, lesbian Chicana.

Jimmy Santiago Baca, of Indio-Mexican descent, has written numerous books of poetry and prose. His writing focuses on his experience in prison, where he learned to read, and the experience of Chicanos in the Southwest. He is the founder of Cedar Tree, a nonprofit that aids people from diverse socioeconomic backgrounds in furthering their education. For more information, visit www.jimmysantiagobaca.com.

Toni Cade Bambara was raised in and around New York City. A social activist and a writer, she did not believe that art and politics should be kept separate. Her writings reveal the complexities of the African American community and of individuals. She published many books; her unfinished novel, *Those Bones Are Not My Child* (Pantheon, 1999), was edited by Toni Morrison and published posthumously.

David Barsamian is Director of Alternative Radio in Boulder, Colorado. He and Arundhati Roy co-authored *The Checkbook and Cruise Missile* (South End Press, 2004). He interviewed Arundhati Roy. For more information, visit http://www.alternativeradio.org.

Becky Birtha is an African American feminist, poet, and short story writer. She has written two books of poems, *Lover's Choice* (Seal Press, 1987) and *Forbidden Poems* (Seal Press, 1991), as well as a book of short stories. Her works often concern African American lesbians, interracial relationships, and strong women. Birtha has also written a children's book and has a Web site directed toward children: www.beckybirtha.net.

Kimberly Blaeser, of Anishinaabe and German ancestry, is an enrolled member of the Minnesota Chippewa Tribe and grew up on the White Earth Reservation in northwestern Minnesota. A professor of English at the University of Wisconsin, Milwaukee, Blaeser is the author of several books of poetry, *Trailing You* (Greenfield Review Press, 1994), winner of the First Book Award from the Native Writers Circle of the Americas, and *Absentee Indians and Other Poems* (Michigan State University Press, 2002), as well as a scholarly study, *Gerald Vizenor: Writing in the Oral Tradition* (University of Oklahoma Press, 1996). Her most recent collection of poetry is *Apprenticed to Justice* (Salt Publishing, 2007).

Jacob Bloom studied social action writing at California State University Monterey Bay. He now lives in the Atlanta area, where he works as a bank teller. He is a student in the Master of Arts in Professional Writing program at Kennesaw State University.

Dennis Brutus, an activist against apartheid during the 1960s, was imprisoned on Robben Island in South Africa along with other notable prisoners, including Nelson Mandela. Following his release, he went into exile, first to England, then to the United States. He is Professor Emeritus at the University of Pittsburgh. Author of four collections of poetry, his most recent is *Leafdrift* (Whirlwind, 2005).

Rafael Campo is a gay, second-generation Cuban-Italian American, a poet, and a physician, who grew up in suburban New Jersey and Venezuela. He has several books of poetry and a memoir, *The Poetry of Healing* (W.W. Norton, 1997). His latest book is *The Enemy* (Duke University Press, 2007). For more information, visit www.rafaelcampo.com.

Daniel Cano has authored *Pepe Rios* (Arte Público, 1991) and *Shifting Loyalties* (Arte Público, 1995). He is a professor in the Spanish Department at Santa Monica College.

Lorna Dee Cervantes was born in San Francisco to a working-class family. She founded Mango Publications and co-edits *Red Dirt*, a multicultural literary journal. Her latest book of poetry is *Drive: The First Quartet* (Wings Press, 2006). Formerly a professor at the University of Colorado, Boulder, she now lives, writes, and works out of San Francisco. For more information, visit lornadice.blogspot.com.

Marilyn Chin was born in Hong Kong and moved to the United States with her family in 1962. Her writing explores cross-culturalism, assimilation, racism, feminism, and issues of patriarchy. Chin has written three collections of poetry, most recently *Rhapsody in Plain Yellow* (W.W. Norton, 2002). Her book of fiction, *Revenge of the Mooncake Vixen* (W.W. Norton), is forthcoming in fall 2009. She co-directs and is a professor of poetry in San Diego State University's MFA program.

Chrystos, of Menominee, Lithuanian, and Alsace-Lorraine descent, is from San Francisco. She is a poet and activist for Native American rights, including disputes concerning land. Her poetry addresses these issues as well as her experiences as a lesbian. She has published five books of poetry, including *Fugitive Colors* (Cleveland State University Poetry Center, 1995).

Judith Clark, a poet, resides in Bedford Hills Correctional Facility in New York State. She is serving a term of 75 years to life for being the get-away driver in a politically motivated armed robbery where two police officers and a Brinks security guard were murdered. Since 1981, when she was arrested, she has worked to acknowledge her role in the incident and the harm she caused. For more information, visit the Friends of Judy Clark Web site: www.judithclark.org.

Lucille Clifton has published several volumes of poetry, children's books, and a memoir. Her writing addresses the African American inner city experience. Her children's books provide examples of African American role models and are intended to help children to navigate the world. In 1999, Clifton won the National Book Award for Poetry for *Blessing the Boats: New and Selected Poems, 1988–2000* (BOA Editions, 2000).

Paola Corso's book of short stories, *Giovanna's 86 Circles* (University of Wisconsin Press, 2005), uses magical realism to depict the lives of working-class women in the rust belt. Corso is also the author of a volume of poetry entitled *Death by Renaissance* (Bottom Dog Press, 2004). For more information, visit www.paolacorso.com.

Jonathan Cott has been a contributing editor to *Rolling Stone Magazine* since its inception. He interviewed Carolyn Forché.

Ann-Marie Cusac, formerly an editor and investigative reporter for *The Progressive,* is currently a professor of communication at Roosevelt University in Chicago. She interviewed Sam Hamill.

Harlon Dalton is a lawyer, Yale Law School professor, and ordained priest of the Episcopal Church. He was an early AIDS activist and co-edited

AIDS and the Law: A Guide for the Public (Yale University Press, 1987) with Scott Burris. Dalton also wrote *Racial Healing: Confronting the Fear Between Blacks and Whites* (Doubleday, 1995).

Mahmoud Darwish was born in Al Birweh, Palestine. During the establishment of the State of Israel in 1948, his village was destroyed and his family fled to Lebanon. They returned the following year, secretly re-entering Israel. He drew the attention of Israeli authorities with a poem written at age fourteen. As an adult, Darwish was imprisoned several times for his poetry before going into exile. He returned to Palestine in 1996 and continued to write about the Palestinian experience until his untimely death in August 2008. Considered Palestine's most eminent poet, Darwish wrote more than thirty books, most recently, *The Butterfly's Burden* (Copper Canyon Press, 2006). For more information, visit www.mahmouddarwish.com/english/index.htm.

Aya de León is a black Puerto Rican writer, poet, performer, and community healer. Renowned for slam poetry and hip-hop theater, de Leon has won many awards and has produced several chapbooks and two CDs. In 1996, she married herself and created an alternative Valentine's Day celebration. De Leon is the director of June Jordan's Poetry for the People at the University of California, Berkeley. For more information, visit www.ayadeleon.com.

Toi Derricotte is the author of five books of poetry and prose—most recently, *Natural Birth* (Firebrand, 2000), *Tender* (University of Pittsburgh Press, 1997), and a literary memoir, *The Black Notebooks* (W.W. Norton, 1997). Together with Cornelius Eady, she founded Cave Canem, a workshop retreat for black poets. She teaches at the University of Pittsburgh.

Chitra Banerjee Divakaruni grew up in Kolkata, India, and moved to the United States in 1976. Divakaruni writes about immigrants and the experiences of Indian women in both countries. She serves on the boards of Maitri and Daya, two organizations that help South Asian and South Asian American women experiencing domestic violence. Her latest novel is *Palace of Illusions* (Doubleday 2008). For more information, visit www.chitradivakaruni.com.

Amy Samala Dixon studied social action writing at California State University Monterey Bay. She lives in the greater Los Angeles area, where she teaches at a special school for autistic toddlers with communication difficulties.

Kelly Norman Ellis is a founding member of Affrilachian Poets, a group of African American poets from the Appalachian region. Ellis's first book of poetry, *Tougaloo Blues* (Third World Press, 2003), celebrates the black southern woman's experience. She is working on a new collection of poetry entitled *The Shoe Cobbler's Daughter*. Ellis is a professor of creative writing at Chicago State University.

Martín Espada is a former trial lawyer and now a professor of English at the University of Massachusetts, Amherst. His poetry explores the experiences of working-class immigrants in this country and the experiences of the dispossessed in both North and South America. Espada is the author of thirteen books, most recently *The Republic of Poetry* (W.W. Norton, 2006). It was a finalist for the 2007 Pulitzer prize. For more information, visit www.martinespada.net.

Margaria Fichtner is a *Miami Herald* features editor. She interviewed Martín Espada.

Carolyn Forché has long been a leading force for "witness" poetry in the United States. In the late '70s, Forché worked for Amnesty International in El Salvador and witnessed human rights abuses and the brutal effects of war. Her book *The Country Between Us* (HarperCollins, 1981) generated both criticism for its political content as well as multiple awards. In addition to writing four volumes of poetry, she edited *Against Forgetting: Twentieth-Century Poetry of Witness* (HarperCollins, 1993). Forché teaches creative writing at George Mason University.

Kate Gale, founding editor and director of Red Hen Press, is a poet and writer with four books of poetry, a novel, and a bilingual children's book. She is editor of three literary anthologies and has recently completed the libretto for the opera *Río de Sangre* by Don Davis.

Henry Louis Gates, Jr., is a renowned scholar of African American studies. He is a professor at Harvard University and has published several books on the African American experience and a memoir, *Colored People* (Knopf, 1994).

Gary Gildner has written several books of poetry, including *Letters from Vicksburg* (Unicorn Press, 1976), a book of sonnets inspired by letters by a semi-literate Civil War soldier. He also wrote a memoir, *Warsaw Sparks* (University of Iowa Press), about coaching a baseball team in communist Poland.

Ray Gonzalez explores his experience as a Chicano growing up in the Southwest. He has written numerous volumes of poetry, most recently, *Faith Run* (University of Arizona Press, 2009). He has also edited several anthologies that feature Latino authors, including *Touching the Fire: Fifteen Poets of Today's Latino Renaissance* (Anchor Books/Doubleday, 1998). He is a professor of creative writing at the University of Minnesota, Minneapolis.

Rigoberto González is the author of several books, including *Butterfly Boy: Memories of a Chicano Mariposa* (University of Wisconsin Press, 2006), which received an American Book Award. The recipient of Guggenheim and NEA fellowships, he lives in New York City and is Associate Professor of English at Rutgers University–Newark.

Forrest Hamer is the author of *Call & Response* (Alice James, 1995), winner of the Beatrice Hawley Award; *Middle Ear* (Roundhouse, 2000), winner of the Northern California Book Award; and *Rift* (Four Way Books, 2007). He is also a psychoanalyst in Oakland, California.

Sam Hamill is the author of several collections of poetry and has edited a number of anthologies, most significantly, *Poets Against the War* (Thunder's Mouth Press, 2003). He has taught in prisons and worked with battered women and children. Founding editor of Copper Canyon Press, he is the recipient of numerous awards, including several National Endowments for the Arts.

Thich Nhat Hanh, originally from Vietnam, is a Buddhist monk who lives in exile in France. He is well known for his writings on mindfulness and social activism based in Buddhist principles. Hanh has also sought to find a place where Christianity and Buddhism meet. He has written many books of spiritual teachings as well as books of poetry and nonfiction concerning Vietnam.

Marc Harshman is a poet, storyteller, and author of many children's books, which have been translated into many languages, along with a book of poetry, *Turning Out the Stones* (State Street Press, 1983). For more information, visit www.marcharshman.com.

Robert Hass has written several volumes of poetry. His most recent collection is *Time and Materials: Poems 1997–2005* (Ecco Press, 2007). Hass has translated both Slavic and Japanese poetry, and as poet laureate of the United States in 1995 and 1996, he sought to improve literacy and community by taking poetry to the business world and encouraging businesses to sponsor poetry contests in schools.

Juan Felipe Herrera is a poet and holds the Tomás Rivera Endowed Chair in Creative Writing at the University of California, Riverside. His recent book *Half of the World in Light: New and Selected Poems* (University of Arizona Press, 2008) won the 2008 National Book Critics Circle award for poetry.

Linda Hogan, poet, playwright, and essayist, draws on her heritage from Native Americans and European settlers of Oklahoma to give her fiction a connection to nature. She writes about spirituality as well as feminism and the working class. Her latest novel is entitled *People of the Whale* (W.W. Norton, 2008).

Langston Hughes grew up in Kansas before moving to Harlem, where he became a central figure of the Harlem Renaissance. While he wrote plays and novels, Hughes is best known for his poetry that captures the rhythm of blues and jazz. His poems often were concerned with poverty and African American culture.

Akasha Gloria Hull is a writer, professor of literature and women's studies, lecturer, and consultant. Her books include *Color, Sex, and Poetry:*

Three Women Writers of the Harlem Renaissance (Indiana University Press, 1987), *All the Women Are White, All the Blacks Are Men, but Some of Us Are Brave* (Feminist Press, 1982), and *Healing Heart: Poems 1973–1988* (Kitchen Table, Women of Color Press, 1989). Her most recent book is *Soul Talk: The New Spirituality of African American Women* (Inner Traditions, 2001).

Francisco Jiménez has written scholarly books and a series for young adults about a migrant worker. The most recent in the series is *Breaking Through* (Houghton Mifflin, 2008). Jiménez is a professor at Santa Clara University in California. For more information, visit www.scu.edu/ethnicstudies/fjimenez.

June Jordan published 28 books in all, including poetry, essays, and a memoir. Her work combines the personal with the political as it explores race, gender, sexuality, economics, social issues, and liberation struggles. She founded Poetry for the People at the University of California, Berkeley, a program that teaches empowerment through artistic expression of writing and reading poetry. For more information, visit www.junejordan.com.

Tracy Kelly studied social action writing at California State University Monterey Bay, and is a domestic violence counselor in New Mexico. She and her spouse were among the first to marry in California following that state's Supreme Court ruling legalizing gay and lesbian marriages in 2008.

Chân Không is a Buddhist nun who was born in Vietnam and is now living in France. In 1972 she helped organize the Buddhist Peace Delegation, which worked for peace in Vietnam. In 1993 she wrote her autobiography, *Learning True Love: How I Learned and Practiced Social Change in Vietnam* (Parallax Press, 1993).

Jamaica Kincaid was born in Antigua, West Indies, and grew up during the time of the British colonization. She left the Caribbean, emigrated to the United States, worked as an au pair, and later as a staff writer for the *New Yorker*. She is the author of many novels dealing with gender, family, colonialism, and the parallels between them. Her most recent novel is *Mr. Potter* (Farrar, Straus and Giroux, 2003).

Zachary Knapp studied social action writing at California State University Monterey Bay. He is passionate about sustainable agriculture, our food system, and the people who work in it. Knapp and his wife now live and tend their backyard "mini-farm" in Los Osos, California.

Katya Komisaruk was arrested, convicted, and imprisoned for vandalizing a nuclear weapons satellite network in California in 1987. While in prison, Komisaruk applied to Harvard Law School, was accepted, and became a lawyer specializing in the defense of radical protesters. Komisaruk has written two books, the most recent being *Beat the Heat: How to Handle Encounters with Law Enforcement* (AK Press, 2004).

Li-Young Lee is the author of four books of poetry, most recently, *Behind My Eyes* (W.W. Norton, 2002). His poetry explores father-son relationships as well as life in exile. The recipient of several literary awards, he lives with his family in Chicago.

Linda Lopez studied social action writing at California State University Monterey Bay, and received her MA in history from San Francisco State University. She is a financial aid counselor at California State University Monterey Bay.

Audre Lorde described herself as "black lesbian, mother, warrior, poet." Of West Indian descent, she was born and raised in New York City. Lorde used her poetry and prose to confront many forms of marginalization and injustice. She published several volumes of poetry, fiction, and essays, including *The Cancer Journals* (Spinsters Ink, 1980), which chronicles her experience with the cancer that caused her death.

David Mas Masumoto grows organic heirloom peaches and grapes in California's San Joaquin Valley. He has written several books suggesting that people take time to experience the world with all of their senses. He has also written an oral history of Japanese farmers in California. His latest book *Heirlooms: Letters from a Peach Farmer* (Heyday Books) came out in 2007.

Jarvis Masters, an African American, has been in California's San Quentin Prison since he was nineteen. While in prison, he was convicted of conspiring to murder a guard and placed on death row, where he both discovered Buddhism and began writing. He won the 1992 PEN Award for Poetry, and his stories and poems have been published in *Tricycle*, *San Francisco Chronicle*, *The Sun*, *Utne Reader*, and *Turning Wheel*. He is the author of *Finding Freedom: Writings from Death Row* (Padma Publishing, 1997). The Campaign to Free Jarvis Jay Masters can be found at www.freejarvis.org.

Linda McCarriston, born in Chelsea, Massachusetts, to working-class Irish American parents, holds both Irish and American citizenship. Her poetry concerns her family history, including the physical and sexual abuse she experienced by her father and her mother's attempts to protect her. Her latest book is *Little River: New and Selected Poems* (Salmon Publishing, 2000). She teaches at the University of Alaska, Anchorage.

Tommi Avicolli Mecca is a radical, southern Italian, working-class, atheist, queer writer, performer, and activist who lives in San Francisco. He is author of *Between Little Rock and a Hard Place* (HarperCollins, 1997), co-editor of *Hey Paesan: Writing by Lesbians and Gay Men of Italian Descent* (Three Guineas Press, 1999), and co-editor of *Avanti Popolo: Italian-American Writers Sail Beyond Columbus* (Manic D Press, 2008).

Janice Mirikitani came to political activism through her family's experience in internment camps for Japanese Americans during World War II. As executive director of Glide Memorial Church in San Francisco, Mirikitani works to aid the marginalized and oppressed people of San Francisco. She is also a choreographer and has written three books of poetry, including *Love Works* (City Lights Foundation, 2002).

Naomi Shihab Nye grew up in St. Louis, Missouri, and Jerusalem. Her poetry explores her heritage and focuses on the Middle East. She has written many volumes of poetry and several children's books. Her latest book is *Honeybee: Poems & Short Prose* (HarperCollins, 2008).

Sharon Olds has written many volumes of poetry that deal with personal and political issues. In 2005 Olds refused an invitation from Laura Bush to read at the National Book Festival in protest of the war in Iraq. Her latest book is *One Secret Thing: Poems* (Alfred A. Knopf, 2008).

Alicia Ostriker, poet, critic, and midrashist, has written several collections of poetry and several books of criticism and Biblical commentary, most recently, *For the Love of God: The Bible as an Open Book* (Rutgers University Press, 2008). She is Professor Emerita of English at Rutgers University.

Leonard Peltier, a citizen of the Anishinaabe and Dakota Nations, is an artist, writer, and activist. He was convicted of the murder of two FBI agents in a shootout on the Pine Ridge Indian Reservation in 1975 and is housed in a federal penitentiary in Pennsylvania. Amnesty International is seeking review of his case based on concerns that he did not receive a fair trial. The Leonard Peltier Defense Committee can be found at www.leonardpeltier.net.

Minnie Bruce Pratt speaks in support of lesbian, gay, bisexual, and transgender issues and against imperialism, racism, and sexism. Pratt has published both essays and poetry. Her latest book is *The Dirt She Ate: New and Selected Poems* (University of Pittsburgh Press, 2003). For more information, visit www.mbpratt.org.

Khadijah Queen holds an MFA in creative writing from Antioch University. She is a Cave Canem Fellow and founding member of the Red Thread Nonfiction Collective. Her published work includes a poetry collection, *Conduit* (Black Goat/Akashic, 2008), and a chapbook, *No Isla Encanta* (dancing girl press, 2007). For more information, visit www.imagesound.tk.

Adrienne Rich has long been a leading voice for poetry and social justice. She is the author of more than seventeen books of poetry and many books of prose. Her awards include a National Book Award, a MacArthur Fellowship, and a Lannan Lifetime Achievement Award. In 1997, Rich turned down the National Medal for the Arts to protest the "cynical politics" in Washington, D.C., and the "increasingly brutal impact of racial and economic injustice in our country." For more information, visit www.barclayagency.com/richwhy.html.

Ethel Rosenberg grew up in a working-class Jewish family on the Lower East Side of New York City. She married Julius Rosenberg, and with him became involved in the union movement. In 1950 Julius was arrested and accused of being a communist spy. Ethel's arrest followed shortly. Both were convicted of conspiracy to commit espionage and executed by the U.S. government.

Arundhati Roy grew up in Kerala, India. Her mother was a Syrian Christian and her father was a Bengali Hindu. Roy is best known for her novel *God of Small Things* (Random House, 1997), which won the Booker Prize. The book brought her fame, which she uses to pursue social activism. She has published several books on the policies of various governments.

Elliot Ruchowitz-Roberts is co-author of *Bowing to Receive the Mountain: Essays by Lin Jensen and Poems by Elliot Roberts* (Sunflower, 1997) and co-editor/co-translator of two works of poetry from the Telugu: Chalam's *Sudha (Nectar)* (South Asia Books, 1990) and *Selected Verses of Vemana* (Sahitya Akademi, 1995). His poems have appeared in various anthologies and journals, most recently *Dancing on the Brink of the World: Selected Poems of Point Lobos* (Point Lobos Natural History Association, 2003). He currently chairs the Monterey county chapter of the American Civil Liberties Union.

Ralph Salisbury, Professor Emeritus at the University of Oregon, is the author of two books of short fiction and eight books of poetry, the most recent being *Light from a Bullet Hole: Poems New and Selected* (Silverfish Review Press, 2009).

Sonia Sanchez was involved in the civil rights movement and the Black Arts movement. She was a pioneer in developing Black Studies courses at San Francisco State University in 1968 and 1969 and taught at Temple University for many years. She has written numerous plays, and many books of poetry, including *homegirls and handgrenades* (Thunder's Mouth, 1984) and *Shake Loose My Skin* (Beacon, 2000).

Esmeralda Santiago was born in rural Puerto Rico. In 1961 she and her siblings moved with their mother to New York City. Santiago's memoirs, *When I Was Puerto Rican* (Addison-Wesley, 1993) and *Almost a Woman* (Perseus, 1998), explore the experience of being caught between two cultures.

Assata Shakur, a Black Panther activist, was convicted as an accomplice to murder in 1977. Two years later, she escaped from prison and was granted political exile by Cuba, where she currently lives and writes. *Assata: An Autobiography* was published in 1987 (Lawrence Hill Books). For more information, visit http://www.assatashakur.org.

Matthew Shenoda is a first-generation Coptic Egyptian American and an activist, poet, and educator. Shenoda explores what it means to be an Arab American in his volume of poetry *Somewhere Else* (Coffee House Press, 2006). He taught the first Arab American literature class at San Francisco State University. His most recent book is *Seasons of Lotus, Seasons of Bone* (BOA Editions Ltd., 2009). For more information, visit www.matthewshenoda.com.

Patricia Smith is the only National Poetry Slam participant to have won the event four times. Smith has written several books of poetry, children's books, and nonfiction. Her latest book, *Teahouse of the Almighty* (Coffee House Press, 2006), explores feminist views, African American life, and more universal themes of love and violence. For more information, visit www.wordwoman.ws.

Gary Soto is the author of eleven poetry collections and numerous books of fiction and nonfiction for children, young adults, and adults. He lives in Berkeley, California. His writing often draws from his background as a working-class Mexican American in the farm town of Fresno, California. His book *Gary Soto: New and Selected Poems* (Chronicle Books, 1995) was a finalist for both the *Los Angeles Times* Book Award and the National Book Award. He recently published *Facts of Life: Stories* (Harcourt, 2008). For more information, visit www.garysoto.com.

William Stafford became a conscientious objector during World War II, a decision that placed him outside the mainstream at the time. The author of 67 books, his collection *Traveling Through the Dark* (Harper and Row, 1962) won a National Book Award in 1963. He taught at Lewis and Clark College for many years. Stafford held the position of Poetry Consultant for the Library of Congress (currently titled Poet Laureate) from 1970 to 1971.

Sekou Sundiata was born in Harlem. While he considered himself a writer rather than a performance or slam poet, Sundiata performed his poetry, often with musicians. Rather than publishing his poetry in book form, he released two CDs of poetry, *Blue Oneness of Dreams* (Polygram, 1997) and *Long Story Short* (Righteous Babe, 2000), which explore the black experience in America and the nation's place in the world community. In spring 2006, he performed his project "the 51st dream state" as his response to 9/11.

Margo Tamez (Lipan Apache–Jumano Apache) is co-founder of Lipan Apache Women Defense-Strength (Tnde' hat'i'i shimaa shini'). Her work critically examines those factors that negatively impact Apache women of the Mexico–U.S. border region. She is the author of several poetry collections, including *Naked Wanting* and *Raven Eye* (both published by the University of Arizona Press, 2003 and 2007). She is completing her PhD at Washington State University with a primary research focus on Native American women and genocide studies of the Mexico–U.S. border region.

Judith Tannenbaum lives in the San Francisco Bay Area, where she works for San Francisco Writers Corps. She is a longtime advocate of the arts in prisons and spent many years teaching poetry in San Quentin prison. Her current project is *By Heart: Poetry, Prison, and Two Lives,* with Spoon Jackson. Tannenbaum has published several books on teaching writing, including *Disguised as a Poem: My Years Teaching at San Quentin* (Northeastern University Press, 2000). For more information, visit www .judithtannenbaum.com.

Viana Enedina Torres studied social action writing at California State University Monterey Bay. She teaches leadership and community service to high school students in the San Diego area.

Natasha Trethewey writes poetry about her experience growing up biracial in Mississippi, her mother's murder by her stepfather, and African American history. She won the Pulitzer Prize for her book *Native Guard* (Houghton Mifflin, 2006). Trethewey is a professor of poetry at Emory University, where she holds the Phyllis Wheatley Distinguished Chair.

Melissa Tuckey is author of *Rope as Witness* (Pudding House Press, 2007). Her poem "Ghost Fishing Louisiana" is in response to a toxic tour of Louisiana led by environmental justice activists Damu Smith and Robert Bullard. Tuckey currently serves as co-director of Split This Rock Poetry Festival and lives in Washington, D.C.

Alice Walker is a prolific essayist, novelist, and poet, and the author of more than 30 books, including *The Color Purple*, which won the Pulitzer Prize in 1983. Her writing draws on her experience growing up in a community of tenant farmers in Eaton, Georgia, and explores the international world as well, addressing issues that span class, race, and gender divisions. She developed the term "womanist" to refer to women of color who, like herself, concern themselves with feminism, audacious acts, and loving the world.

Evelyn C. White is the author of *Chain, Chain, Change: For Black Women Dealing with Physical and Emotional Abuse* (Seal Press, 1985), *The Black Women's Health Book: Speaking for Ourselves* (Seal Press, 1990), and most recently, the biography *Alice Walker: A Life* (W.W. Norton, 2005).

Hisaye Yamamoto (DeSoto), a first-generation Japanese American, was raised in California; her parents were tenant farmers. As a young adult during World War II, she and her family were placed in Japanese internment camps. She writes of the camps and other experiences growing up Japanese American in her collection of short stories, *Seventeen Syllables and Other Stories* (Kitchen Table: Women of Color, 1988).

Gary Young's books include *Hands* (Illuminati, 1979), *The Dream of a Moral Life* (Copper Beech, 1990), *Days* (Silverfish Review, 1997), *Braver Deeds* (Gibbs Smith, 1999), and *No Other Life* (Heyday, 2005), which won the William Carlos Williams Award. His most recent books are *Pleasure* (Heyday, 2006) and *Bear Flag Republic: Prose Poems and Poetics from California* (co-edited with Christopher Buckley, Greenhouse Review, 2008). He has twice received National Endowment of the Arts fellowships. Other awards include a Pushcart Prize and a National Endowment for the Humanities fellowship. He edits the *Greenhouse Review Press* and teaches at the University of California, Santa Cruz.

Index